Nova Scotia, New Brunswick, and Prince Edward For Dummies, 1st Edition

S0-BAT-501

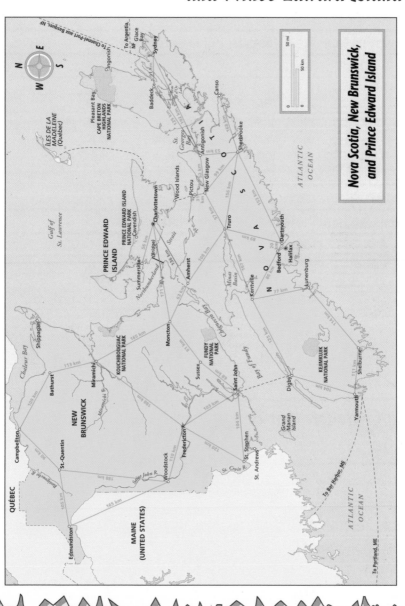

Nova Scotia, New Brunswick, and Prince Edward Island

Nova Scotia, New Brunswick, and Prince Edward Island

For Dummies: Bestselling Book Series for Beginners

Nova Scotia, New Brunswick, and Prince Edward Island For Dummies® 1st Edition

Cheat Sheet

Ferry Schedules

Departing from Wood Islands, PEI to Caribou, NS

Date	Time								
May 1–June 12	06:30	09:30	13:00	16:30	19:30				
June 13–June 30	06:30	09:30	11:00	13:00	14:30	16:30	19:30		
July 1–Sept. 6	(06:30)	08:00	09:30	11:00	13:00	14:30	16:30	18:00	19:30
Sept. 7–Oct. 11	06:30	09:30	11:00	13:00	14:30	16:30	19:30		
Oct. 12–Nov. 30	06:30	09:30	13:00	16:30	19:30				
Dec. 1–Dec. 20	08:00	12:00	16:00						

Departing from Caribou, NS to Wood Island, PEI

Date	Time								
May 1–June 12	08:00	11:15	14:45	18:00	21:00				
June 13–June 30	08:00	11:15	12:45	14:45	16:15	18:00	21:00		
July 1–Sept. 6	(08:00)	09:30	11:15	12:45	14:45	16:15	18:00	19:30	21:00
Sept. 7–Oct. 11	08:00	11:15	12:45	14:45	16:15	18:00	21:00		
Oct. 12–Nov. 30	08:00	11:15	14:45	18:00	21:00				
Dec. 1–Dec.20	10:00	14:00	17:30						

( ) Brackets indicate no Sunday departures
* All departures in Atlantic Time

The Confederation Bridge Fares

Auto	$39.00
RV	$44.50
Motorcoach Bus	$223.00
Motorcycle	$15.50

For Dummies: Bestselling Book Series for Beginners

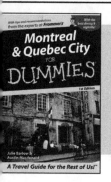

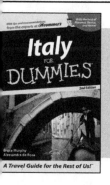

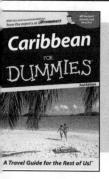
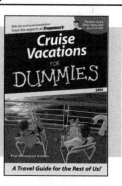

Nova Scotia, New Brunswick & Prince Edward island

FOR

DUMMIES®

1ST EDITION

by Andrew Hempstead

John Wiley & Sons Canada, Ltd

Nova Scotia, New Brunswick & Prince Edward Island For Dummies®

Published by
John Wiley & Sons Canada, Ltd
6045 Freemont Boulevard
Mississauga, Ontario, L5R 4J3
www.wiley.ca

National Library of Canada Cataloguing in Publication

Hempstead, Andrew

Nova Scotia, New Brunswick and Prince Edward Island for dummies / Andrew Hempstead.

Includes index.

ISBN 0-470-83399-8

1. Maritime Provinces–Guidebooks. I. Title.

FC2024.H44 2004   917.1504'4   C2003-906731-9

Printed in Canada

1 2 3 4 5 TRI 07 06 05 04 03

Distributed in Canada by John Wiley & Sons Canada, Ltd.

For general information on John Wiley & Sons Canada, Ltd., including all books published by Wiley Publishing, Inc., please call our warehouse, Tel 1-800-567-4797. For reseller information, including discounts and premium sales, please call our sales department, Tel 416-646-7992. For press review copies, author interviews, or other publicity information, please contact our marketing department,
Tel: 416-646-4584, Fax 416-236-4448.

About the Author

Andrew Hempstead is a travel writer and photographer who has traveled widely throughout Canada from his home in Banff, Alberta. His research trip for this book took him to every corner of the Maritimes, and along the way he found himself surrounded by whales in the Bay of Fundy, surfing along Nova Scotia's east coast, and golfing the fairways of Prince Edward Island.

In addition to this book, Hempstead has authored guidebooks to Alberta, British Columbia, the Canadian Rockies, and Vancouver, and has co-authored guidebooks to Atlantic Canada, Australia, and New Zealand. His writing and photography has also appeared in many national and international publications.

Author's Acknowledgments

Thanks to the following people for helping out with information and planning at various stages of my research trip: Judy Dougan, Tourism Moncton; Carol Horne and Tracy Stretch, Tourism PEI; Susan Jeffries, Nova Scotia Department of Tourism and Culture; Margaret Totten, Tourism Saint John; and Angela Watson, Fredericton Tourism. Thanks also to staff at information centers, innkeepers, and others on my travels who guided me in the right direction, all of whom contributed to making this book as useful and comprehensive as it could possibly be.

Publisher's Acknowledgments

We're proud of this book; please send us your comments at canadapt@wiley.com. Some of the people who helped bring this book to market include the following:

Acquisitions and Editorial

Associate Editor: Michelle Marchetti

Developmental Editor: Sandra Braun, Colborne Communications

Copy Editor: Jennifer Warren, Colborne Communications

Cover Photo: Thomas Fricke/First Light

Back Cover Photo: Andrew Hempstead

Production

Publishing Services Director: Karen Bryan

Publishing Services Manager: Ian Koo

Project Manager: Elizabeth McCurdy

Project Coordinator: Robert Hickey

Layout and Graphics: Pat Loi

Proofreader: Allyson Latta

Indexer: Belle Wong

John Wiley & Sons Canada, Ltd.

Bill Zerter, Chief Operating Officer

Robert Harris, General Manager, Professional and Trade Division

Publishing and Editorial for Consumer Dummies

Diane Graves Steele, Vice President and Publisher, Consumer Dummies

Joyce Pepple, Acquisitions Director, Consumer Dummies

Kristin A. Cocks, Product Development Director, Consumer Dummies

Michael Spring, Vice President and Publisher, Travel

Suzanne Jannetta, Editorial Director, Travel

Publishing for Technology Dummies

Andy Cummings, Acquisitions Director

Composition Services

Gerry Fahey, Executive Director of Production Services

Debbie Stailey, Director of Composition Services

Contents at a Glance

Maps at a Glance

· ·

Table of Contents

Introduction

. . . .

*T*he most common term used to describe the Maritimes as a tourist
destination is "underrated." After spending your vacation traveling
through Nova Scotia, New Brunswick, and Prince Edward Island, I'm sure
you'll agree. This area of Canada possesses a subtle magnetism that is
impossible to define — you just have to experience it to understand —
and offers spectacular scenery to rival that of many other top destinations. Each of the three provinces has its own distinct character, and
yet they come together to create a single destination like no other
place on earth.

How do you distill the essence of the Maritimes into one book? That
was the challenge I faced as I sorted through my experiences to bring
you only the best and most unique accommodations, restaurants, and
attractions. And they are just the tip of the iceberg; you won't go wrong
at any of the places described in this book, but you will return home
from your memorable Maritimes adventure with your own favorites.

About This Book

Nova Scotia, New Brunswick, & Prince Edward Island For Dummies is a
reference guide. It is not designed to be a comprehensive, tell-all guidebook that weighs you down. Each of the three provinces is discussed
separately in individual parts, laid out in a logical sequence so you can
refer quickly to a particular region, or skip a chapter completely if it is
off your route (although you may want to reconsider after reading up
on it). History is a big part of the Maritimes and travel, but I have only
dwelled on the past when it is necessary.

Conventions Used in This Book

To help you get the information you need easily and quickly, I have
taken the liberty of using a few conventions throughout this book.

- ✔ I use the accepted term "Maritimes" to collectively describe the
  provinces of Nova Scotia, New Brunswick, and Prince Edward Island.

- ✔ All prices in this book are given in both Canadian and U.S. dollars.

✔ Dollar sign ($) symbols preceding each listing are designed to give you an approximate price for a night's stay in a hotel or a meal in a restaurant. In the hotel section, the rates I quote are the rack rates (the hotel's official rates) for one night for a double room, although after reading Chapter 8, I would hope you never pay this full amount. When recommending restaurants, I give the range of main course prices; appetizers, desserts, drinks, and tips are not included in this amount unless explicitly stated. If a restaurant doesn't serve dinner, the price range refers to the lunch menu. Lobster causes a small problem (not to eat, that's for sure!) — in almost every restaurant it's sold at "market price," so my price ranges do not include this Maritimes delicacy.

Here's what the dollar signs represent:

Dollar Signs	Hotel	Restaurant
$	$75 or less	$10 or less
$$	$75–$150	$10.00–$17.50
$$$	$150–$225	$17.50–$25.00
$$$$	$225 or more	$25 and up

I also use abbreviations for credit cards. I only include the major ones, so if your particular card is not listed here, it may or may not be accepted. Call ahead to make sure. The credit cards and their corresponding abbreviations are as follows:

✔ AE   American Express

✔ DC   Diners Club

✔ DISC   Discover

✔ M   MasterCard

✔ V   Visa

Assumptions

In writing this book, I took the liberty of making some assumptions about you, the reader, and what you may need from a Maritimes guidebook. Here's what I assumed:

✔ You are an inexperienced traveler who needs general travel advice as well as specific guidance on visiting the Maritimes, or

✔ You've traveled a lot but never to the Maritimes, and you want expert advice on maximizing your time there, and

✔ Regardless of your travel experience, you don't want a book that dwells on history or describes every hotel and restaurant. You simply want concise descriptions of the very best places in a variety of price ranges.

If you identify with any of my assumptions, then *Nova Scotia, New Brunswick, & Prince Edward Island For Dummies* is the book for you.

How This Book Is Organized

Nova Scotia, New Brunswick, & Prince Edward Island For Dummies is divided into six parts. The chapters within each part cover specific topics or regions in detail. You can read each chapter or part without reading the others — after all, there's no need to read about Prince Edward Island if you're heading for Cape Breton Island.

Part I: Getting Started

This part introduces you to the three provinces, and highlights — well, the highlights. I tell you about the best times of year to visit, and describe the top festivals and events. I also propose four itineraries (a one-week trip, a two-week trip, a special trip for families, and another for seafood-lovers). I also offer tips for travelers with special needs, such as seniors and those with disabilities, as well as budget-planning advice that all travelers can use.

Part II: Ironing Out the Details

Call it Trip-Planning 101. Here, I'll lay out the basics and delve into details to help you get started on the right path. By the end of Part II, you will know:

✔ Whether or not to use a travel agent to help plan your trip

✔ The pros and cons of taking an escorted or package tour

✔ How to get to the Maritimes, and how to get around after you arrive

✔ The different lodging types available to you, and how you can save money when booking a room

✔ Other details, such as the best way to carry your money and what type of travel insurance will meet your particular needs

Parts III, IV, V: The Provinces

These three parts form the bulk of the book, with each one devoted to a separate province. I've then broken the parts down further into chapters that focus on specific regions. In each chapter, you'll find all the information you need to make the most of your visit, including:

- ✔ How to get there
- ✔ Where to stay
- ✔ Where to eat
- ✔ What there is to see and do

Part VI: The Part of Tens

Skip ahead to this part for the best of the Maritimes condensed into a few pages: ten classic Maritimes experiences and my ten favorite seafood restaurants — with ten people you probably didn't know were from the Maritimes thrown in as a bonus.

Quick Concierge

Use this section as a quick reference for emergency phone numbers, useful Web sites, and contacts for further information.

Have a look at the pages with bright yellow borders at the back of the book. They're worksheets designed to help you formulate a travel budget, create itineraries, and make notes of your favorite stops.

Icons Used in This Book

I've used five icons throughout this book to call your attention to different types of information. Here's what they mean:

This icon points out useful advice you probably wouldn't otherwise know. Keep an eye out for these to make the most of your trip.

This icon calls attention to tourist traps or potential pitfalls.

Next to a hotel recommendation, this icon means that the establishment welcomes children. Next to a restaurant, it indicates that kids are offered their own menu. In front of an attraction, it emphasizes somewhere your kids will (hopefully) enjoy.

If you see this icon, you'll know you're about to save some money. It doesn't necessarily mean that something is cheap — just that it is particularly good value.

This is my favorite icon. When you spot it, you'll know you're in for a special Maritimes welcome.

Where to Go from Here

As you begin to plan your Maritimes vacation, consider my recommendations while keeping your own interests in mind. Pore over maps and plot out an itinerary — the idea is to plan ahead, book your transportation and lodgings, and leave the rest until you get there.

This book is designed to help you juggle the practicalities of advance planning (like the security of knowing you have a comfortable room to retire to) with spontaneity (like a spur-of-the-moment restaurant stop or an exhilarating whale-watching excursion). That way, you won't have to worry about the nitpicky details; you can just relax and enjoy the magnificent Maritimes.

Part I
Getting Started

In this part...

Okay, it's time to get excited about traveling to the Maritimes! This part breaks it down, nice and easy, by listing the best places to go and sights to see in each province. It'll also highlight the pros and cons of traveling to the region at different times of year, provide four itineraries to help you make the most of your time, and suggest tips for travelers with special needs or those on a budget.

Chapter 1

Discovering the Best of Nova Scotia, New Brunswick, & Prince Edward Island

- -

In This Chapter

▶ Discovering the different provinces

▶ Learning what there is to do and see

▶ Focusing on the best lodgings and restaurants

- -

*I*n the Maritimes, spectacular coastal scenery, rural serenity, and the historic appeal of some of North America's oldest towns combine to create a destination like no other. The people, who call themselves "Maritimers" or "East Coasters," are a bonus. They are some of the friendliest folks you're ever likely to meet — extremely proud of their heritage and even prouder to share it with visitors.

Maritimes tourist literature is filled with pictures of lighthouses and seafood, and you'll see lots of the former and eat lots of the latter. But in addition, each of the three provinces covered in this book — Nova Scotia, New Brunswick, and Prince Edward Island — offers something unique that goes beyond anything you've ever known.

Introducing Nova Scotia

Almost cut off from the rest of Canada by the Bay of Fundy, Nova Scotia is compact and easy to get around. You'll never be more than 60km (37 miles) from what best defines the province — the ocean. Picturesque fishing villages, abundant seafood, and the stark beauty of Cape Breton Island are highlights of a visit to Nova Scotia.

Checking out the scenery

One of the best things about Nova Scotia's most spectacular natural features is that they are all very accessible.

Along the South Shore (Chapter 12), **Peggy's Cove, Mahone Bay,** and **Lunenburg** get all the attention for their postcard-perfect oceanfront settings, but many other South Shore villages you won't see in the tourist brochures are equally scenic and a lot quieter. Stroll the waterfront sections of **West Dover, Prospect Point,** or **Blue Rocks** to experience Nova Scotia without the crowds. The **Bay of Fundy** is no scenic gem, but with the world's highest tides and resident populations of **whales**, it offers huge attractions. The best place to see whales is on a tour from Digby Neck, while the **tidal bore** (a wall of water that builds up as the tide comes in against the waters of a river) can be viewed at **Truro** (Chapter 13).

Cape Breton Island (Chapter 14) is one of Nova Scotia's biggest draws. The island's most spectacular scenery lies within the protection of **Cape Breton Highlands National Park.** The **Cabot Trail,** one of the world's most scenic drives, passes through the park, allowing roadside views of high sea cliffs, endless ocean, white-sand beaches, and occasionally whales frolicking in the water far below.

Stepping back in time

I don't plan to bore you with too much history in this book. If I mention a museum or historic site, you know it's a good one (or very important).

Halifax (Chapter 11) is a hotbed of history. It is home to many *Titanic*-related sights, from the mainstream (**Maritime Museum of the Atlantic**) to the offbeat (the final resting place of third-class seaman J. Dawson, who was immortalized by a fictionalized character of the same name, played by Leonardo DiCaprio in the movie version of the tragedy). **Citadel Hill,** a nineteenth-century fort that is Canada's most visited National Historic Site, is worth visiting for the views alone.

Along the South Shore (Chapter 12), the waterfront core of attractive **Lunenburg,** home to the famous schooner *Bluenose II,* is a UNESCO World Heritage Site. Further south, the shipbuilding center of Shelburne is a lesser-known but equally interesting destination. The British and French struggled for control of **Annapolis Royal** for almost a century, and many buildings from this era remain along the main street, including Canada's oldest wooden building.

The **Fortress of Louisbourg** (Chapter 14), Canada's largest historic reconstruction, is also one of its most remote, situated as it is on the northeastern tip of Cape Breton Island. The island is also home to the **Alexander Graham Bell National Historic Site,** a top-notch museum commemorating one of the world's best-known inventors.

The best places to stay

In Halifax (Chapter 11), the **Lord Nelson Hotel & Suites** is an excellent choice for upscale lodging within walking distance of downtown. If you don't mind being outside city limits, **Prospect Point Bed & Breakfast** has a delightful ocean setting.

After hearing a glowing recommendation from a fellow traveler, I spent on of the most enjoyable nights of my Maritimes research trip at **Whispering Waves Cottages** near Shelburne (Chapter 12). Along the Bay of Fundy, **Brier Island Lodge,** near Digby, is a great spot for wildlife enthusiasts. In Annapolis Royal, the **Queen Anne Inn** is soaked in Victorian charm.

In Pictou (Chapter 13), the **Consulate Inn** mixes history with a waterfront setting, making it the preferred overnight option in that town.

On Cape Breton Island (Chapter 14), accommodations range from rustic cottage complexes to the upscale grandeur of the **Keltic Lodge** at Ingonish. Nearby, **Glenghorm Beach Resort** lacks the name recognition of its famous neighbor but provides all the elements of a memorable beach vacation. Of the many historic lodgings in Baddeck, you can choose the **Dunlop Inn** for comfort and location, or a budget-conscious room in the old wing of **Telegraph House**.

The best places to eat

As you'd expect in a provincial capital set by the ocean, seafood is available at almost every Halifax restaurant (Chapter 11). Of those that specialize in seafood, go to **Five Fishermen** for the cuisine, **Murphy's on the Water** for the views, or **Salty's** for the atmosphere.

Along the South Shore (Chapter 12), the **Salt Spray Café** dishes up one of the province's better breakfast deals, while down the road in Lunenburg, the **Old Fish Factory** has a view to match the food. Continuing around southwestern Nova Scotia, Digby is famous for its sweet, plump scallops. There's no better place to try this delicacy than right on the Digby docks at the **Fundy Restaurant**.

Truro (Chapter 13) may be away from the coast, but **Murphy's** is well worth searching out for delicately battered fish. To the north (east of Pictou), **Jost Vineyards** is the Maritimes' finest winery.

On Cape Breton Island (Chapter 14), Baddeck has a choice of touristy restaurants, including the **Baddeck Lobster Suppers,** where you pay a set price for a lobster with all the trimmings. **Restaurant Acadian** in Chéticamp is a great place to try traditional Acadian cuisine. Two restaurants near Ingonish, the **Chowder House** and the **Muddy Rudder,** are low on frills but big on seafood.

Introducing New Brunswick

The largest of the three Maritimes provinces, New Brunswick is also the most varied in terms of landscape, and it offers diverse experiences. An excellent highway system links the three largest cities — **Moncton, Fredericton** (the capital), and **Saint John** — with other worthwhile destinations close at hand.

Checking out the scenery

The Acadian Coast of New Brunswick, northeast of Moncton (Chapter 15), has long stretches of sandy beaches and some of Canada's warmest ocean water. **Parlee Beach,** near Shediac, is especially popular for its warm water, making it the busiest beach in the Maritimes. If it's solitude you're after, head north to the beaches in **Kouchibouguac National Park.**

The world's highest tides are found in the **Bay of Fundy** (Chapter 16). **Fundy National Park** and **Hopewell Rocks** are the best spots to view the effects of this natural phenomenon.

North of Fredericton (Chapter 17), the **Miramichi River** is a scenic waterway renowned for salmon fishing. New Brunswick's most dramatic scenery is still further north, where a northern extension of the Appalachian Mountains rises to 820 meters (2,700 feet) at **Mount Carlton,** the highest point in the Maritimes.

The best places to stay

Moncton (Chapter 15) is the first highway stop beyond Nova Scotia and the gateway to Prince Edward Island, so at some stage of your Maritimes travels you will likely find yourself there. For downtown accommodations, the **Chateau Moncton** is a solid choice. Along the Acadian Coast, the **Governor's Mansion Inn** offers up plenty of atmosphere at a reasonable price.

In Saint John, **Homeport Historic Bed and Breakfast** is an excellent choice along the Fundy Coast (Chapter 16). South of the city, St. Andrews has been a fashionable seaside resort since the late 1800s, and this is reflected in the lodging (and prices). The **Kingsbrae Arms** is the ultimate splurge, while places like the **Treadwell Inn** offer historic charm at a fraction of the price.

Fredericton (Chapter 17), the provincial capital, offers no real surprises when it comes to accommodations. The downtown area holds the usual upscale chain hotels catering to business travelers and politicos, while roadside motels line all the main arteries. An attractive alternative is the **Carriage House Inn,** a historic bed-and-breakfast close to downtown. If you're looking for a cheapie motel, you won't go wrong at **Fort Nashwaak Motel,** across the river and within sight of downtown.

The best places to eat

The hordes of university students living in Moncton (Chapter 15) gravitate to Main Street for cheap drinks and good times, but local bars such as the **Pump House** also cook up good food. In nearby Shediac, **Captain Dan's** attracts a young, hip crowd of New Brunswickers with its prime waterfront location, well-priced seafood, and live music.

Although Saint John (Chapter 16) is an industrial city through and through, it has a selection of excellent restaurants. The obvious choices are in **Market Square,** along the harbor; but it's also worth seeking out places like **Billy's** for seafood or **Church Street Steak House** for a break from the tried-and-true (but sometimes tired) seafood routine.

In Fredericton (Chapter 17), most of the big hotels have dining rooms, or you can veer off the main street to **Rye's,** a fancy pub known as much for its food as its beer.

Introducing Prince Edward Island

Prince Edward Island (PEI) is Canada's smallest province, just one-tenth the size of Nova Scotia. It's linked to the mainland by a bridge, but is a world away from the rest of the country in look and feel. The island was immortalized by Lucy Maud Montgomery in her popular *Anne of Green Gables* novel, and in many ways retains the charms she wrote of almost 100 years ago.

Checking out the scenery

Don't come to Prince Edward Island expecting dramatic scenery and stunning natural wonders. Instead, you will be greeted by a gently rolling landscape of cultivated fields surrounded by stark red cliffs that drop into blue ocean. Many of the island's most scenic byways, like coastal Highway 14 through Prince County or any of the roads in Kings County running south from Highway 2, are unassuming rural roads.

Prince Edward Island National Park protects a long sliver of the island's northern coastline. The park's widest — and busiest — beaches are near **Cavendish** (Chapter 19), while the less-visited portion of the park lies to the east, around **Tracadie Bay** (Chapter 21).

Highway 2 leads west from Charlottetown through the pretty farmland of Prince County (Chapter 20) to **North Cape,** a remote point of land jutting into the Gulf of St. Lawrence.

Exploring Anne's Land

Canadians take great pride in their heritage, which makes **Charlottetown** (Chapter 18) a popular destination. It was here in 1864 that the Fathers of Confederation met to discuss uniting the British North American colonies to establish the Dominion of Canada. The meeting took place at **Province House,** still home to the PEI legislature and open to the public. Charlottetown's top attraction is **Founders' Hall,** which tells the story of Canada from before Confederation to modern times.

Few places in the world are as closely associated with a fictional character as PEI is with Anne of Green Gables. Lucy Maud Montgomery, who wrote the classic in 1908, used her childhood home of **Cavendish** (Chapter 19) as an inspiration for the young girl who comes to live on a farm in the village of Avonlea. Tens of thousands of fans visit Montgomery-related sites annually, including **Green Gables,** Montgomery's cousin's farm and the principal setting for the book; the nearby foundations of the farmhouse where she was raised; and her grave in the local cemetery.

The best places to stay

With over 2,000 bed-and-breakfast options available, there's no lack of choice on Prince Edward Island. But you should still reserve ahead of time.

Many fine old buildings in Charlottetown (Chapter 18) have been turned into inns and bed-and-breakfasts. My favorite is the **Shipwright Inn,** a centrally located oasis of luxury. **Inns on Great George** is another good choice, offering a wide range of room styles two blocks from Province House.

In Cavendish (Chapter 19), do what vacationing island families have done for decades, and stay in a self-contained cottage within walking distance of the ocean. **Lakeview Cottages** is a practical, well-priced option. At nearby **Kindred Spirits Country Inn,** choose between cottages or bed-and-breakfast rooms in the main lodge.

In Kings County (Chapter 21), **A Place to Stay** is one of the province's most comfortable accommodations for travelers on a budget. In the vicinity, but in a different league price-wise, is **Inn at Bay Fortune,** a once-grand summer estate converted to luxurious lodging.

The best places to eat

McAssey's shares a building with Founders' Hall, the most popular tourist attraction in Charlottetown (Chapter 18). This usually isn't a good sign, but the seafood there is excellent and surprisingly well priced. **Peake's Quay** serves standard pub fare but offers a delightful harborfront setting and lively atmosphere.

Plan on giving the touristy restaurants in Cavendish a miss and head to North Rustico Harbour (Chapter 19), where the **Blue Mussel Café** dishes up fresh, innovative seafood to the lucky few who nab a table on its small deck. Nearby, **Fisherman's Wharf Lobster Suppers** is a great spot to take the kids.

In Kings County (Chapter 21), the restaurant at **Inn of Bay Fortune** stands out for exceptional food and refined service, while the **Bluefin Restaurant** in Souris is notable for its homey atmosphere and inexpensive seafood.

Chapter 2

Deciding When to Go

* *

* *

*O*nce you have an idea of *where* you'd like to go on your Maritimes vacation, you need to decide *when* to visit. That's where this chapter comes to the rescue. I describe the pros and cons of each season and use a table to show monthly temperature differences in a simple format. I end this chapter with a roundup of popular festivals and events (along with a few personal favorites).

Knowing the Secrets of the Seasons

Sure, it may be bright and sunny in one part of the region while raining in another, but as a whole, the Maritimes are under the influence of a single weather pattern whose biggest influencing factor is the Atlantic Ocean. In spring, the cold ocean water creates a lag in the warming of land. In fall, the opposite occurs, as the warmth from the ocean delays the onset of cooler temperatures by a few weeks.

Each of the four seasons is very distinct. Summer is far and away the most pleasant time of year to visit. The vast majority of visitors and local residents take advantage of this season — more visitors arrive in July and August than during the rest of the year combined.

If possible, plan your trip for either late June or early September. Most attractions are already (or are still) open, the crowds are thinner, and lodgings offer discount prices. If you were to ask me which of these two times of year I prefer, I'd do what all good politicians do and sit on the fence, suggesting I like June for the long hours of daylight and September for the fall colors.

Handy weather information is provided on the following government Web sites:

- ✔ **Environment Canada Atlantic Region** (Internet: www.ns.ec.gc.ca) features general information, such as forecasts and storm warnings.
- ✔ **Canadian Hydrographic Services** (Internet: www.charts.gc.ca) displays tide charts for the Bay of Fundy.
- ✔ **Marine Services On-Line** (Internet: www.marineservices.gc.ca) provides a log of marine forecasts.

The following table shows the average daytime temperatures and precipitation levels in Halifax, which gives you a rough idea for the Maritimes as a whole.

Table 2-1	Halifax's Temperature and Precipitation	
Month	*Daytime Mean Temperature*	*Total Monthly Precipitation*
January	–5°C (22°F)	147 mm (5.8 in)
February	–6°C (21°F)	119 mm (4.7 in)
March	–2°C (29°F)	121 mm (4.8 in)
April	4°C (39°F)	124 mm (4.9 in)
May	9°C (49°F)	111 mm (4.4 in)
June	15°C (59°F)	99 mm (3.9 in)
July	18°C (65°F)	96 mm (3.6 in)
August	18°C (65°F)	109 mm (4.3 in)
September	14°C (57°F)	94 mm (3.7 in)
October	11°C (47°F)	130 mm (5.1 in)
November	3°C (38°F)	155 mm (6.2 in)
December	–3°C (27°F)	168 mm (6.6 in)

As a general rule, the farther inland you go, the greater the temperature differential over the year. For example, Moncton has a hotter average July temperature than Halifax but is generally colder than Halifax in winter.

What time is it?

All three provinces are on Atlantic Standard Time (AST), which is one hour ahead of Eastern Standard Time, two hours ahead of Central Standard Time, three hours ahead of Mountain Standard Time, and four hours ahead of Pacific Standard Time.

Clocks are moved forward one hour for Daylight Saving Time on the first Sunday in April. They are turned back on the last Sunday in October.

Spring

As the long days of spring begin to warm the land, the snow melts quickly, giving way to fresh growth and a certain feeling of optimism in the air.

Spring is wonderful because:

- ✔ The crowds of summer have yet to arrive.
- ✔ Gardens are in full bloom.
- ✔ Days are long, with up to 16 hours of daylight.

But this season can also have its drawbacks, such as:

- ✔ Foggy days, especially along the Nova Scotia coast and the Bay of Fundy.
- ✔ A lot of rain, especially on Cape Breton Island.
- ✔ Cool temperatures that rule out swimming in the ocean or sunbathing.

Summer

The climate from mid-June onward makes travel comfortable throughout the Maritimes. Locals and visitors alike take full advantage of long hours of daylight and temperatures that often reach 30°C (86°F). Sea breezes and moderate temperatures along the coast create an agreeable climate.

Summer is the busiest travel season for the following reasons:

- ✔ July and August are the sunniest and warmest months.
- ✔ The Maritimes come alive with outdoor activities and festivals.

However, keep these points in mind:

- ✔ Crowds are at their peak.
- ✔ Prices are at their highest and lodging reservations must be made well in advance.

Fall

The ocean climate creates relatively warm temperatures, prolonging fall in the Maritimes. The famous fall colors begin appearing in mid-September and often linger well into October.

Fall is a favorite time of year because:

- ✔ Temperatures remain pleasant well into October.
- ✔ Turning leaves put on an incredible display of color.
- ✔ Crowds thin out dramatically.
- ✔ Lodging rates are discounted.

But remember:

- ✔ Many summer-only lodgings begin closing in September, and attractions shorten their operating hours.
- ✔ Daylight hours become shorter.
- ✔ You can get caught up in the tail end of a hurricane (like Juan, which hit Halifax in late September 2003, leaving 300,000 people without power).
- ✔ Come October, there's a distinct chill in the air.

Winter

When winter hits the Maritimes, it does so with a vengeance, dumping up to 300 centimeters (118 inches) of snow on some areas in a single season. The biggest 24-hour snowfall recorded in Halifax was in February 2004, when 95 centimeters (37.4 inches) fell during a single blizzard.

Winter is wonderful for the following reasons:

- ✔ Crowds are nonexistent.
- ✔ Airlines lower their prices and hotels offer discounted rooms.
- ✔ Winter temperatures are moderated by the Atlantic Ocean.
- ✔ The snow is great for cross-country skiing.

Keep the following in mind, however:

> ✔ Most outdoor attractions are closed.
>
> ✔ Blizzards can make driving dangerous.
>
> ✔ Daylight hours are short.

Hitting the Big Events: A Maritimes Calendar

The Maritimes calendar is brimming over throughout summer, so I've focused my efforts there to give you the cream of the crop. However, the other seasons also offer their own special taste of Maritimes culture: Spring and fall bring various festivals and events to the region, while winter is trade show and exhibition time.

The following major annual events are just the beginning. Local and regional events take place around the region on a weekly basis, so check individual provincial tourism Web sites (see Appendix) for more information.

May

Nova Scotia

One of the province's most colorful events (literally) is the **Truro Tulip Festival.** Look for tours of private and public gardens, a tulip-themed art display, and an antique fair. Middle week of May. For details, call ☎ **902-798-9440** or visit www.nstulips.com.

Prince Edward Island

Charlottetown Festival Port-Lajoie is a gathering of Acadian musicians from around Atlantic Canada at venues as varied as the bandstand at Peake's Quay to the ballroom of the Delta Hotel. Second week in May. Call ☎ **902-368-1895** or visit www.festivalacadiendecharlottetown.ca for a schedule and ticket details.

June

Nova Scotia

The **Nova Scotia International Tattoo** is not what you might think. It has nothing to do with body art, but instead brings together military and civilian marching bands for what is billed as the world's largest indoor show. Over ten days starting on the last Friday in June. Call ☎ **800-563-1114** or visit www.nstattoo.ca.

July

Virtually every town and city across the Maritimes holds **Canada Day** (July 1) celebrations. The typical schedule may include a free breakfast in the morning, a parade at midday, musicians performing on outdoor stages during the afternoon and evening, and finally, a fireworks display. Contact the local information center in the town you plan to visit to see what's going on.

Nova Scotia

The biggest Maritimes music gathering, the **Stan Rogers Folk Festival** (best known as "Stanfest"), is hosted by one of the region's most remote towns, Canso. Over 10,000 fans gather for outdoor performances of all genres by Canada's leading musicians, with Celtic music getting an extra-special welcome. First weekend in July. Call ☎ **888-554-7826** or visit www.stanfest.com for details.

New Brunswick

Shediac Lobster Festival: The name alone is tempting. A local tradition for over half a century, it's a culinary salute to the Maritimes' best-known delicacy. You can enjoy the nightly lobster supper, or compete for prizes in the lobster-eating competition. Kids will love the parade, themed especially for them, as well as appearances by Mr. Lobster, the event mascot. Second week of July. Call ☎ **506-532-1122** or visit www.lobsterfestival.nb.ca.

The **Summer Shakespeare Festival** brings the Bard's work to life in an 1883 Gothic church in Saint John. Performances take place over the middle two weekends of July. Tickets are just C$10 (US$7.10). For information, visit www.summershakespeare.com.

The **Loyalist Heritage Festival** commemorates the founders of Saint John, who came to Canada in 1783. Highlights include an outdoor mock court proceeding and a parade of floats filled with costumed performers. Third weekend of July. Call ☎ **506-632-9018** for information.

The **New Brunswick Highland Games & Scottish Festival** centers on the grounds of Old Government House in Fredericton. Pipe bands, Highland dancing, and heavy-duty sports events like caber-tossing are all scheduled. Late July. Call ☎ **888-368-4444** or visit www.nbhighlandgames.com.

Prince Edward Island

Historic St. Mary's Church in Indian River provides the perfect setting for the **Indian River Festival.** Various types of music — chamber ensembles, Celtic, jazz, and more — are featured every Friday and Sunday evening through July and August. Call ☎ **800-565-3688** or visit www.indianriverfestival.com for a schedule.

August

Nova Scotia

Hundreds of enthusiasts gather at Mahone Bay for the **Wooden Boat Festival.** Boat-building demonstrations and finished boats cover the Town Wharf, while the harbor is filled with wooden boats of all shapes and sizes. Races take place across the weekend, including the Fast and Furious event, in which teams of two are given just four hours to build their craft. First weekend of August. Log on to www.woodenboatfestival.org for details.

Digby Scallop Days celebrate Digby's most famous export. The fun includes scallop-shucking demonstrations and competitions, a parade of scallop boats, and, of course, the crowning of the Scallop Queen. Early August. Contact the town office for information, ☎ **888-463-4429**, www.townofdigby.ns.ca.

New Brunswick

Moncton's **Atlantic Seafood Festival** features celebrity chefs from around the world — whose cooking lives up to their fame. Seafood tastings and demonstrations take place at various city venues, along with a Saturday night Cajun street party and a Sunday cooking competition. Middle week of August. Call ☎ **506-853-3516** for information.

For over 100 years, Acadians have celebrated their heritage and rich culture on August 15, but it wasn't until 2003 that **National Acadian Day** was officially recognized by federal and provincial governments. Look for celebrations in downtown Saint John and Moncton.

Prince Edward Island

Attending the **Atlantic Fiddler's Jamboree** in Abram Village is a wonderful way to immerse yourself in Acadian culture. Expect lots of fiddling, food, and fun, all crammed into the first weekend of August. Call ☎ **902-854-3321** for details.

The same weekend that fiddlers are strutting their stuff in Abram Village, the annual **Oyster Festival** is in full swing across the island at Tyne Valley. The crowd is at its loudest during the Canadian Oyster Shucking Championships. First weekend of August. Call ☎ **902-831-2848** for information.

The **L.M. Montgomery Festival** in Cavendish celebrates the life of PEI's best-known author. Join a writing workshop on the grounds of Green Gables, enjoy strawberries and ice cream in the garden of Montgomery's childhood home, or have your children participate in a coloring competition at Avonlea School. Second weekend in August. For details, call ☎ **902-963-7874** or www.lmmontgomeryfestival.com.

September

Nova Scotia

New Scotland Days commemorate the arrival of Pictou's first settlers, who traveled from Scotland aboard the *Hector*. Activities include woodworking demonstrations, walking tours, a children's art center, a reenactment of the arrival of the *Hector,* and a dockside *ceilidh* (a traditional Celtic celebration of singing and dancing). Second weekend of September. Call ☎ **902-485-6057** or go to www.townofpictou.com for details.

New Brunswick

Fredericton's biggest annual event is the **Harvest Jazz & Blues Festival**. Musicians take over downtown, performing on dozens of stages, both indoors and out. Second week in September. Call ☎ **506-454-2583** or visit www.harvestjazzandblues.com.

Prince Edward Island

The **PEI International Shellfish Festival,** centered on the Charlottetown waterfront, is a good place to watch the world's fastest oyster shuckers compete in various events. For C$15 (US$10.70) you can give it a go yourself with a dozen oysters and the guidance of a pro. Other event highlights include the International Chowder Championship and boat tours to the shellfish grounds. Third weekend in September. Call ☎ **902-892-0420** or go to www.peishellfish.com for all the details.

October

Nova Scotia

The **Windsor–West Hants Pumpkin Festival** is a crowd-pleasing event that includes a pumpkin weigh-off (first Saturday in October), where winning weights regularly top 450 kilograms (1,000 pounds), and a "boat" race (second Sunday in October) where participants compete in huge half-pumpkins with the insides scooped out. Call ☎ **902-798-9440** for details, or visit www.worldsbiggestpumpkins.com for a schedule and photos of last year's winners.

Cows and cowboys may seem out of place in Halifax, but the country comes to this port city for the annual **Maritime Fall Fair.** Children will love the Kid's Corral, the Super Dogs, and the large midway. Second week of October. Go to www.maritimefallfair.com for a schedule of events.

With the stunning colors of fall as a backdrop, Celtic musicians from around the world descend on Cape Breton Island for the **Celtic Colours International Festival.** Performances take place in bandstands, town halls, and theaters at over 40 island towns. Third week of October. Call ☎ **877-285-2321** or 902-539-9388, or visit www.celtic-colours.com.

November

Nova Scotia

The **Atlantic Christmas Fair,** held at Halifax's Exhibition Park, features over 400 booths filled with antiques and the work of Nova Scotian artisans. First weekend of November. For details, call ☎ **902-463-2561.** Similar events take place throughout November across the province, including **Christmas by the Sea,** also the first weekend of November, along the Pictou waterfront.

New Brunswick

The **Tidal Wave Film Festival** takes place at various theaters around Fredericton. It focuses primarily on New Brunswick filmmakers, but additional international films fill out a busy screening schedule. Early November. Call ☎ **506-455-1632** or visit www.tidalwavefilmfest.ca.

The **World Wine Festival**, at the Moncton Coliseum–Agrena Complex, attracts a blend of connoisseurs and ordinary folks looking to learn more about the world's favorite drink. More than 150 wineries participate, while seminars and foodie shows add to the mix. Call ☎ **800-258-5684** or visit www.winefestivaldesvins.

Prince Edward Island

The **Charlottetown Christmas Parade** is the biggest in Atlantic Canada. It starts downtown at 1 p.m. on the last Saturday in November.

December

Prince Edward Island

Most cities in the Maritimes organize some sort of family-oriented celebration for New Year's Eve. Charlottetown hosts one of the biggest draws, **Capital New Year in the Park,** with lots of games, sleigh rides, and a group countdown to midnight.

Table 2-2	Public Holidays
Date	*Name*
January 1	New Year's Day
March/April	Good Friday and Easter Monday
Monday preceding May 25	Victoria Day
July 1	Canada Day
First Monday in August	Civic Holiday
First Monday in September	Labour Day
Second Monday in October	Thanksgiving
November 11	Remembrance Day
December 25	Christmas Day
December 26	Boxing Day

Chapter 3

Four Great Itineraries

● ●

In This Chapter

▶ Hitting the highlights in one week

▶ Exploring the Maritimes in two weeks

▶ Doing the Maritimes with the family

▶ Taking a seafood-themed sojourn

● ●

*E*ven though the Maritimes comprise Canada's three smallest provinces, you can't expect to see everything in a single trip. If you have a specific destination or activity in mind, such as visiting Cape Breton Island for the Celtic Colours International Festival or golfing on Prince Edward Island, then you're well on your way to planning your trip. For those of you who are still pondering the best way to spend your time or which route you should take, this chapter's for you. I'll suggest some itineraries to give you an idea of where you can go and what you can see in the time you have, as well as a trip geared toward families and another specifically designed for seafood lovers.

For each itinerary, I assume you're flying into Halifax, the transportation hub of the Maritimes, and then renting a vehicle.

Seeing the Maritimes in One Week

If you have one week, you can visit each of the three provinces — but only to hit the highlights.

On **Day 1,** after arriving in **Halifax** (see Chapter 11), plan on making your first stop **Halifax Citadel National Historic Site.** Then wander down to the harbor and enjoy lunch at **Salty's**. Spend the early afternoon browsing the **Historic Properties** or taking in the **Maritime Museum of the Atlantic.** Drive to **Lunenburg** (see Chapter 12), stopping at **Peggy's Cove** to snap the famous **lighthouse** picture without the maddening midday crowds. Spend the night at the **Lunenburg Arms Hotel,** dining in-house on the patio at **Rissers.**

On **Day 2**, strike out early from Lunenburg and cut across southwestern Nova Scotia to **Digby**, walking the docks and then enjoying a scallop lunch at the **Fundy Restaurant**. Catch the ferry across the **Bay of Fundy** to **Saint John** (see Chapter 16). Spend the night at the **Homeport Historic Bed and Breakfast**, asking your friendly hosts for a dinner recommendation.

On the morning of **Day 3**, head north from Saint John to **Moncton** (see Chapter 15). If your mid-morning arrival corresponds with the incoming tide (check at the information center), hang around for the **tidal bore**. Continue north to **Shediac**. Plan a dip in Canada's warmest ocean water at **Parlee Beach**. Cross **Confederation Bridge** to **Prince Edward Island** and continue to **Charlottetown** (see Chapter 18). Dinner at the **Lucy Maud Dining Room**, a couple of drinks at **Peake's Quay**, and a bed at the **Shipwright Inn** are an ideal combination for your first night on the island.

On **Day 4**, drive north from Charlottetown to **Cavendish** (see Chapter 19). Visit the grounds of **Green Gables House** and select other "Anne" attractions; then spend the afternoon at your leisure — maybe exploring adjacent **Prince Edward Island National Park** or golfing at **Green Gables Golf Course**. Give Cavendish's touristy restaurants a miss and enjoy dinner in nearby North Rustico at the **Blue Mussel Café**, then retire to **Kindred Spirits Country Inn**.

Begin **Day 5** by driving to **Wood Islands** for the ferry trip to **Caribou**. Stop at **Pictou** (see Chapter 13), visiting **Hector Heritage Quay**. Jump aboard Highway 104 and cross Canso Causeway to **Cape Breton Island** (see Chapter 14). Continue along Highway 105 and take the signed turn to **Chéticamp**. Spend the night at the **Parkview Motel**.

On **Day 6**, rise early for the short but spectacular drive through **Cape Breton Highlands National Park** to **Pleasant Bay**, where you have a mid-morning whale-watching tour booked. Continue along the **Cabot Trail** and take lunch at the **Chowder House** in Neil's Harbour. Spend the rest of the afternoon leisurely making your way down the coast to **Glenghorm Beach Resort**.

On **Day 7**, take an early-morning walk along **Ingonish Beach**, or rise at your leisure and begin driving the final stretch of the Cabot Trail to **Baddeck**. Visit the **Alexander Graham Bell National Historic Site**, then enjoy lunch at an outside table at the **Lakeside Café**. Leave the island and overnight at **Truro** (see Chapter 13), an hour's drive from Halifax International Airport.

Exploring the Maritimes in Two Weeks

On **Day 1,** fly into **Halifax**, and spend the remainder of that day along with **Day 2** enjoying Nova Scotia's capital. Chapter 11 provides a detailed sightseeing plan for Halifax.

On **Day 3,** head along the **South Shore** to **Lunenburg** (see Chapter 12), stopping at **Peggy's Cove** and **Mahone Bay** along the way. That gives you plenty of time to visit the **Fisheries Museum of the Atlantic** and to wander the streets before checking into one of Lunenburg's historic inns.

The destination on **Day 4** is **Shelburne**, an easy two-hour drive from Lunenburg, so rise at your leisure — but be sure to hit the road in time to reach Shelburne's **Charlotte Lane Café** for lunch. Spend some time along the waterfront, watching boatbuilders at work. Leave Shelburne and continue south to **Whispering Waves Cottages,** where you can order a lobster dinner delivered to your oceanfront cabin.

On **Day 5,** continue around the South Shore to **Digby.** Explore the waterfront, stepping aboard the *Lady Vanessa* to see what a scallop boat looks like up close. Pick up fresh seafood from **O'Neil's Fundy Fish Market**, then check into the **Mountain Gap Inn** where you can cook up a storm on one of the supplied barbecues.

Plan on catching the first ferry of the morning on **Day 6,** crossing the Bay of Fundy to **Saint John** (see Chapter 16) with enough time to go through the **New Brunswick Museum** before lunching at **Market Square**. Continue down the coastline to **St. Andrews.** It's easy to soak up the village's bustling resort atmosphere by walking along the main street (although if you're staying at the upscale **Inn on the Hiram Walker Estate,** you may not want to leave the grounds).

On **Day 7,** drive to **Fredericton** (see Chapter 17) and join a guided walking tour of downtown sights such as the **Military Compound**; then spend an hour or so on your own exploring the leafy downtown streets of the provincial capital. From Fredericton, follow the **Miramichi River** north to **Miramichi** and hang a right down the **Acadian Coast** (see Chapter 15). With a room booked in **Bouctouche** at **Le Gîte de l'Oasis Acadienne**, you should have time for a beach walk along neighboring **Bouctouche Dune.**

On **Day 8,** take a dip in the warm water off **Parlee Beach** before crossing the **Confederation Bridge** to **Prince Edward Island.** Spend the afternoon catching up with your childhood memories at **Green Gables** in Cavendish (see Chapter 19). Spend the night in a room overlooking **Rustico Bay** at **Barachois Inn**. Nearby, **Fisherman's Wharf Lobster Suppers** is a good choice for a casual dinner.

Arrive in **Charlottetown** (see Chapter 18) early on **Day 9**, and park at the waterfront information center. A good starting point for exploring Charlottetown is **Province House,** in the heart of the historical precinct. Enjoy lunch at **McAsseys,** knowing you'd be paying a lot more for the same dishes at dinnertime. **Brundell River Resort** (see Chapter 21) is a world away from the capital but is easily reached in well under an hour. Make the most of long summer days by fitting in a round of golf at one of the resort's two courses.

On **Day 10,** catch the ferry to **Caribou** and spend the rest of the morning at **Hector Heritage Quay** in **Pictou** (see Chapter 13). Leave Pictou for **Cape Breton Island** (see Chapter 14) and **Baddeck.** Check into the **Dunlop Inn,** and then walk over to the **Alexander Graham Bell National Historic Site.** Have dinner at the **Lynwood Inn Dining Room.**

The next morning, **Day 11,** drive to **Ingonish.** You have two nights here; choose **Glenghorm Beach Resort** for its casual beachside atmosphere, or the **Keltic Lodge** for its historic grandeur. Spend the rest of the day at your leisure, taking a trip with **North River Kayak Tours,** golfing at **Highland Links,** or just doing absolutely nothing at all down on the beach.

Day 12 is a good one. Rise early to beat the crowds along the **Cabot Trail** in **Cape Breton Highlands National Park.** Drive all the way through the park — stopping at lookouts, maybe doing a short hike or two (the Skyline Trail if you're energetic, **Benjie's Lake Trail** if it's foggy); take a whale-watching tour at Pleasant Bay, and just generally soak up the magnificent scenery. The turnaround point is **Chéticamp.** Back in Ingonish, dine at **Seascapes Restaurant.**

On **Day 13,** drive back to **Halifax** (443km/275 miles). This is the longest day's drive in this itinerary, but it will get you back to your starting point the night before your flight leaves (and give you a few extra hours to shop in Halifax). Book a room at the **Airport Hotel Halifax** for an early morning flight, or downtown at the centrally located **Waverly Inn** for last-minute shopping.

On **Day 14,** catch your plane home.

Enjoying the Maritimes with Kids

The attractions and activities incorporated into this itinerary are designed to appeal to traveling families — a combination of learning experiences and fun times at a leisurely pace. Like the first itinerary, it spans seven days.

As with the first two itineraries, **Day 1** starts in Halifax (see Chapter 11). After getting oriented, plan on lunch at the **Harbourside Market,** where everyone can choose their favorite food (seafood, pizza, and so on). Start your vacation off with a splash on a **Harbour Hopper Tour.** If the weather is colder, head to the **Discovery Centre,** in the same building as Halifax's main information center. Drive south to **Mahone Bay** and spend the night at the family-friendly **Ocean Trail Retreat.**

On **Day 2,** visit **Lunenburg** (see Chapter 12), and then backtrack through Halifax to Highway 102, reaching **Hopewell Rocks** (see Chapter 16) by mid-afternoon. This natural attraction has to be explored at low tide; if it's high tide when you arrive, you will need to wait till the following morning. From Hopewell Rocks, drive through **Pictou** (see Chapter 13) to **Pictou Lodge Resort,** where the beach and water sports will keep everyone busy for the rest of the day.

On **Day 3,** catch the ferry to **Prince Edward Island.** It's a one-hour trip, which is enough time to find your way to the upper observation deck and award a prize to the first one in your family to spot the red-and-white lighthouse beside the ferry dock at **Wood Islands** (see Chapter 21). Stop at **Rossignol Estate Winery** for a bottle of island wine, and enjoy it on the deck of your cabin at **Lakeview Cottages** in **Cavendish** (see Chapter 19) while the kids burn off energy in the playground.

On **Day 4,** children (and many grown-ups) familiar with *Anne of Green Gables* will want to spend a full morning at **Green Gables.** Pick one of the many surrounding commercial attractions for an afternoon of fun — **Avonlea** for Anne fans, **Rainbow Valley** for the under-12's, or **Sandspit** for the older kids. Spend another night in Cavendish.

Day 5 kicks off with a drive to **Charlottetown** (see Chapter 18). For a bit of history, a visit to Founders' Hall is a must, while animal lovers may enjoy a trip searching out seals with **Peake's Wharf Boat Tours.** Stop at **Gateway Village** (see Chapter 20) to pick up last-minute souvenirs before crossing **Confederation Bridge** and heading up New Brunswick's **Acadian Coast** (see Chapter 15) to the **Rodd Miramichi River** at Miramichi.

Day 6 mixes nature and fun. Take the boardwalk through **Kouchibouguac National Park** to reach a remote stretch of beach with water warm enough for swimming, and then jump back in the car to head to **Moncton.** Let the kids go crazy at **Magic Mountain Water Park,** and then retire to one of the surrounding family-friendly motels.

On **Day 7,** it's an easy three-hour drive back to Halifax. Depending on your flight time, stagger the drive with a stop to watch the **tidal bore** in **Truro** (see Chapter 13) or a visit to **Shubenacadie Wildlife Park.** If your flight doesn't depart until early the next day, make reservations at the **Airport Hotel Halifax.**

Cruising the Coast: In Search of Seafood

Even die-hard seafood lovers like myself might not be able to keep up with the following one-week itinerary. It's designed for true devotees of the sea and all it offers up. But even if you're not a seafood fanatic, this itinerary will give you some ideas for taking advantage of the Maritimes' best-loved export.

Day 1 begins by heading north from Halifax along the **Eastern Shore** (see Chapter 13). Make your first stop the **Fisherman's Life Museum** in **Jeddore Oyster Pond.** In **Tangier,** drop by **J. Willy Krauch & Sons** to stock up on smoked salmon. If the weather is good, take a stroll along the beach in **Taylor Point Provincial Park** before continuing on to the **Salmon River House Country Inn,** where you dine at the in-house **Lobster Shack.**

On **Day 2,** take Highway 7 to **Antigonish,** then cross to **Cape Breton Island** (see Chapter 14) via the Canso Causeway. At **Baddeck,** check into **Bethune's Boathouse Cottage.** Wander along the waterfront and take an afternoon sailing trip aboard the *Amoeba,* returning to shore in time for dinner at **Baddeck Lobster Suppers.**

Day 3 starts out with a short drive along St. Anns Bay to **Ingonish.** Have some cash on hand for mussels and crab at the **Muddy Rudder,** a unique outdoor restaurant where you can watch your lunch being boiled to order. Then hit the fairways of **Highland Links.** An evening walk to **Middle Head** is a perfect way to walk off dinner from the **Atlantic Restaurant.** Spend the night at the **Keltic Lodge.**

The morning of **Day 4** is spent driving the famous **Cabot Trail** through **Cape Breton Highlands National Park.** Wander down to the docks in **Chéticamp** to watch crab boats unloading their precious catch. Head to the **Restaurant Acadian** for a feast of *Croquettes de Morue* (cod fish cakes) served by women in traditional Acadian dress. From Chéticamp, drive to **Pictou** (see Chapter 13). Learn about the traditions of fishing at the **Northumberland Fisheries Museum,** and spend the night at the **Consulate Inn.**

Day 5 starts with a ferry trip to **Prince Edward Island.** Drive through **Kings County** (see Chapter 21) and catch a tour boat from **Montague** to visit a large **seal colony,** or take a **kayak tour** at **Brundell River Provincial Park.** Plan on enjoying the most formal meal of your trip (tuck into Malpeque Bay oysters to start, then get serious with the seared Atlantic salmon) and a comfortable night's rest at **Dalvay-by-the-Sea.**

Rise early on **Day 6** for the drive to **Shediac** (see Chapter 15) and book a lobster-fishing trip with **Shediac Bay Cruises.** After the traps are hauled up, the lobsters are boiled for an onboard feast. On the way out of town, have someone snap a shot of you in front of the world's biggest lobster. Drive to **Saint John** and cross the **Bay of Fundy,** then drive along **Digby Neck** (see Chapter 12) to **Brier Island Lodge.**

On **Day 7,** plan on taking an early morning **whale-watching trip**, returning to **Digby** in time to enjoy a dockside takeout lunch of scallops from **O'Neil's Fundy Fish Market.** This gives you plenty of time to get back to Halifax for an evening flight home, or to drive only as far as **Annapolis Royal** and stay at the **Garrison House,** where the in-house restaurant does wonders with local seafood.

Chapter 4

Planning Your Budget

· ·

In This Chapter

▶ Estimating your costs

▶ Uncovering hidden charges

▶ Cutting expenses

· ·

*L*et's kick off this tiresome subject with some good news: it costs less to travel in the Maritimes than anywhere else in Canada. If you're from the United States or Europe, throw in a favorable exchange rate, and you have an inexpensive vacation destination.

Prices in this book are listed in both Canadian and U.S. dollars, with all U.S. dollar amounts rounded out to the nearest US10¢. I did my calculations using an exchange rate of US$1 to C$1.40 (or going the other way, C$1 to US71¢).

Some accommodations and tour companies quote prices in both Canadian and U.S. dollars. This can sometimes work in your favor, other times not, depending on the exchange rate of the day. Where this is the case, I have stuck with my formula of C$1 equals US71¢.

Adding Up the Elements

Budgeting for your Maritimes vacation isn't hard, and a few hours spent with pen and paper before leaving home will prevent any surprises.

To come up with the total amount that you plan to spend, begin with transportation costs, starting from your front door. Include flight costs (see Chapter 6 for tips on how to fly for less), airport shuttles at both ends, and car rental. Then add in gas, hotel rates, meals, admissions to attractions, and the cost of activities you want to participate in (whale-watching or golf, for example). The following table shows some examples of what your money will buy you in the Maritimes.

Table 4-1	What Things Cost in the Maritimes
Accommodations	
Double room at Halifax's Lord Nelson Hotel ($$$$) on a weekday	C$250 (US$178.60)
Bed-and-breakfast package for two at Halifax's Lord Nelson Hotel ($$$$) on a weekend	C$159 (US$113.60)
Self-contained unit at Lakeview Cottages, Cavendish, PEI, in August ($$)	C$115 (US$82.10)
Self-contained unit at Lakeview Cottages, Cavendish, PEI, in September	C$60 (US$42.90)
Dorm bed at Halifax Backpacker's Hostel ($)	C$20 (US$14.30)
Dining	
Dinner for two without drinks, tax, or tips at da Maurizio ($$$$), Halifax	C$120 (US$85.70)
Lobster dinner for one (including a full lobster, mussels, and dessert) at Baddeck Lobster Suppers ($$), Cape Breton Island	C$25 (US$17.90)
A six-pack of Moosehead beer	C$19 (US$13.60)
A pint of Alexander Keith's beer	C$5 (US$3.60)
Activities and Attractions	
Greens fees at Brundell River golf course in July	C$60 (US$42.90)
Greens fees *and* accommodations at Brundell River golf course in October	C$80 (US$57.10)
Adult admission to Fortress of Louisbourg	C$13.50 (US$9.60)
Whale-watching in the Bay of Fundy	C$30 (US$21.40)
Adult admission to Province House, Charlottetown	free

You'll find a budget worksheet, Making Dollars and Sense of It, in the yellow pages at the end of this book. Use it to help get a ballpark figure for how much your trip will cost.

Transportation

Costs for transportation, which will likely be the single largest cost associated with your trip, are easy to estimate. If you're arriving by air, begin with the cost of your plane ticket. Next, add your car rental costs (Chapter 7 deals with these in detail), including the rental itself, taxes, and gas expenses. If you are planning to fly from province to province, transportation costs will be an even bigger chunk of your budget.

If you're driving your own vehicle, begin by calculating its fuel consumption. To do this:

1. Fill the gas tank and zero the trip odometer.
2. Drive until the tank is nearly empty.
3. Fill the tank again and note the odometer reading.
4. Divide the distance you've driven by the number of gallons (or liters) it took to fill up the second time. This will give you a miles per gallon (or kilometers per liter) amount.

Lodging

Accommodation costs will be the biggest variable in your budget. Where you stay and, to a lesser degree, *when* you stay are the determining factors. Staying midweek at full-service city hotels is going to take a much bigger bite out of your budget than choosing rooms in rural bed-and-breakfasts with shared bathrooms.

In general, rates are at their peak from late June through mid-September. A month either side is "shoulder season" (intermediate, between high and low). The rest of the year is low season, but many bed-and-breakfasts and inns close down completely through the winter. See Chapter 2 for seasonal specifics and Chapter 8 for lodging categories and costs.

In this book, I use dollar signs ranging from $ to $$$$ to express the approximate cost for a double room in high season (excluding taxes). Hostels and some bed-and-breakfasts outside of cities fall into the $ (under C$75/US$53.60) category. (So do many nondescript roadside motels, but I steer clear of those in this book — you can find them easily enough using the Internet or accommodation guides.) Moving into the $$ range, which runs up to C$150 (US$107.10), you have a choice of most bed-and-breakfasts as well as historic inns. In Halifax, the top end of the $$ category will get you a room within walking distance of the harbor. Moving up to the $$$ (C$150 to C$225/ US$107.10 to US$160.70) and $$$$ (C$225/US$160.70 or more) categories, you will find yourself in a fine city hotel or at an upscale oceanfront resort. Very few standard rooms anywhere in the Maritimes cost more than C$250 (US$178.60).

Do-it-yourself dining

Wander down to the docks at most coastal towns and you'll find a fish market of sorts, selling everything from filleted fish to live lobsters. If you are staying in a self-contained unit, cooking fresh lobster, crab, or mussels is as easy as boiling up a big pot of salted water (okay, mussels are better when steamed with wine, but you get the idea), at a fraction of the price of dining out. Some accommodations keep a supply of pots especially for their lobster-boiling guests. Many resorts and smaller bed-and-breakfast inns have barbecues, allowing you to get a little more creative in your selection of seafood. Expect to pay around C$10 to C$12 (US$7.10 to US$8.60) per pound for fresh lobster, crab, or scallops, and around half that amount for mussels and clams.

Dining

Seafood dominates the restaurant menus across the Maritimes (for the highlights, see Chapter 1, or Cruising the Coast: In Search of Seafood in Chapter 3) and is generally well priced, even in the top restaurants. If you can do without the niceties associated with fine-dining restaurants, seafood is downright inexpensive. When it comes to dishes like lobster, you're really not sacrificing culinary quality by eating at a cheaper restaurant — it doesn't take a master chef to dunk a lobster in boiling water for a few minutes and prepare a side of melted butter.

Attractions

Let's face it, the real reason you're traveling to the Maritimes is to see the sights. So it's a good thing they are so affordable; in fact, they'll probably make up the smallest portion of your overall costs. Small town museums often have no admission fee, or else they request a simple donation to cover costs.

Count on paying around half-price admission for children and teens up to the age of 16, while entry for children under the age of six is usually free.

The definition of "child" can drop to as low as 2 years old when that child fills an actual seat (on a tour boat, for example), so you can't always expect a deal.

If you plan on visiting lots of national parks and historic sites, consider purchasing an annual pass. After all, the Maritimes have five national parks (out of 37 in all of Canada). A day pass costs C$3.50 to C$5 (US$2.50 to US$3.60), while entry to each of the Maritimes' 30 national historic sites ranges from C$2 to C$13.50 (US$1.40 to US$9.60). With these factors in mind, you can decide which, if any, of the following passes best serve your interests:

- The **National Parks of Canada Pass,** valid for entry to all Canadian national parks, is C$45 (US$32.10) adults, C$38 (US$27.10) seniors, C$22 (US$15.70) children aged 6 to 16, to a maximum of C$89 (US$63.60) per family.

- The **National Historic Sites of Canada Pass** is C$35 (US$25) adults, C$29 (US$20.70) seniors, C$18 (US$12.90) children aged 6–16, to a maximum of C$69 (US$49.30) per family.

- The **Discovery Pass** combines annual entry to both national parks and national historic sites for one price — C$59 (US$42.10) adults, C$49 (US$35) seniors, C$29 (US$20.70) children aged 6 to 16, to a maximum of C$119 (US$85) per family.

Passes can be purchased at all national parks and national historic sites. For more information, click through the Planning Your Visit links on the Parks Canada Web site, www.pc.gc.ca.

Activities and tours

Although your costs can start adding up if your tastes run to guided tours and sporting endeavors, the Maritime provinces are still a relatively inexpensive destination. A four-hour whale-watching tour in the Bay of Fundy, for example, may cost C$30 (US$21.40), but compared to C$70 (US$50) for a similar trip on the West Coast of Canada, it's an excellent value. Golfing is another relative bargain: at Highland Links (Cape Breton Island), which is rated one of the world's top 100 courses, twilight greens fees during peak summer season are a steal at C$50 (US$35.70).

You can save on some tours, golfing, and big-city options like spa treatments if you book them as part of a hotel package. Hotel Web sites are the best place to search out these deals.

Shopping

Shopping can make or break your budget. You can spend anywhere from C$2 (US$1.40) on a fridge magnet to well over C$2,000 (US$1,430) for an oil painting. Original artwork aside, you will find plenty to buy that doesn't break the bank (or stick on your fridge).

Nightlife

Keeping your costs down when it comes to after-dark entertainment is easy. In the Maritimes, it's not about what you wear or which is the hippest nightspot. The quintessential night out involves simply relaxing with a pint of beer while listening to traditional Celtic music at a local bar (that doesn't charge a cover).

Keeping a Lid on Hidden Expenses

No matter how carefully you plan, there always seem to be hidden costs you'd never considered. This section is designed to inform you about additional costs that aren't always apparent, so that you don't unwittingly blow your budget.

Talking taxes

Two taxes are added onto almost every purchase and transaction made in the Maritimes. (Notable exceptions include liquor and gas purchases, which have taxes built into the posted price.) These taxes are collected in different ways. Each province applies a **Provincial Sales Tax** on top of the Canada-wide 7% **Goods and Services Tax (GST)**. In Prince Edward Island, the provincial tax is 10%, for a grand total of 17%. In Nova Scotia and New Brunswick, the provincial tax is 8% and is blended with the GST to create what is known as a **Harmonized Sales Tax** (HST) of 15%. So, since most prices you see quoted do not include tax, you must factor in an extra 15% to 17%, depending on the province, to come up with a final price.

Now for the good news, at least for those visiting from outside Canada: HST that is paid in Nova Scotia and New Brunswick, and GST that is paid in Prince Edward Island, are refundable on accommodations and on most consumer goods (not meals or gas) for foreign visitors. Be aware, though, that you must be very organized in order to claim this refund. First and foremost, keep all your receipts. To qualify for the rebate, purchases must be at least C$50 each and total over C$200 combined. They must also be dated less than 60 days before your departure from Canada. Rebates can be claimed any time within one year from the date of purchase.

Most visitors apply for the rebate at duty-free shops (at the U.S. border or at Halifax International Airport) when exiting the country. Duty-free shops can rebate up to C$500 on the spot. For rebates of more than C$500, you'll need to mail a completed GST rebate form directly to the Canada Revenue Agency. These forms are available at city hotels and airports, and online from the Web site noted below. If claiming from outside of Canada, you must have receipts (except for accommodations) validated upon leaving Canada. For more information, contact **Canada Revenue Agency** ☎ **800-668-4748** or 902-432-5608; Internet: www.ccra-ardc.gc.ca/visitors.

Tips on Tipping

Tipping in the Maritimes is no different from anywhere else in North America. A good standard tip for service providers such as waiters and cab drivers is 15% to 20%. A smaller tip is enough for a beer at a bar, and C$1 to C$2 (US70¢ to US$1.40) per bag is a sufficient tip for a city hotel bellhop.

In the Maritimes, you can use a very simple method to calculate an average restaurant tip: in Nova Scotia and New Brunswick, leave the same amount as the HST, and in Prince Edward Island, leave double the amount of the GST. Both of these are clearly marked on the bill.

The deal on dialing

Many city hotels charge for local calls, often over C$1 (US$.70), even if you're dialing a toll-free number or using a prepaid phone card. Per-minute charges from hotel room phones for long distance calls can be exorbitant. Always check with reception before dialing out.

The least expensive way to make phone calls is to use prepaid phone cards. Available from gas stations, drug stores, and some grocery stores, they come in amounts ranging from C$5 (US$3.60) to C$50 (US$36), and can be an exceptional value if you choose the one that best suits your needs; some are designed for international calls, others for regional connections. Most can be activated by keying in a serial number at public or private phones, but the latter will incur a cost if your hotel charges for local calls.

Cutting Costs

Want to cut vacation costs without cutting corners? Don't we all. Look for the Bargain Alert icon throughout this book for hints on keeping costs down. In addition, here are some general money-saving tips:

✔ **Go off-season.** Outside of the summer (late June through mid-September) high season, you'll find hotel prices almost half the price of those in peak months. But don't push it — many smaller places close down completely in winter.

✔ **Travel mid-week.** If you can travel on a Tuesday, Wednesday, or Thursday, you may find cheaper flights to the Maritimes. When you ask about airfares, see if you can get a cheaper rate by flying on a different day. For more tips on getting a good fare, see Chapter 6.

✔ **Try a package tour.** For many destinations, you can book airfare, hotel, ground transportation, and even some sightseeing just by making one call to a travel agent or packager — and often you'll pay much less than if you put the trip together yourself. (See Chapter 6 for more on package tours.)

✔ **Reserve a room with a kitchen.** Most motels have a few rooms with cooking facilities, or at the very least a fridge and microwave. Buying supplies for breakfast will save you money (and probably calories).

✔ **Always ask for discount rates.** Membership in the Canadian Automobile Association, CAA (or its American counterpart, AAA), frequent-flyer plans, trade unions, the American Association of Retired Persons (AARP), or other groups may qualify you for savings on car rentals, plane tickets, hotel rooms, and even meals. Ask about everything; you may be pleasantly surprised.

✔ **Ask if your kids can stay in the room with you.** A room with two double beds usually doesn't cost any more than one with a queen-size bed, and many hotels won't charge you the additional-person rate if the additional person is pint-size and related to you. Even if you have to pay C$10 (US$7.10) or $15 (US$10.70) extra for a roll-away bed, you'll save big bucks by not taking two rooms.

✔ **Try expensive restaurants at lunch instead of dinner.** Lunch usually costs a lot less than what dinner would cost at a top restaurant, and the menu often boasts many of the same specialties.

✔ **Don't rent a gas-guzzler.** Renting a smaller vehicle is cheaper, and you save on gas to boot. Unless you're traveling with kids and need a lot of space, don't go beyond the economy size offered by most rental companies. For more on car rentals, see Chapter 7.

✔ **Don't use exchange bureaus.** Exchange bureaus will give unfavorable rates and then add on a commission. Instead, get your Canadian cash at an ATM, which will always give you the exchange rate of the day.

✔ **Walk a lot.** A good pair of walking shoes can save you a lot of money in taxis and other local transportation. As a bonus, you'll get to know your destination more intimately, as you explore at a slower pace.

✔ **Skip the souvenirs.** If you're concerned about money, pass on the T-shirts, key chains, salt and pepper shakers, and other trinkets. Your photographs and memories should be the best mementos of your trip.

Chapter 5

Planning Ahead for Special Travel Needs

· ·

In This Chapter

▶ Bringing the family

▶ Discovering seniors' tours

▶ Seeking out accessible travel options

▶ Searching out gay-friendly resources

· ·

*I*f you have special needs or interests, this chapter will make your travel planning a little easier. There are so many resources available now, especially online, that whatever your needs, you should be able to find the information and the support you need to ensure that your trip is safe, stress-free and, most of all, fun!

Traveling with Kids: Are We There Yet?

If you have enough trouble getting your kids out of the house in the morning, dragging them thousands of kilometers away may seem like an insurmountable challenge. But family travel can be immensely rewarding, giving you new ways of seeing the world through more youthful pairs of eyes.

Here are a few pre-trip planning tips for families:

  ✔ **Look for the Kid-Friendly icon.** I've marked lodgings, restaurants, and attractions especially suited to children throughout the book.

  ✔ **Read books set in the Maritimes.** Books such as *Anne of Green Gables* are a great introduction to the Maritimes, and kids will love visiting Cavendish after reading about it (as do thousands of adults).

✔ **Surf the Internet.** Each of the three provincial tourism Web sites has a section devoted to family travel, including kid-friendly attractions or ideas for entire vacations.

You can find good family-oriented vacation advice on the Internet from sites like the **Family Travel Network** (www.familytravelnetwork.com) and **Traveling Internationally with Your Kids** (www.travelwithyourkids.com), a comprehensive site offering sound advice for long-distance and international travel with children.

✔ **Pack favorite toys and games.** Something simple from home can act as a security blanket for a child traveling in a strange place.

✔ **Reserve a child-safety seat.** If your kids are small, be sure to arrange a car seat for your rental car.

Seeing the Maritimes Senior-style: The Age Advantage

Getting older certainly doesn't have to mean slowing down, and it even has money-saving benefits. If you're a senior citizen, mention that fact when you make your travel reservations. Most major chain hotels offer discounts for seniors (at Best Western, those over 55 enjoy a discounted stay). In most cases, people over the age of 60 qualify for reduced admission to theaters, museums, and other attractions, as well as discounted fares on public transportation and access to national parks.

Members of **AARP** (American Association of Retired Persons) get discounts on hotels and car rentals. Anyone over 50 can become a member and receive a wide range of benefits, including *AARP: The Magazine* and a monthly newsletter. You can contact AARP at 601 E Street NW, Washington, D.C. 20049 (☎ **800-424-3410** or 202-434-2277; www.aarp.org). In Canada, **Mature Outlook** is a program for over-55's that costs C$25 and includes preferred rates at Sears Travel and some hotels, as well as over C$300 in Sears coupons.

Elderhostel (☎ **877-426-8056**; Internet: www.elderhostel.org) arranges study programs for those aged 55 and over (and a spouse or companion of any age) in more than 80 countries around the world, including Canada. The courses in Nova Scotia last five to ten days, and many include accommodations (in modest inns), meals, and tuition.

Here are some recommended publications offering travel resources and discounts for seniors:

- ✔ The quarterly magazine *Travel 50 & Beyond* (Internet: www.travel50andbeyond.com)

- ✔ *Travel Unlimited: Uncommon Adventures for the Mature Traveler* (Avalon Travel Publishing) and its associated Web site, www.travelwithachallenge.com

- ✔ *101 Tips for Mature Travelers,* available from Grand Circle Travel (☎ 800-221-2610 or 617-350-7500; Internet:)

- ✔ *Unbelievably Good Deals and Great Adventures That You Absolutely Can't Get Unless You're Over 50* (McGraw-Hill)

Traveling Without Barriers

If you have special needs, finding accessible travel options takes a little research, but there are more options and resources out there than ever before. Many travel agencies offer customized tours and itineraries for travelers with disabilities. **Flying Wheels Travel** (☎ 507-451-5005; Internet: www.flyingwheelstravel.com) is a full-service travel agency that caters exclusively to travelers with disabilities. Similarly, **Accessible Journeys** (☎ 800-846-4537 or 610-521-0339; Internet: www.disabilitytravel.com) accommodates the travel needs of slow walkers and wheelchair travelers and their families and friends. The **Access-Able Travel Source** (Internet: www.access-able.com) is a comprehensive compendium of travel agents who specialize in travel for the disabled. The site also has an extensive database of lodgings around the world, including the Maritimes, that are suited to travelers with disabilities.

The following organizations offer assistance to disabled travelers:

The **Moss Rehab Hospital** (Internet: www.mossresourcenet.org) provides an online library of accessible-travel resources.

The **Society for Accessible Travel and Hospitality** (☎ 212-447-7284; Internet: www.sath.org; annual membership fees: US$45 adults, US$30 seniors and students) offers a wealth of travel resources for people with all types of disabilities, as well as informed recommendations on destinations, access guides, travel agents, tour operators, vehicle rentals, and companion services.

The **American Foundation for the Blind** (☎ 800-232-5463; Internet: www.afb.org) provides information on traveling with Seeing Eye dogs. In Canada, the **Canadian National Institute for the Blind** (☎ 416-486-2500; Internet: www.cnib.ca) offers a wide variety of services from division offices in Halifax (☎ 902-453-1480) and Fredericton (☎ 506-458-0060).

Operated by the Canadian government, **Access to Travel** (☎ 800-465-7735; Internet: www.accesstotravel.gc.ca) is an information clearinghouse of accessible travel information.

For general information specifically targeted to travelers with disabilities, the community Web site **iCan** (Internet: www.icanonline.net/channels/travel/index.cfm) has destination guides and several regular columns on accessible travel.

Twin Peaks Press (☎ 360-694-2462; Internet: http://disabilitybookshop.virtualave.net) offers a catalog of travel-related books for travelers with special needs. Also check out the quarterly magazine *Emerging Horizons* (US$14.95 per year, US$19.95 outside the U.S.; Internet: www.emerginghorizons.com) and the book *Barrier-Free Travel: A Nuts and Bolts Guide for Wheelers and Slow Walkers,* published by the same company.

Advice for Gay and Lesbian Travelers

The university cities of Halifax, Fredericton, and Charlottetown tend to have the most resources in the Maritimes for gay and lesbian travelers. Even in these centers, you won't find gay or lesbian neighborhoods, but specific hangouts like nightclubs, coffee shops, and bookstores do exist. Outside of the cities, attitudes are generally conservative but accepting.

A good source of gay- and lesbian-friendly Canadian businesses, including accommodations and restaurants, is the Web site www.gayfriendly.com, which has links to each of the Maritimes provinces. A similar database specifically for Halifax is http://welcome.to/gayhalifax. **Gay Crawler** (Internet: www.gaycrawler.com) is a search engine with a searchable database of over 17,000 gay-themed Web sites, many of which are travel-related. The **International Gay & Lesbian Travel Association (IGLTA)** (☎ 800-448-8550 or 954-776-2626; Internet: www.iglta.org) is the trade association for the gay and lesbian travel industry, and offers an online directory of gay- and lesbian-friendly travel businesses. Go to their Web site and click "Members."

Some companies offer tours and travel itineraries specifically for gay and lesbian travelers. One of these is **Freewheeling Adventures**, based in Nova Scotia (☎ **800-672-0775** or 902-857-3600; Internet: www.freewheeling.ca). **Now, Voyager** (☎ **800-255-6951** or 415-626-1169; Internet: www.nowvoyager.com) is a well-known San Francisco–based gay-owned and -operated travel service.

The following travel guides are available at most travel bookstores and gay and lesbian bookstores, or you can order them from **Giovanni's Room** bookstore, 1145 Pine Street, Philadelphia (☎ **215-923-2960**; Internet: www.giovannisroom.com):

Out and About (☎ **800-929-2268** or 415-644-8044; Internet: www.outandabout.com) offers guidebooks and a monthly newsletter packed with solid information on the global gay and lesbian scene.

Spartacus International Gay Guide and *Odysseus* (Internet: www.odyusa.com) are both good, annual English-language guidebooks for gay men.

The *Damron* guides feature separate annual books for gay men and lesbians.

Gay Travel A to Z: The World of Gay & Lesbian Travel Options at Your Fingertips (Ferrari International) is a very good gay and lesbian guidebook series.

Part II
Ironing Out the Details

The 5th Wave   By Rich Tennant

In this part...

You know you're going to the Maritimes, you've done some reading, and you have an idea of where you want to travel; now, it's time to start the actual planning. This section deals with the different ways to get there, your transportation options once you arrive, the types of lodging options and the rates you can expect to pay, the best ways to deal with your money while on the road, and assorted odds and ends that are easy to ignore — but good to be reminded about.

Chapter 6

Getting to the Maritimes

● ●

In This Chapter

▶ Talking with a travel agent

▶ Deciding on a package or escorted tour

▶ Flying in for less

▶ Traveling by land or by sea

● ●

*T*he first steps in vacation planning can be tough. You have to make a lot of commitments early on — and often back them up with your hard-earned money. You probably have questions: Should you use a travel agent? Will a self-guided or group tour suit your needs? Which tour company will provide the vacation you're dreaming of? Do you want to be totally independent, either because you're a control freak and can't stand even a single detail being out of your hands, or because you're into spontaneity and hate to have things prearranged? Whatever your goals, this chapter will help you break them down and decide what you really want to do.

If you do decide on a tour, how do you find a deal? I suggest some strategies in the next sections, but every embarkation point and destination province is different, and the tour operators I mention may not offer deals convenient to your city. If that's the case, check with a local travel agent, who will likely have a thorough knowledge of your options and how best to bundle packages, such as escorted tours and airline fares.

Using a Travel Agent

A good travel agent is like a good mechanic or a good plumber: They're hard to find, but invaluable when you locate the right one. The best way to find one is the same way you find any professional — through word of mouth.

To get the most out of your travel agent, do a little homework. Read up on your destination (you've already made a sound decision by buying this book) and pick out some accommodations and attractions that appeal to you. If you have access to the Internet, check prices on the Web yourself (see "Getting the best deal on your airfare" later in this chapter) to get a sense of ballpark figures. Then take your guidebook and Web information to the travel agent, and ask him or her to make the arrangements for you. Because they have access to more resources than even the most complete travel Web site, travel agents generally can get you a better price than you can get by yourself. Also, they can issue your tickets and vouchers right in the agency. If they can't get you into the hotel of your choice, they can recommend an alternative, which you can then check out by looking for an objective review in your guidebook.

Most travel agents work on commission. The good news is that you don't pay the commission — the airlines, hotels, and tour companies do. The bad news is that unscrupulous travel agents will try to persuade you to book the vacations that nab them the most money in commissions. Over the past few years, many airlines and resorts have begun to limit or altogether eliminate these commissions. The immediate result has been that some travel agents don't bother booking certain services unless the customer specifically requests them; others have started charging customers for their services.

Choosing an Escorted Tour

Say the words "escorted tour" and you may automatically feel as though you're being forced to choose: your money or your lifestyle. Think again. Times — and tours — have changed.

An **escorted tour** does, obviously, involve an escort, but that doesn't mean it has to be constricting. Escorted tours range from cushy bus trips, where you sit back and let the driver worry about the traffic, to adventures that include biking around Prince Edward Island or sea kayaking on Cape Breton Island — situations where most of us could use a bit of guidance. The main point is, you travel with a group, which may be just the thing if you're single and want company. In general, your costs are taken care of after you arrive at your destination, but you have to cover your airfare to get there.

Many people love escorted tours. The tour company takes care of all the details and tells you what to expect at each leg of your journey. You know your costs up front and, in the case of the tame tours, you don't get many surprises. Escorted tours can take you to the maximum number of sights in the minimum amount of time with the least amount of hassle.

If you decide to go with an escorted tour, I strongly recommend purchasing travel insurance, especially if the tour operator asks to you pay up front. But don't buy insurance from the tour operator! If the operator doesn't fulfill its obligation to provide you with the vacation you paid for, there's no reason to think that it will fulfill its insurance obligations either. Get travel insurance through an independent agency. (I tell you more about the in's and out's of travel insurance in Chapter 10.)

When considering an escorted tour, find out if you have to put down a deposit, and ask when final payment is due. In addition, there are a few simple questions you should ask before you buy:

- ✔ **What is the cancellation policy?** Can they cancel the trip if they don't get enough people? How late can you cancel if you are unable to go? Do you get a refund if you cancel? If they cancel?

- ✔ **How jam-packed is the schedule?** Does the tour schedule try to fit 25 hours into a 24-hour day, or does it give you ample time to shop or relax by the pool? If starting your day at 7 a.m. for 10 to12 hours of nonstop sightseeing sounds like a grind, certain tours may not be for you.

- ✔ **How large is the group?** The larger the group, the more time you will spend waiting for people to get on and off the bus. Tour operators may be evasive about this, because they may not know the exact size of the group until everybody has made reservations, but they should be able to give you a rough estimate.

- ✔ **Is there a minimum group size?** Some tours have a minimum size, and may cancel if they don't book enough people. If a quota exists, find out what it is and how close the tour operator is to reaching it. Again, operators may be evasive in their answers, but the information can help you select a tour that's sure to happen.

- ✔ **What exactly is included?** Don't assume anything. You may have to pay to get yourself to and from the airport. A box lunch may be included in an excursion, but drinks could be extra. Beer may be included, but not wine. How much flexibility do you have? Can you opt out of certain activities, or does the bus leave once a day, with no exceptions? Are all your meals planned in advance? Can you choose your entree at dinner, or does everybody get the same chicken cutlet?

Picking the right escorted tour is a very personal choice. I won't pretend to know what you like, but here are a few reputable companies (in alphabetical order) to get you started:

✔ **Atlantic Tours** (☎ 800-565-7173 or 902-423-6242; Internet: www.atlantictours.com) is the Atlantic Canada arm of the Grayline conglomerate. Typical offerings include an eight-day Nova Scotia tour for C$1,945 (US$1400) and the Taste of the Maritimes tour that hits the hot spots in each of the three provinces over eight days for C$2,100 (US$1,500).

✔ **Collette Vacations** (☎ 800-340-5158; Internet: www.collettetours.com) offers many tours that include the Maritimes. The six-day Best of New Brunswick tour is US$700 per person, and the Atlantic Coastal Experience hits all three provinces as well as Maine over ten days for US$1,350.

✔ **Cosmos** (Internet: www.cosmosvacations.ca) is an upscale company offering escorted tours to destinations around the world. Their nine-day Nova Scotia Adventure is C$1,200 (US$860), including some meals. Check their Web site for details, but book through your local travel agent.

✔ **Horizon Holidays** (☎ 800-387-2977 or 416-585-9911; Internet: www.horizon-holidays.com) is a Canadian tour company with an excellent reputation. Expect to pay around C$4,600 (US$3,290) for a 14-day, all-inclusive tour that visits each of the three provinces.

✔ **VBT** (☎ 800-245-3868; Internet: www.vbt.com) offers a seven-day bike tour of Prince Edward Island for US$1,345. The biking is easy, and upscale accommodations and all meals are included.

You can also check ads in the travel section of your local Sunday newspaper or in the back of national travel magazines such as *Travel & Leisure, Outside, National Geographic Traveler,* and *Condé Nast Traveler.*

Choosing a Package Tour

Unlike escorted tours, **package tours** are simply a way to buy the airfare, accommodations, and other elements of your trip at the same time and often at a discounted price. There are companies that bundle every aspect of your trip, including tours to various sights, but most deal just with selected aspects. This allows you to get a good deal by putting together an airfare and hotel arrangement, say, or a lodging and greens-fee package. Most packages tend to leave you a lot of leeway, while saving you money.

For the Maritimes, package tours can be a smart way to go. In many cases, a package tour that includes airfare, hotel, and transportation to and from the airport costs less than the price of a hotel alone that you book yourself. That's because packages are sold in bulk to tour operators, who resell them to the public. It's kind of like purchasing your vacation at a bulk store — except the tour operator is the one who buys the 1,000-count box of garbage bags and resells them ten at a time at a cost that undercuts the local supermarket.

Package tours can vary as much as those garbage bags, too. In a comparison of any two tours, one may offer a better class of hotels for the same price, or provide the same hotels for a lower price. Some book seats on scheduled airline flights; others sell charters. In some packages, your choice of accommodations and travel days may be limited. Some let you choose between escorted vacations and independent vacations; others allow you to add on just a few excursions or escorted day trips (also at discounted prices) without booking an entirely escorted tour.

Following are some recommendations (in alphabetical order) for companies offering package tours:

- ✔ **Air Canada** (☎ **888-247-2262;** Internet: www.aircanada.ca), Canada's national airline, offers numerous ways to book package tours incorporating Air Canada flights. **Destina.ca** (☎ **800-563-5633** or 514-845-5633; Internet: www.destina.ca) is an online travel site with Maritimes package deals; **Air Canada Vacations** (Internet: www.aircanadavacations.com) offers packages that can be booked through travel agents as well as an online search tool for air–car rental combos; and **Air Canada's Canada** (☎ **888-271-1584**; Internet: www.aircanadascanada.com) is a reservation service that incorporates airfares from U.S. destinations with car rental–hotel packages in Canada.

- ✔ **Hillcrest Vacations** (Internet: www.hillcrestvacations.com) combines rail travel with car rental and accommodations for independent travelers. Its Web site has details, but bookings must be made through travel agents.

- ✔ **Liberty Travel** (☎ **888-271-1584;** Internet: www.libertytravel.com) is one of the biggest packagers in the Northeast. It offers separate package tours to each of the three Maritimes provinces.

- ✔ **Rodd Hotels and Resorts** (☎ **800-565-7633** or 902-892-7448; Internet: www.rodd-hotels.ca) is an upscale Maritimes hotel chain with golf and "leisure" packages that usually include breakfast and passes to local attractions.

✓ **VIA Rail** (☎ **888-842-7245** or 514-871-6000; Internet: www.viarail.ca) and Canadian tour operators combine forces to offer some interesting packages that originate in Toronto and Montreal. Click the "Adventure and Outdoor Activities" link on the Web site for details.

✓ **WestJet** (☎ **866-787-1277**; Internet: www.westjet.com) partners with Worldwide Travel Exchange (an arm of Expedia), offering its own flights along with car rental–hotel packages throughout the Maritimes.

Several big online travel agencies — **Expedia**, **Travelocity**, **Orbitz**, and **Site59** — also do a brisk business in packages.

Traveling by Plane

All Canadian and several major U.S. carriers serve Halifax, the main air hub for the Maritimes. You can also fly into Saint John, Moncton, or Charlottetown. With plenty of competition, prices are usually reasonable and sometimes very good.

Halifax International Airport (Internet: www.hiaa.ca), the busiest airport in the Maritimes, handles three million passengers annually in two modern terminals. It is served with direct flights by major Canadian and U.S. airlines (Table 6.1 lists them all) from 30 locations. The Web site www.flyhalifax.com is an excellent resource that allows you to search for flights to Halifax from specific destinations and also check flight arrival and departure times.

The other major airports are **Greater Moncton International Airport** (Internet: www.gma.ca), served by Air Canada, CanJet, and WestJet; **Saint John Airport** (Internet: www.saintjohnairport.com), served by Air Canada and Pan Am (☎ **800-359-7262**; Internet: www.flypanam.com); **Greater Fredericton Airport** (Internet: www.frederictonairport.ca), served by Air Canada and Delta; and **Charlottetown Airport** (www.charlottetownairport.ca), served by Air Canada and Jetsgo.

If you're Maritimes-bound from Europe, your flight will be routed through Toronto or Montreal. Flights originating in Asia and the South Pacific will require a plane-change in Vancouver or Toronto.

Table 6-1	Airlines Serving Halifax	
Carrier	**Phone**	**Web Site**
Air Canada	☎ 888-247-2262	www.aircanada.ca
Air Canada Jazz	☎ 888-247-2262	www.flyjazz.com
CanJet	☎ 800-809-7777	www.canjet.com
Continental	☎ 800-784-4444	www.continental.com
Delta	☎ 800-221-1212	www.delta.com
Jetsgo	☎ 866-440-0441	www.jetsgo.com
Northwest	☎ 800-225-2525	www.nwa.com
WestJet	☎ 888-937-8538	www.westjet.com

Now that you know a little about who flies into the Maritimes, it's time to start searching out the best fares. Read the advice below, then use the worksheet titled "Fare Game: Choosing an Airline" located at the back of this book to do some comparison shopping.

Getting the best deal on your airfare

Competition among major airlines is unlike that of any other industry. Every airline offers virtually the same product (basically, a coach seat is a coach seat is a . . .), yet prices can vary by hundreds of dollars.

Business travelers who need the flexibility of last-minute changes, or those who want to get home before the weekend, pay (or at least their companies pay) the premium rate, known as the *full fare*. But if you can book your ticket far in advance, stay over a Saturday night, and are willing to travel with restrictions such as non-changeable flights, you can save big bucks. Quotes from Air Canada illustrate this point well: A full-fare return ticket from Boston to Halifax costs US$890, while the least expensive "Web saver" fare costs just US$165 for the same dates. The difference shows how it pays to plan ahead and to be flexible.

The airlines also periodically hold sales, in which they lower the prices on their most popular routes. These fares have advance purchase requirements and date-of-travel restrictions, but you can't beat the prices. As you plan your vacation, keep your eyes open for these sales, which tend to take place in seasons of low travel volume, November to March. You almost never see a sale around the peak summer vacation months of July and August, or around Thanksgiving or Christmas, when many people fly regardless of the fare they have to pay.

Buying from a consolidator

Consolidators buy seats in bulk and sell them to the public at discounted rates. Several reliable consolidators have worldwide locations and are available on the Internet. In the United States, **STA Travel** (☎ **800-781-4040**; Internet: www.statravel.com) is a world leader in student travel. The Canadian equivalent is **Travel Cuts** (☎ **866-246-9762**; Internet: www.travelcuts.com). In both cases, you don't need to be a student to take advantage of their good fares. **Flight Centre** is a large consolidator with offices around the world and competitive online fares. Contacts are: U.S. ☎ **866-967-5351**; Internet: www.flightcentre.us; Canada ☎ **888-967-5355**; Internet: www.flightcentre.ca; United Kingdom ☎ **0870-499-0040**; Internet: www.flightcentre.co.uk. London-based **Trailfinders** (☎ **020-7937-5400**; Internet: www.trailfinders.com) always has competitive fares to North America, along with easy-to-understand rental car and hotel packages. They also produce an informative travel magazine, or you can sign up for their e-mail service.

Buying your ticket online

If you are simply buying a flight from one point to another, you'll find it hard to beat prices that are available online. Searching out the best online airfares can be more time-consuming than using a travel agent, but it gives you more flexibility and you won't be stuck with any additional charges. Most sites prompt you to enter a departure point and destination along with your dates of travel, so if you're not sure of thespecifics of your trip, you can play with the variables until you find the best price. The displayed results usually include a number of flight and fare options.

Travel Web sites

When looking for flights, I begin with the airlines that I know fly to my destination; then I go to an agency site like Expedia and start my comparison shopping. For an itinerary that is more complicated than a simple round trip, such as ending the trip somewhere other than your starting point, or flying home from somewhere other than your first destination (known as an "open-jaw" itinerary), it's usually easier to use a local travel agent.

The "big three" online travel agencies are **Expedia** (Internet: www.expedia.com), **Travelocity** (Internet: www.travelocity.com), and **Orbitz** (Internet: www.orbitz.com). For travelers already in Canada, try www.expedia.ca or www.travelocity.ca; U.K. residents can go for www.expedia.co.uk. Each has different business deals with the airlines and may offer different fares on the same flights, so shopping around is wise.

Of the smaller travel agency Web sites, **SideStep** (Internet: www.sidestep.com) receives good reviews from users. It's a browser add-on that claims to "search 140 sites at once," although in reality it only beats competitors' fares as often as other sites do.

If you're in no rush to book your vacation, you can sign up for sale alerts at some of the major travel Web sites. Two of the big three, Expedia and Travelocity, will send you an e-mail notification when a cheap fare to your favorite destination becomes available.

Opaque-fare services

If you're willing to give up some control over your flight details, use an *opaque fare service* such as **Priceline** (Internet: www.priceline.com) or **Hotwire** (Internet: www.hotwire.com). Both offer rock-bottom prices in exchange for travel on an airline that will remain unknown to you until you purchase your ticket. Be assured that the "mystery airlines" are all major, well-known carriers, and the possibility of traveling from Detroit to Halifax via Vancouver is remote. On the other hand, your chances of getting a 6 a.m. or 11 p.m. flight are pretty high. Hotwire tells you flight prices before you buy; Priceline usually has better deals than Hotwire, but you have to play their "name our price" game.

Last-minute specials

Great last-minute deals are available through free weekly e-mail services provided directly by the airlines, including **Air Canada** (Internet: www.aircanada.ca). Usually, these deals are announced on a Tuesday or Wednesday, and must be purchased online. Most are only valid for travel that weekend, but some can be booked weeks or months in advance. Sign up for weekly e-mail alerts at airline Web sites, or check mega-sites that compile comprehensive lists of last-minute specials, such as **Smarter Living** (Internet: www.smarterliving.com) and **Webflyer** (Internet: www.webflyer.com).

Traveling by Other Means

Though flying is the primary means of getting to the Maritimes, some people enjoy a road trip, or have mobility issues that make flying impossible, or simply prefer not to fly. Here's the lowdown on traveling to the Maritimes by train, car, and ferry.

Taking the Train

VIA Rail (☎ **888-842-7245** or 514-871-6000; Internet: www.viarail.ca) operates the *Ocean* between Montreal and Halifax up to six times weekly, with stops in Moncton and Truro en route. The two classes of travel are Comfort (lots of leg room, reclining seats, reading lights, pillows and blankets, and a Skyline Car complete with bar service) and Easterly (daytime seating, nighttime sleeping room, a domed lounge, and a dining car for passengers in this class). The Comfort Class fare between Montreal and Halifax is C$234 (US$167), while the fare in Easterly Class is C$476 (US$340). Discounts of up to 35% applied to bookings made more than seven days in advance. Children, seniors, and students also enjoy discounted travel.

If you are planning extensive rail travel in Canada, VIA Rail's **Canrailpass** may be a worthwhile investment. It allows for unlimited rail travel across Canada for 12 days over any given 30-day period for C$719 (US$513) in high season (June to mid-October) and C$448 (US$320) the rest of the year.

 While the Canrailpass can be a good deal if you plan to do a lot of rail traveling, it comes with a few hitches: If you travel on the Montreal–Halifax service, for example, it counts as two days of travel, and travel on the Bras d'Or to Cape Breton Island incurs a surcharge. So check to see that the routes you plan to take don't incur extra charges that will make this pass a not-so-smart investment.

Driving in

You can drive to the Maritimes via numerous highways, all of which enter the region through New Brunswick.

- ✓ **Trans-Canada Highway,** which takes on different numbers as it crosses the country, enters New Brunswick near Edmundston as Highway 2. Using this route, it's 1,238km (769 miles) from Montreal and 1,757km (1,092 miles) to Halifax. Planning on driving across Canada via the Trans-Canada Highway? Gas up. It's 6,187km (3,846 miles) from Vancouver to Halifax.

- ✓ **Interstate 95** links Portland and Bangor, Maine, with the Maritimes, crossing the Canadian border west of Fredericton at the Houlton/Woodstock crossing.

- ✓ **Highway 1** winds its way along the Maine coastline to the Calais/St. Stephen border, crossing in the southern corner of New Brunswick. From this point, it's 90 km (56 miles) to Saint John, and a little farther to Fredericton.

- ✓ **Highway 189** branches off Maine's Highway 1, 77km (48 miles) south of Calais. It makes for an interesting approach to New Brunswick. At Lubec, it crosses a bridge to Campobello Island, across the border in New Brunswick. From this point, it's a short ferry ride to Deer Island, and then another to reach the mainland. Both ferries are summer-only.

Arriving by Ferry

A glance at a map will make it obvious that catching a ferry from Maine to Yarmouth, on the southwestern tip of Nova Scotia, will shorten the journey considerably. You have two options, both convenient and probably less expensive than you may expect. Reservations are strongly recommended on both routes. They are:

- ✔ **Bay Ferries (☎ 888-249-7245;** Internet: www.catferry.com) operate a service between Bar Harbor, Maine, and Yarmouth, twice daily in each direction between mid-May and mid-October. It is North Amercia's fastest car ferry, doing the journey in under three hours (a traditional ferry would take twice as long). Sample one-way fares are US$55 adults, US$50 seniors, US$25 children 5 to17, US$120 for vehicles up to 6.4 meters (21 feet) long. Discounts apply in the shoulder season.

- ✔ *Scotia Prince* **(☎ 800-341-7540;** Internet: www.scotiaprince.com) is more like a cruise ship than a ferry, with fine dining, self-contained cabins, and rooftop hot tubs. It departs once daily from Portland, Maine for Yarmouth, and the crossing takes 11 hours. High season one-way fares are US$90 adults, US$45 children 5 to 12, US$110 for vehicles up to 2.1 meters (7 feet) high, US$40 to US$160 for a cabin. The *Scotia Prince* runs from May through mid-October.

Chapter 7

Getting Around the Maritimes

• •

In This Chapter

▶ Exploring the Maritimes by car

▶ Taking the ferry

▶ Flying or riding the rails between provinces

• •

So, you know how you're getting *to* the Maritimes: now you need to know how to get around. This chapter covers driving (really the only way to explore beyond the downtown core of the major cities) as well as two important ferry routes. If you're willing to shell out big bucks, flying between provinces is an option, as is catching the train, although the latter is limited in its options.

Driving Around

Unless you're on an escorted tour, driving is the best way to get around the Maritimes. All you need is a vehicle, a good set of maps, a full tank of gas, and a sense of adventure.

Motoring in the Maritimes is similar to that in other parts of Canada or in the United States. Major thoroughfares are kept in excellent condition, and all towns and minor highways are well marked. Gas stations are regularly spaced — you'll find one in almost every town — so running out of gas won't be a problem if you keep an eye on the gauge. Expect to pay around C80¢ to C90¢ per liter (US$2.30 to US$2.60 per gallon) for gas, though prices can fluctuate quite dramatically.

Apart from other drivers, the most important thing to watch for on the roads is wildlife, most commonly deer, moose, and bears, especially if you're driving at dawn or dusk. Areas with lots of animal activity are usually signposted, but it is always best to scan both sides of the road just to make sure. In winter, blowing snow and blizzards can make driving extremely dangerous.

Wearing a seat belt is compulsory in Canada, and the fine for not wearing one is steep. Most drivers voluntarily travel with their headlights on at all times; motorcyclists are required by law to ride with their lights on. Traffic in both directions must stop when school buses have their red lights flashing. Pedestrians have the right-of-way at crosswalks.

Renting a car

The good news is that every major car rental company is represented in the Maritimes, so you can easily shop around for the best deal. The bad news is that demand is high during the peak summer months (mid-June to early September), so prices can be high. Rental car companies and their contact numbers and Web sites are listed in the Appendix.

Getting the best deal

Car rental rates vary even more than airline fares. The price depends on the size of the vehicle, the length of time you keep it, where and when you pick it up and drop it off, where you take it, and a host of other factors. The following tips could help save you hundreds of dollars:

- ✔ Check your rental car company's weekend rates — they may be lower than the weekday rates. If you're keeping the car for five or more days, a weekly rate may be cheaper than the daily rate.

- ✔ Ask about drop-off conditions: Some companies may add a drop-off charge if you don't return the car to the same rental location.

- ✔ Rent your vehicle from someplace other than the airport. At Halifax International Airport, for example, a Concession Recovery Fee adds 10.5% to all airport rentals. To save this charge, rent a vehicle at one of dozens of downtown agencies.

- ✔ Find out whether age is an issue. Many car rental companies add on a fee for drivers under 25, while some don't rent to them at all.

- ✔ If you see an advertised price in your local newspaper, be sure to ask for that specific rate; otherwise you may be charged the standard (higher) rate. Don't forget to mention membership in AAA, AARP, and trade unions. These memberships usually entitle you to discounts ranging from 5% to 30%.

- ✔ Check your frequent-flier accounts. Airlines often team up with rental car companies to offer you incentives to use their services. Not only are your favorite (or at least most-used) airlines likely to have sent you discount coupons, but most car rentals add at least 500 air miles to your account.

✔ As with other aspects of planning your trip, using the Internet can make comparison shopping for a car rental much easier. You can check rates at most of the major agencies' Web sites. Plus, all the major travel sites, such as **Travelocity** (Internet: www. travelocity.com), **Expedia** (Internet: www.expedia.com), **Orbitz** (Internet: www.orbitz.com), and **Smarter Living** (Internet: www.smarterliving.com), have search engines that can dig up discounted car-rental rates. Just enter the car size you want, the pickup and return dates, and the location, and the server returns a price. You can even make the reservation through any of these sites.

Adding up the charges

In addition to the standard rental prices, other optional charges apply to most car rentals (along with some not-so-optional charges, such as taxes). The *Loss Damage Waiver* (LDW), which requires you to pay for damage to the car in a collision, is covered by many credit card companies. Check with your credit card company before you go, to see if you can avoid paying this hefty fee (as much as C$25/US$17.90 a day).

The car rental companies also offer additional *liability insurance* (if you harm others in an accident), *personal accident insurance* (if you harm yourself or your passengers), and *personal effects protection* (if your luggage is stolen from your car). Your insurance policy on your car at home probably covers most of these unlikely occurrences. However, if your own insurance doesn't cover you for rentals or if you don't have auto insurance, definitely consider the additional coverage (ask your car rental agent for more information). Unless you're toting around the Hope diamond (and you wouldn't want to leave that in your car trunk anyway), you can probably skip the personal effects insurance, but driving around without liability or personal accident coverage is never a good idea. Even if you're a good driver, other people may not be, and liability claims can be complicated.

 Most companies also offer refueling packages, in which you pay for your initial full tank of gas up front and then return the car with an empty gas tank. The prices can be competitive with local gas prices, but you don't get credit for any gas remaining in the tank. If you reject this option, you pay only for the gas you use, but you have to return the car with a full tank or face charges that are around 50% higher per liter than at the pump to make up for the shortfall. If you tend to run late and a fueling stop may make you miss your plane, you're a good candidate for the fuel-purchase option.

Ferrying Between Provinces

The three provinces are linked not only by road (or bridge, in the case of PEI) but also by ferry. This is a fun, affordable way to travel while cutting down on driving.

Nova Scotia to New Brunswick

The ferry across the Bay of Fundy between Digby, Nova Scotia, and Saint John, New Brunswick, can cut a considerable chunk from your driving mileage if your itinerary takes you either up the Maine coast (and you didn't use the ferry systems detailed in Chapter 6) or on a circuitous route through both Nova Scotia and New Brunswick.

The *Princess of Acadia* plies this route year-round, with up to three sailings daily, depending on the season. The trip takes 2–3 hours and is C$20 to C$35 (US$14.30 to US$25) for adults, C$17.50 to C$25 (US$12.50 to US$17.90) for seniors, C$10 to C$15 (US$7.10 to US$10.70) for children 5 to 17, and C$70 to C$75 (US$50 to US$53.60) for vehicles under 6.4 meters (21 feet). Fare variations reflect seasonal pricing (July to early October is high season). Contact **Bay Ferries** (☎ **888-249-7245** or 902-245-2116; Internet: www.nfl-bay.com) for information and reservations.

Nova Scotia to Prince Edward Island

Although Prince Edward Island is linked to mainland New Brunswick by a bridge, the ferry link between Caribou (north of Pictou, Nova Scotia) and Wood Islands (on the southeastern corner of PEI) is also a viable way of crossing Northumberland Strait.

In July and August, there are eight sailings daily in each direction, with less frequent service in spring and fall. Drifting ice closes the service down completely between mid-December and April. Once the vessel gets going, the crossing takes little more than an hour. The round-trip fare is C$49.50 (US$35.40) per vehicle including passengers. For walk-on passengers, the cost is C$12 (US$8.60) for adults, C$10 (US$7.10) for seniors; no charge for children under five. For information, contact **Northumberland Ferries** (☎ **902-566-3838**; Internet: www.nfl-bay.com). No reservations are taken, so plan on catching a mid-week (except Friday afternoon) or early morning sailing to avoid a long wait.

Getting to Prince Edward Island is free, regardless of whether you cross the Confederation Bridge or take the ferry. The bridge toll and ferry fare are only collected when you leave the island. The bridge toll (C$38.50/US$27.50) is less expensive than traveling by ferry, so if you cross to the island aboard the ferry and return to the mainland via the bridge, you'll save a bit of money.

To Newfoundland

I didn't forget about Newfoundland when writing this book. It was simply that it was impossible to comprehensively cover the three Maritime provinces as well as their northern neighbor in the page count I was allotted. (Collectively, the province of Newfoundland and Labrador and the Maritime provinces are known as Atlantic Canada.)

For those who plan on visiting Newfoundland, this section details ferry routes and rates from Nova Scotia.

Marine Atlantic (☎ 800-341-7981 or 902-794-5200; Internet: www.marine-atlantic.ca) operates the following ferries between North Sydney and the Newfoundland docks (reservations are required for all sailings):

- ✔ **Port aux Basques,** located at the southwestern tip of Newfoundland. This ferry ride takes between five and seven hours, with departures twice daily year-round. Costs are (one-way) C$25 (US$17.90) for adults, C$22.75 (US$16.30) for seniors, and C$12.50 (US$8.90) for children 5 to 12. Vehicles up to 6 meters (20 feet) cost C$72.75 (US$52), and accommodations range from a dorm bed for C$14.50 (US$10.40) to an ensuite cabin for C$90 (US$64.30).

- ✔ **Argentia,** situated a couple of hours' drive from the capital, St. John's (not to be confused with Saint John, New Brunswick). This route is much longer and more of an adventure, taking around 16 hours and crossing sometimes-rough open ocean. Ferries depart twice a week between mid-June and mid-October. Sample one-way fares are: C$68.50 (US$49) adults, C$61.75 (US$44) seniors, C$34.25 (US$24.50) children 5 to 12, C$16 (US$11.40) reclining chair, C$25 (US$17.90) dorm bed, C$125 (US$89.30) ensuite cabin, and C$146 (US$104.30) for vehicles up to 6 meters (20 feet).

Before leaving home, request an information package from **Newfoundland & Labrador Tourism (☎ 800-563-6353** or 709-729-2831; Internet: www.gov.nf.ca/tourism). The recommended guidebook is *Frommer's Newfoundland and Labrador.*

Getting Around by Other Means

If you aren't on an escorted tour and don't want to drive, your options for travel in the Maritimes are limited to flying between provinces or catching the train along one of two main routes.

Traveling by plane

Air Canada (☎ 888-247-2262; Internet: www.aircanada.ca) or one of its partners such as Air Canada Jazz flies daily between Halifax, Moncton, Fredericton, Saint John, Charlottetown, and Sydney. At each of these airports, you'll find transportation to downtown, car rental desks, and an information booth or a bank of phones linked to a directory of local accommodations.

Taking the train

VIA Rail (☎ 888-842-7245 or 514-871-6000; Internet: www.viarail.ca) service between Montreal and Halifax stops in Truro, Moncton, Miramichi, and Bathurst, making it a viable transportation option. From Moncton, bus connections can be made to Charlottetown, Saint John, and Fredericton. Fares are reasonable, especially if purchased seven or more days in advance.

VIA Rail also operates the summer-only **Bras d'Or** between Halifax and Sydney. It is mostly used by vacationers on package or escorted tours, but anyone can book. Huge windows and a special dome car are perfect for taking in the scenery, and an onboard guide gives a running commentary. A light breakfast and lunch are included in the one-way adult fare of C$232 (US$165.70).

Chapter 8

Deciding Where to Stay

. . . .

In This Chapter

▶ Choosing the best overnight option

▶ Wheeling and dealing for a good night's sleep

. . . .

*I*t's easy to find accommodations that meet the basic criteria of being clean and comfortable — the Maritimes has all the chain hotels and motels you already know. But unless you're traveling there to have the same experience you can have anywhere else, you should consider my recommended lodgings in Chapters 11 to 21. The chains are sure to lack Maritime charm, which is why I recommend them only when there are no other options.

Finding the Place That's Right for You

People have different ideas about the type of places they want to stay at, so no lodging I recommend in this book will appeal to everyone. I've included a wide cross-section of options to suit all tastes and budgets — not hard to do, as the Maritimes has everything from big-city luxury hotels to rustic wilderness cabins. And compared to other North American destinations, hotel rooms in the Maritimes are reasonably priced.

Remember to add taxes to all quoted prices — the 15% Harmonized Sales Tax in Nova Scotia and New Brunswick and 17% worth of taxes on Prince Edward Island. Halifax accommodations also add a 1.5% **Destination Halifax Marketing Levy** to your bill.

Hotels and motels

You'll find a plethora of luxury hotels in the major cities. Most international chains are represented in each province, along with **Fairmont Hotels and Resorts** (Internet: www.fairmont.com) and **Delta Hotels** (Internet: www.deltahotels.com), both upscale Canadian chains with impeccable credentials. These hotels have rack rates in the top $$$$ (over C$225/US$160) category, but generally offer discounts on weekends or for online bookings.

Reliable mid-priced chains like **Holiday Inn** (Internet: www. holiday-inn.com) and **Best Western** (Internet: www.bestwestern. com) are also plentiful. The Maritimes' own **Rodd Hotels and Resorts** (Internet: www.rodd-hotels.ca) is in this same $$ to $$$ price bracket. On the edge of the cities and in smaller towns, you'll find hotels in the middle of the $$ category. Their rooms usually come with fewer amenities and the furnishings may be older.

If you just need somewhere to spend the night or you can't get a room at one of my recommended lodgings, a roadside motel will do. Access to the room is normally from the parking lot. In general, motels don't have attached dining rooms. They are common throughout the Maritimes, other than in Prince Edward Island. Always in the $ or $$ range but rarely over C$100 (US$71.40), you will find them listed in provincial tourism guides, or look for their brochures displayed in local information centers.

Bed-and-breakfasts

Some travelers plan their vacations around bed-and-breakfasts; others avoid them like the plague. If you fall into the first category, you will have plenty of scope in the Maritimes. Literally hundreds of homes in each of the three provinces have been converted to bed-and-breakfast accommodation, with a wide range of services and prices to match (anywhere from C$50/US$35.70 to over C$200/US$142.90 double). By doing some research and asking the right questions, you can easily avoid unpleasant surprises. If you follow my recommendations, you won't have to worry about ending up in a room left vacant by the owner's college-bound kid. My picks are all proper businesses with more than two guest rooms, not individuals looking to rent an extra room to make some quick cash.

Bed-and-breakfasts are a great place to meet fellow travelers, learn more about the area from knowledgeable hosts, and enjoy a hearty breakfast before hitting the road. It is a perceived lack of privacy that puts most people off this type of accommodation. Most North American travelers do not relish the idea of sharing a bathroom with other guests — but this is not the case at all bed-and-breakfasts. Here are the accepted definitions (I use them throughout this book), but it's always best to double-check when reserving so you know exactly what you're getting:

- ✔ **Ensuite bathroom:** A bathroom that is accessed directly from the guest room, and only used by the guests in that room.

- ✔ **Private bathroom:** A bathroom that is for the sole use of one room, but may be down a hallway.

- ✔ **Shared bathroom:** A bathroom that is used by guests in more than one room.

If you're traveling with children or have a disability, it is very important that you make the proprietor aware of your situation before making a reservation. Children may not be appreciated by other guests (who may be vacationing from their own kids!). Many bed-and-breakfasts are converted residences, so wheelchair access is often limited.

Cottages, cabins, and chalets

This type of accommodation is perfect for families or those who don't need the luxuries of resort living.

The words "cabin" and "cottage" are mostly interchangeable, but "cottage" sounds somehow more inviting (sort of like using "home" instead of "house"). Either way, you can expect a freestanding unit with a bathroom and linen provided. Some may have extras like a kitchen or a private veranda. Generally, a chalet will be a larger unit with more amenities and some attention to décor.

Many cabin resorts pre-date World War II, and became increasingly popular as families began to vacation together in the coastal resort towns. These old cabins, loaded with character, remain; some have been combined with newer and bigger units to suit a wider range of budgets and needs, and feature facilities that may include a restaurant or canoe rentals. For this reason, pricing runs the full spectrum. A good example is **Glenghorm Beach Resort** on Cape Breton Island (Internet: www.capebretonresorts.com), where the most basic cabins are at the bottom end of the $$ price range while luxurious chalets cost well into the top $$$$ category at C$395 (US$282).

Expect older, more basic cabins to be in the $ category (under C$75/US$53.60). The addition of cooking facilities doesn't usually affect the price that much, with many self-contained cabins costing around C$100 (US$71.40). By the time you reach the $$$ category, you will be getting a modern, self-contained cabin with a separate bedroom.

Cabins and cottages are priced seasonally throughout the Maritimes, with peak season in July and August. Many close completely after September, reopening in April or May.

Resorts

While most hotels and motels are set up for overnight stays, resorts are designed to keep you happy for an entire vacation. The Maritimes' top resorts do this well, with golf courses, activity programs, spa services, and a choice of dining rooms. Resorts are generally kid-friendly, with children's programs and menus as well as baby-sitting services.

Of course, you pay for all this pampering. Rack rates at most resorts are in the $$$ to $$$$ range, with decent savings for booking a package that may include meals or greens fees. Resorts are the first to offer discounts outside of summer, so look for bargains in June and September, while the property is still functioning fully. You will find my resort recommendations liberally spread throughout this book, but the Web sites for **Rodd Hotels and Resorts** (Internet: www.rodd-hotels.ca), **Cape Breton Resorts** (Internet: www.capebretonresorts.com), and **Signature Resorts** (Internet: www.signatureresorts.com) are a good place to decide if this type of accommodation seems suited to your needs.

Booking Your Accommodations

Some people book a room by calling a hotel, asking for a reservation, and paying whatever price is quoted. That won't be you, though, because after reading this section, you'll know how to find the best rates available.

Uncovering the truth about rack rates

The *rack rate* is the maximum rate a hotel charges for a room. It's the rate you get if you walk in off the street and ask for a room for the night. (You sometimes see these rates printed on the fire/emergency exit diagrams posted on the back of your door.) Hotels are happy to charge you the rack rate, but you can almost always do better. Perhaps the best way to avoid paying the rack rate is surprisingly simple: Just ask for a cheaper or discounted rate. You may be pleasantly surprised.

Some lodgings, especially bed-and-breakfasts and hostels, really mean what they say. The rates they publish are what everyone pays.

The price is right

In all but the smallest accommodations (mostly bed-and-breakfasts), the rate you pay for a room depends on many factors — chief among them being when you travel and how you make your reservation. The following are some strategies you can use to find the best rate possible.

Shop early for the greatest choice

If you are planning on traveling to the Maritimes in summer, it's not too early to start making bookings at the beginning of the year. Some chain hotels sell a percentage of rooms at a discounted rate, and when they're gone, they're gone — everyone else pays a higher rate. Booking early won't get you a discount at that quaint little bed-and-breakfast, but it will ensure that you get the room you want, rather than, say, their smallest room with a bathroom down the hallway, which is always last to go.

Travel off-peak

As shown as an example in Table 4-1 in Chapter 4, Lakeview Lodge, in Cavendish on Prince Edward Island, rents self-contained cottages for C\$115 (US\$82.10) in July and August. If you make your booking anytime outside of these two months — even for the first week of September — the rate drops to C\$60 (US\$42.90), a saving of almost 50%. The difference isn't always this abrupt — many accommodations discount a bit during "shoulder season" (June and September), then further discount rates the rest of the year (or close altogether).

Luxury hotels and big resorts often charge less than half their peak rates during the off-season, which often puts them in competition with mid-range chain hotels. Check the Web sites of the major chains as well as of Canadian companies such as **Delta Hotels** (Internet: www.deltahotels. com) and **Rodd Hotels and Resorts** (Internet: www.rodd-hotels.ca), who lead the way in this regard.

See Chapter 2 for more information on what rates you can expect during different times of year in the Maritimes.

Ask for discounts

Hotels usually offer discounts for people with travel club or other memberships. In most cases, you can expect a 10% to 15% discount simply for flashing your AAA card. Going gray has its advantages too — Best Western offers an automatic 10% discount to all travelers over 55, with upgrades, late checkouts, and complimentary breakfasts thrown in for good measure. Most major hotel chains have loyalty programs, but you usually don't really need to be loyal to reap the benefits. Members of Holiday Inn's Priority Club and Fairmont's President Club, for example, enjoy daily papers, free local calls, late checkouts, and more, simply for signing up.

Guesthouses and bed-and-breakfasts are a little different. You can ask for a discount if you want to stay more than one night or pay with cash, but don't push it.

Surf the Web for hotel deals

The Internet is your best friend when it comes to gathering information about accommodations. Start with the Web sites of my recommended lodgings. They will often provide you with up-to-date pricing, special offers, and online reservation forms. Many bed-and-breakfasts post pictures of every room, so you can see exactly what you're getting.

Web sites of the chain hotels (see the Appendix) are the best place to search out discounted rates ("Web savers," advance bookings, and last-minute deals). Another way to pay less for your room is to have it bundled as a package with an activity like golfing or with passes to a local attraction. See Chapter 6 for discussion on booking a package.

For smaller places, check out **Bed & Breakfast Online** (Internet: www.bbcanada.com) and **Innsite** (Internet: www.innsite.com), where you'll find a list of independent establishments you might not otherwise find on your own. Although you can't book online through these sites, you can follow the links to individual lodgings' Web sites and book directly with them.

Although the major travel booking sites, such as **Destina.ca** (Internet: www.destina.ca), **Travelocity** (Internet: www.travelocity.com), **Expedia** (Internet: www.expedia.com), and **Orbitz** (Internet: www.orbitz.com), offer hotel bookings, you may be better off going directly to the source and booking online with the property itself.

Getting the most for your money

Now you know how to wrangle a great price, but how about the quality of the room? When making your reservation, ask a couple of pointed questions to make sure you get the best room in the house. Here are some tips that can help, whatever lodging you choose:

✔ **Always ask for a corner room.** They're usually larger, quieter, and have more windows and light than standard rooms, and they don't always cost more.

✔ **Avoid renovations.** If the hotel is renovating, request a room away from the work. Of course, they probably won't offer up this information when you're making your reservation, so it's up to you to ask.

✔ **Inquire about the location of the hotel's restaurants and bars.**
This can go either way — fine if you want to be close to the action, but if sleep is what you're after, the hotel's hot night spots are potential sources of annoying noise.

If you aren't happy with your room when you arrive, talk to the front desk. If they have another room, they should be happy to accommodate you, within reason.

Chapter 9

Money Matters

● ●

In This Chapter

▶ Learning about the loonie

▶ Carrying your money wisely

▶ Coping with a lost or stolen wallet

● ●

*T*his chapter describes the Canadian currency, which is similar to that of the United States, only more colorful and with goofier names. Then, I'll look at how you can use the Canadian banking system to get your money or to pay for purchases using your hometown financial institution. Finally, I'll cover what do to if your money or banking cards are lost or stolen.

Making Cents of the Loonie

Canadian currency is easy to get used to. Coins come in 1¢, 5¢, 10¢, and 25¢ denominations, as well as $1 and $2. The $1 is a gold-colored coin that depicts the loon (a common species of bird), and is known as the "loonie." The $2 coin has a gold-colored core with a silver-colored rim and is best known as the "toonie." Bills come in the usual denominations of $5, $10, $20, $50, and $100; they're all the same size but vary in color. The $100 bill can sometimes be difficult to cash at smaller businesses or early in the morning, especially if you're only buying something inexpensive, like a cup of coffee.

At press time, the Canadian dollar was roughly equal to US71¢, the conversion rate I used throughout this book. However, exchange rates fluctuate often (and sometimes dramatically), so it's always a good idea to check before you go.

The best online tool I know of for checking exchange rates is the **Universal Currency Converter** at www.xe.com/ucc.

Cash or Credit? How to Pay While You're Away

You're the best judge of how much cash you feel comfortable carrying or what form of currency is your favorite. That's not going to change much on your vacation, and it doesn't need to — you can use cash, credit, debit, and traveler's checks in the Maritimes with little trouble. The only type of payment that won't be quite as useful to you away from home is your personal checkbook.

Doting on debit cards

Using a debit card (also known as an ATM or banking card) is hands-down the easiest way to manage your money while traveling and is extremely popular in Canada (in fact, Canadians are the world's biggest users of this type of banking). You can use your debit card to withdraw cash at ATMs or to pay for purchases at point-of-sale terminals installed at participating merchant locations (over 300,000 in Canada). The national organization responsible for the network in Canada is Interac (similar to the **Cirrus** and **Plus** networks elsewhere in the world), so you'll sometimes hear it referred to as "paying by **Interac**." Before relying solely on debit and ATMs, check with your bank to find out which Canadian banks honor your card system. The following is a list of the major Canadian banks and the system(s) they use:

- **Bank of Montreal:** Cirrus
- **Scotiabank:** Plus
- **Canada Trust:** Cirrus and Plus
- **CIBC:** Plus
- **Royal Bank:** Cirrus and Plus
- **TD Bank:** Plus

ATMs

These days, far more people use ATMs than traveler's checks. Most cities have these handy 24-hour cash machines linked to an international network that almost always includes your financial institution back at home. You can use your debit or credit card to withdraw the money you need every couple of days, which eliminates the insecurity of carrying around a large stash of cash. Of course, many ATMs are little money managers (or dictators, depending on how you look at it), imposing limits on your spending by allowing you to withdraw only a certain amount of money per day.

One important reminder before you go ATM crazy, however: Canadian banks charge a fee of up to C$1.50 (US$1.07) whenever a non-account holder uses their ATMs. Your own bank may also charge a fee for using an ATM that's not one of their branch locations. In some cases, you may get charged twice. Check out your bank's policy before ruling out traveler's checks altogether, since they may be a cheaper — though certainly less convenient — option for you.

Do not use privately owned ATMs. Also known as white-label ATMs, these banking machines are most often placed in gas stations, corner stores, restaurants, and bars. Fees can be up to C$4 (US$2.90) for a single transaction, in addition to the fee your own bank charges. The businesses that install these machines split the "convenience fee" you pay with the machine owners, making a tidy profit for themselves along the way. Because they are money-makers, some businesses don't use point-of-sale terminals, instead forcing you to withdraw cash from one of these privately owned ATMs hidden away in a corner to pay for your purchase.

Toting traveler's checks

Traveler's checks are something of an anachronism from the days when people wrote personal checks instead of going to an ATM. Because traveler's checks could be replaced if lost or stolen, they were a sound alternative to cash, and as long as vendors continue to accept them, they are still a viable alternative to cash or banking cards. Service charges are fairly low, or even nonexistent if you know where to go.

The best way to ensure a fair rate of exchange is to purchase your traveler's checks in Canadian dollars. You can get Canadian-currency traveler's checks at most major banks and organizations such as AAA. The most common denominations are $20, $50, and $100. Commissions range from 1% to 4%, although this is often waived if you bank with the issuing institution or if you're an Amex gold or platinum cardholder. AAA members can get checks without a fee at most AAA offices. For details, contact your local office or go online to www.aaa.com.

Charging ahead with credit cards

Credit cards can be invaluable when traveling: They're a safe way to carry money and they provide a convenient record of all your travel expenses after you arrive home. Of course, the disadvantage is that they're easy to overuse. Credit cards let you indulge in a lot more impulse buying than any other form of payment — taking you as far as your credit limit, which may not bear much relation to your actual financial resources.

You can also get cash advances from your credit card at any ATM if you know your *personal identification number* (PIN). If you've forgotten it or didn't even know you had a PIN, call the phone number on the back of your credit card and ask the bank to send the number to you. You'll then have the number in about five to seven business days. Some banks can give you your PIN over the phone if you tell them your mother's maiden name or provide some other security clearance.

Use your credit card for a cash advance in emergencies only. Interest rates for cash advances are often significantly higher than rates for credit-card purchases. More importantly, you start paying interest on the advance from the moment you receive the cash. On airline-affiliated credit cards, a cash advance doesn't earn frequent-flyer miles.

Coping with Loss or Theft

While on vacation, there are few events more stressful than losing your wallet. Though you can rarely prevent this from happening, knowing what to do if it does occur can save you a lot of headaches.

Most credit card companies have an emergency toll-free number to call if your card is lost or stolen. They may be able to wire you a cash advance immediately or deliver an emergency credit card in a day or two. Make sure you have the numbers with you (but not in your wallet!) so that, if a theft occurs, you can deal with the situation immediately. Check the following Canadian toll-free emergency numbers and note down those that apply to you:

✔ **American Express** ☎ **800-668-2639**

✔ **Diners Club** ☎ **800-363-3333**

✔ **Discover Card** ☎ **800-347-2683**

✔ **MasterCard** ☎ **800-307-7309**

✔ **Visa** ☎ **800-847-2911**

Be sure to contact all of your credit card companies the minute you discover your wallet has been lost or stolen. You'll also want to file a report at the nearest police precinct. Your credit card company or insurer may require a police report number or record of the loss.

If you need emergency cash over the weekend when all banks and American Express offices are closed, you can have money wired to you via **Western Union** (☎ **800-325-6000;** Internet: www.western unioncanada.ca). Agents are scattered across all three Maritime provinces; check the Web site for locations.

Chapter 10

Tying Up Loose Ends

● ●

In This Chapter

▶ Securing travel documents

▶ Covering your assets with insurance

▶ Staying healthy while you travel

▶ Packing for your trip

▶ Measuring in metric

▶ Crossing into Canada

● ●

*T*here's nothing worse than that feeling that you've forgotten something but can't remember what it is. In this chapter, I'll discuss a variety of often-overlooked planning elements. So relax and read on — it's all covered.

Getting a Passport

Citizens of the United States do not require a passport for entry to Canada, but it is highly recommended that you carry one. For travelers from other countries, a valid passport is the only form of identification accepted at Canadian borders.

Applying for a U.S. passport

Getting a passport is easy, but the process takes some time. If you're applying for your first passport, you can complete a passport application in person at a U.S. passport office; a federal, state, or probate court; or a major post office. The best sources of information are the U.S. State Department Web site (http://travel.state.gov) and the National Passport Information Center (☎ 877-487-2778; Monday to Friday, 8 a.m. to 8 p.m. eastern standard time). Passport applications can be downloaded from the U.S. State Department Web site or picked up from passport acceptance facilities.

Allow plenty of time before your trip to apply for a passport; processing normally takes three weeks but can take longer during busy periods (especially spring).

If you have a passport in your current name that was issued within the past 15 years (and you were over age 16 when it was issued), you can renew the passport by mail for US$55.

American Passport Express (☎ **800-841-6778;** Internet: www.americanpassport.com) can process your first passport application in two to eight business days for US$145, plus a US$55 to US$135 service fee, depending on how quickly you need it done.

Applying for other passports

The following list offers more information for citizens of Australia, New Zealand, and the United Kingdom.

- ✔ **Australians** can visit a local post office or passport office. For further details, call the **Australia Passport Information Service** (☎ **131-232** toll-free from Australia), or log on to www.passports.gov.au. Passports cost A$148 for adults and A$74 for those under 18.

- ✔ **New Zealanders** can pick up a passport application at any travel agency or Link Centre. For information, contact the **New Zealand Passports Office,** Department of Internal Affairs, (☎ **0800-22-50-50;** Internet: www.passports.govt.nz). Passports are NZ$71 for adults and NZ$36 for those 16 and under.

- ✔ **United Kingdom** residents can pick up applications for a standard 10-year passport (£42) or 5-year passport for children under 16 (£25) at passport offices, major post offices, or travel agencies, or from the **United Kingdom Passport Service** (☎ **0870-521-0410;** Internet: www.ukpa.gov.uk).

Travel and Medical Insurance

Three kinds of travel insurance are available: trip cancellation, medical, and lost luggage. Here is my advice on all three:

- ✔ **Trip cancellation insurance** is a good idea if you signed up for an escorted tour and paid a large portion of your vacation expenses up front (for information on escorted tours, see Chapter 6). Trip cancellation insurance covers three types of emergencies: death or sickness that prevents you from traveling, bankruptcy of a tour operator or airline, or a disaster that prevents you from getting to your destination.

✔ **Medical insurance** doesn't make sense for most travelers. Your existing health insurance should cover you if you get sick while on vacation (although if you belong to an HMO, check to see whether you're fully covered while out of the country).

✔ **Lost luggage insurance** is not necessary for most travelers. Your homeowner's or renter's insurance should cover stolen luggage if you have off-premises theft coverage. Check your existing policies before you buy any additional coverage. If an airline flying between Canada and the U.S. or another international destination loses your luggage, the airline is responsible for paying US$20 per kilogram to a maximum of US$1,280. On flights within Canada, this liability is limited to C$1,500 (US$1,070) for checked baggage. In either case, the carrier's liability does not exceed your loss.

Some credit cards (American Express and certain gold and platinum Visa and MasterCards, for example) offer automatic flight insurance against death or dismemberment in case of an airplane crash — if you charged the cost of your ticket, that is.

If you're interested in purchasing travel insurance, try one of the following companies:

✔ **Access America** (☎ **866-807-3982;** Internet: www.accessamerica.com)

✔ **Travel Guard International** (☎ **800-826-4919;** Internet: www.travelguard.com)

✔ **Travel Insured International** (☎ **800-243-3174;** Internet: www.travelinsured.com)

✔ **Travelex Insurance Services** (☎ **800-457-4602;** Internet: www.travelex-insurance.com)

Don't pay for more insurance than you need. For example, if you need only trip cancellation insurance, don't buy coverage for lost or stolen property. Trip cancellation insurance costs about 6% to 8% of the total value of your vacation.

Staying Healthy When You Travel

Getting sick will ruin your vacation, so I *strongly* advise against it (of course, last time I checked, the bugs weren't listening to me any more than they probably listen to you).

If you have health insurance, be sure to carry your insurance card in your wallet. Most U.S. health insurance plans and HMOs cover at least part of the cost of out-of-country hospital visits and procedures if insured become ill or are injured while out of the country. Most require that you pay the bills up front at the time of care, issuing a refund only after you return and file all the paperwork.

Talk to your doctor before leaving on a trip if you have a serious and/or chronic illness. For conditions such as epilepsy, diabetes, or heart problems, wear a **MedicAlert Identification Tag** (☎ 800-825-3785; Internet: www.medicalert.org), which immediately alerts doctors to your condition and gives them access to your records through MedicAlert's 24-hour hotline.

Packing for the Maritimes

To be succinct, pack as lightly as possible but be prepared for a variety of weather conditions. Start by assembling all the clothing you think you'll need. Then put half away, and you will have an ideal amount for your vacation.

What to bring

Pack clothing that is comfortable and practical. In summer, a rain jacket, sweater, and a pair of worn-in walking shoes are sufficient accompaniments to your regular casual clothing choices. Pack fragile items between layers of clothes and things that may leak, like shampoo bottles, in sealable bags. You should also remember to bring the following:

- Tickets, car and hotel confirmations
- Discount membership cards
- Credit and debit cards
- Prescription medications and a copy of your prescriptions in case you lose them or run out

Though these are not really essential (believe it or not, you *can* buy film in the Maritimes, too), here's a list of handy items you'll be glad to have on hand:

- Open-toed shoes, such as sandals
- Binoculars
- Spare film and batteries for your camera
- Insect repellent
- Extra pair of contacts or glasses and a copy of your prescription

What not to bring

Disregard everything you've heard about Canada and the cold. In summer, there is absolutely no need to carry a down parka or heavy winter boots (as proof, see Chapter 2 for average Maritime temperatures); you can make do with comfortable, casual spring and summer clothing. And unless you plan on attending the theater or dining in the finest restaurants, you won't need a suit or formal wear either. Khakis and a golf shirt for men, and dress slacks or a skirt for women, are sufficiently dressy.

Meeting airline baggage requirements

Security measures at airports vary from country to country and even from airport to airport. All major airlines include up-to-date lists of permitted and prohibited items, as well as procedures for boarding flights, on their Web sites. Another option is to go straight to the source:

- ✔ United States: **Transportation Security Administration,** www.tsa.gov/public
- ✔ Canada: **Canadian Air Transport Security Authority**, www.catsa-acsta.gc.ca

If you need to have medical equipment like syringes or oxygen bottles on your person when you fly, contact your airline at least seven days prior to your departure.

Checked bags

Most airlines allow each passenger two pieces of checked luggage at no charge. Maximum weights and dimensions vary with each airline, but Air Canada's guidelines are typical. They allow a maximum measurement (combined length, height, and width) of 158 centimeters (62 inches) for each piece. The weight of each piece must not exceed 32 kilograms (70 pounds) and the two pieces combined may not weigh more than 45 kilograms (100 pounds).

Sporting equipment like golf clubs, skis, and snowboards is allowed at no extra cost but counts as one of your two checked bags. Larger items like bikes and surfboards incur an extra charge. Contact your airline for details.

On flights originating in the U.S., checked luggage is often screened by hand. Therefore, make sure it is not locked when you check in. If you are transporting a gift (as either checked-in or carry-on luggage) and it is wrapped, you may be required to unwrap it. So plan ahead, and carry the wrapping paper separately.

In addition to an identification tag, a piece of ribbon tied to your suitcase makes spotting it on the baggage carousel easy. I've seen a dozen bags come off the same flight with yellow ribbon, so be creative and tie yellow and red, or a combination of colors that represent your country or favorite football team.

Carry-on luggage

Every airline is different when it comes to carry-on luggage allowances, but Air Canada's guidelines, once again, are typical. Each passenger is allowed one carry-on bag that measures less than 55 x 40 x 23 centimeters (21 x 16 x 9 inches) and weighs a maximum of 10 kilograms (22 pounds), and one "personal article" (like a laptop computer or briefcase). Items like cameras and coats are allowed but aren't included in the allowance. Check with your airline (Web sites are easiest) for specifics.

In your carry-on bag, pack valuables, like jewelry and cameras; documents, such as return tickets and car rental reservations; prescription drugs; and a sweater. Throw in a magazine or good book, a bottle of drinking water, and a snack for good measure.

Keep your boarding pass and photo identification (passport or driver's license) handy at all times after checking in your main bags.

Sizing Things Up: Converting to Canadian

Well, actually, it's converting to **metric**. This section is only relevant to readers from countries that have not adopted the global measurement system — the United States, Liberia, and Myanmar.

Metric works on the decimal system, which means that all measurements have a base of 10. The basic unit of measurement is a meter (a little longer than one yard), which can be divided into 100 centimeters (2.5 centimeters equals 1 inch) or 1,000 millimeters. One thousand meters equals one kilometer (approximately 0.6 miles).

The difference between kilometers and miles when driving is probably the most important conversion you'll need to know. All speed limits and distance signs in Canada are posted in kilometers. If the sign dictates a limit of 100, that means 60 miles per hour. At the pump, gas is sold in liters. Approximately 3.8 liters equals one U.S. gallon.

In 1975, rain began falling in Canada in millimeters and snow in centimeters. And, while you'll still hear older Canadians talk in Fahrenheit, **Celsius** is the official scale of measuring temperature, with water freezing at 0°C and boiling at 100°C. To convert from Celsius to Fahrenheit, multiply by 1.8 and then add 32.

The only Canadian holdouts to metric conversion are golfers (golf courses are measured in yards), seamen (boat speeds are measured in knots and distances in nautical miles), and grocery stores (bulk retail food like fresh vegetables is priced in ounces and pounds — but weighed at the cash register in metric).

Getting Through Immigration and Customs

Canada is a welcoming country, but officers at the border are still likely to ask some pointed questions, like the purpose of your stay and what you are bringing into the country.

Crossing the border

U.S. citizens need proof of citizenship for entry into Canada. A passport is best, although a birth certificate, baptismal certificate, or voter registration card *and* photo ID such as driver's license is also acceptable. A driver's license alone isn't considered proof of citizenship, but it may help in a tight spot.

All other foreign visitors require a valid passport and will be asked to produce onward tickets and sufficient funds upon arrival in Canada.

Citizens from some countries are required to apply for a Temporary Resident Visa (TRV) before arriving in Canada (if you're from Britain, a Commonwealth country, or somewhere in Western Europe, the answer is probably "no"). For details, as well as contact information for consulates and embassies around the world, contact **Citizenship and Immigration Canada** (☎ **888-242-2100;** Internet: www.cic.gc.ca/english/visit/index.html).

If you travel with a passport, keep it with you at all times. The only time you should give it up is at the border, for officers to examine. If you lose your passport while in Canada, go directly to the nearest embassy or consulate of your own country. (See the Appendix for embassy and consulate locations in the Maritimes.)

Passing through customs

Although there is no limit to the amount of loot you can take into Canada, the customs authority does have limits on how much you can bring in for free (to separate the tourists from the importers).

Entering Canada

If you are bringing goods other than clothing and personal effects into Canada, you'll need to fill out a declarations form. Here's the threshold on some common items: 50 cigars, 200 cigarettes, and either 1.14 liters (40 oz) of liquor or wine or one case (12 bottles or cans) of beer. It is not illegal to bring more than the equivalent of C$10,000 (approximately US$7,100) into Canada, but you must report it if you do so.

Temporary visitors are permitted to bring their pet cat or dog into Canada without it being quarantined. The department responsible for overseeing the import of animals is the **Canada Food Inspection Agency** (Internet: www.inspection.gc.ca). Check their Web site for current regulations.

Revolvers, pistols, and fully automatic firearms are definitely not allowed, and, needless to say, neither are narcotics. For more information, contact the **Canada Firearms Centre** (☎ 800-731-4000; Internet: www.cfc-ccaf.gc.ca). For more information on general customs regulations, check with the **Canada Border Services Agency** (☎ 800-461-9999 or 204-983-3500; Internet: www.cbsa-asfc.gc.ca).

Returning home

If you're a citizen of the United States, you may bring home US$400 worth of goods duty-free, providing you've been out of the country at least 48 hours. This includes one liter of an alcoholic beverage, 200 cigarettes, and 100 cigars. You may mail up to US$200 worth of goods to yourself (marked "for personal use") and up to US$100 to others (marked "unsolicited gift") once each day. You'll have to pay an import duty on anything over these limits.

If you have further questions, or for a list of specific items that you cannot bring into the United States, check the **Customs & Border Protection** Web site, www.customs.ustreas.gov.

Customs regulations are different in every country. Here are some contacts for returning citizens of other countries:

- ✔ **Australian Customs Service** (☎ 1300-363-263; Internet: www.customs.gov.au).

- ✔ **HM Customs & Excise** (☎ 0845-010-9000; Internet: www.hmce.gov.uk) for the United Kingdom.

- ✔ **New Zealand Customs Service** (☎ 0800-42-87-86; Internet: www.customs.govt.nz).

Part III
Nova Scotia

"We had it in the guest bedroom, and then in the hallway, but for now we're leaving it in here until we figure out which room it seems to want to be in."

In this part...

Life in Nova Scotia revolves around the ocean, and chances are, so will your travels in this East Coast province. In this part, I'll unveil the best of Halifax with tips on the top sights, the best places to stay, and dining experiences you won't want to miss. But don't despair, I'll also cover the spectacular Cabot Trail on Cape Breton Island and famous shipbuilding towns like Lunenburg. Nova Scotia offers more than spectacular scenery and quaint seaside towns, so I've thrown in a few bonus tips, like where to see the world's largest pumpkins and which outdoor restaurant boils its lobster on barbecues — just to make sure you don't miss a thing!

Chapter 11

Halifax

• •

In This Chapter

▶ Getting to Halifax

▶ Finding your way around the city

▶ Choosing the best places to stay and dine

▶ Sightseeing, shopping, and spending a night on the town

▶ Taking day-trips out of the city

• •

*H*alifax may look like any other city as you approach the runway, but after you've landed, there's no doubt you're in the Maritimes. This port city does a wonderful job of combining work and play. Although large chunks of shoreline are taken up by industrial endeavors, a prime stretch of waterfront is the epicenter for locals and visitors alike. Museums, boutiques, restaurants, and pubs fill historic waterfront warehouses, with a seawall promenade winding past tour boats, tall ships — and even the occasional seal!

Although the harbor dominates the landscape, it's easy to see past the working port areas to uninhabited islands, with glimpses of the Atlantic Ocean in the distance. Overlooking the harbor is a compact downtown core, with no point more than a few blocks from the water. Here, you find all the trappings of a modern metropolis, delicately interspersed with rows of 200-year-old stone buildings and abundant green space. Downtown is first and foremost a business core, but the streets are perpetually alive with friendly faces and the catchy sounds of traditional East Coast music wafting out from darkened drinking holes.

Plan on spending two (preferably three) days in Halifax. Maritime weather will have some bearing on what you do, so check the forecast and plan your time at indoor attractions to coincide with rainy spells.

Nova Scotia

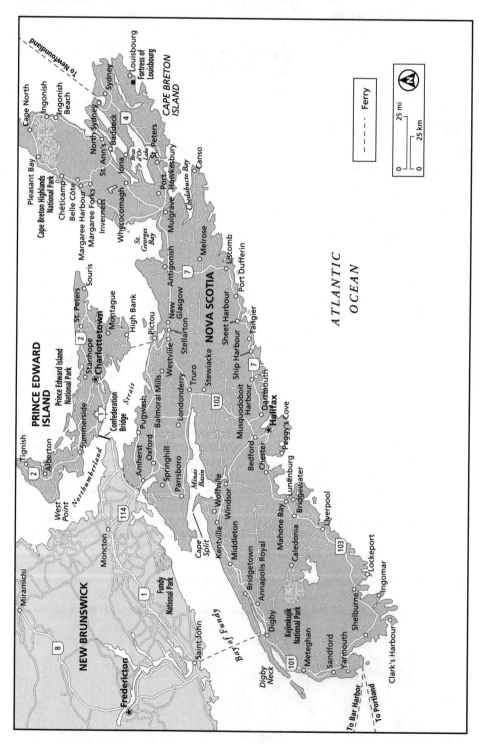

Halifax

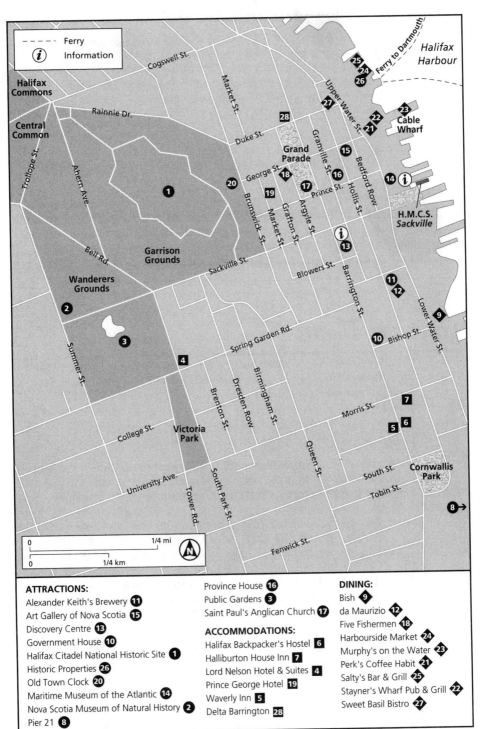

ATTRACTIONS:
Alexander Keith's Brewery **11**
Art Gallery of Nova Scotia **15**
Discovery Centre **13**
Government House **10**
Halifax Citadel National Historic Site **1**
Historic Properties **26**
Old Town Clock **20**
Maritime Museum of the Atlantic **14**
Nova Scotia Museum of Natural History **2**
Pier 21 **8**

Province House **16**
Public Gardens **3**
Saint Paul's Anglican Church **17**

ACCOMMODATIONS:
Halifax Backpacker's Hostel **6**
Halliburton House Inn **7**
Lord Nelson Hotel & Suites **4**
Prince George Hotel **19**
Waverly Inn **5**
Delta Barrington **28**

DINING:
Bish **9**
da Maurizio **12**
Five Fishermen **18**
Harbourside Market **24**
Murphy's on the Water **23**
Perk's Coffee Habit **21**
Salty's Bar & Grill **25**
Stayner's Wharf Pub & Grill **22**
Sweet Basil Bistro **27**

Historic Halifax

The sight of arriving immigrant ships and the echoes of horse-drawn carts down cobbled streets may be long gone, but the port city of Halifax retains its historic appeal. Nowhere are the city's traditions better preserved than at the Maritime Museum of the Atlantic, which is flanked by Canada's oldest waterfront warehouses, aptly named the Historic Properties.

But behind the museums and old buildings lies Halifax's colorful history . Now home to popular boutiques and restaurants, Halifax's stone warehouses once stored pirate booty. The British government commissioned private vessels to cruise against their enemies (usually the French or the U.S.) and called it "privateering" — really just a pleasant name for piracy.

The story of Halifax is punctuated by intriguing footnotes like this. The 1997 movie *Titanic* brought renewed attention to the disaster and its numerous Halifax links, most of which are actively promoted as tourist attractions. Other links are more subtle, such as the Five Fishermen restaurant, located in a former funeral home where the *Titanic's* first-class passengers were embalmed.

Getting There

Halifax is a transportation hub for all of the Maritimes. Most visitors arrive by plane at Halifax International Airport or drive into the city on one of four major highways.

By plane

Traveling from **Halifax International Airport** to the heart of downtown takes around 40 minutes, but allow slightly longer during the morning rush hour. Public transportation options are:

- **Bus.** Because Metro Transit buses don't reach the airport, try the **Airbus** (☎ 902-873-2091), which offers service between the airport and major downtown hotels. The fare is C$12 (US$8.60) one-way, C$20 (US$14.30) round-trip. The first bus leaves the airport at 6 a.m., the last at 11:15 p.m. Heading back to the airport, shuttles depart from most accommodations up to 20 times daily between 5 a.m. and 10 p.m. (plan on catching a bus at least 90 minutes before your flight departs). You don't need advance reservations.

- **Taxi.** After collecting your baggage from the carousel, head through the exit doors to the lineup of taxis out front. The set fare to downtown is C$41 (US$29.30).

Most of the major **car-rental** companies have check-in counters near the baggage carousels and vehicles can be picked up in a parking lot within easy walking distance. The exception is Discount, which operates out of the nearby Airport Hotel; if your reservation is with this company, call for a pickup at the hotel phone bank in front of the information booth.

By car

Highway 102 cuts across Nova Scotia from New Brunswick, bringing you right into the heart of Halifax. Allow three hours nonstop from the border. You may discover plenty of worthwhile stops en route, but the only one you *must* make is at the tollgates east of Amherst (C$3/US$2.10). As Halifax looms on the horizon, Highway 118 branches left off Highway 102. This alternative route draws traffic into the city of Dartmouth, but also provides a final approach to downtown.

Two highways lead into Halifax from the west: **Highway 101** from along the Bay of Fundy; and **Highway 103**, which runs along the South Shore from Yarmouth. Both routes pick up ferry traffic from farther afield. Ferries from Saint John (New Brunswick) terminate at Digby, a three-hour drive along Highway 101 to Halifax. Travelers arriving by ferry at Yarmouth from either Portland or Bar Harbor, both in Maine, are faced with a four-hour drive on Highway 103.

By train or bus

If you choose to travel into Halifax by train, VIA Rail runs two routes into Nova Scotia from Montreal; one terminates in Halifax, the other on Cape Breton Island. In Halifax, the station is at 1161 Hollis Street (☎ **888-842-7245**; Internet: www.via.ca) on the southern edge of downtown.

Acadian Lines (☎ **902-454-9321**) provides bus service to Halifax from Moncton (New Brunswick), where connections can be made from Montreal or Maine (the closest that Greyhound services get to the Maritimes). These two cities are the closest that **Greyhound** services get to the Maritimes. Through tickets to Halifax can be purchased from Greyhound and connections are seamless. Acadian Lines also run buses to Halifax from points throughout the province, including the ferry ports of Yarmouth and Digby. The Halifax bus depot is west of downtown at 6040 Almon Street and is open daily 6:30 a.m. to 7:00 p.m.

Orienting Yourself in Halifax

Most of Halifax's attractions and major hotels are within walking distance of the touristy downtown waterfront precinct between Cogswell Street in the north and South Street in—you guessed it—the south. The main thoroughfare along this ten-block stretch is Water Street. This narrow, winding road set back slightly from the harbor is dotted with public parking lots (that's a hint — downtown is compact enough that most sights can be seen on foot).

Halifax is small and easy to navigate. The city center clings to a hilly peninsula within Halifax Harbour. From here, built-up areas spread in all directions.

Downtown

Most attractions, accommodations, and restaurants are within walking distance of one another in the downtown core. The basic grid pattern of streets laid out over 200 years ago remains, bounded very roughly by the harbor to the east and Citadel Hill to the west, with Cogswell Street and Spring Garden Road creating man-made boundaries to the north and south respectively. Water Street, as you may suspect, runs along the harborfront. South of Sackville Street, it's known as Lower Water Street, while to the north it's Upper Water Street. Between Water Street and the harbor are numerous pay parking lots, the Maritime Museum of the Atlantic, restaurants, and gift shops.

Dartmouth

Two bridges and a ferry service link downtown Halifax with Dartmouth, across the harbor to the east. Although Dartmouth has its own distinct industrial, business, and residential districts, it is not a separate city, but combines with Halifax to form the Halifax Regional Municipality. Less picturesque than Halifax, it offers parks, lakes, and a few eccentric attractions — head here if Quaker history, ocean research, or rocks from around the world are your thing.

Bedford and Sackville

Bedford is a picturesque community at the head of Bedford Basin and north of Halifax proper. Settled as early as 1749, its streets are lined with well-kept middle- and upper-class homes, many with views of the harbor. If you detour into Bedford, be sure to find your way down to the water's edge, much of it protected by parkland.

There's little reason to visit Sackville, north of Bedford, but a quick overview may be helpful for highway travelers entering Halifax from the north along Highway 102. If you're heading for the city, follow Highway 102 through Sackville. Don't be tempted by "Halifax via the bridges signage", which detour through Dartmouth and make the approach to downtown confusing.

Getting Around Halifax

Although downtown can get congested with traffic, this is more to do with the narrow, hilly streets than any great volume of vehicles. The best advice I can give you is to not plan on driving at all. Public transportation schedules and routes are designed to get residents to and from work, so, aside from the ferry to Dartmouth, you can leave this form of transportation to the locals.

Driving (and parking)

If you're staying downtown, park your car and walk. Your best bet is the city-operated parking lots along Upper and Lower Water streets.

 Admission to Halifax Citadel includes parking. You can visit this top-of-the-town attraction early in the day, then leave your vehicle there while you spend the rest of the day exploring downtown. Just remember, it's an uphill walk (or an inexpensive cab ride) at the end of the day, and keep your Citadel entry receipt.

 If Halifax International Airport is the starting point of your Maritimes adventure, reserve your vehicle to be picked up at a downtown location just before heading out of the city. Not only will you save a few days' rental charge, you'll save on the airport rental surcharge.

On foot

Downtown Halifax is a great place to get around on foot. You can easily do without a vehicle and not miss any of the popular attractions. If you're staying downtown, then the main information center and all the best restaurants are within easy reach. If you tire of walking, jump aboard a tour bus or take to the water for a break. Only a few attractions are out of reach by walking — save these up and visit them in one go.

Catching cabs

Cabs are easy to hail anywhere in the downtown area, especially along Upper and Lower Water streets, or head for one of the major hotels where taxis wait. Rates begin at C$2.50 (US$1.80), increasing based on time and distance to around C$7 (US$5) for a trip across downtown. Cab companies include:

- ✓ **Casino Taxi** (☎ 902-425-6666)
- ✓ **Co-op Taxi** (☎ 902-444-0001)
- ✓ **Maritime Taxi** (☎ 902-456-4248)
- ✓ **Yellow Cab** (☎ 902-420-0000)

Transit tips

Metro Transit (☎ 902-490-6600) provides inexpensive bus and ferry transportation to all parts of the city. The fare for any single sector is adults C$1.75 (US$1.25), exact change only. The main transit interchange is at the corner of Upper Water and George streets. Call or pick up a schedule from the information center.

From June to September, Metro Transit and the Downtown Halifax Business Commission sponsor a free shuttle service known as **fred** (short for "free rides everywhere downtown"). Hop on and ride the loop through Lower Water Street, Spring Garden Road, South Park Street, and South Street for a free tour of the downtown core.

Staying in Halifax

The following recommendations are a cross-section of accommodation choices in various price categories. Prices fluctuate with supply and demand. Most downtown hotels cater to business travelers, with rack rates matching Monday-to-Friday work schedules. Weekend packages are offered year-round, but look for the best deals outside of the summer tourist season. As always, hotel Web sites are the best places to start searching out deals.

Ask about additional charges for parking and local calls, since they may not be included in your room's rate.

To the rate quoted, count on 16.5% in taxes being added to your final hotel bill.

First-Choice Lodgings

Airport Hotel Halifax
$$ Airport

As the name suggests, this hotel is right by the airport, 40km (25 miles) north of downtown. A free shuttle transports guests between the two terminals and the hotel 24 hours a day. The exterior and public areas are a little tired, but spacious, comfortable rooms provide a relaxing stay before or after a long flight. Aside from the adjacent aircraft museum, this property is isolated — meaning you're stuck eating at the in-house restaurant (so-so food at best). On the plus side, facilities include indoor and outdoor pools, a small fitness room, and a lounge that opens to a pleasant patio.

60 Bell Blvd. (take Exit 6 from Highway 102) ☎ **800-667-3333** *or 902-873-3000. Internet:* www.atlific.com. *Parking: Above ground, free. Rack rates: C$90– C$140 (US$64.30–US$100) double. AE, DC, MC, V. Wheelchair-accessible rooms.*

Halifax Backpacker's Hostel
$ Downtown

A 10-minute walk north of the waterfront, this renovated residence is perfectly suited to budget travelers who don't mind being a little away from the night-time action offered by the Hostelling International hostel (on Barrington Street). Facilities include a well-equipped communal kitchen, a lounge room with television and lots of games, Internet access, and a small garden. Bike rentals are C$15 (US$10.70) for a full day. The Airport Shuttle drops hostel guests at the nearby Citadel Hotel.

2193 Gottingen St. (north of Cogswell St) ☎ **888-431-3170** *or 902-431-3170. Internet:* www.halifaxbackpackers.com. *Parking: Streetside. Rack rates: C$20 (US$14.30) dormitory bed, C$25 (US$17.90) single, C$35 (US$25) double, C$65 (US$46.40) family room.*

Halliburton House Inn
$$–$$$$ Downtown

Three adjoining townhouses, one dating to 1809, make up this well-located accommodation. The inn has 29 guest rooms, each elegantly decked out in period antiques, with in-room coffee and super-comfortable beds topped out with goose-down duvets. Most are at the lower end of the price range; the one-bedroom suite comes with its own wood-burning fireplace (C$225/US$161). If you've chosen one of the other rooms, plan on relaxing in the inviting lounge, which also has a fireplace, or in the private garden courtyard. The downstairs restaurant serves up a complimentary breakfast and the dinner menu features local seafood and game prepared with a European flare.

5184 Morris St. (between Barrington and Hollis sts). ☎ *902-420-0658. Fax: 902-423-2324. Internet:* www.halliburton.ns.ca. *Rack rates: C$140–C$350 (US$100–US$250) double. AE, DC, MC, V.*

Inn on the Lake
$$$–$$$$ Waverly

Set on 2 hectares (5 acres) of lakefront parkland north of Halifax, this country-style retreat is a world away from the bustle of city living (although I have heard complaints about highway noise). You can sunbathe on a white-sand beach, lounge on chairs surrounded by well-manicured gardens, or crank up the energy level on the tennis courts and then cool off in the large outdoor pool. Some of the standard rooms have poolside patios, while others have lake-view balconies. Upgrade for C$40 (US$29) to a Deluxe Room and enjoy a king-size bed and jetted tub. Dining options include poolside snacks, an English-style pub, or a more formal dining room. The inn is a 10-minute drive from the airport, a short free shuttle ride away.

3009 Lake Thomas Dr. (take Exit 5 from Hwy 102) ☎ *902-861-3480. Fax: 902-861-4883. Internet:* www.innonthelake.com. *Rack rates: C$159–C$320 (US$114–US$229). AE, MC, V.*

Lord Nelson Hotel & Suites
$$$$ Downtown

Dating to 1928, this landmark hotel has a reputation as one of Halifax's finest. Standard rooms are large and elegantly furnished; bathrooms are particularly well equipped. Amenities include all the usual business services, free local calls, a concierge, and a British-style pub with good, inexpensive food. Despite its size (243 rooms), service and attention to detail is flawless. As is so often the case, disregard the rack rates and book online to snatch deals such as a room, parking, breakfast, and a city tour for two for around C$200 (US$142.90). Make sure you request a room with views of the adjacent Public Gardens.

1515 South Park St. (at Spring Garden Rd.) ☎ *800-565-2020 or 902-423-6331. Fax: 902-423-7148. Internet:* www.lordnelsonhotel.com. *Parking: C$7.50 (US$5.40) per day. Rack rates: C$250–C$420 (US$178.60–US$300). AE, DISC, MC, V.*

Prince George Hotel
$$$$ Downtown

This place, halfway between the waterfront and Citadel Hill, is my fave among downtown hotels. Even the standard guest rooms are spacious and well appointed with lots of stylish mahogany furniture. For a few extra dollars, you can opt for a Crown Service room, with upgrades like a CD player, evening turndown service, and breakfast delivered to your door. Other in-house amenities include a bistro-style restaurant, an indoor pool, and a business center. Service is also a step above what you'd expect from a hotel. Don't be scared off by the rack rates — the hotel Web site offers rooms for well under C$200 (US$142.90) year-round, making them an excellent downtown deal.

1725 Market St. ☎. ***800-565-1567*** *or 902-425-1986. Fax: 902-429-6048. Internet:* www.princegeorgehotel.com. *Rack rates: C$240–C$450 (US$171.40–US$321.40) double. AE, DISC, MC, V.*

Prospect Bed & Breakfast
$$ Prospect

If you have your own transportation, an overnight stay in seaside Prospect, near Peggy's Cove, is a delightful escape from city living. Housed in a 150-year-old covent, five guest rooms each have a private bathroom and the more expensive ones also have a fireplace. The ocean is nearly always in sight, from your bedroom window, from the dining room, and from the Adirondack chairs scattered around the grounds, or wander down to the private beach and dip your toes in the Atlantic. Hot breakfast and afternoon tea are included in the price of your stay.

1758 Prospect Bay Rd., Prospect. ☎ ***800-725-8732*** *or 902-423-1102. Internet:* www.nsinns.com. *Parking: Free. Rack rates: C$125–C$145 (US$60.70–US$103.60) double. AE, MC, V.*

Waverly Inn
$$–$$$ Downtown

Originally home to a society couple, Halifax's grandest residence was converted to the Waverly Inn in 1876 and has been taking guests ever since. All rooms come with extravagant Victorian touches such as four-poster beds and lace curtains, while some feature more modern conveniences like jetted tubs. A deck catches the afternoon sun and the parlor is a wonderful place to relax in the evening. A continental breakfast is included in the rates.

1266 Barrington St. ☎ ***800-565-9346*** *or 902-423-9346. Fax: 902-425-0167. Internet:* www.waverlyinn.com. *Parking: Free. Rack rates: C$110–C$220 (US$78.60–US$157.10) double. AE, DISC, MC, V.*

Runner-up Lodgings

Delta Barrington
$$$ Downtown

The Delta Barrington is ideally located one block from the harbor. Rooms are smallish but well appointed. An upgrade to Signature Club (bigger room, continental breakfast, and so on) only costs a few extra dollars.

1875 Barrington St. ☎ **877-814-7706** *or 902-429-7410. Fax: 902-420-6524. Internet:* www.deltahotels.com.

Fountain View Guest House
$ **Near Citadel Hill**

In a renovated residence, seven guest rooms share three bathrooms and parking is on the street, but at under C$50 (US$35.70) for double occupancy, no one complains.

2138 Robie St. ☎ *902-422-4169.*

Howard Johnson Hotel Halifax
$$ **West of Downtown**

An inexpensive choice along the road to Peggy's Cove and the South Shore, with a downtown transit stop out front. Although the rooms are unremarkable, rates include breakfast and other niceties.

20 St. Margaret's Bay Rd. ☎ **888-561-7666** *or 902-477-5611. Fax: 902-479-2150. Internet:* www.hojohalifax.com.

King Edward Inn
$$ **West of Downtown**

Partially destroyed in the Halifax Explosion, this hotel has 40 older rooms with private baths and televisions. Rates include a light breakfast and admission to nearby pool complexes.

5780 West St. ☎ *800-565-5464 or 902-484-3466. Internet:* www.kingedward.com.

Dining in Halifax

The eateries along the harbor are the easiest to find and have the best views. Considering their prime tourist locale, these restaurants are surprisingly popular with Haligonians, both during the weekday lunch hour and for an evening meal, and the reasonable prices are a pleasant treat.

Bish
$$$–$$$$ **Downtown**   **GLOBAL**

Aside from the unusual name, a few things stand Bish apart from Halifax's other waterfront restaurants — it's well away from the crush of the Historic Properties, the setting is elegant, and the menu offers a lot more than seafood. The cooking itself is excellent. The roasted rack of lamb with feta couscous stars as a main course; there's seafood if you must, with choices such as arctic char amandine, a delicate-tasting fish from northern waters baked in an almond-based sauce.

1475 Lower Water St. (Bishop's Landing) ☎ *902-425-7993. Reservations recommended. Main courses: C$23–C$30 (US$16.40–US$21.40). AE, DC, DISC, MC, V. Mon–Sat 5:30–10:00 p.m.*

da Maurizio
$$$$ **Downtown ITALIAN**

Halifax's finest Italian restaurant, da Maurizio, is in the historic Alexander Keith's Brewery building, across from the waterfront. Little has been done to alter the structure, yet the dining room is pleasing to the eye, with clean, simple lines set off by exposed red brick and lots of richly finished woods. Begin with *fiore di salmone* (smoked salmon in a balsamic vinaigrette), then get serious with upscale pasta presentations or main courses like *chicken scaloppine*, thin slices of chicken in a port-based demi-glaze. *Crème brûlée* with fresh fruit is a fitting way to end this decadent splurge. The wine list has many Italian choices, while sensibly also including bottles from around the world.

1496 Lower Water St. ☎ *902-423-0859. Reservations recommended. Main courses: C$28–C$32 (US$20–US$22.90). AE, DC, DISC, MC, V. Mon–Sat 5–10 p.m.*

Five Fishermen
$$–$$$ **Downtown SEAFOOD**

Five Fishermen is one of Halifax's better seafood restaurants, and the only one housed in a building that once served as a funeral home for some of the *Titanic*'s doomed passengers. Table settings are spread through a number of different rooms (one recreates a cruise ship's dining room), all with high ceilings and lots of brass and dark woodwork. You can't go wrong with any of the seafood or steak choices, although I imagine the baked medley of seafood covered in a lobster butter sauce would be hard to top. Take a break from seafood with any of the Alberta beef dishes, or enjoy the best of both worlds by ordering a half-lobster side. Don't be put off by the price of main courses — they include unlimited salad and steamed mussels.

Little Fish, in the same building (☎ 902-425-4025), is an inexpensive off-shoot of the Five Fishermen, with seafood mains under C$20 (US$14.30). It's open weekdays for lunch, with innovative choices like po' boys stuffed with oysters.

1740 Argyle St. ☎ *902-422-4421. Reservations recommended. Main courses: C$27–C$32 (US$19.30–US$22.90). AE, DC, DISC, MC, V. Daily from 5 p.m.*

In the market for a cheap meal?

One of the best places to find inexpensive food is **Harbourside Market,** occupying a prime waterfront spot within the Historic Properties complex at 1869 Upper Water Street. Seating is inside or out, with the outdoor tables sitting right above the water. This glorified food court is anchored by **Captain John's** (☎ 902-420-9255), where choices range from a halibut burger (C$8/US$5.70) to a full lobster with all the trimmings (C$22/US$15.70). Looking for something to share? Try the mussels, steamed in a tomato broth (C$7/US$5). Across the way is **Brisket Boardwalk Deli** (☎ 902-423-7625) with healthy wraps, soups, and sandwiches. The market even has its own brewpub, **John Shippey's** (☎ 902-423-7386), which serves up draft (C$6/US$4.30 a pint) brewed on site and offers table service at one outside corner. The food outlets are open daily 11:00 a.m. to 9:30 p.m.

Murphy's on the Water
$–$$$ **Downtown   SEAFOOD**

Located on a wharf jutting into Halifax Harbour, this restaurant's panoramic water views from its outside seating area at the very end of the building can't be beat. Though the menu isn't the city's most upscale offering, combined with the location, dining here will not dissappoint. Keep it simple and stick to classics like clam linguini or seafood bouillabaisse. Aside from a few additional dinner entrees, the same menu is offered all day, meaning you can order a burger for dinner or share a platter of Nova Scotian seafood for lunch.

1751 Lower Water St. ☎ *902-420-1015. Reservations accepted. Main courses: C$8–C$27 (US$5.70–US$19.30). AE, DC, MC, V. Daily 11 a.m.–10 p.m.*

Perk's Coffee Habit
$ **Downtown   COFFEEHOUSE**

The delicious coffee concoctions on offer would ensure Perk's popularity wherever it was located. Since it's in the heart of the city near the exit from Dartmouth commuter ferries, the crowds are continuous. In the morning, suited workers simply stop by to grab a coffee on their way to the office. The rest of the day and late into the night, the pace is more subdued, with tables inside and out (well positioned for the morning sun) always crowded. In addition to the standard coffeehouse bagels and muffins, friendly staff serve up daily soup specials and sandwiches made to order. Even at the local coffeehouse you can't get away from seafood — here it comes with a salad on a croissant.

1781 Lower Water St. (at the foot of George St.). ☎ *902-429-9367. Reservations not taken. Lunches: C$4–C$8 (US$2.90–US$5.70). MC, V. Daily 6:30 a.m.–11:30 p.m.*

Salty's Bar & Grill
$-$$$ **Downtown** **SEAFOOD**

This popular waterfront eatery is in the heart of the action at the front of the Historic Properties complex. The most sought-after seating is out on the wharf, where, for the price of a beer, you can watch the watery world of Halifax Harbour go by. The menu is typical pub fare, but with lots of local seafood. Considering the location, it's great value, with choices ranging from simple salads (under C$8/US$5.70) to entrees like baked salmon casserole (C$13/US$9.30). This inexpensive menu is available for both lunch and dinner. An upstairs dining room uses the same menu until 5 p.m., and then things get creative (and more expensive) with a menu that features dishes such as blackened halibut doused in a mango salsa and rack of lamb roasted in a herb crust. Of course, steamed lobster is available anytime. Salty's is a good choice for families looking for water-front dining — the kid's menu is C$5 (US$3.60), including drink and dessert.

1869 Upper Water St. ☎ *902-423-6818. Reservations recommended for the upstairs restaurant after 5 p.m. Main courses: C$8–C$26 (US$5.70–US$18.60). AE, DC, DISC, MC, V. Daily 11 a.m.–11 p.m.*

Stayner's Wharf Pub & Grill
$-$$ **Downtown** **SEAFOOD/PUB FARE**

Head to Stayner's for all the usual East Coast pub fare, like fish and chips or mashed potatoes topped with roasted onions. It's also a good choice if you're in the mood for a more refined take on seafood favorites, like baked salmon glazed with maple syrup or Digby scallops fried in lemon herb butter.

5075 George St. ☎ *902-492-1800. Reservations not necessary. Main courses: C$8–C$16 (US$5.70–US$11.40). MC, V. Daily 11:00 a.m.–11:30 p.m.*

Sweet Basil Bistro
$$-$$$ **Downtown** **ITALIAN/ASIAN**

Casual and brightly decorated, this funky dining room is in a historic brick building across from the Historic Properties. It's the perfect spot for an inexpensive meal when you want a break from seafood. The menu features lots of fresh, healthy cooking with classic pastas balanced by lighter choices. Vegetarians will love the tofu stir-fry topped with roasted peanuts, or the daily crepe special, which is often meatless. After 5 p.m., the menu expands to include creative dishes like Slash N' Burn Salmon — blackened salmon served on a bed of Thai noodles. Save room for a banana split doused in rum and sprinkled with coconut.

1866 Upper Water St. ☎ *902-425-2133. Reservations recommended. Main courses: C$15–C$20 (US$10.70–US$14.30). AE, DC, MC, V. Daily 11:30 a.m.–11:00 p.m.*

Exploring Halifax

Alexander Keith's Brewery
Downtown

When Alexander Keith arrived in Halifax from Scotland, he put his experience brewing beer for British troops in India to work, establishing a brewery on the the Halifax harborfront in 1820. Keith's signature beer, India Pale Ale, is still brewed at what is now North America's oldest working brewery, along with other English-style ales and seasonal brews. Led by costumed guides, brewery tours are as much about the history of the city as they are about the brewing process, making them popular with everyone. (And the two free mugs of beer presented at the end of the tour have nothing to do with it.)

Keith's legacy is celebrated by the raising of mugs across city pubs, often for no particular reason. Keith's birthday, October 5, is celebrated more officially at nearby Pier 22 with Nova Scotian music, marching bands, dancing, and—you guessed it— lots of India Pale Ale.

1496 Lower Water St. ☎ *902-455-1474. Internet:* www.keiths.ca. *Admission: C$11 (US$7.90) adults, C$8 (US$5.70) children. Tours depart every 30 minutes June–Aug Mon–Sat 10 a.m.–9 p.m., Sun 10 a.m.–5 p.m.; Sept–May Fri 5–8 p.m., Sat noon–8 p.m.*

The Great Explosion

On December 6, 1917, Halifax was scarred by the largest man-made explosion prior to the atomic age. The *Mount Blanc,* a French munitions ship, collided with a Belgian relief ship in the middle of Halifax Harbour. The accident itself wasn't major, but it started a fire aboard the *Mont Blanc* and the crew, well aware of the cargo on board, took to the water in lifeboats. As crowds gathered toward the waterfront to watch the spectacle, the ship exploded, leveling over 100 hectares (250 acres) at the northern end of Halifax.

The force of the blast was almost incomprehensible: It was felt on Cape Breton Island and heard as far away as Prince Edward Island. The initial explosion was followed by fire, much of it fueled by coal stored in cellars for the approaching winter. The final death toll was 2,000, with an additional 10,000 injured.

Art Gallery of Nova Scotia
Downtown

Much of the art you see in Maritime galleries depicts lighthouses and fishing boats. This gallery proves that regional artists have a much broader range of subject matter. The 5,000-strong permanent collection is displayed in two buildings separated by a courtyard. A highlight is the colorful folk art of Maude Lewis. The gallery also hosts touring and temporary exhibits and is home to a small cafe serving up tasty lunches.

*1741 Hollis St. ☎ **902-424-7542**. Internet:* www.agns.gov.ns.ca. *Admission: C$10 (US$7.10) adults, C$8 (US$5.70) seniors, C$2 (US$1.40) children. Daily 10 a.m.–5 p.m. (Thurs until 9 p.m.).*

Discovery Centre
Downtown

Geared toward kids, this hands-on science museum is a great place to while away an afternoon if the weather is unfavorable. It's filled with fun activities that will fascinate (and educate!) the younger generation. Two favorites are the Ames Room (which distorts perceptions through a series of optical illusions) and Building Edification (an adventure playground where the emphasis is on basic construction principles). Other exhibits let kids blow massive bubbles or take a ride in a spinning chair (to teach momentum, of course).

*1593 Barrington St. ☎ **800-565-7487** or 902-492-4422. Internet:* www.discoverycentre.ns.ca. *Admission: C$6 (US$4.30) adults, C$4 (US$2.90) children. Mon–Sat 10 a.m.–6 p.m., Sun 1–5 p.m.*

Fairview Cemetery
Fairview

You can read the names on some of the 121 headstones at the back of Fairview Cemetery, but most only have numbers. All, however, have the same date — April 15, 1912. Halifax was the port where many bodies from the *Titanic* were brought for identification. Victims were identified by number, in the order they were pulled from the cold waters of the North Atlantic. Graves of the unknown victims are marked with these numbers.

For almost a century, these tombstones lay quietly at the back of the Fairview Cemetery, visited only by the occasional tourist. Everything changed with the release of the 1997 movie *Titanic* — suddenly, the final resting place of victim number 227, Joseph Dawson, became very popular. He coincidentally shared a name with third-class seaman Jack Dawson (portrayed by Leonardo DiCaprio in the movie) and has, as a result, garnered his own share of the actor's fan base. The grave is impossible to miss — just look for the fresh flowers left by weeping teenage girls.

Cemetery entrances are on Connaught and Chisholm avenues. Admission: Free.

A brochure detailing Titanic-related sights is available at the Maritime Museum and local visitor centers. Included are details and driving directions to Fairview Cemetery, along with Mount Olivet Cemetery, the final resting place of John Clarke, one of the Titanic band members famous for continuing to play as the ship was sinking.

Government House
Downtown

Completed in 1805, this house has been the official residence of Nova Scotia's Lieutenant-Governor longer than any other North American government residence. Built of Nova Scotian stone, it has been extensively restored inside and out, and although access is restricted, feel free to admire the exterior from surrounding gardens.

1451 Barrington St. Not open to the public.

Halifax Citadel National Historic Site
Downtown

I recommend starting your exploration of Halifax at the top, literally, by visiting Citadel Hill, which sits atop a high point of land overlooking the harbor. The original fortifications, built in 1749, have been replaced numerous times, with the most recent renovations completed in 1856 as a deterrent to a perceived threat from the United States. The fort was decommissioned in 1906, but has continued to serve as a proud symbol of the Canadian military ever since. History comes alive at the Citadel in summer through the haunting reverberations of bagpipers, a variety of interpretive programs, and colorful kilted soldiers following shouted marching orders. Indoor exhibits are tucked away in rooms built into the walls. A good starting point is the Fortress Halifax display, which tells the story of the complex. Other highlights are the school room and the adjacent magazines, where gunpowder and cannon charges were stored. A trail follows the top of the casement, encircling the courtyard and passing cannon emplacements. Looking outward, views extend across downtown to the harbor. In the middle of the courtyard, the two-story Cavalier Building holds an information center, a cafe, and a gift shop.

The **Old Town Clock,** below the Citadel's George Street entrance, is a city landmark.

Enter off Sackville St., immediately west of Brunswick St., and follow signs to public parking at the rear of the fortifications. On foot, walk up George St. from the waterfront. ☎ *902-426-5080. Admission: C$9 (US$6.40) adults, C$7.75 (US$5.50) seniors, C$4.50 (US$3.20) children; fees are reduced during shoulder seasons and admission is free Nov–early May. July–Aug 9 a.m.–6 p.m.; Sept–June 9 a.m.–5 p.m. Although the grounds are open year-round, no services are available Nov–May.*

Maritime Museum of the Atlantic
Downtown

Everyone will find something of interest at this museum, one of Halifax's premier attractions. The exhibits in this restored waterfront warehouse include numerous vessels that once plied the coastline, as well as displays exploring Nova Scotia's seafaring legacy through chronicles of ship-wrecks, the Canadian Navy, the Great Explosion, and the fishing industry. Because of Halifax's numerous links to the *Titantic*, a good portion of the museum is dedicated to the tragedy. A highlight is *Titanic 3-D,* a 15-minute documentary taken at the wreck site, shown at regular intervals throughout the day.

Moored at the wharf in front of the museum is the 1913 hydrographic steamer **Acadia,** which spent most of its life charting the ocean floor. Parts of the ship are open for public inspection, including the deck area and the chart room. At the next wharf is the **HMCS** *Sackville*, a speedy escort used during WW II. Admission to both vessels is free with a museum ticket.

1675 Lower Water St. ☎ *902-424-7490. Internet:* www.museum.gov.ns.ca/mma. *Admission: a very worthwhile C$8 (US$5.70) adults, C$7 (US$5) seniors, C$4 (US$2.90) children. May–Oct 9:30 a.m.–5:30 p.m. (Tues until 8 p.m.); Nov–April Tues–Sat 9:30 a.m.–5:30 p.m., Sun 1:00-5:30 p.m.*

McNab's Island
Halifax Harbour

On McNab's Island you'll find an 1888 fort built to defend Halifax Harbour from seaborne attacks. It's also a provincial park that provides a quick escape from the bustle of the city. You can enjoy numerous hiking trails, spectacular views, and good beaches. A teahouse serves snacks and light meals, or you can bring your own picnic lunch to one of the many designated day-use areas.

Access is by ferry departing Cable Wharf June–Sept, daily at 9 a.m. and 2 p.m. ☎ *902-420-1015; C$12.50 (US$8.90) round-trip. From Fisherman's Cove, McNab's Island Ferry,* ☎ *800-326-4563 or 902-465-4563, departs on demand; C$8 (US$5.70) round-trip. Admission: Free.*

Nova Scotia Museum of Natural History
Downtown

Natural history comes alive at this musuem, situated west of Citadel Hill. The skeleton of a pilot whale and dinosaur fossils take center stage in the main gallery, with geology, anthropology, and history displays filling out an interesting facility. Some exhibits change with the season (it was exotic butterflies in the Butterfly Pavilion when I visited), but one regular is Gus, an 80-year-old tortoise.

1747 Summer St. ☎ *902-424-7353. Internet:* www.nature.museum.gov.ns.ca. *Admission: C$5 (US$3.60) adults, C$4.50 (US$3.20) seniors, C$3 (US$2.10) children. Mon–Sat 9:30 a.m.–5:30 p.m., Sun 1:00–5:30 p.m. (closed Mon, Oct–April).*

Pier 21

Downtown

Between 1928 and 1971, over one million immigrants first stepped foot in Canada at Pier 21. This historic locale has since been turned into a museum dedicated to these people and the trials and tribulations they encountered on the journey to Canada. The Exhibition Hall is filled with interactive displays that trace the immigration process. Even if you're not researching your roots, plan on spending a little time here, especially at the compelling audiovisual presentations that relate personal immigrant stories. The Research Centre sounds more scholarly than it is. Computers and microfilm hold a database of ship arrivals and some passenger lists (1925–1935).

1055 Marginal Rd. ☎ *902-425-7770. Internet:* www.pier21.ca. *Admission: C$7.75 (US$5.50) adults, C$6.60 (US$4.70) seniors, C$4.30 (US$3) children. Mid-May–mid-Nov 9:30 a.m.–8:00 p.m.; mid-Nov–mid-May Tues–Sat 10 a.m.–5 p.m., Sun noon–5 p.m.*

Point Pleasant Park

Downtown

At the southern end of the downtown peninsula, the name sums up this wooded waterfront park perfectly. Within its 75-hectare (180-acre) boundary are numerous picnic spots, a sandy beach, a restaurant, and the remains of various fortifications. You can stroll along the 40km (25 miles) of trails that lace the park, or check out the view from the centrally located Prince of Wales Martello Tower. To explore Halifax's industrial port area, take advantage of the several trails that run close to the harborfront.

2km (1.2 miles) south along Young Ave. from downtown; parking is plentiful, or take Bus 9 from Scotia Centre. Daylight hours. Admission: Free.

Province House

Downtown

Famously described by Charles Dickens in 1842 as "like looking at Westminster through the wrong end of the telescope," this small, symmetrical tree-shaded building is Canada's oldest seat of government, having been used as the meeting place of the provincial legislature since 1819. Inside the rather dour sandstone building are a number of inspiring exterior features, including ornamental plasterwork.

1726 Hollis St. ☎ **902-424-4661.** Internet: gov.ns.ca/legislature. Admission: Free. July–Aug Mon–Fri 9 a.m.–5 p.m., Sat–Sun 10 a.m.–4 p.m.; Sept–June Mon–Fri 9 a.m.–4 p.m.

Public Gardens
Downtown

Generally regarded as North America's finest original Victorian garden, this 7-hectare (17-acre) green-space was created as a private garden in 1753, just four years after the founding of Halifax. Carefully tended rose-bushes bloom in formal Victorian-style beds, rhododendrons grow so lush they form a canopy over the path, and small streams link ponds inhabited by ducks and swans. In the center of the gardens, an old-fashioned bandstand hosts free Sunday afternoon concerts, but any sunny afternoon of the week is a perfect opportunity to while away some time here. Across Sackville Street from the north side of the gardens stands a sandstone cottage, the home of gardener Richard Power, who designed the original layout.

Bordered by Sackville St., Summer St., Corner South Park St. and Spring Garden Rd. The main entrance is at the corner of the latter two streets. Admission: Free. May–Nov daylight hours.

Saint Paul's Anglican Church
Downtown

Founded in 1749, Saint Paul's was the first cathedral built outside Great Britain. Grand, white, and dotted with stained-glass windows, it's now surrounded by modern highrises. Above the north-facing porch is a piece of metal embedded during the explosion of the *Mont Blanc* (see The Great Explosion sidebar on page 104).

1749 Argyle St. ☎ **902-429-2240.** Internet: www.stpaulshalifax.org. Admission: Free. Mon–Fri 9 a.m.–4 p.m.

Shopping

Shopping in Halifax tends to center around the waterfront, with a couple of notable exceptions. You can buy a wide variety of Maritimes creations — everything from ceramic fishermen to one-of-a-kind artworks. The city has a number of excellent art galleries, as well as quirky shops.

Checking out the scene

Shopping hours in Halifax are generally longer than elsewhere in the Maritimes, but vary greatly depending on the clientele. The touristy waterfront area is busy every day of the week, while many shops (and some restaurants) in the business district follow business hours, closing in the early evening and not opening at all on weekends.

Don't forget that you must add the 15% harmonized sales tax to all quoted prices (actually, it's done at the cash register). That's the bad news. The good news is that you may be able to get a portion back via the Visitor Rebate Program.

What to look for

Although Halifax is not renowned for any particular specialty items, these Maritimes' products find their way into Halifax's many shops:

- ✔ **Seafood.** The only sensible thing to do with seafood is to eat it, and that's what you'll probably find yourself doing most of time. Some seafood, such as smoked salmon, is prepared to last, allowing you to take it home to hungry relatives. You can also get dried dulse (seaweed), live lobster boxed specially for travel, or canned lobster, mussels, and oysters.

- ✔ **Books and Music.** Most bookstores have sections dedicated to Atlantic Canada literature. Secondhand and antiquarian bookstores often have large collections of nautical nonfiction. Traditional folk music is also abundant in music stores as well as nearly all souvenir shops, which often have listening stations so you can get a taste of the music before you buy.

- ✔ **Tacky souvenirs.** Whether it's a lighthouse Christmas decoration, a city-branded T-shirt, or a fluffy moose that you're after, there's no lack of touristy shops to fulfill your needs. Start your search in the Historic Properties along Upper Water Street.

Where to find it

This section details some of my favorite Halifax shopping experiences.

Arts and crafts

Jennifer's of Nova Scotia, 5635 Spring Garden Rd. (☎ **902-425-3119**), is Nova Scotian all over. Pottery, fabric patchwork, jewelry, soaps, and just about everything else is handcrafted. Many items are seasonal, focusing on such occasions as Easter or Christmas.

You'll find a selection of crafty shops along pedestrian-only Granville Mall. One of these is **Pewter House**, 1875 Granville St. (☎ 902-423-8843). Pewter products are crafted in the delightfully named village of Pugwash, on Nova Scotia's northern shore, and sold at this outlet in Halifax.

Clothing

Island Beach Co. started out selling T-shirts from an old log church, but has since grown into a 30-store chain with outlets across Atlantic Canada. Head to their stores at 1903 Barrington St. (☎ 902-423-0908) and 1781 Lower Water St. (☎ 902-422-4060) in downtown Halifax for casual, contemporary clothing in a subtly themed nautical setting.

If you're in the market for a kilt, or maybe a length of tartan to make your own, **Plaid Place**, in Barrington Place at 1903 Barrington St. (☎ 902-429-6872), is a good choice. They also stock other plaid clothing such as ties, scarves, and sweaters.

Antiques

Urban Cottage, at street level of the 1911 Old Merchant's Bank at 1819 Granville St. (☎ 902-423-3010), offers an eclectic mix of antiques from around the world.

At **henhouse**, south of downtown at 5802 South St. (☎ 902-423-4499), antiques are mixed with beautiful hand-built furniture constructed using traditional techniques. They also sell hand-dyed cotton linens, ceramic kitchenware, and porcelain dog dishes.

Crystal

It's difficult to miss **Nova Scotian Crystal**, along the waterfront at 5080 George St. (☎ 888-977-2797 or 902-492-0416), when crowds gather to watch artisans turn molten crystal into delicate masterpieces using century-old techniques. The factory doors open for public inspection daily between 8:00 a.m. and 4:30 p.m., but the most intriguing part of the process — glass-blowing — takes place Tuesday, Thursday, and Saturday. The adjacent shop sells a wide variety of unique pieces such as glasses, vases, and paperweights.

Camping and sporting gear

Halifax's largest outdoor retailer is **Mountain Equipment Co-op,** 1550 Granville St. (☎ 902-421-2667). MEC, as it's best known, is a co-operative owned by its members, similar to the American R.E.I. stores. Expect a range of high-quality clothing and camping gear, canoes and kayaks, books and maps, and a huge number of accessories.

Smaller **Chilkoot Pass**, 5523 Spring Garden Rd. (☎ 902-425-3674), is a more personal shopping experience, but with a wide range of outdoor and travel gear. You can also rent camping equipment such as tents and sleeping bags.

SportChek is a big-box sporting goods retailer offering popular brand names for reasonable prices at over 100 stores across Canada. The store features a wide variety of sporting goods for various recreational pursuits, including golfing and mountain biking; the selection of footwear is particularly strong. In Halifax, SportChek is in the Halifax Shopping Centre at 1001 Mumford Rd. (☎ 902-455-2528).

Halifax City Farmers' Market

North America's oldest farmers' market takes place every Saturday in a courtyard at the Alexander Keith's Brewery (1496 Lower Water St.; ☎ 902-492-4043). Hundreds of stands are filled with local produce and crafty creations. Search out Nova Scotian maple syrup and specialty soaps. The market operates every Saturday 7 a.m. to 1 p.m.

Nightlife

Mainly due to a healthy population of students, Halifax has a huge number of pubs and nightclubs. Beer aficionados will love the selection of local brews, most available on tap. Live music is a big part of the local nightlife scene, with bands playing every night of the week somewhere in town. Local bands to watch for include the Kilkenny Krew, the Navigators, McGinty, and Clam Chowder.

Most pubs open at 10 a.m. or 11 a.m. and close at midnight through the week and at 1 a.m. on weekends. Nightclubs generally stay open later, closing between 2 a.m. and 4 a.m.

For complete listings of everything that's happening after dark, pick up the free *Coast* newspaper, where you'll find a full schedule of music, stage, and film performances as well as club listings. Another source of information is the waterfront visitor center, where a map is dedicated to city drinking holes.

Pubbing and clubbing it

There's no better place to start this exploration of the local bar scene than down at the harborfront. The **Lower Deck,** in the Privateer's Warehouse at 1869 Upper Water Street (☎ 902-425-1501), is part of a three-story restaurant complex, with a few tables spread out on the adjacent wharf. It's the quintessential Halifax pub — good tunes, lots of local beer on tap, and smart, friendly service. Bands belt out traditional East Coast music nightly from 9:30 p.m., with afternoon patio parties scheduled on summer Saturday afternoons from 3 p.m. It's popular with locals, so arrive early to get the best seats. **John Shippey's Brewing Company** (☎ 902-423-7386) is tucked into a corner of the Harbourside

Market at 1869 Upper Water Street. Beer is brewed on-site, with large brew tanks filling the small booth. As part of the food court, the beer is served at tables spread inside and outside along the dock. A few are set aside for brewery patrons, with table service available. I recommend the Piper's Pale Ale, a light and refreshing beer that is the perfect accompaniment to a seafood meal. Continuing along the harborfront, **Stayner's Wharf,** 5075 George Street (☎ **902-492-1800**), is as popular for its food as it is for its beer. Monday and Tuesday nights are dedicated to improv comedy while Maritimes music draws crowds the rest of the week.

The **Granite Brewery**, two blocks from the water at 1662 Barrington Street (☎ **902-422-4954**), pours beer from its in-house brewery in a relaxed, upmarket atmosphere. Upstairs is **Ginger's Tavern**, which is the reincarnation of a pub of the same name that was popular in Halifax during the 1980s. On any given night, it could be the same 1980s crowd, too, listen to the same music. Just down the road, Granite Brewery's original location is now **Henry House**, 1222 Barrington Street (☎ **902-423-5660**), with a pub downstairs and a restaurant upstairs. It is as authentic as any of the British-style pubs in town, with an exposed brick and beam interior, cozy nooks, private booths, muted lighting, comfortable seating, and of course the Granite's popular Peculiar Ale on tap.

Local brews

Finding an authentic pint in Halifax is easy and I really encourage you to forgo the big brewery products familiar to most of us (through advertising as much as anything else) and try local brews.

Best-known is Alexander Keith's India Pale Ale, brewed in Halifax since 1820 (see "Exploring Halifax" for tour information) and available on draught throughout the city and at liquor stores across Canada. This beer has a distinctive "hoppy" flavor, a hangover (pun intended) from the original recipe. The style of beer was developed in Britain, with extra hops added to preserve the beer during its long journey to troops stationed in India (hence the name).

Propeller and Garrison are known as microbreweries. Their output is a fraction of Keith's; look for these beers on tap at many pubs, and in local liquor stores.

Ingredients are sourced from as far away as England for Granite Brewery's Peculiar Ale. This darker ale has a smooth, malty-sweet taste and is usually served only slightly below room temperature.

The **Thirsty Duck,** 5472 Spring Garden Road (☎ **902-422-1548**), is best for its sunken rooftop patio, a pleasant escape from the noisy street below. The decibel level does go up on weekends, when crowds gather and bands strum their stuff inside. ("The Duck," as it's usually known, gets its name from a pond in the nearby Public Gardens where ducks gather for a refreshing drink). In perfect position for a pub crawl (but be careful crossing the road) is nearby **Rogue's Roost** at 5435 Spring Garden Road (☎ **902-492-2337**). Beyond the rather unassuming facade is a friendly brewpub with a choice of British-style and seasonal ales brewed in-house. **Your Father's Moustache,** 5686 Spring Garden Road (☎ **902-423-6766**), is a big, bright pub, with a rooftop patio complete with its own bar. Admiring the ocean-themed mural behind the main stage is a good excuse to visit.

Other bars and nightclubs

Bitter End, 1570 Argyle Street (☎ **902-425-3039**), is a hip hangout that tries for a European air of elegance. The drink selection is impressive (good Caesars), cool contemporary art hangs on the walls, and candles create a distinctive atmosphere that sets this pub apart from those detailed above. **Velvet Olive,** below Citadel Hill at 1770 Market Street (☎ **902-492-2233**), features a DJ spinning disco and funk on Thursday while on Friday and Saturday, lighter "dinner music" plays until 10 p.m. when a band hits the stage. Crowds thin during the week, when you can expect drink specials and promotions such as theme nights. An extensive menu includes delicious Thai dishes under C$20 (US$14.30) and irresistible desserts like Smooth Chocolate Silk for C$7 (US$5).

Reflections Cabaret, at 5184 Sackville Street (☎ **902-422-2957**), is Halifax's premier venue for gays and lesbians. Through the working week, expect game and theme nights as well as karaoke, while on weekends a DJ spins the latest dance hits.

The arts

Halifax more than makes up for its lack of major theater companies with semiprofessional theater groups and a packed schedule of summer arts festivals.

Theater

The **Neptune Theatre** calls a historic theater at 1593 Argyle Street (☎ **902-429-7070**) home. The main season runs October to May with a smattering of performances ranging from classic to contemporary throughout the summer. Tickets range from C$15 to C$35 (US$10.70 to US$25).

For lighter theater fare (historically themed musical comedy anyone?) that comes with a substantial three-course meal, make reservations for the **Grafton Street Dinner Theatre**, at 1741 Grafton Street (☎ **902-425-1961**). Tickets are C$35 (US$25) adults, C$16 (US$11.40) children; plan to be seated by 6:45 p.m.

Seeing Halifax by Guided Tour

If your time in Halifax is limited, joining a guided tour ensures you see all the major attractions. You can get an overview of the city in a variety of ways — by land, sea, or a combination of the two — but even if you only have one day in town, plan on spending at least some of it exploring on foot. A trip out onto the harbor is also a must.

By bus

For a quick, complete tour of the city, **Gray Line** (☎ **902-425-9999;** Internet: www.atlantictours.com) offers a three-hour Deluxe Historic Halifax City Tour for C$31.30 (US$22.40) adults, C$28.70 (US$20.50) seniors, C$8.70 (US$6.20) children. A kilted guide provides a running commentary as a trolley car whizzes you around the city. While this tour provides a good overview, you may not get to linger as long as you'd like at some of the best stops — Citadel Hill alone (one of the stops; admission included) easily deserves a two-hour visit. Departures are daily at 9 a.m. and 1 p.m. from major downtown hotels. Another Gray Line option is a downtown loop tour aboard an old British-style double-decker bus. You can get on and off as you please at any of 12 stops. Tickets cost C$24.34 (US$17.40) adults, C$21.74 (US$15.50) seniors, C$6.09 (US$4.40) children. The main ticketing office for these tours is a kiosk in front of the Maritime Museum on Upper Water Street.

By boat

One the most pleasurable ways to view Halifax is from sea level. Jump on a commuter ferry, ride a tugboat with personality, or sail off into the sunset aboard one of the world's most famous yachts. However you do it, get out on the water for a true feel of this seaside town!

The least expensive way to enjoy Halifax Harbour is from the upper deck of the passenger ferry between Halifax and Dartmouth. Operated by **Metro Transit** (☎ **902-490-4000**), ferries depart for Dartmouth every 30 minutes between 6:30 a.m. and 9:30 p.m. from the terminal at the foot of Duke Street. The 12-minute trip costs just C$1.75 (US$1.25) each way.

For a wide variety of tour boat options, head to Cable Wharf at 1751 Lower Water Street and the **Murphy's on the Water** (☎ **902-420-1015**; Internet: www.murphysonthewater.com) ticket kiosk. The *Harbour Queen* sternwheeler departs for a two-hour cruise daily at 10 a.m. and 2 p.m. costing C$19.95 (US$14.30); daily at 4:30 p.m. for a one-hour cruise costing C$15.95 (US$11.40); Thursday to Sunday at 6:30 p.m. for a two-hour dinner cruise costing C$39.95 (US$28.50); and Friday and Saturday at 9:30 p.m. for a 2.5-hour party cruise complete with live music for C$17.95 (US$12.80). Murphy's also offers nature cruises, fishing trips, and boats to Peggy's Cove.

If the *Bluenose II* is away from Halifax (see "The *Bluenose*" sidebar in the Lunenburg section of the following chapter), or you miss one of the precious few times when this famous schooner is in town, the *Mar II* is a good alternative. Operated by Murphy's (see above), this wooden ketch that has circumnavigated the world now departs Cable Wharf daily at 2:00 p.m., 4:00 p.m., and 6:30 p.m. for a 90-minute sailing trip. The cost is C$19.95 (US$14.30).

By amphibious craft

I'm sure that the engineers who developed the *Larc V* for transporting supplies and troops in the Vietnam War never imagined one of their boats would end up as a colorfully painted tourist attraction. But that's what's happened in Halifax with **Harbour Hopper Tours**, whose amphibious vehicles will drive you around the streets of Halifax and then plunge into the water for a harbor cruise. You'll find the ticket kiosk on Cable Wharf (☎. **902-490-8687**). The bus (or is that boat?) departs up to 20 times daily between 9:00 a.m. and 9:30 p.m. Rides are C$22.50 (US$16) adults, C$21.50 (US$15.40) seniors, C$13.95 (US$10) children .

Side Trips from Halifax

Halifax is an ideal base for coastal excursions to the northeast and southwest. Highway 7 (known as Marine Drive) winds for over 300km along the **Eastern Shore** to the Canso Causeway, while a string of minor roads beckon from Highway 103 to form the Lighthouse Route along the **Southern Shore**. It's possible to drive either route and return to Halifax in a single day. If you want to take more time to appreciate these areas (and you really should), have a look at the chapters on each region, which will discuss these scenic driving routes more fully. For now, here are some reasonable half-day round-trip excursions that will whet your appetite for more Maritime charm.

Taking a tour to Peggy's Cove

If you don't have your own vehicle (or even if you do), consider taking a tour to Peggy's Cove. **Gray Line Halifax** (☎ 902-425-9999; Internet: www.atlantic tours.com) offers transportation that includes a running commentary for C$26.09 (US$18.60) adults, C$23.48 (US$16.80) seniors, C$14.78 (US$10.60) children. It's a flexible tour, with the option to return at your own leisure on buses scheduled to leave Peggy's Cove for Halifax every 90 minutes. An alternative to the bus is a return trip by boat, with the captain searching out whales, dolphins, and puffins. This option is an additional C$59.95 (US$42.80) for adults, C$53.95 (US$38.60) for seniors and children.

To Peggy's Cove

Less than an hour's drive southwest of Halifax is Peggy's Cove, a village of just 60 people, renowned for its postcard-perfect composition. On the way there you'll encounter several towns — including Prospect, East Dover, and West Dover — that are worth a look.

Finding your way out of Halifax and onto Highway 103 along the South Shore is simply a matter of map-reading — follow Cogswell Street to Quinpool Road, then merge across to Highway 3 (Margaret's Bay Road) at the large traffic circle. After 3km (1.9 miles), Highway 333 to the left is signposted to Peggy's Cove. Take this route, and you quickly leave the city behind; miss the turn and you end up on Highway 103, which zips down the coast on an inland route that misses some of Nova Scotia's best scenery.

Prospect

Overshadowed by its famous neighbor (or maybe because it is on the Lighthouse Route and doesn't have a lighthouse), the village of Prospect receives only a fraction of the visitors that Peggy's Cove does. But that's a good thing for the few visitors who venture the 8km (5 miles) from Highway 333. Like dozens of other villages along Nova Scotia's Atlantic Coast, Prospect is picturesque, with a cluster of colorful fishing cottages clinging to edges of a rocky harbor. Aside from a bed-and-breakfast, Prospect has no tourist services.

The Dovers

Continuing toward Peggy's Cove from the Prospect junction, **East Dover** lies 2km (1.2 miles) from Highway 333, while the main road passes through the heart of **West Dover**. Both are quintessential fishing villages comprising smartly kept homes separated from the ocean by a rocky shoreline. Even if you don't stop to wander the wharves, at least slow down and soak up the atmosphere.

Peggy's Cove

Ocean views from the approach to Peggy's Cove are impressive. But don't be tempted to drive to the end of the road. Instead, leave your vehicle in the parking lot to the left as you enter the village. From this point, the road narrows and descends to the harbor, with its boats, nets, and lobster traps. At the end of the road is a restaurant that tries hard not be touristy and an octagonal **lighthouse** surrounded by rounded granite boulders that is the main attraction for most visitors. It's also the only lighthouse in North America to have a post office.

Beyond the turnoff into Peggy's Cove is the touching **Swissair Memorial** dedicated to the 229 passengers and crew who lost their lives when Swissair Flight 111 crashed into the ocean within sight of land off Peggy's Cove on the night of September 2, 1998.

Because the village is popular with tour buses, it can get extremely busy after 9 a.m., especially when the cruise-ship crowd is docked in Halifax. Plan on an early morning excursion to miss the worst of the crowds and also to have the best light for photographing the "world's most photographed lighthouse." Of course, if you'd rather join the tourists than fight them, see the sidebar "Taking a Tour to Peggy's Cove."

Dartmouth

Dating to 1750 (just one year after Halifax was founded), the city of Dartmouth lies across Halifax Harbour from downtown. The working waterfront is dominated by industrial complexes with a population of 65,000 sprawling through to city limits. The city itself lacks the charm of Halifax, but boasts numerous lakes and parks.

Getting there and around

The ferry from Halifax terminates at the **Alderney Gate** quayside complex. A small visitor booth (☎ 902-490-4433) dispenses information on local attractions and transit routes and schedules for buses headed to the sights listed below. You'll also find numerous shops, an indoor play park, and a Saturday farmers' market (7 a.m. to 2 p.m.).

Show out-of-town identification and you can check e-mail for free at **Dartmouth Public Library,** upstairs in the Alderney Gate complex (☎ 902-490-5765; open Tuesday to Thursday 10 a.m. to 9 p.m., Friday and Saturday 10 a.m. to 5 p.m., Sunday 2 to 5 p.m.). There's usually a free terminal, and if not, newspapers from around the world will let you catch up on local goings-on while you wait your turn.

Exploring Dartmouth

From Alderney Gate, a short harborfront walking trail offers views back across the water to Halifax and the impossible-to-miss Imperial Oil refinery. In the adjacent Ferry Terminal Park is the World Peace Pavilion, which includes stones of substance from over 60 countries, including chunks of the Berlin Wall and the Great Wall of China.

Within walking distance of Alderney Gate, **Quaker Whaler House**, 59 Ochterloney Street at Edward Street (☎ **902-464-2300**), is a good little museum open Tuesday to Sunday mid-June through August 10 a.m. to 5 p.m. Quakers were drawn to Nova Scotia from New England for the whaling industry and this 1786 home tells their story. Costumed guides lead visitors out back to a herb and vegetable garden planted with the same varieties that were planted there over 200 years ago. Admission is C$2 (US$1.40). Keep your receipt, because entry to nearby **Dartmouth Heritage Museum** is included. It's a just few blocks away at the corner of Alderney Drive and Wyse Road (☎ **902-464-2300**); hours are the same as at Quaker Whaler House. Displays catalog the natural and human history of the Dartmouth region, including a small collection of native artifacts.

The **Bedford Institute of Oceanography**, under the MacKay Bridge at 1 Challenger Drive (☎. **902-426-2373**; Internet www.bio.gc.ca), is definitely worth checking out. It is Canada's largest ocean research center, targeting a wide range of disciplines from ocean surveillance techniques for the Department of Defence to the monitoring of cod fisheries for the Department of Oceans and Fisheries. The public is welcome to take a self-guided tour of the facility. The Sea Pavilion contains a series of touch tanks holding sea life collected from the Nova Scotia coastline, while another interesting display depicts the *Titanic* on the ocean floor. It is open Monday to Friday from 9 a.m. to 4 p.m. and, best of all, admission is free.

Fisherman's Cove

Jump aboard bus 60 at Alderney Gate to reach this photogenic fishing village, 7km (4.3 miles) south of Dartmouth. Though many of the older dockside buildings have been renovated, an authentic atmosphere prevails. The waterfront itself is the main attraction, but you can find plenty of activities, including a sandy beach and kayak rentals. A ferry link across the Eastern Passage provides access to **McNab's Island. A&M Sea Charters** (☎ **902-465-6617**) takes visitors on weekend whale-watching excursions for C$20 (US$14.30) adults, C$10 (US$7.10) children, while **Spirit of the East Kayaks** (☎ **902-478-7330**) rents kayaks for C$10 (US$7.10) per hour and leads three-hour calm-water kayak trips for C$30 (US$21.40) per person.

Suggested One-, Two-, and Three-Day Itineraries

Here are some of the best ways to spend one, two, or three days in Halifax, assuming you're visiting in summer (along with almost everyone else). For details on the attractions, restaurants, and activities mentioned in these itineraries, see the corresponding sections earlier in this chapter.

One-day itinerary

If you have just a single day in Halifax, start at the top and hit **Halifax Citadel National Historic Site** as soon as it opens (9 a.m.) to get a taste of the city's colorful past. Spend an hour exploring this fort, then head down George Street, taking detours along Granville Street and Bedford Row to admire heritage buildings such as **Province House.** Spend another hour or so at the Maritime Museum of the Atlantic. At lunchtime, choose from the many stands at Harbourside Marketplace (it's hard to bypass the seafood — splurge and share a lobster platter for two) and find a table outside. Afterward, hop aboard a boat to **Peggy's Cove,** returning to Halifax via a Gray Line bus. Plan on returning in time to catch the 6:30 p.m. *Mar II* departure. After returning to the dock, it's a short walk to Salty's, where your reservation ensures a waterfront table.

Two-day itinerary

If you have two days in Halifax, you can take a more leisurely approach to the attractions covered in the one-day itinerary, while saving Peggy's Cove for day two. Across Sackville Street from the Halifax Citadel, the **Public Gardens** are an ideal addition to your pre-lunch itinerary. After lunch, walk south along the docks to **Alexander Keith's Brewery** for a tour, and then continue to **Pier 21** and **Point Pleasant Park**.

On day two, rise early for the drive to **Peggy's Cove** (or take Gray Line's first departure). Spend the morning exploring the village and its famous lighthouse before returning to Halifax. Eat dinner at the **Upper Deck,** then, if you're still feeling active, head downstairs to the **Lower Deck** and catch one of the regular bands entertaining the crowd with traditional Maritime music.

Three-day itinerary

For the first two days, follow the two-day itinerary. If you happen to be there on Saturday, head to **Halifax City Farmers' Market,** wandering through stands of fresh produce and local arts and crafts. If not, enjoy browsing in shops scattered throughout downtown. Enjoy an early lunch at whichever waterfront restaurant strikes your fancy, then jump aboard a ferry for Dartmouth and visit the **Bedford Institute of Oceanography.**

Having your own vehicle expands your options: Continue beyond Dartmouth to **Fisherman's Cove,** then drive along the coast to **Lawrencetown Beach**, a good turn-around point for a four-hour excursion. Back in the city, enjoy dinner at one of the many restaurants listed in the "Dining in Halifax" section of this chapter, then head over to **Henry House** for a pint or two of the Granite Brewery's Peculiar Ale. If you're feeling up to it, continue the night by catching a cab up to Spring Garden Road, which is lined with pubs and clubs.

Fast Facts

ATMs

Most banks, along with a growing number of grocery stores and gas stations, have ATMs.

Emergencies

Dial ☎ **911** for all emergencies.

Hospital

The Halifax Infirmary (☎ **902-473-3383**) is the 24-hour emergency department of the Queen Elizabeth II Health Services Centre, at 1796 Summer St.

Information

Tourism Halifax operates the International Vistor Centre at 1595 Barrington St. (☎ **902-490-5946**; Internet: www.halifaxinfo.com). **Tourism Nova Scotia** (☎ **902-424-4248**) has an information booth by the baggage carousels at Halifax International Airport and another on the waterfront at 1655 Lower Water St.

Internet Access

Downtown, **Ceilidh Connection,** at 1672 Barrington Street (☎ **902-422-9800**), has a bank of public computers with high-speed connections.

Police

For emergencies, dial ☎ **911.**

Post Office

The main post office is between Sackville and Prince sts. at 1680 Bedford Row.

Restrooms

Along the waterfront, public restrooms are located in the Harbourside Marketplace and the ferry terminal. The public restrooms in hotel lobbies are also a good bet.

Taxis

See "Orienting Yourself," earlier in this chapter, for a discussion on using local taxis. One company is **Yellow Cab** (☎ **902-420-0000**).

Transit Info

Public buses are operated by **Metro Transit** (☎ **902-490-6600**). See "Orienting Yourself," earlier in this chapter for details.

Weather

Environment Canada maintains a Web site at www.weatheroffice.ec.gc.ca with a link to Halifax's forecast.

Chapter 12

Southwestern Nova Scotia

. . . .

In This Chapter

▶ Strolling the streets of Mahone Bay

▶ Exploring Lunenburg

▶ Stepping back in time at Shelburne

▶ Enjoying the sea life along Digby Neck

▶ Brushing up on the history of Annapolis Royal

. . . .

The southwestern portion of Nova Scotia has a raw magnetism unlike anywhere else in Canada. You'll find an endless line of picturesque seaside villages clinging to the rocky shorelines of sheltered bays. The region is mostly rugged and often remote, yet it holds some of Canada's oldest towns. Unhurried and unchanged for decades, they are living proof of Nova Scotia's nautical traditions.

Glance at a map of Nova Scotia and you'll see that the southwestern part of the province is encircled by a single highway that is rarely more than a few kilometers from the ocean. If you drive along this route, beginning and ending in Halifax, you'll get more than a taste of Maritimes history and charm. In this section, I'll explore some of the notable towns you'll encounter on the way.

The farther you travel from Halifax, the less touristy it becomes. This is a good thing when it comes to crowds, but it also means you should plan ahead by making accommodation reservations in advance and carrying a small amount of cash — just in case that craft shop with the wooden whale doesn't accept credit cards.

What's Where: Southwestern Nova Scotia and Its Major Attractions

In a clockwise direction from Halifax, the region's highway passes each of the following towns.

Mahone Bay

Mahone Bay is a historic shipbuilding town set around a protected waterway. Although its setting is similar to other villages along the South Shore, its close proximity to Halifax has led to the creation of a bustling village center in an otherwise staid old seafaring town. Make sure to check out:

- The **three churches,** perfectly placed beside the harbor
- **Shopping** for local art and crafts
- **Chester,** a short drive from Mahone Bay (See sidebar "Charming Chester" later in this chapter)

Lunenburg

Lovely Lunenburg. Just over an hour's drive from Halifax, this colorful port is one of the Maritimes' most popular destinations. After checking in at one of the many historic inns, don't miss:

- **Strolling the streets of Old Town,** protected as a UNESCO World Heritage Site
- The **Fisheries Museum of the Atlantic** and historic vessels tied up on the adjacent wharf
- *Bluenose II,* a symbol of Canada
- **Lobster fishing** aboard a working fishing boat

Shelburne

Famous for its shipbuilding heritage, Shelburne sits on a bay near the southern end of the South Shore. Many visitors turn around at Lunenburg, leaving Shelburne and the following sights delightfully unaffected by tourism:

- **Pre-1800 wooden buildings,** the largest such concentration in Canada
- The **Dory Shop,** where craftsmen still ply their historic trade
- **Muir Cox Shipyard,** in operation since 1820

Digby

Digby is a fishing town through and through, which, if you love seafood, is reason enough to drop by. When you're here, plan on:

- ✔ **Dining on scallops** at a harborfront restaurant
- ✔ Seeing the world's largest fleet of **scallop boats,** one of which is open for inspection
- ✔ Driving the **Digby Neck**
- ✔ **Whale-watching** in the Bay of Fundy

Annapolis Royal

The site of Canada's first permanent settlement, Annapolis Royal is under the grand delusion that it is still the Victorian era. In addition to admiring tree-lined streets of gracious homes, check out:

- ✔ **Annapolis Tidal Generation Station,** which uses the massive Fundy tides to generate electricity
- ✔ **Fort Anne National Historic Site,** beside Canada's oldest thoroughfare
- ✔ **Howard Dill Enterprises,** famous for producing the world's biggest pumpkins

Mahone Bay

Picturesque Mahone Bay is a small village with a big-time reputation for its charmingly restored private homes and businesses set around a narrow inlet filled with boats. The main street wends its way around the water, passing art galleries, craft shops, cafes, and restaurants housed in historic buildings, many dating from the days when Mahone Bay was a major shipbuilding center. At the head of the inlet, the towering spires of three adjacent churches make for one of Canada's most photographed scenes.

Getting there

Follow Highway 103 southwest from Halifax for 80km (50 miles) and take Exit 10 to reach Mahone Bay. Parking is permitted along the streets, but a better option is the parking lot opposite the churches just before downtown.

Staying in Mahone Bay

While day-trippers from Halifax fill the streets of Mahone Bay, only those smart enough to have made advance reservations are able to take advantage of the limited number of guest rooms in the village.

Mahone Bay Bed and Breakfast

$$ **Mahone Bay**

Watch the world go by from the veranda of this distinctive yellow and white inn along the main street. Constructed in 1860 by a shipbuilder, it's a solid old home that has been spruced up with "gingerbread" trim — elaborate swirls of wood below the roofline and around the veranda. Beyond the photogenic exterior are four adequate guest rooms, two with ensuites and two with private bathrooms down the hall. Bathrobes are a nice touch and rates include a full breakfast.

558 Main St. ☎ *866-239-6252 or 902-624-6388. Fax: 902-624-0023. Rack rates: C$75–C$95 (US$53.60–US$67.90). MC, V. May–Oct.*

Nature's Cottage Bed and Breakfast

$$ **Mahone Bay**

Set on almost 1 hectare (2.5 acres) of forest across from the water, guests can find plenty of space to relax in the gardens, in an outdoor hot tub, or on a private dock. My favorite of the three guest rooms is the Safari Room, with bright decor, African furnishings, and a private bathroom. Above the garage, the Loft has a private entrance, cooking facilities, and television/VCR combo.

906 Main St. (toward Lunenburg) ☎ *877-607-5699 or 902-624-0196. Internet:* www.naturescottagebb.com. *Rack rates: C$100–C$150 (US$71.40–US$107.10) double. AE, MC, V.*

Ocean Trail Retreat

$$-$$$ **Mahone Bay**

You won't find a better setting than this sprawling resort high above Mahone Bay. What the resort's motel rooms lack in cutting-edge decor, they make up for with stunning water views (two of the rooms even have balconies) and reasonable prices. The two-bedroom chalets are more comfortable and each has a kitchen and separate living area with gas fireplace. For a splurge, book the Balcony Suite that comes with a jetted tub, expansive deck with barbecue, and full kitchen.

Maders Cove (between Mahone Bay and Lunenburg) ☎ *888-624-8824 or 902-624-8824. Fax: 902-624-8899. Internet:* www.oceantrailretreat.com. *Rack rates: C$89–C$200 (US$63.60–US$142.90) double. Minimum stay applies on some units in July and Aug. AE, MC, V. April–Nov.*

Dining in Mahone Bay

Mimi's Ocean Grill
$$–$$$ Mahone Bay   CONTEMPORARY

Everyone leaves Mimi's raving about the food. I did too, after a cucumber and roasted red pepper puree and grilled lamb chops with peach chutney. Can't resist more seafood? Not a problem, Mimi's has that covered, too. The restaurant itself is a converted residence, with table settings spread between connected rooms, a veranda, and in a courtyard out back. The atmosphere inside is casually dignified, with paintings by local artists on whitewashed walls.

662 South Main St. ☎ *902-624-1342. Main courses: C$14–C$23 (US$10–US$16.40). MC, V. April–Dec daily noon–9 p.m.*

Salt Spray Café
$–$$ Mahone Bay   SEAFOOD/CANADIAN

The Salt Spray is my all-time favorite breakfast spot in Nova Scotia. Sitting on the back deck soaked in morning sun with the ternary of harborside churches reflecting on the water is simply divine. The food is tasty and very well priced too. Typically, breakfast for two, with all the trappings, will cost well under C$20 (US$14.30), *including* tip. The rest of the day, the menu features soups, salads, and healthy sandwiches — with emphasis on the seafood, of course.

621 South Main St. ☎ *902-624-9902. Main courses: C$8.50–C$13.50 (US$6.60–US$9.60). MC, V. Daily 7:30 a.m.–6 p.m.*

Exploring Mahone Bay

You could easily walk from one end of Mahone Bay to the other in ten minutes, but that's not the point. Instead, plan on spending at least two hours admiring the fine architecture and making the following stops (listed from the parking lot in front of the churches):

  ✔ **Jo-Ann's Deli.** Located at 9 Edgewater St. (☎ **902-624-6305**), this is the place to pick up picnic supplies like baked goodies and healthy wraps, as well as jams and preserves. Of special note are the blueberry scones (delicious!) and the bag of carrots (not for general consumption) used as a counterweight for the front door.

✔ **Tea Brewery.** On Main St. opposite the end of Clairmont St., the Tea Brewery (☎ 902-624-0566; daily 9:30 a.m.–5:30 p.m.) is crammed with teas and tea-brewing paraphernalia from around the world. Two tables and a selection of cakes may tempt you to linger longer.

✔ **Bandstand.** Behind the grocery store parking lot, you'll find the flower-encircled waterfront bandstand. From this vantage point, you can take the classic Mahone Bay photo of the three churches reflected on the water.

✔ **Mahone Bay Trading Company.** Opposite the bandstand on Main St. (☎ 902-624-8425), walk past the potting soil and laundry detergent in this general store to admire the massive boat-shaped counter. It's open Mon–Sat 10 a.m.–6 p.m., Sun 11 a.m.–5 p.m.

✔ **Amos Pewter.** The ancient art of casting, spinning, and finishing pewter can be viewed at this waterfront workshop at 589 Main Street (☎ 902-624-9547; Internet: www.amospewter.com). Open: June–Aug Mon–Sat 10 a.m.–6 p.m., Sun 10 a.m.–5 p.m.

✔ **Mahone Bay Settlers Museum.** Admission is free to this small museum in a 150-year-old home. Displays trace the history of the local shipbuilding industry and highlight local architecture. It's at 578 Main St. (☎ 902-624-6263; June–Aug Tues–Sat 10 a.m.–5 p.m., Sun 1–5 p.m.).

✔ **Redden's Fine Whale Sculptures Studio.** Stop by the studio of Susan Redden, at 788 Main St. (☎ 902-624-1232; June–Sept), to admire her mahogany carvings, which reflect the enchanting personality of whales and dolphins through clean, polished lines.

Charming Chester

In the late 1700s, Chester, north of Mahone Bay along Highway 3, was an infamous hub for pirates, privateers, and smugglers. The village matured over time into a resort town dominated by imposing waterfront mansions and sprawling summer estates. Today, Chester still has a distinctive moneyed feel. Local real estate is among the highest priced east of Montreal, well-heeled guests stay at exclusive lodges such as **Haddon Hall Resort Inn** (☎ 902-275-3577; Internet: www.haddonhallinn.com), and yachters from around the world tie up at the local marina. Through it all, the community itself remains very approachable — children splash around in a tidal swimming pool beside million-dollar boats, locals mix with Hollywood stars on the waterfront deck of the **Captain's House** pub (☎ 902-275-3501), and a mid-August yachting regatta attracts as many spectators as boat owners.

Lunenburg

A stay in Lunenburg, famous for its colorful, perfectly preserved private homes and commercial buildings overlooking a bustling harbor, is a Maritime highlight.

Lunenburg successfully juggles an active working harbor with a prosperous tourism industry — and does it well. The town brims with excellent accommodations, lively restaurants, and artsy shops.

Getting There

Lunenburg is 92km (57 miles) southwest of Halifax. To drive from the capital, take Highway 103 to Exit 10 (if you want to visit Mahone Bay) or Exit 11. From either of these exits, it's a ten-minute drive along well-signposted rural roads to Lunenburg.

DRL Coachlines (☎ **877-450-1987** or 902-450-1987) offers daily bus service between Halifax and Lunenburg. The cost is C$18 (US$12.90) each way.

Orienting Yourself in Lunenburg

Commercial enterprises are concentrated on four main streets: Bluenose Drive, along the waterfront, and Pelham Street and Montague Street, both running parallel to Bluenose, are of most interest, with restaurants, boutiques, and craft shops; Lincoln Street, one block up from Pelham Street, is the original thoroughfare.

The location of **Lunenburg Visitor Information Centre** (take Pelham Street east through town) on Blockhouse Hill Road (☎ **902-634-8100**) affords good views, but is a little inconvenient for arriving visitors. It's open May to October 9 a.m.to 8 p.m. The Web site www.town. lunenburg.ns.ca has lots of information on the town's history and links to tourist services.

Staying in Lunenburg

A couple of factors make staying in Lunenburg more expensive than staying elsewhere in the province — most lodgings are in grand old homes (no chain motels here) and demand is high for a limited number of rooms. Reservations are a must in July and August, but also recommended for June and September.

Captain Westhaver Bed and Breakfast

$ Lunenburg

Backed by quiet gardens with a rural outlook, this lodge offers three clean, simple rooms that share a bathroom. My favorite room is Hollyhock, which opens to a private sundeck. Built in 1910 for a sea captain, the home's historic character shines through best in the comfy parlor or out on the wide veranda.

102 Dufferin St. ☎ ***902-634-4937.*** *Fax: 902-634-8640. Rack rates: C$65–C$75 (US$46.40–US$53.60). MC, V.*

Lunenburg Arms Hotel

$$–$$$$ Lunenburg

This gracious 18th-century hotel has been renovated inside and out, yet retains its historic character. Original hardwood floors combine well with modern amenities such as plush mattresses and high-speed Internet access to create a memorable stay. Bathrooms are well appointed and all rooms are air-conditioned. Only some rooms have harbor views (404 is the least expensive room with a view of the water). Breakfast (extra) is served in the downstairs restaurant, and you'll find it easy to relax in the adjacent lounge.

94 Pelham St. ☎ ***800-679-4950*** *or 902-634-3333. Fax: 902-640-4041. Internet:* www.lunenburgarms.com. *Rack rates: C$130–C$250 (US$92.90–US$178.60). AE, MC, V.*

Lunenburg Inn

$$–$$$ Lunenburg

An attractive Victorian home in a leafy setting, this bed-and-breakfast is away from the bustle of Old Town yet within a five-minute walk of the waterfront. Built in 1893, the inn features seven guest rooms, some opening to a second-floor sundeck, all richly decorated with lots of polished wood. The two suites are extra-large and come with jetted tubs. This inn has five rate levels over a six-month season, with rooms dipping as low as C$80 to C$115 (US$57.10–US$82.10) in April. Rates include a cooked breakfast.

26 Dufferin St. ☎ ***800-565-3963*** *or 902-634-3963. Fax: 902-634-9419. Internet:* www.lunenburginn.com. *Rack rates: C$140–C$180 (US$100–US$128.60). MC, V. April–Sept.*

Lunenburg Oceanview Chalets
$$–$$$$ Lunenburg

I've included this one because it's a better option for families than the historic downtown inns, which make up the bulk of Lunenburg's lodgings. The complex comprises six newish log chalets, each with a full kitchen, fireplace, separate bedrooms, and deck with gas barbecue. One is wheelchair accessible. From the lofty location atop a high ridge behind town, it's a ten-minute walk to the waterfront.

78 Old Blue Rocks Rd. ☎ *902-640-3344. Fax: 902-640-3345. Internet:* www.lunenburgoceanview.com. *Rack rates: One-bedroom cottage C$139 (US$99.30), two-bedroom cottage C$229 (US$163.60). MC, V.*

Spinnaker Inn
$$–$$$ Lunenburg

Water views and central location are the good news. The bad news is there are only four units, so you will need to book well in advance for summer. The highlight of the rooms are the big windows and the expansive views (the best in town). The rooms themselves are simply furnished with antique-style beds and hardwood floors, and the bathrooms have been thoroughly updated. The more expensive units are split-level and have a jetted tub and kitchenette (although Suite 4 has limited views). The Spinnaker is one of the few small inns open year-round; rates drop as low as C$60 to C$100 (US$42.90–US$71.40) in winter.

126 Montague St. ☎ *902-634-4543. Fax: 902-640-2022. Internet:* www.spinnakerinn.com. *Rack rates: C$120–C$175 (US$85.70–US$125). AE, MC, V.*

Dining in Lunenburg

Big Red's
$–$$ Lunenburg   FAMILY DINING

If you're traveling with a family in tow and looking for an inexpensive meal, it's hard to beat Big Red's, a big restaurant with great views. Of course there's seafood, but you can also choose from hamburgers, pizza, and an extensive kids' menu.

80 Montague St. ☎ *902-634-3554. Main courses: C$9–C$21 (US$6.40–US$15). AE, DC, MC, V. Daily 9 a.m.–10 p.m.*

Old Fish Factory
$$$–$$$$ Lunenburg   SEAFOOD

Overlooking Lunenburg Harbour from a converted fish factory (also home to the Fisheries Museum), this touristy restaurant has a varied menu with plenty of seafood choices. Mussels or oysters are a good choice to start, with mains ranging from grilled halibut to a seafood platter for two (C$80/US$57.10) that comes with a full lobster. The pricing is a little higher than comparable seafood restaurants, but the tables on the enclosed patio are a pleasant place to relax over an evening meal.

68 Bluenose Dr. ☎ *902-634-3333. Reservations recommended for dinner. Main courses: C$19–C$32 (US$13.60–US$22.90). AE, DC, DISC, MC, V. Daily 11:30 a.m.–9:00 p.m.*

Rissers

$$–$$$ **Lunenberg   SEAFOOD/MODERN CANADIAN**

Rissers is away from the water, which isn't necessarily a bad thing — you're not paying for a view and the atmosphere is distinctly more mellow than down the hill. Dining is in a casually elegant room or on a tiered patio. The quality of food is equal to anywhere else in town, with choices running the gamut of Canadian cuisine from lamb to lobster. Rissers has no dessert menu. Instead, samples of each are presented to your table, which makes them almost impossible to resist.

Lunenburg Arms Hotel, 94 Pelham St. ☎ *902-634-3333. Main courses: C$13–C$24 (US$9.30–US$17.10). AE, DC, MC, V. Daily 7:30 a.m.–10:00 p.m.*

Rum Runner Restaurant

$–$$$ **Lunenburg   SEAFOOD**

Set on the lower level of the Rum Runner Inn, this restaurant is a little bit old fashioned in decor and cuisine, but the menu is well priced and the unobstructed views are unbeatable. The prime seats are outside on the covered veranda. Local seafood takes precedence on the menu. Lobster is served in various ways, including in a bisque. A seafood platter for two is only C$33 (US$23.60) or take your pick from any of a variety of non-seafood mains, like chicken curry and Vienna schnitzel.

66 Montague St. ☎ *902-634-9200. Main courses: C$9–C$25 (US$6.40–US$17.90). AE, DC, MC, V. Daily 11 a.m.–9 p.m.*

Exploring Lunenburg

Lunenburg's biggest attraction is the town itself, so take some time to stroll around and appreciate its historic architecture. Or, soak up authentic Maritimes fishing culture at the Fisheries Museum. If you run out of things to do in town, there's plenty to see and do out on the water or at any of the nearby attractions.

Fisheries Museum of the Atlantic
Downtown

If wandering along the waterfront doesn't give you a good enough feeling for the region's heritage, this harborside museum in a former fish-processing plant will. As the name suggests, it highlights the fishing industry, using exhibits of boat-building (including a shop where you can watch carpenters at work), whales and whaling, commercial fishing equipment, and rum-running during the era of prohibition. In the Millennium Aquarium, commercially important fish species, super-sized lobsters, and a variety of crabs reside in large tanks, and a touch tank allows you to get up close and personal with tidal pool species like starfish. And the museum takes advantage of its harborfront location — a small fleet of historic vessels is tied up out front, including the *Teresa E. Connor*, a wooden schooner that spent her life on the famous Grand Banks fishery. You can also take your pick from a busy schedule of daily events such as knot-tying and seafaring storytelling out on the dock.

68 Bluenose Dr. ☎ *902-634-4794. Internet:* www.museum.gov.ns.ca/fma. *Admission: C$9 (US$6.40) adults, C$7 (US$5) seniors, C$3 (US$2.10) children. May–Oct daily 9:30 a.m.–5:30 p.m.*

Historic buildings of note

Some buildings in the oldest part of town (known as Old Town) date to the 18th century, but most are pre-1900. Aside from the colorful palate of paint, restoration work is unpretentious (no fancy woodwork or fake facades). What you see is what you would have seen a century ago, which creates a real visual sense of history. Although most of the restoration has been done by individual owners, the town as a whole achieved the ultimate accolade in 1995 — when Old Town was declared a World Heritage Site by UNESCO for being "the best example of a British colonial settlement in North America."

While it was Old Town as a whole that was recognized by UNESCO as a World Heritage Site, the following individual buildings are especially noteworthy:

- ✔ **Scotia Trawler Shipyard.** The *Bluenose* was built at this sprawling complex at 250 Montague St. (☎ **902-634-4914**). Today, it also incorporates boat construction and repair with the Yacht Shop, primarily serving the needs of local seamen but with a range of marine-themed souvenirs unlike anything in the more touristy shops. The actual shipyards are off-limits, but access to the adjacent Government Wharf is permitted.

- ✔ **Knaut Rhuland House.** Aside from commercial enterprises, this historic home at 125 Pelham St. (☎ **902-634-3498**) is the only historic building in Old Town Lunenburg open to the public. Considered to be the finest example of Georgian architecture anywhere in the Maritimes, it's open June–early September daily 10 a.m. to 5 p.m. Admission costs C$3 (US$2.10).

- **Bailly House.** Built in 1780, this privately owned home at 134 Pelham St. is the oldest building in Lunenburg. It is owned by the brother of artist Earl Bailly, whose work is displayed in civic buildings (including the library and museum) through town.

- **St John's Anglican Church.** Tragically destroyed by fire in November 2001, this 1753 Lunenburg landmark on the corner of Duke and Cumberland streets has been carefully rebuilt in its gothic revival grandeur.

- **Lunenburg Academy.** This striking building at 97 Kaulbach St. is a rare example of a large wooden school. Dating to 1895, it still operates as a center for education. The black and white turreted structure is easy to recognize from anywhere around the harbor.

The *Bluenose*

The dime is the only Canadian coin that doesn't feature one of the country's flora or fauna. It depicts the *Bluenose*, a famous sailing ship that represents East Coast nautical traditions and is about as Canadian as the maple leaf. Built as a fishing schooner, the *Bluenose* was actually designed for winning the International Fishermen's Trophy, an America's Cup-style racing series between working ships from Canada and the U.S. After its launch from Lunenburg in 1921, the *Bluenose* enjoyed a tremendously successful career and was retired from racing after 17 undefeated years, then ingloriously lost off Haiti in 1946.

Back in Lunenburg, construction of the *Bluenose II* began in the 1960s, using the original plans to create an exact replica of her predecessor, right down to the sails and rigging. The *Bluenose II* now spends June through September mixing public cruises with appearances at festivals and events around the Nova Scotian coast. The public cruise portion of her schedule is divided between Lunenburg and Halifax. Half of all tickets are allotted for advance sales (☎ **800-763-1963** or 902-634-1938), with the remainder sold dockside 90 minutes prior to sailing from the Bluenose II Company Store, corner of Bluenose Drive and King Street, Lunenburg, or the ticket booth behind the Maritime Museum of the Atlantic at 1675 Water Street, Halifax. The cost is C$20 ($US$14.30) adults, C$10 (US$7.10) children. The *Bluenose II* schedule is posted on the Web site, www.bluenose2.ns.ca. To ensure a spot, you will either need to make advance reservations at least three months prior to sailing or be in line for the standby tickets at least two hours before the posted departure time. Don't say I didn't warn you.

Wondering where the boat's unusual name originated? So do the experts, but I like one theory in particular — local fishermen would wipe their noses when wearing blue mittens and in the cold, wet conditions on board, the dye would often run.

Other cool things to do in and around Lunenburg

In addition to browsing nautically themed shops and walking the fairways of **Bluenose Golf Club** (☎ 902-634-4260), here are a few other activities to keep you busy in and around Lunenburg.

Boat tours

If the *Bluenose II* is out of port, or you missed a spot, don't despair, there is another option. The ***Eastern Star,*** a classic 15-meter (48-foot) wooden ketch, departs Lunenburg up to five times daily for a sailing trip around the harbor (the 7 p.m. Sunset Cruise is two hours and travels to Ovens Natural Park). Buy tickets from the dockside booth at the foot of King Street (☎ 902-634-3535). The cost is C$22 to C$25 (US$15.70 to US$17.90) adults, C$11 to C$12 (US$7.90 to US$8.60) children.

Exactly as the name suggests, **Lobstermen Tours** (☎ 902-634-3434) are trips in a working fishing boat. Led by local fishermen, you get to learn firsthand about lobsters and the industry from the experts before pulling traps (hopefully) filled with lobsters. The two-hour tour departs four times daily from the foot of King Street and the cost is C$25 (US$17.90) adults, C$12 (US$8.60) children.

If you're not planning on traveling as far as Digby or Cape Breton Island, then Lunenburg is the next best option for a whale-watching trip. **Lunenburg Whale Watching Tours** (☎ 902-527-7175) has an excellent record for spotting humpback, finback, minke, and pilot whales. Regular sightings of sunfish, turtles, porpoises, dolphins, seals, and puffins round out what can be a very exciting tour. The cost is C$45 (C$32.10) adults, C$30 (US$21.40) children.

Blue Rocks

In this pretty hamlet, you'll find a jumble of fishing cottages clinging to a rocky shoreline, with small fishing boats in a protected bay, and the shoreline dotted with fishing nets and lobster traps. In other words, this is exactly what Nova Scotia is supposed to look like — minus the crowds of Peggy's Cove. Take Pelham Street eastbound through Lunenburg and follow Blue Rocks Road.

Ovens Natural Park

The "ovens" are sea caves that have been carved into cliffs over thousands of years by the ocean's waves. A trail leads to various overlooks while another ends at the mouth of one of the larger caves. Also at the site is a small gold rush museum and a restaurant. To get to this commercialized natural attraction, take Route 332 south from Lunenburg for 16km (10 miles) (☎ 902-766-4621). Admission is C$6 (US$4.30) adults, C$3 (US$2.10), seniors and children. A guided walk costs an additional C$3 (US$2.10) or view the caves from sea level on a boat tour for C$18 (US$12.90) adults, C$14 (US$10) children. Open: mid-May to early October daily 8 a.m. to 9 p.m.

Shelburne

The small South Shore town of Shelburne is as attractive and interesting as its better-known counterparts to the north, but because it's that much farther from Halifax, it remains untouristy.

Founded in 1783, by 1900 Shelburne had grown into one of the most important shipbuilding centers in North America. Local boatbuilders were renowned for quality wooden boats, with some of the world's first and fastest yachts coming from local shipyards (some consider Shelburne the birthplace of the yacht). The waterfront remains remarkably unchanged from its halcyon years.

Getting there

Take Exit 26 from Highway 103 to access downtown Shelburne. This turnoff is 133km (83 miles) southwest of Lunenburg and 123km (76 miles) east of Yarmouth.

Staying in Shelburne

Loyalist Inn
$ Shelburne

Don't anticipate too much from this 200-year-old hotel. You'll get the basics — budget rooms with private bath, television, and air-conditioning. On weekends, request a room as far away from the downstairs bar as possible if you want a good night's sleep. The in-house dining room is open Tues–Sun 7:30 a.m.–8:30 p.m., or use the money you've saved on a room for dinner at Charlotte Lane Café.

160 Water St. ☎ *902-875-2343. Fax: 902-875-1473. Rack rates: C$65 (US$46.40) double. MC, V.*

Whispering Waves Cottages
$$$ Ingomar

If you want a modern, well-equpped cottage with panoramic ocean views, Whispering Waves is hard to beat. Beautifully located on the ocean south of Shelburne, the property runs right down to the rocky shoreline, with sandy beaches and mackerel fishing within easy walking distance. The cottages are in three subtle themes — wilderness, seaside, and romance — and are carefully designed to take advantage of ocean views while also offering a certain amount of privacy. Inside, the practical layout includes a separate bedroom, small kitchen, and living area with electric fireplace. Sliding doors open to a veranda. Congenial hosts Jo-Anne and Paul Goulden will go out of their way to make you feel comfortable. They will organize sea kayaking with a local operator, tee times at the local golf course, appointments at a nearby spa, and evening beachside bonfires. When I'm on the the road researching a book, there's no time for golfing or the like, but I did take the Goulden's up on one option — a lobster dinner (complete with strawberry shortcake) delivered to my cottage.

Black Point Rd., Ingomar (take Exit 27 or 28 from Highway 103) ☎ ***866-470-9283*** *or 902-637-3535. Internet:* www.whisperingwavescottages.com. *Rack rates: C$150–C$165 (US$107.10–US$117.90) double. AE, MC, V. One cottage is wheelchair accessible.*

Dining in Shelburne

Charlotte Lane Café
$$–$$$ Shelburne SEAFOOD/FUSION

Tucked between Shelburne's main street and the waterfront, this delightful dining room is a great find. The Swiss chef concentrates on combining local seafood with cooking styles from around the world. Starters range from a rich but simple chowder (with real scallops and shrimp) to a creative East-meets-West fish sampler, which includes smoked salmon and sushi. The biggest concern is finding room for dessert (the almond fruit torte is a must).

13 Charlotte Lane ☎ ***902-875-3314***. *Main courses: C$13–C$21 (US$9.30–US$15). Tues–Sat 11:30 a.m.–2:30 p.m. and 5–8 p.m.*

Exploring Shelburne

Head down to Dock Street, which runs along the waterfront, and you'll find yourself in the middle of the largest concentration of wooden buildings from the late-1700s remaining in Canada. Many are private residences, while others are still home to a variety of boat-building endeavors. Four buildings are open to the public. Admission to each is C$3 (US$2.10), or buy a combined pass for C$8 (US$5.70). They are:

- ✔ **Shelburne County Museum,** 8 Maiden Lane (☎ **902-875-3219**; June–mid-Oct 9:30 a.m.–5:30 p.m., mid-Oct–May Mon–Fri 10 a.m.–noon and 2–5 p.m.), is the best place to learn about the earliest Loyalist settlers and the subsequent years of shipbuilding fame.

- ✔ **Dory Shop,** 11 Dock St. (☎ **902-875-3219**; June–Sept daily 9:30 a.m.–5:30 p.m.), has been churning out dory boats since the 1880s, when they were first used on the Grand Banks to help lay fishing nets from a mother ship. Admission is free on Sunday mornings.

- ✔ **Muir Cox Shipyard,** south end of Dock St. (☎ **902-875-1114**; June–Sept daily 9:30 a.m.–5:30 p.m.), has been in continuous operation since 1820. Inside, the Shipbuilding Interpretive Centre describes the history of the industry while the Boatshop, which once turned out enormous full-rigged barques, now takes orders for smaller wooden boats (viewing year-round Mon–Fri 8 a.m.– 4 p.m.).

- ✔ **Ross Thomson House,** Charlotte Lane (☎ **902-875-3219**; June–mid-Oct daily 9:30 a.m.–5:30 p.m.), was a general store built by Scottish brothers in 1784. The interior recreates the time (complete with staff in period costume behind the counter) when locals flocked in to purchase goods such as salt and tobacco.

Digby and Digby Neck

Best-known for its plump, sweet-tasting scallops, this bustling town of 2,200 has been an important fishing center since its founding by Loyalists in 1783.

Getting there

Digby is near the entrance to the Annapolis Basin, just off Highway 101, halfway between Yarmouth and Wolfville.

Bay Ferries (☎ **888-249-7245** or 902-245-2116; Internet: www.nfl-bay.com) operates the *Princess of Acadia* year-round between Saint John (New Brunswick) and Digby, with one to three departures in each direction daily. The crossing takes two to three hours. Depending on the time of year (Julyto early Oct is high season) the one-way cost is C$20 to C$35 (US$14.30 to US$25) for adults, C$17.50 to C$25 (US$12.50 to US$17.90) for seniors, and C$10 to C$15 (US$7.10 to US$10.70) for children aged 5 to 17. The fare for vehicles under 6.4 meters (21 feet) is C$70 to C$75 (US$50 to US$53.60) one-way.

Staying in and around Digby

Bayside Inn
$–$$ Digby

Within walking distance of the Digby harborfront, you won't go wrong at this small lodging that has been taking in guests for over 100 years. Historic character blends with modern touches in the 11 rooms, some outfitted with antiques, others in a floral theme. Every room has a television and ensuite bathroom, while an enclosed porch awaits you downstairs.

115 Montague Row ☎ *888-754-0555 or 902-245-2247. Internet:* www.baysideinn.ca. *Rack rates: C$60–C$100 (US$42.90–US$71.40) double. AE, DC, DISC, MC, V.*

Brier Island Lodge
$–$$ Brier Island

Nature lovers should plan on spending at least one night on Brier Island, preferably at Brier Island Lodge, perched atop sea cliffs and surrounded by native woodlands. Staying here, you can spot whales from your room, go birdwatching, or hike down to a narrow cove where seals haul themselves onto the rocks. The motel-like rooms are a little plain, but they are clean and comfortable and most have ocean views. The more expensive rooms have either a king-size bed or a jetted tub.

Meals are taken in a casual restaurant (7 a.m.–9:30 p.m.) featuring lots of exposed wood and snappy-colored fabrics. Mains are mostly under C$20 (US$14.30), including smoked pollock, a local delicacy that is poached in milk and served with a creamy white sauce.

Westport, Brier Island ☎ *800-662-8355 or 902-839-2300. Fax: 902-839-2006. Internet:* www.brierisland.com. *Rack rates: C$60–C$129 (US$42.90–US$92.10) double. MC, V. April–Oct.*

Mountain Gap Inn
$$–$$$$ Smith's Cove

Set along the edge of Annapolis Basin, this sprawling resort does a good job of keeping guests occupied. Activities include hiking, biking, tennis, swimming at the beach or in the outdoor heated pool; or you can just relax in the hot tub or at tables spread throughout the grounds. Most units were revamped in 2003, including the regular motel rooms and older cottages, many with kitchens and water views. The dining room is contained in the original 1915 lodge building and is open daily 7:30 a.m. to 9:30 p.m. For something more casual, pick up seafood at the fish market in Digby and boil or grill it at one of the resort's barbecue areas.

Smith's Cove (Exit 25 from Highway 101 east of Digby) ☎ ***800-565-5020*** *or 902-245-5841. Fax: 902-245-2277. Internet:* www.mountaingap.ns.ca. *Rack rates: C$125–C$300 (US$89.30–US$214.30) double. AE, MC, V. May–Oct.*

Olde Village Inn
$$ Sandy Cove

An attractive inn with panoramic views, you won't need to go anywhere for a meal — breakfast is included and the in-house restaurant does wonders with local seafood. Accommodations range from cabins that share bathrooms to a spacious modern suite in the main building with a balcony and water view.

387 Sandy Cove Rd., Sandy Cove ☎ ***800-834-2206*** *or 902-834-2202. Fax: 902-834-2927. Internet:* www.oldevillageinn.com. *Rack rates: C$85–C$130 (US$60.70–US$92.90). MC, V. June–mid-Oct.*

Dining in Digby

Fundy Restaurant
$$–$$$ Digby   SEAFOOD

With a harbor full of trawlers, finding fresh seafood in Digby is not an issue. What really matters is the view, and the Fundy Restaurant wins hands down. Located right on the harborside boardwalk, the restaurant has an upstairs dining room that opens to a wide deck, or the downstairs Dockside Restaurant with tables spread right to the water's edge. For an evening meal, stick to the upstairs section. The menu is scallop-centered, whether you're looking for breakfast (scallop omelette), lunch (scallop wrap), or dinner (scallop stir-fry, fettuccini, or casserole).

34 Water St. ☎ ***902-245-4950.*** *Main courses: C$14.50–C$21 (US$10.40–US$15). MC, V. Daily 7 a.m.–11 p.m.*

O'Neil's Fundy Fish Market
$–$$ Digby   SEAFOOD

Primarily a fish market, also has a few tables set aside for in-house dining. Scallops (pan- or deep-fried) and chips is the obvious choice, but you can also order steamed mussels, lobster, or a platter of fish, scallops, and shrimp. The market also sells a wide variety of seafood (fresh scallops are around C$10/US$7.10 per pound), perfect if you are staying somewhere with cooking facilities. Otherwise, grab Digby chicks (smoked herring) for C$1 (US70¢) each and eat them on the go.

Prince William St. ☎ *902-245-6528. Main courses: C$6–C$15 (US$4.30–US$10.70). Mon–Sat 9 a.m.–9 p.m., Sun 11 a.m.–3 p.m.*

Exploring Digby

Although Digby offers a couple of worthwhile sights, the main local attraction is the drive out along Digby Neck.

Along the Harborfront

The **Admiral Digby Museum,** an 1850s home at 95 Montague Row (☎ 902-245-6322), documents a local history dominated by the ocean. On display are model ships, recreated 1880s living quarters, and a large collection of photographs. It's open June to August, Tuesday to Saturday 9 a.m. to 5 p.m, Sunday 1– 5 p.m; the rest of the year Tuesday and Friday only, 9 a.m. to 5 p.m.

In front of the Fundy Restaurant at 34 Water Street, the *Lady Vanessa,* a retired wooden scallop boat, is open for inspection June to September daily 9 a.m. to 7 p.m. In addition to simply clambering over and into the boat, you can view video footage of fishermen at work, and displays include the claws of a 20-kilogram (45-pound) lobster. Admission is a worthwhile C$2 (US$1.40).

Driving Digby Neck

Digby Neck is a narrow finger of land that extends around 50km (31 miles) into the Bay of Fundy. Most visitors are drawn to the end of the road by its diversity of wildlife.

Along the way, you'll encounter a string of villages. The most picturesque is **Sandy Cove,** overlooking a beach with good swimming. Ask directions to the local waterfall, one of the highest in the Maritimes.

Highway 217 reaches right to the end of Digby Neck. From there it's a short ferry ride to **Long Island,** then an 18km (11.2-mile) drive to another ferry that crosses to **Brier Island.** Both ferries run 24 hours a day, year-round. Departures are timed to link up with drivers who don't stop in between. The fare on either ferry is C$3 (US$2.10) round-trip, per vehicle (including passengers).

Around the world in 1,160 days

Born near Digby in 1844 and raised on Brier Island, Joshua Slocum left home at 16 for a life on the high seas. After a distinguished career as captain, he set off on April 24, 1895, in the 11-meter (37-foot) sloop *Spray* on a journey that would make him famous well beyond the sailing community. He was at sea for over three years, returning to his starting point on June 27, 1898, thus becoming the first person to sail single-handedly around the world.

Although Slocum remains one of the best-known sailors of all time, his feat is not well-promoted in Annapolis County — a plaque on Brier Island makes note of his Nova Scotian links; the ferry to Brier Island is named in his honor, as is a bar at Mountain Gap Inn; and the one-room school he attended in Hanley is now a museum. You won't find his grave around these parts — he was lost at sea off the South American coast in 1909.

The ferry from the mainland docks on Long Island at **Tiverton,** a small fishing village with a couple of whale-watching operations and a museum. Around 2km (1.2 miles) beyond the village is a trail to the **Balancing Rock.** This striking natural feature is an outcrop of igneous (volcanic) rock that rises 7 meters (22 feet) from a narrow ledge above the ocean. The 2km (1.2-mile) trail leading to the lookout platform is somewhat tricky to negotiate, but the round trip can easily be made in 90 minutes.

If you're feeling hungry as you approach the far end of Long Island, make a stop in Freeport at **Lavena's Catch Café** (☎ **902-839-2517;** mid-May to mid-Dec daily 9 a.m. to 8 p.m., summer until 11 p.m.) for well-priced fresh seafood without a deep-fryer in sight.

The ferry from Freeport docks at **Westport**, the only settlement on **Brier Island.** The island is renowned for high populations of seabirds and excellent hiking.

Whale-watching

The Bay of Fundy teems with plankton, which attracts an abundance of marine life — fish, whales, and dolphins are all common in the area. Of course, that means the whale-watchers aren't far behind. Finback, minke, and humpback are the most common types of whales, but right and sperm whales are also present. The main whale-watching season is June through October, with August considered the prime month.

A number of companies based along Digby Neck and on the two islands take people to see the whales. Most use former fishing boats, with the captains keeping in contact with one another by radio to help track down the whales. Trips last three to five hours (depending on how quickly whales are found) and cost C$25 to C$35 (US$17.90 to US$25) for adults and C$15 to C$20 (US$10.70 to US$14.30) for children.

Operators include: **Freeport Whale & Seabird Tours,** at Freeport, Long Island (☎ **866-866-8797** or 902-839-2177); **Brier Island Whale and Seabird Cruises,** at Westport (☎ **800-656-3660** or 902-839-2995); and **Mariner Cruises,** also at Westport (☎ **800-239-2189** or 902-839-2346). Tours with **Ocean Explorations,** at Tiverton (☎ **877-654-2341** or 902-839-2417), are led by biologist Tom Goodwin in large, stable Zodiac boats. The advantage of this type of craft is speed — reaching the whales takes less time. In August, when North Atlantic right whales (the world's rarest whale) congregate in the middle of the Bay of Fundy, this is the only company that can get out far enough to see them. Tour cost is C$50 (US$35.70) adults, C$25 (US$17.90) children.

Annapolis Royal

The French and British fought for control of this town for over a century. In 1710, the British finally took control and renamed it in honor of Queen Anne. Despite its age, less than 1,000 people call Annapolis Royal home, although the streets swell with summer visitors wandering the compact downtown core.

Getting there

Annapolis Royal is 29km (18 miles) northeast of Digby Neck. Take Exit 23 from Highway 101 to follow the Annapolis Basin shoreline to town or Exit 22 for a more direct approach.

Staying in Annapolis Royal

Garrison House Inn
$$ **Annapolis Royal**

Unlike most local bed-and-breakfasts, the 1854 Garrison House was designed originally as a guesthouse. Careful renovations have restored its Victorian-era feel. In total there are seven guest rooms, each with a private bathroom and shower and some with canopy beds. Choose Room 2 for its spaciousness and views across to Fort Anne, or Room 4 for its quiet, nicely cozy feel. The in-house restaurant is Annapolis Royal's premier dining room.

350 St. George St. ☎ 902-532-5750. Fax: 902-532-5501. Internet: www.garrison house.ca. *Rack rates: C$99–C$149 (US$70.70–US$106.40) double. AE, MC, V. May–Oct.*

Queen Anne Inn
$$–$$$ **Annapolis Royal**

Named for the Queen of England at the time the British were ceded Acadia, this 1865 landmark lodging is set back from the road and surrounded by expansive gardens. A grand stairway leads from the lobby and parlor to 10 guest rooms, 9 of which are extremely spacious (Number 10 is not). While furnishings and fabrics reflect the Victorian era, the rooms have been thoroughly modernized, some featuring amenities like a jetted tub. Rates include a full breakfast and nice touches, such as plush bathrobes and the use of a DVD player on request.

494 St. George St. (across from the Historic Gardens) ☎ *877-536-0403 or 902-532-7850. Fax: 902-532-2078. Internet:* www.queenanneinn.ns.ca. *Rack rates: C$120–C$170 (US$85.70–US$121.40) double. AE, MC, V. Mid-April–mid-Oct.*

Dining in Annapolis Royal

Fort Anne Café
$–$$ **Annapolis Royal** **CAFE FARE/SEAFOOD**

The decor might not have changed since the 1970s, but that's not a concern to the locals who gather here for hearty and well-priced, no-frills food. Served until noon, breakfast choices include a three-filling omelette for just C$4 (US$2.90); even the biggest, meanest cooked breakfast is only C$7 (US$5). The rest of the day, tuck in to a clam burger for C$5 (US$3.60) or pay C$12 (US$8.60) for a big pile of juicy Digby scallops.

298 St. George St. ☎ *902-532-5254. Main courses: C$5–C$16 (US$3.60–US$11.40). Daily 8 a.m.–8 p.m.*

Garrison House
$$–$$$ **Annapolis Royal** **SEAFOOD/GLOBAL**

At this lovely three-room restaurant, in the lodging of the same name, seafood and local produce are served in all kinds of creative ways. The menu changes every few weeks, but usually includes a rich Acadian seafood chowder and mains ranging from the simple (pan-fried haddock) to Greek-inspired (Digby scallops, feta cheese, and olives on a bed of pasta) to Asian (scallop and shrimp Vietnamese curry). Most dishes are accompanied by local, farm-fresh produce.

350 St. George St. ☎ *902-532-5750. Main courses: C$15–C$20 (US$10.70–US$14.30). AE, MC, V. Daily 5:30–8:30 p.m.*

Exploring Annapolis Royal

Make your first stop the generating station, home to a **Nova Scotia Tourist Information Centre** (☎ 902-532-5769; mid-June to mid-Oct daily 10 a.m. to 6 p.m.). Here you can pick up the brochure Footprints with Footnotes, an excellent reference for a self-guided tour of **St. George Street,** one of Canada's oldest streets. Of dozens of historic buildings, the most notable is the **Sinclair Inn,** at 230 St. George Street (☎ 902-532-7754). Built in 1710, it's the oldest wooden building in Canada.

Annapolis Tidal Generating Station
North of Downtown

The Bay of Fundy's record-breaking tides are used to generate electricity at the world's second-largest tidal generating station (actually, there's only three, but it's bigger than the one in Russia), on a causeway north of Annapolis Royal. Although it continues to generate electricity, the station was originally built as an experiment, as a precursor to a more ambitious project that has been stalled by environmental concerns. An upstairs interpretive center explains the generation process in a straight-forward manner, with large picture windows allowing views of the holding pond. "Down Under" tours into the bowels of the plant are offered a couple of times daily.

Prince Albert Rd. (Highway 1) ☎ *902-532-5769. Admission: Free. Mid-June–mid-Oct daily 10 a.m.–6 p.m.*

Fort Anne National Historic Site
Downtown

Preserving the site of settlements dating back to 1629, this accessible attraction is centrally located on a lowrise beside the main street. Star-shaped earthen fortifications and a moat dating to 1702 are the oldest visible remains of 200 years of struggle between the French and British. In a more modern building is a mid-sized museum with rooms representing different eras, including the period between 1713 and 1749 when the settlement was the capital of Nova Scotia. If you are staying overnight in town, ask at the museum about entertaining nighttime tours of the Garrison Graveyard, led by a top-hatted "undertaker."

St. George St. ☎ *902-532-2397. Admission: C$3.50 (US$2.50) adults, C$3 (US$2.10) seniors, C$1.75 (US$1.25) children. Mid-May–mid-Oct 9 a.m.–6 p.m.*

Historic Gardens
Downtown

These "historic" gardens were actually created in the 1980s, but they have been laid out to represent distinct eras in the history of Annapolis Royal, including Acadian (pre-1700s), British (early 1700s), and Victorian (late 1880s). Also on the grounds is a rose garden that comes alive with color in mid-summer, a small maze that will keep children on their toes, and a marshland trail dotted with interpretive panels explaining Acadian dyking techniques. A restaurant with a pleasantly shaded patio serves lunch.

441 St. George St. ☎ 902-532-7018. Internet: www.historicgardens.com. *Admission: C$6 (US$4.30) adults, C$5 (US$3.60) seniors and children. Mid-May–mid-Oct daily 9 a.m.–5 p.m. (July–Aug until dusk).*

Port-Royal National Historic Site

This is the actual site of Canada's first permanent settlement. It was founded in 1605 by French explorer Samuel de Champlain. Destroyed by the British eight years later, it has been reconstructed to look as it did in Champlain's day, complete with costumed interpreters. One of the most interesting exhibits describes how the Mi'kmaq helped the settlers adapt to the new land.

Follow Granville Rd. for 10km (6.2 miles) from the north side of the causeway ☎ 902-532-2898. Admission: C$3.50 (US$2.50) adults, C$3 (US$2.10) seniors, C$1.75 (US$1.25) children. Mid-May–mid-Oct 9 a.m.–6 p.m.

Continuing around the Bay of Fundy from Annapolis Royal

From Annapolis Royal, Highway 101 continues to make its way along the southern edge of the Bay of Fundy. It's just over 200km (125 miles) back to Halifax along this direct route. A more enticing option is Highway 1, which heads in the same direction but at a more relaxing pace. The following are easily reached from both highways:

✔ **Cape Split**. Reaching the end of this narrow finger of land extending almost across the Minas Channel entails an 8km (5-mile) one way hike, but you will be rewarded with magnificent views down to the Bay of Fundy. On the protected side of the spit, **Blomidon Provincial Park** protects an impressive lineup of red cliffs. To get to either spot, take Exit 11 from Highway 101 and follow the signs from Highway 358.

✔ **Wolfville.** This university town has an impressive array of Victorian- era homes, the **Randall House Museum** at 171 Main Street (☎ 902-542-9775), which catalogue the colonists who came after the Acadians had been expelled, and a pleasant waterfront area where interpretive boards describe the natural and human history of Minas Basin. Built by an apple baron, **Victoria's Historic Inn** at 600 Main Street (☎ 902-542-5744; Internet: www.victorias historicinn.com) can be an inexpensive overnight stop or a decadent splurge, depending on your room choice. Regardless of how much you pay, everyone enjoys the same gourmet breakfast.

✔ **Grand Pré National Historic Site.** Once the principal population center of Acadia, this site east of Wolfville off Highway 1 (☎ 902-542-3631) remembers the expulsion of Acadians in 1755. Although the English burned their villages, the clever dyking system Acadians developed to farm land below sea level is still present. Also on the grounds are a church, various statues and monuments, a blacksmith's shop, and an information center with Acadian literature for sale. Admission C$3.50 (US$2.50) adults, C$3 (US$2.10) seniors, C$1.75 (US$1.25) children. Mid-May–Oct daily 9 a.m.–6 p.m.

✔ **Howard Dill Enterprises.** If you're tiring of history, maybe it's time for a detour to one of Nova Scotia's quirkiest, yet most impressive attractions. Howard Dill is famous for developing pumpkin seeds that go on to produce some of the world's largest pumpkins, including the current world record-holder at 606 kilograms (1,337 pounds). He's no slouch himself in the growing department, with four world records in the books. The best time to visit his farm at 400 College Road (☎ 902-798-2728) is late September through early October, when the pumpkins are at their biggest.

Keji what?

Pronounced "Kedge-im-a-KOO-jik" (and sensibly known simply as "Keji"), Kejimkujik National Park protects a remote inland region scarred by glacial action from the last Ice Age.

A single road penetrates the park, branching off Highway 8 halfway between Annapolis Royal and the South Shore near Liverpool. Along its length are numerous easy hikes, a lookout tower with expansive views, a large campground, and supervised swimming at Merrymakedge Beach. The park's extensive system of shallow lakes and rivers is ideal for canoeing. Rentals are available at **Jakes Landing**, 8km (5 miles) from Highway 8 (☎ 902-682-2196) for C$6 (US$4.30) per hour and C$30 (US$21.40) per day, including paddles and life jackets.

Stop at the **Visitor Reception Centre** by the park entrance (☎ 902-682-2772; Internet: www.pc.gc.ca; daily 8:30 a.m. to 4:30 p.m., summer until 9 p.m.) for schedules of guided walks and paddles and the evening interpretive program.

Chapter 13

Central Nova Scotia

. . . .

In This Chapter

▶ Watching the tidal bore in Truro

▶ Poking around Pictou

▶ Exploring the wild and rugged Eastern Shore

. . . .

*C*entral Nova Scotia is a somewhat arbitrary designation that encompasses the region north of Halifax and extends east to Cape Breton Island. This portion of the province is served by main highways that lead to major population centers like Truro, New Glasgow, and beyond. In this chapter, you will be encouraged to explore towns and attractions that lie beyond the highways but are still close at hand. Highlights are as varied as watching the tidal bore created by massive tides in the Bay of Fundy, clambering over a replica of the boat that transported early Scottish settlers to North America, and learning to surf in the Atlantic Ocean.

What's Where: Central Nova Scotia and Its Major Attractions

Truro

The historic downtown area of Truro, Nova Scotia's third-largest city, is worth a leg-stretch, but the region's best attractions lie in the surrounding areas. Local highlights include:

✔ The **tidal bore,** an intriguing natural phenomenon (although you should know that jaded locals call it "the total bore")

✔ **Balmoral Mills,** a picture-perfect gristmill north of Truro

✔ The **Glooscap Trail,** a coastal drive along Cobequid Bay

Pictou

Just a ten-minute detour from Nova Scotia's major highway, the harbor town of Pictou is noteworthy for a choice of wonderful accommodations and a rich history. Don't miss:

✔ The *Hector,* moored along the Pictou harborfront

✔ **Jost Vineyards,** the Maritimes' premier winery

Eastern Shore

A lightly settled coastline, the Eastern Shore is easily accessible from Halifax and well worth exploring for the following:

✔ **Grassy Island National Historic Site,** a once-bustling 1700s fishing town

✔ **Lawrencetown Beach,** famous for its surfing waves (yes, you're allowed to just watch)

Truro

Two major highways merge at Truro, but many tourists pass right on by. That's a shame, because the Truro area offers a few notable attractions that make a visit worthwhile.

Getting there

Highway 102 from Halifax (90km/56 miles to the south) passes west of Truro, while the east–west Trans-Canada Highway, here called Highway 104, passes north of it. To get downtown from Highway 102, take Exit 14; if you're on Highway 104, take Exit 15 to Highway 102 and then Exit 14.

Staying in Truro

Truro lodgings are designed to fill the needs of overnighting highway travelers. You'll find some decent, well-priced motel rooms along the roads linking downtown to the main highways.

Comfort Inn Truro
$$ Truro

This low-slung, two-story chain motel is handy to Highway 102, but far enough away from it for traffic noise to be at a minimum. The mid-sized rooms come with lots of amenities (in-room coffee, hairdryers, ironing facility), and a light breakfast is included in the rates.

12 Meadow Dr. (Exit 14 from Highway 102) ☎ *902-893-0330. Fax: 902-897-0176. Rack rates: C$100 (US$71.40). AE, DC, DISC, MC, V.*

Palliser Motel
$ Truro

It's certainly not the older-style rooms that are the attraction here: it's quite simply the location. Set on a low bluff above the Salmon River, this is the prime local spot for viewing the tidal bore (the river in front of the motel is lit at night for this purpose). The Palliser also has a restaurant, where motel guests are offered a complimentary hot breakfast.

Tidal Bore Rd. (Exit 14 from Highway 102) ☎ *902-893-8951. Fax: 902-895-8475. Rack rates: C$60 (US$42.90) double. AE, DC, MC, V.*

Dining in Truro

Give all the usual chain restaurants on the outskirts of Truro a miss, and take the time to search out the only local restaurant I recommend.

Murphy's
$ Truro   SEAFOOD

Who says it's all about location? One of Nova Scotia's best-known seafood restaurants is in Truro, which isn't even on the ocean — and it's in a strip mall to boot. Inside, the fish nets, model boats, and bright maritime murals leave no one guessing at this restaurant's specialty. The menu offers a wide range of all the usual seafood suspects, but it's the perfectly cooked deep-fried fish (usually cod) that brings in a constant flow of locals and travelers in the know.

112 The Esplanade ☎ *902-895-1275. Main courses: C$10–C$22 (US$7.10–US$15.70) dinner. MC, V. Daily 11 a.m.–8 p.m.*

Exploring Truro

Start your visit at the local **information center** (Victoria Square, ☎ 902-893-2922), and take a downtown walking tour that focuses on an unfortunate history with a silver lining. A few years back, Dutch elm disease struck many of the stately elm trees lining Truro's streets. While trees afflicted with the same disease in other towns were destroyed, an imaginative group of locals commissioned a wood carver to create art from the trunks. Today, over 30 tree-trunk sculptures dot the downtown streets.

There aren't many reasons to linger too long in Truro, though. See the tidal bore, and then hit the road for some quick out-of-town sightseeing.

Tidal Bore

Truro

Some of the world's highest tides rise through the Bay of Fundy. When the ocean water in the bay is forced up adjacent low-lying rivers, a wall of water surges across the mudflats and funnels into the local river systems, and you can actually see the water changing direction. Truro's location beside the Salmon River at the far end of the "funnel," combined with easy access from the highway, make the local **Tidal Bore Park** a favorite viewing spot for this intriguing sight.

Tides change just over every six hours, so the bore occurs twice daily. It arrives approximately 50 minutes later each day, so be sure to check at the local visitor center (☎ 902-893-2922) for tide times.

South Tidal Bore Rd. (Exit 14 off Highway 102 or west from downtown along Prince St.) Admission: Free.

Balmoral Mills

Balmoral Mills

Step back in time at this underrated, off-the-beaten-path attraction which was built in 1874 and restored to working order. Water tumbles over a dam, turning a waterwheel linked by a pulley system to a solid granite millstone that grinds wheat and oats. Various demonstrations take place daily, with the finished product used in a variety of baked goodies sold at the site. Not only is Balmoral Mills worth visiting for its historical interest, the location is delightful. Plan on enjoying a picnic lunch in the adjacent park.

38km (24 miles) north of Truro off Hwy. 311 ☎ 902-637-3016. Admission: C$3 (US$2.10) adults, C$2 (US$1.40) seniors and children. June–mid-Oct, Mon–Sat 9:30 a.m.–5:30 p.m., Sun 1:00 p.m.–5:30 p.m.

Glooscap Trail
West from Truro

Named for a mythical Mi'kmaq spirit who controlled the tides, this route (Highway 2) follows the northern shoreline of Cobequid Bay and Minas Basin west from Truro to Parrsboro before taking a jog north to rejoin the Trans-Canada Highway (104) near Springhill. Although the Glooscap Trail is in the geographical center of the Maritimes, it passes through a relatively remote region, with verdant forests running down to sea cliffs.

An obvious attraction along this stretch of highway is the scenery, but the most interesting features are less obvious. In the 1980s, this region came into the paleontological spotlight when more than 100,000 bone fragments from dinosaurs were unearthed. The **Fundy Geological Museum** in Parrsboro (☎ 902-254-3814) explains the importance of the 200-million-year-old fossil beds. In addition, agate and amethyst are common along this stretch of coast. **Parrsboro Rock and Mineral Shop** (☎ 902-254-2981), operated by local legend Eldon George, displays various dinosaur fossils (including thumbnail-sized dinosaur footprints) along with lots of gemstones. Eldon will sell you rock-collecting gear or, if he's not busy, will take you out to his favorite collecting grounds for around C$25 (US$17.90) per person.

Riverview Cottages in Parrsboro (☎ 902-254-2388) is a good overnight choice for travelers on a budget. The cabins are basic, but the setting is delightful.

Pictou

In 1773, about 250 hardy Scottish settlers stepped ashore at Pictou Harbour after a treacherous transatlantic journey aboard the *Hector*. They were brought to the area by a Philadelphia company looking to fulfill the terms of a land grant. Few people from North America were willing to move to the area, so the company began to look farther afield; Acadia was renamed Nova Scotia ("New Scotland" in Latin) in a desperate effort to attract Scots.

Getting there

Pictou lies on a protected harbor 12km (7.5 miles) north of Highway 104. The road to Pictou is busier than you might expect, because it continues through town to the Caribou ferry terminal, one of two gateways to Prince Edward Island.

Staying in Pictou

This town has a good selection of historic properties that offer comfortable lodging without going over the top in decor or price.

Consulate Inn

$–$$ **Pictou**

This ivy-covered 1810 building was once a consulate for the United States, and later a prominent local judge called it home for 50 years. Perhaps as a result, it has a somewhat jaded air of having been-there, done-that. The cheaper rooms may not be designer-chic, but you'll get a good night's rest. The Lower Garden Suite with basic cooking facilities is good value, but has a low ceiling. Rooms in the new wing have a more modern look, and all have a jetted tub and varying water views. Out back, the garden runs all the way to the water's edge, with outdoor furniture, a gazebo, and a barbecue area. For families on a budget, the adjacent house can be rented through the Consulate Inn for C$100 (US$71.40).

115 Water St. ☎ *800-424-8283 or 902-485-4554. Fax: 902-485-1532. Internet:* www.consulateinn.com. *Rack rates: C$69–C$125 (US$49.30–US$89.30) double. AE, MC, V.*

Pictou Lodge Resort

$$–$$$ **East of Pictou**

This sprawling resort occupies a prime position on Northumberland Strait. Pictou Island is visible in the distance and water surrounds the property on three sides, with a man-made pond thrown in for good measure. Activities include canoeing, sea kayaking lessons, horseback riding, hiking along nature trails, biking, or just relaxing on the private beach. The oldest units date to the 1920s; some have been given a thorough going-over (the one-bedroom deluxe cottages, complete with a kitchen and screened veranda, are my favorite), but more modern motel units and snazzy log cabins have the better views. A summer activity program makes the lodge a great place for families.

Braeshore Rd. (5km/3.1 miles east of Pictou) ☎ *888-662-7484 or 902-485-4322. Fax: 902-485-4945. Internet:* www.maritimeinns.com. *Rack rates: C$115–C$169 (US$82.10–US$120.70) double. AE, MC, V. Mid-May–mid-Oct.*

Dining in Pictou

Pictou Lodge Resort Dining Room

Even if you're not staying here, it's worth the short drive just for a meal. While the rest of the resort has undergone numerous upgrades through the years, the restaurant hasn't, which is a good thing. Breakfast and lunch are taken on the screened-in veranda, while the main dining room, with its high ceiling, exposed log work, and massive fireplace, has a distinctly historic charm. The menu also reflects an earlier era, with steak, chicken, and seafood dishes cooked to perfection and served without frills. The salmon, basted in maple syrup and herbs and broiled on a cedar plank, is a real treat.

Braeshore Rd. ☎ *902-485-4322. Reservations recommended for dinner. Main courses: C$24–C$30 (US$17.10–US$21.40). AE, MC, V. Mid-May–mid-Oct. daily 7 a.m.–9 p.m.*

Exploring Pictou

Pictou's biggest draw is the waterfront. Plan on spending at least half a day poking around the harbor.

Hector Heritage Quay
Pictou

This harbor complex is anchored by a full-sized floating replica of the 33.5-meter (110-foot) *Hector,* the sailing ship that transported Nova Scotia's first Scottish settlers across the Atlantic. The three-masted ship was constructed using traditional tools and techniques, making it the most faithful reconstruction project of its kind ever undertaken in North America. Admission includes access to the ship itself, but it's also worth spending time "on land," reading interpretive panels that narrate the story of the original ship and its passengers and watching blacksmiths and carpenters at work in their dockside shops. It's perfect for families — interesting for adults, but the kids will have fun too.

33 Caladh Ave., Pictou ☎ *902-485-4371. Admission: C$5 (US$3.60) adults, C$4 (US$2.90) seniors, C$2 (US$1.40) children 6–12. June–Aug Mon–Sat 9 a.m.– 5 p.m., Sun 10 a.m.–5 p.m., May and Sept–Oct Mon–Sat 9 a.m.–5 p.m., Sun 1 p.m.–5 p.m.*

Northumberland Fisheries Museum
Pictou

At one time, this redbrick railway station was the eastern end of the rail line across Canada. Now it's an unassuming museum that's actually pretty interesting. You'll find an impressive collection of exhibits on diverse ocean-related topics ranging from local marine life to the whaling and fishing industries and racing boats. Kids will love the model boats and tank of live lobsters. It's easy to spend an hour at this museum, even if you're not a maritime buff.

71 Water St., Pictou ☎ *902-485-4972. Admission: C$4 (US$2.90) adults, C$3 (US$2.10) seniors, C$2 (US$1.40) children 6–12. Mid-June–mid-Oct Mon–Sat 9 a.m.–7 p.m., Sun noon–5 p.m.*

Not Jost another winery

Everyone loves promoting a local product — that's why you'll see wines from Jost Vineyards (pronounced "yost") featured in many Nova Scotia restaurants. Though it's situated well away from Canada's better-known wine-producing regions, Jost has produced some award-winning products. They're only available in Nova Scotia, so be sure to get a sample while you're here, especially of their award-winning ice wine. Frost is the enemy in most vineyards, but at Jost it is a vital part of the ice wine process. The frozen grapes are left on the vines for a few days, then gently pressed to extract just a few drops of concentrated juice from each grape. The result of this low-yield process is an intense, sweet wine that pairs well with dessert. Ice wine is only a small part of the Jost repertoire. Many classic European varietals that reflect the owner's German roots, including a classic Riesling, are picked at a more traditional time of year to produce wines in the C$10 to C$15 (US$7.10–US$10.70) range.

Free winery tours are offered daily at noon and 3 p.m. throughout the summer. Afterward, you can browse the wine shop, pick up some gourmet goodies at the deli, and enjoy a picnic on the grounds.

Jost Vineyards is at Malagash, east of Pictou along Highway 6 (☎ **902-257-2636**; Internet www.jostwine.com). Monday to Saturday, 9 a.m. to 6 p.m.; Sunday, noon to 6:00 p.m.

Touring along the Northumberland Strait

East of Pictou, the Northumberland Strait is bordered by a convoluted coastline that extends all the way to Canso Causeway, gateway to Cape Breton Island. Highway 104, the main route to Cape Breton, sensibly follows a direct route well away from the coastline, leaving a variety of options for casual touring. Here are some suggested detours along the way:

   ✔ **New Glasgow.** The first town east of Pictou along Highway 104, this sprawling town has a pleasant downtown core centered on a river. An 1841 building constructed from ship ballast has been converted to the **Dock, Food, Spirits, and Ales** pub. Its historical origins are ignored by most patrons, who gravitate to the sun-drenched patio.

- ✔ **Stellarton.** New Glasgow and Stellarton are separated by Highway 104, though linked by commercial sprawl. Take Exit 24 on Highway 104 to get to Eastern Canada's largest museum, the **Nova Scotia Museum of Industry** (☎ 902-755-5425). This may not sound like an exciting stop, but kids will love every minute of it. In keeping with the theme, you must punch a time card upon entry. Allow at least an hour to explore. Open: Mon–Sat 9 a.m.–5 p.m. Admission: C$7 (US$5) adults, C$4 (US$2.90) seniors, C$3 (US$2.10) children.

- ✔ **Antigonish.** Pronounced An-tee-gun-ish, this busy highway town becomes even busier during the middle weekend of July for the **Highland Games,** the biggest and oldest such games outside of Scotland. Heavyweight events like tug-o'-war and caber-tossing are balanced by pipe bands and performances by some of the biggest names in Celtic music.

- ✔ **St. Georges Bay beaches**. If the sun is out, take Exit 35 north off Highway 104 to **Pomquet Beach Park** or Exit 36 to **Bayfield Provincial Park**. Both spots are just a few minutes from the highway and have picnic areas, sandy beaches, and swimming in some of Canada's warmest ocean water.

Eastern Shore

Promoted as the **Marine Drive** (Highway 7, then Highways 211 and 316), the route between Halifax and Canso looks relatively tame on a big map, but when it comes to negotiating the narrow, winding 320km (200-mile) route you should allow a full day — *without* stops. But don't let the pace put you off: the slow going is the perfect excuse to take your time and spend the night in one of the charming villages en route.

Getting there

From Dartmouth, across the harbor from downtown Halifax, take Exit 7 from Highway 111. The highway is occasionally in sight of the ocean, but the most scenic areas are along side roads. Consult a good map, and enjoy!

Staying along the Eastern Shore

The Eastern Shore has a few excellent lodging options, but make sure you've reserved ahead of time or you'll end up spending the night in a nondescript roadside motel.

Liscomb Lodge
$$ Liscomb Mills

Its location halfway between Halifax and Canso makes Liscomb Lodge a good place for an overnight stop. Standard rooms are comfortable but unexceptional. It's worth paying extra for the much larger cottages, even if you don't have a family in tow. Activities like hiking and boating will tempt you to stay longer. The resort restaurant is one of the few dining choices along this stretch of coast, so it's worth enquiring about meal packages when booking a room.

Highway 7, Liscomb Mills ☎ *800-665-6343 or 902-779-2307. Fax: 902-779-2700. Internet:* www.signatureresorts.com. *Rack rates: C$125–C$150 (US$89.30–US$107.10) double. AE, DISC, MC, V. Mid-May–late Oct.*

Salmon River House Country Inn
$$ Salmon River Bridge

Less than an hour's drive from Halifax, this lodging has been a popular getaway for almost 100 years. The rooms have been modernized, but décor remains a bit old-fashioned. Still, the additions of ensuite bathrooms and televisions aren't a bad thing. Water views and a wonderful restaurant are the real reason this place makes the cut. The self-contained guesthouse may appeal to those looking for a little more privacy.

Highway 7, Salmon River Bridge ☎ *800-565-3353 or 902-889-3353. Fax: 902-889-3653. Internet:* www.salmonriverhouse.com. *Rates: C$90–C$150 (US$64.30– US$107.10) double. AE, MC, V. April–Nov.*

Seaboard Bed and Breakfast
$$ Lawrencetown Beach

Popular with active travelers on a budget, this converted 1912 farmhouse is less than 1km (0.6 miles) from the waves of Lawrencetown Beach. Guests are welcome to use bikes or the canoe the hosts leave at a lake across the road. You'll find basic, comfortable accommodations, a communal television room, a small library, and a lounge with fireplace. A hearty breakfast with lots of homemade baked goodies will get you going in the morning.

2629 Cromwell Rd. ☎ *902-827-3747. Internet:* www.seaboardbb.com. *Rack rates: C$75–C$85 (US$53.60–US$60.70) double. AE, MC, V. May–Aug.*

St. Mary's River Lodge
$–$$ Sherbrooke

The five rooms in this renovated residence all have private bathrooms and television, and all but one are air-conditioned. The rooms are a little cutesy for my liking, but the price is right and it's handy to historical Sherbrooke Village, right next door. Rates include a cooked breakfast.

21 Main St., Sherbrooke ☎ *902-522-2177. Fax: 902-522-2515. Internet:* www.riverlodge.ca. *Rack rates: C$70–C$100 (US$50–US$71.40) double. MC, V.*

Dining along the Eastern Shore

Gold Coast Seafood Restaurant
$–$$ Jeddore Oyster Pond   SEAFOOD

If you like seafood, the menu at this inexpensive eatery offers something for everyone. It's a good spot to head for lunch after visiting the Fisherman's Life Museum, which is across the road. Eat in or order to go.

Highway 7, Jeddore Oyster Pond ☎ *902-889-2386. Main courses: C$8.50–C$18 (US$6–US$12.90). Daily 11 a.m.–9 p.m.*

J. Willy Krauch & Sons Ltd.
$ Tangier   SEAFOOD

You'll often see salmon in restaurants referred to as "Krauch" salmon, and this is where it comes from. Krauch salmon is cold-smoked, which means the fish has been salted and then smoked for up to a week at very low temperatures. The process is very different from normal smoking, where the fish literally cooks as it is smoked. Cold-smoking creates a subtle, savory flavor and a firm texture — perfect for slicing thinly and serving on crackers (it is the most divine smoked salmon you will ever taste). If you're worried about consuming your purchase before it makes it home, you'll be pleased to know that the company ships worldwide.

Highway 7, Tangier ☎ *902-772-2188. Mon–Fri 10 a.m.–5 p.m.*

Lobster Shack
$$–$$$ Salmon River Bridge   SEAFOOD

Ahoy, matey! Even landlubbers are made to feel at home in this small-town restaurant with a big-time reputation. The dining room is in a small clapboard building overlooking the water and attached to the Salmon River House Country Inn. The walls are decorated with all manner of maritime memorabilia — the sort of stuff you'd expect to find washed up on the beach after a big storm. As the name suggests, lobster is a menu feature. To start, choose from super-creamy lobster chowder or rich seafood dip with pita bread. If you're serious about your lobster, choose one from the tank and order it as a main course. Boiled lobster is boiled lobster; what sets the Lobster Shack apart from other restaurants is the variety of sizes — up to 5 pounds on my last visit (I was told they often hold them up to 10 pounds).

Highway 7, Salmon River Bridge ☎ *902-889-3353. Main courses: C$13–C$25 (US$9.30–US$17.90). AE, MC, V. April–Nov daily 8 a.m.–9 p.m.*

Exploring the Eastern Shore

Like the rest of the province, the Eastern Shore has a long and interesting history that can be relived at numerous attractions. But it is the smell of salt in the air, the long stretches of sandy beach, and the quiet coves that are the real draw.

Fisherman's Life Museum
Jeddore Oyster Pond

Life for an East Coast fisherman and his family 100 years ago was not easy. This museum recreates the simple, self-sufficient lifestyle of one such family. Ervin Myers, the husband, spent long days at sea while his wife Ethelda raised 13 daughters in this small house. Details such as the family's woodstove and small pipe organ and the surrounding gardens planted with root vegetables add to the museum's authentic quality.

58 Navy Pool Loop, Jeddore Oyster Pond ☎ *902-772-2344. Admission: C$3 (US$2.10) adults, C$2 (US$1.40) seniors and children. June–mid-Oct Mon–Sat 9:30 a.m.–5:30 p.m., Sun 1 p.m.–5:30 p.m.*

Grassy Island National Historic Site
Canso

The Canso Islands, within sight of the small town of Canso, have a long and colorful history, but today sit empty beyond the end of one of Nova Scotia's most remote roads. The British established an outpost on one of them, Grassy Island, in the early 1700s, harvesting and processing 8 million cod annually. They also made a lackadaisical attempt at fortifying the settlement, but were unable to protect it against a 1774 attack by the French, who destroyed the entire town. Stop by the Visitor Reception Centre beside the wharf in Canso to learn more about the history, then take the free 15-minute boat ride across to the island. It's an interesting trip for the stark, end-of-the-world feel of the site.

Access by boat from Canso ☎ *902-366-3136. Admission: C$2 (US$1.40) to the Visitor Reception Centre; boat ride is free. June–mid-Sept daily 10 a.m.–6 p.m.*

Sherbrooke Village
Sherbrooke

What makes this historic park stand out from others is that the village is an actual community, with real live Nova Scotians going about their daily business. Sherbrooke was the site of an 1860s gold rush, and many of the original buildings have been faithfully restored in the style of this era. Costumed guides are on hand to talk about the village and its history, or to give demonstrations of traditional crafts such as candle-making and old-time photography. One of the most interesting displays is the workshop, where carpenters combine traditional skill with modern technology to produce reproductions in demand at historic sites across the province.

Highway 7, Sherbrooke ☎ *888-743-7845 or 902-522-2858. Internet:* www.museum. gov.ns.ca/sv. *Admission: C$8.25 (US$5.90) adults, C$6.75 (US$4.80) seniors, C$3.75 (US$2.70) children. June–mid-Oct daily 9:30 a.m.–5:30 p.m.*

More cool things to do along the Eastern Shore

While the historic sites are worth a stop, it's the ocean that takes center stage along the Eastern Shore. Apart from the coastal scenery, it's a great area for trying your hand at surfing or sea kayaking, and boasts some great beaches:

- ✔ **Surfing.** After surfing on both coasts of Canada, I'm not sure if it's possible to say one is better than the other. One thing is for certain, though: **Lawrencetown Beach,** a half-hour drive from Halifax, is Canada's best-known surf spot. Waves break along a rocky point as well as on the beach, with the biggest swells rolling through in winter. **DeCane Sports** (☎ 902-431-7873) charges around C$50 (US$35.70) per day for rental of surfboard and wetsuit (you'll need one, even in summer). Lessons are also offered.

- ✔ **Sea kayaking.** Even if you've never been near a sea kayak, the guides at **Coastal Adventures,** based at Tangier (☎ 902-772-2774; Internet www.coastaladventures.com), will make you feel comfortable in the water. The full-day beginner course (C$100/ US$71.40 per person) is as much a tour as a lesson, with an introduction to basic paddling skills followed by a trip to an uninhabited island. You're in safe hands with co-owner Dr. Scott Cunningham, who could write a book on the subject — and in fact has (*Sea Kayaking in Nova Scotia*).

✔ **Beach walking.** Okay, this activity is a little less adventurous than the others, but there's nothing like feeling sand between your toes and breathing in the smells of the ocean. Best of all, it's free. As Canada's longest stretch of sand (5km/3.1 miles), **Martinique Beach**, south of Musquodoboit Harbour, is a good option for an extended beach walk. It is protected as a provincial park and is dotted with day-use areas and access paths. Continuing north from Martinique Beach, **Taylor Head Provincial Park** protects a narrow spit of land ringed by glorious white-sand beaches. The ones on the east side of the headland are most protected.

Chapter 14

Cape Breton Island

● ●

In This Chapter

▶ Taking in the life and times of Alexander Graham Bell at Baddeck

▶ Driving the Cabot Trail through Cape Breton Highlands National Park

▶ Stepping back in time at the Fortress of Louisbourg

● ●

C ape Breton Island is a Maritimes gem. It offers plenty of breathtaking coastal scenery and a dash of Canadian history, coupled with that unmistakable down-home East Coast charm you've heard so much about. Joined to the mainland by a causeway, the island is renowned for its rugged coastline, while mountains, lakes, and salmon-filled rivers add to the diversity inland. The Cabot Trail, a 300km (186-mile) road that winds its way around Cape Breton Highlands National Park, is the island's top attraction.

History buffs will be satiated at Canada's largest historical reconstruction, the Fortress of Louisbourg National Historic Site, which reminds us that the French once held sovereignty to the island after ceding the rest of the province to the British in 1713.

A big part of this region's appeal is the people ("Cape Bretoners"), many of them proudly descended from Scots who were attracted by the island's strong resemblance to their homeland. The island's most famous resident was born in Scotland himself: Alexander Graham Bell, like so many others, was captivated by this unique part of the country and called Baddeck home for much of his life.

You need your own vehicle to make the most of a visit to Cape Breton Island.

Plan on spreading the wealth around when it comes to lodging. One night at a historic inn at Baddeck and another at a beachy resort along the Cabot Trail would be the perfect combination for a two-night stay.

Cape Breton Island

What's Where: Cape Breton Island and Its Major Attractions

After crossing the Canso Causeway to Cape Breton Island, highways head up the island in three different directions. Interesting sights are spread throughout the island, but so long as you top off your sojourn with a loop around the Cabot Trail, you shouldn't miss anything major.

Baddeck

Baddeck is an old resort town with lots of fine lodging and dining choices, as well as:

- ✔ **Alexander Graham Bell National Historic Site,** a museum dedicated to one of the world's most prolific inventors
- ✔ **Bras d'Or,** an inland sea that laps at the edge of town
- ✔ **Celtic music,** nightly at the local parish hall

Cape Breton Highlands National Park

Undoubtedly Nova Scotia's premier destination for outdoor lovers, this park protects a wide swath of land at the top of Cape Breton Island. It is ringed by the Cabot Trail, which allows you to get up close and personal with some of North America's most dramatic coastal scenery. Highlights along the way include:

- ✔ **Whale-watching tours** from Pleasant Bay
- ✔ **Golfing at Highland Links,** with ocean views
- ✔ **Beaches near Ingonish,** reputed to be the finest in Canada
- ✔ **Quiet inland lakes,** ideal to explore on foggy days

Louisbourg

Built by the French as a "new Paris" almost 300 years ago, Louisbourg was a bustling center of commerce on the remote east coast of Cape Breton Island until the British attacked, destroying the entire town. Today, a visit is worthwhile for:

- ✔ **Fortress of Louisbourg**, Canada's largest historic park
- ✔ **Hiking** beyond the fortress walls to the site of the original settlement

Baddeck

Halfway up the island, the delightful resort town of Baddeck is a good central location to plan an overnight (or longer) stay. The town's most famous resident was Alexander Graham Bell, who spent summers and then the last three decades of his life at a stately waterfront mansion across the bay from Baddeck. The home is owned by Bell's descendants, but in town one of the province's best museums tells his interesting life story. Down on the waterfront, a free ferry shuttles visitors to Kidston Island for hiking and swimming, while other tour boats can take you to search out nesting bald eagles.

Getting there

Take Highway 105 north from the Canso Causeway, and in less than an hour you'll be greeted by a bombardment of Baddeck billboards.

Staying in Baddeck

Whether you're looking to spend your day at a waterfront resort or a character-laden historic lodging, you'll find something in Baddeck.

Summer is very busy in Baddeck, so reservations are necessary for local lodging. If you do arrive without having booked a room, stop at the centrally located **Baddeck Welcome Centre** (☎ 902-295-1911) for suggestions.

Bethune's Boathouse Cottage
$$ Baddeck

The name says it all: this small cottage is a converted boathouse on the Baddeck waterfront. Inside, you'll find a double bed, bathroom, and living area with a television and radio. Cooking is done on an outdoor barbecue. The cottage sits on its own small lot, but is not particularly private. If you feel like getting away, simply take to the water in the complimentary rowboat.

49 Water St. ☎ *902-295-2687. Rack rates: C$110 (US$78.60) double. No credit cards. Mid-May–mid-Oct.*

Dunlop Inn
$$–$$$ Baddeck

The Dunlop Inn enjoys a prime location at the bottom end of the main street, in a relaxing waterfront setting. It's also the closest lodging to the Alexander Graham Bell museum. My favorite of five guest rooms is the Lighthouse Room, which has a crisp blue and white color scheme. The ideal place to while away a warm afternoon is on an Adirondack chair on the waterfront deck. Breakfast is self-serve continental.

552 Chebucto St. ☎ *888-263-9840 or 902-295-1100. Fax: 902-295-1136. Internet:* www.dunlopinn.com. *Rack rates: C$120–C$160 (US$85.70–US$114.30) double. AE, MC, V. May–Oct.*

Inverary Resort
$$–$$$$ **Baddeck**

Kids in particular will enjoy this resort on the south side of Baddeck. It's not really within walking distance of town, but why would you want to leave when you've got tennis courts, a spa facility, an indoor pool, a fitness center, a large playground, boat and kayak rentals, and sailing trips aboard a boat once owned by Alexander Graham Bell? The rooms vary from those in an original building to modern, fully equipped suites with private balconies. The resort also has two restaurants and a lounge. Golf and meal packages can be a good deal.

Shore Rd. ☎ *800-565-5660 or 902-295-3500. Fax: 902-295-3527. Internet:* www.capebretonresorts.com. *Rack rates: C$110–C$300 (US$78.60–US$214.30) double. AE, DISC, MC, V.*

Telegraph House
$–$$$ **Baddeck**

Built in 1861 and now run by the fifth generation of the same family, this imposing gray-and-white inn on the main street was once a telegraph office. Rooms in the main lodge are basic and some are very small, but all are clean and comfortable, and the location couldn't be more central. Alexander Graham Bell often stayed in Room 1 when in town — do you need a better recommendation? Behind the main lodge is a wing of more modern motel rooms with vaguely Victorian decor. They may lack the history of those in the original building but are good value, especially the extra-large ones which are ideal for families.

9 Chebucto St. ☎ *888-263-9840 or 902-295-1100. Fax: 902-295-1136. Internet:* www.baddeck.com/telegraph. *Rack rates: C$80–C$200 (US$57.10–US$142.90) double. AE, MC, V.*

Dining in Baddeck

Restaurants line the main street through Baddeck, but some of the better dining choices are associated with local lodgings.

Baddeck Lobster Suppers
$$ Baddeck   SEAFOOD

In typical lobster-supper style (or lack of it), this traditional Maritimes feast is replayed for tourists in a dining hall across from the waterfront. At dinner, pay C$25 (US$17.90) for one full lobster and all-you-can-eat mussels, chowder, dessert, and non-alcoholic drinks. Lunch offers similar choices from a regular menu.

Ross St. ☎ *902-295-3307. Lobster supper: C$25 (US$17.90). MC, V. June–Oct daily 11:30 a.m.–1:30 p.m. for lunch and 4 p.m.–9 p.m. for dinner.*

Lakeside Café
$$ Baddeck   GLOBAL

Drive down through the Inverary Resort to reach this casual waterfront restaurant, which has lots of outdoor tables. The lunch menu is made up of fancy sandwiches such as a Lobster Clubhouse and appetizers from the dinner menu. The evening menu takes its roots from around the world, with an emphasis on local produce. Choose from dishes such as a Thai stir-fry tossed with scallops, or go Greek with grilled halibut topped with feta cheese and olives.

Inverary Resort, Shore Rd. ☎ *902-295-3500. Main courses: C$12–C$20 (US$8.60–US$14.30). AE, MC, V. Daily 11:30 a.m.–3:30 p.m. and 4:30–10:00 p.m.*

Lynwood Inn Dining Room
$$–$$$ Baddeck   CANADIAN

Tucked inside a historic residence that has been converted to an inn, this smallish dining room features subtle Victorian furnishings with the modern addition of a deck wrapped around two sides. For starters, the menu covers all bases, with nachos, mussels, and chicken soup (with loads of chicken). Entrees are no less diverse, with choices ranging from a charbroiled T-bone to grilled rainbow trout splashed with a corn salsa.

23 Shore Rd. ☎ *902-295-1995. Main courses: C$11–C$19 (US$7.90–US$13.60). AE, MC, V. Daily 11 a.m.–9 p.m.*

Exploring Baddeck

Baddeck isn't big on traditional official "sights," but that doesn't mean it's not a delightful town to visit. Chebucto Street is the main thoroughfare, but walk one block down Jones Street to reach the waterfront and you'll find yourself in the real heart of the town.

Alexander Graham Bell National Historic Site
Baddeck

Like most kids, I learned in school that Alexander Graham Bell invented the telephone, but it wasn't until I'd spent a few hours in this museum that I realized the extent of his contribution to the world of science and engineering. The first exhibit explains Bell's achievements in teaching the deaf (including Helen Keller) to speak, using a phonetic alphabet developed by his father. Spend some time at this display, as the interpretive panels go on to explain how this early work was inextricably linked to his later experimenting with transmitting sound along wire using voice pulsations. This, of course, led to Bell's patenting of the world's first telephone in 1876. The rest of the museum is devoted to his lesser-known inventions, such as the world's first hydrofoil and first seaplane. Among the various replicas and original parts on display is the *Silver Dart*, with which Bell broke the world speed record on Bras d'Or Lake. As a symbol of Bell's work with children, part of the museum is set aside for kids, with puzzles, experiments, and kite-making.

Chebucto St. ☎ ***902-295-2069****. Internet:* www.pc.gc.ca/lhn-nhs/ns/grahambell*. Admission: C$5.75 (US$4.10) adults, C$5 (US$3.60) seniors, C$3 (US$2.10) children. June daily 9 a.m.–6 p.m; July–mid-Oct daily 8:30 a.m.–6:00 p.m.; mid-Oct–May daily 9 a.m.–5 p.m.*

Cape Bretoners and their music

You'll hear Celtic-based music wherever you travel on Cape Breton Island. It's incredibly popular with the local population, and so catchy that you can't help but be captivated by its spirit and energy. Cape Bretoners Natalie McMaster, Ashley MacIsaac, The Rankins, and the Irish Descendents have introduced this music to the world, but there's no place like the island itself to immerse yourself in the traditions of Celtic song and dance. To find the best place to go for a night out, ask a local, check entertainment listings in newspapers, or simply wander the streets listening for live music.

One event worth noting is the **Celtic Colours International Festival (☎ 877-285-2321** or 902-539-9388; Internet: www.celtic-colours.com), which is held the third week of October with the magnificent backdrop of fall's blazing colors. Celtic musicians from around the world perform in over 40 island towns in churches, halls, and theaters. After their regular gigs, musicians often turn up at Baddeck's Festival Club for a jam that rarely ends before 3 a.m.

Other cool things to see and do in Baddeck

Relax at an outdoor cafe, wander down to the waterfront, or, if you're feeling more active, consider one of the following:

✔ **Set Sail.** The *Amoeba* (☎ 902-295-2481) is a 15-meter (50-foot) sailing ship that departs Baddeck Wharf four times daily for a 90-minute journey on Bras d'Or. Keep an eye out for Alexander Graham Bell's mansion and the odd bald eagle along the way. The cost is C$20 (US$14.30) per person.

✔ **Paddle over to Kidston Island.** Protected as a park, this uninhabited island lies just across the channel from Baddeck. It has a beach, nature trails, and even a lighthouse. A free ferry departs Government Wharf for the island every 20 minutes, but it's more enjoyable to rent a canoe or kayak from **Harvey's,** beside Government Wharf (☎ 902-295-3318), and reach the island under your own steam.

✔ **Take a drive through the Margaree Valley.** West of Baddeck, the southernmost section of the Cabot Trail follows the Margaree River, famed in fishing circles for its high concentrations of salmon. At the **Margaree Salmon Museum** in North East Margaree (☎ 902-248-2848) you can learn about the salmon's life cycle from guides or on your own. It's open daily 9 a.m. to 5 p.m., and entry is just C$1 (US71¢). North of the museum, potter Bell Fraser sells her distinctive ocean-inspired pieces at **Cape Breton Clay** in the village of Margaree Valley (☎ 902-235-2467).

✔ **Dance the night away.** The **Baddeck Gathering Ceilidhs** is a nightly performance by local musicians in St. Michael's Hall on Main Street. (☎ 902-295-2794). Entry costs just C$7 (US$5); tea, coffee, and oatcakes are each C$1 (US71¢), and all the action gets under way at 7:30 p.m., July and August only.

Cape Breton Highlands National Park and the Cabot Trail

It is impossible not to fall in love with this spectacular national park which stretches across the top of Cape Breton Island. Sea cliffs and rocky coves dominate the west side and long sandy beaches run down the east side, with a vast plateau of wilderness in between. The Cabot Trail, one of Canada's most scenic drives, loops through the park and weaves along both coasts, ensuring you miss nothing. Wildlife viewing is excellent: most visitors spot moose, whales, and bald eagles, often without even leaving their vehicles.

Getting there

Unless you're planning to traverse the Cabot Trail by bike, you'll need your own vehicle. To reach the main park gate, turn off Highway 105, south of Baddeck.

Paying entrance fees

The **park entry fee** of C$5 (US$4) adults, C$4.25 (US$3) seniors, C$2.50 (US$1.80) youths, to a maximum of C$12.50 (US$8.90) per vehicle, is good until 4 p.m. the day following its purchase. If you are planning to spend more than a few days in the park, a season pass pays for itself in five days. Passes can be purchased at the information center north of Chéticamp or at the toll booths at both park entrances. If you have a **National Parks of Canada Pass** (see Chapter 4), you'll be waved right on through.

Arriving at the park's main entrance

Make your first stop the **Park Information Centre** (☎ 902-224-2306), 5km (3.1 miles) north of Chéticamp. It's open daily 8 a.m. to 8 p.m. Inside, natural history exhibits provide a good introduction to the park, and posted activities schedules will help in planning your time. Friendly staff at the information desk supply free maps and will help you decide which hiking trails best suit your abilities. Off to one side is **Les Amis du Plein Air** (☎ 902-224-3814), a bookstore that stocks park-related literature and a wide selection of general outdoor and nature guides.

Staying along the Cabot Trail

Glenghorm Beach Resort
$$–$$$$ **Ingonish Beach**

Set on a sprawling property that extends from the Cabot Trail to a beautiful sandy beach, this resort has activities for the whole family and accommodations to suit all tastes. It offers canoe and kayak rentals, an outdoor pool, volleyball courts, a large playground, a fitness room, an esthetics salon, and nightly beachside bonfires. The least expensive units are roadside motel rooms. Older cottages come with a kitchen and up to two bedrooms; some are within sight of the ocean. The Beach House Suites are among the best guest rooms in all of the Maritimes: luxuriously appointed, they still manage to maintain a casual air — you can happily tramp sand in without feeling guilty. Each air-conditioned unit has a private veranda or balcony, separate sleeping quarters, a jetted tub, a kitchen, and comfortable couches set around a gas fireplace. Resort dining includes a restaurant open for three meals and a downstairs bar with live Celtic music most nights.

Ingonish Beach ☎ *800-565-5660 or 902-285-2049. Fax: 902-285-2395. Internet:* www.capebretonresorts.com. *Rack rates: High season C$99–C$395 (US$70.70–US$282) double, low season C$82–C$295 (US$58.60–US$210.70) double. AE, MC, V. May–Oct.*

Keltic Lodge

$$$–$$$$ **Ingonish Beach**

Sharing a narrow peninsula that juts into Ingonish Bay with the famous Highland Links golf course, the Keltic Lodge is one of Canada's most fashionable resorts. A short drive from the Cabot Trail leads to the perfectly positioned main lodge, on an isthmus high above the ocean and with water views to the north and south. The nationalistic red and white exterior contrasts starkly with the surrounding blues and greens. Dating to the 1940s, this is the original lodge, with older rooms, a restaurant and lounge, and the main lobby. Guests also have the use of a heated outdoor pool, and the concierge can make bookings for tennis, whale-watching, and fishing. You don't need to be a registered guest to get a tee time at Highland Links or to hike out to the tip of Middle Head, but you'll feel more like you belong if you are. Price-wise, you may expect more from the rooms. On the other hand, you'll find yourself enjoying the outdoors for much of your stay. Rooms in the main lodge are a little old-fashioned, while those in the Inn at Keltic are motel-like, but air-conditioned and just steps away from a grassy area with a gazebo and colorful Adirondack chairs. The four-bedroom cottages can be rented as an entire unit or with guests sharing a communal living area.

Ingonish Beach ☎ *800-565-0444 or 902-285-2880. Fax: 902-285-2859. Internet:* www.signatureresorts.com/keltic. *Rack rates: High season C$190–C$320 (US$135.70–US$228) double, low season C$100–C$150 (US$71.40–US$107.10) double. AE, DISC, MC, V. June–Oct.*

Parkview Motel

$$ **Chéticamp**

Choose from older rooms or upgrade to air-conditioned creek-side deluxe rooms at this motel complex within walking distance of the park information center. The on-site restaurant and lounge save you from having to drive anywhere.

West entrance, 5km (3.1 miles) north of Chéticamp ☎ *902-224-3232. Fax: 902-224-2596. Internet:* www.parkviewresort.com. *Rack rates: C$80–C$110 (US$57.10–US$78.60) double. AE, MC, V. June–mid-Oct.*

Salty Mariner's Motel & Inn

$$–$$$ **Pleasant Bay**

Don't be perturbed by the bland, salmon-pink exterior of the Salty Mariner. Inside, the 18 rooms are tastefully decorated using bright color schemes. All feature four-piece bathrooms, and some have balconies with ocean views. The property lies on a slight rise between the Cabot Trail and Pleasant Bay, so you would be well located for an early morning whale-watching excursion. The adjacent Tin Pan Gallery Restaurant has a seafood-dominated menu, but also some decent steaks.

23475 Cabot Trail ☎ *800-292-3222 or 902-224-1252. Internet:* www.salty mariner.com. *Rack rates: C$109–C$159 (US$77.90–US$113.60) double. AE, MC, V. May–Oct.*

Seascape Coastal Retreat

$$$ **Ingonish**

Set on a grassy slope that ends at a private beach on Ingonish Bay, this resort is a little piece of heaven beside the busy Cabot Trail. The well-tended grounds are dotted with outdoor seating and a hot tub. In one corner, a garden produces vegetables and herbs used in the adjacent restaurant. The cottages have solid, modern furnishings; amenities such as jetted tubs, fireplaces, ocean-view verandas, and special touches like bathrobes add to their charm. All have a veranda with ocean view. Prices include seafood hors d'oeuvres upon arrival, a cooked breakfast, and the use of kayaks and mountain bikes.

36083 Cabot Trail, Ingonish ☎ *866-385-3003 or 902-285-3003. Internet:* www.seascapecoastalretreat.com. *Rack rates: High season C$189 (US$135) double, low season C$149 (US$106.40) double. MC, V. May–Oct.*

Dining along the Cabot Trail

It's seafood and more seafood along the Cabot Trail. If you feel like a break from the catch of the day, try the major resorts, most of which have restaurants with wide-ranging menus.

Atlantic Restaurant

$$–$$$ **Ingonish Beach   SEAFOOD/CANADIAN**

Looking in, this place could be an upmarket family restaurant anywhere in North America. Looking *out*, the drop-dead gorgeous ocean view through big windows could only be Cape Breton. Low prices are the only real surprise on the seafood-dominated menu. You can order favorites like beer-battered fish and chips for as little as C$10 (US$7.10), but I encourage you to be more adventurous. The grilled halibut, bookended by crab cakes to start and a slice of blueberry shortcake for dessert, will set you back around C$35 (US$25).

Keltic Lodge, Ingonish Beach ☎ ***902-285-2880.*** *Main courses: C$10–C$22 (US$7.10– US$15.70). June–Oct. 11 a.m.–9 p.m.*

Chowder House
$ **Neil's Harbour   SEAFOOD**

This is casual Cape Breton dining at its very best. The Chowder House is in a weather-beaten building on a headland through the village of Neil's Harbour. Don't be put off by the pine-paneled decor: the food is super-fresh and very well priced. The clam chowder is chockablock with juicy clams and costs just C$4 (US$2.90) per bowl; a lobster burger will set you back C$9 (US$6.40); or you can order the most expensive item on the menu board, a full lobster with fries and coleslaw, for C$20 (US$14.30). Once you've made a decision, order at the counter and listen for your number. The restaurant is totally enclosed, which is a bit of a shame — if it's a nice day, I'd recommend spreading a blanket out on the grassy headland.

Neil's Harbour, beside the lighthouse ☎ *902-336-2463. Main courses: C$6–C$20 (US$4.30–US$14.30). May–Sept 11 a.m.–8 p.m.*

Muddy Rudder
$–$$ **South Ingonish Beach   SEAFOOD**

The delightfully named Muddy Rudder is part restaurant, part attraction, and totally unique. It's simply a roadside shanty at the head of Ingonish Harbour with a few plastic outdoor table settings off to one side. Choose from lobster, crab, mussels, or clams, all of which are cooked to order in big pots of boiling water out front. Prices are a little higher than you'd pay at a local seafood market, but a lot lower than at a regular restaurant. While researching this book, my wife and I enjoyed the biggest plate of mussels I've ever seen (C$6/US$4.30), followed by a full crab that came with tea cakes and coleslaw (C$16/US$11.40), and we just happened to have a bottle of red from Jost Vineyards (see page 156) in the car, which the owner happily opened for us.

Cabot Trail, South Ingonish Beach ☎ ***902-285-2266.*** *Main courses: C$7–C$15 (US$5–US$10.70). Cash only. May–Sept 10 a.m.–7 p.m. (later if the owner doesn't have other engagements).*

Restaurant Acadian
$–$$ Chéticamp   ACADIAN

Attached to a craft shop, this casual restaurant is a wonderful place to try Acadian cuisine. Adding to the charm, the women who work there all dress in traditional clothing. Mains like *Croquettes de Morue* (cod fish cakes) and *Chaudrée au Poisson* (haddock chowder) are mostly under C$10 (US$7.10). Plan on saving room for dessert — the raisin pudding (C$3/US$2.10) is as good as it gets.

774 Main St., Chéticamp ☎ *902-224-3207. Main courses: C$8–C$14 (US$5.70–US$10). MC, V. Mid-May–mid-Oct. daily 7 a.m.–9 p.m.*

Seascapes Restaurant
$$$ Ingonish   SEAFOOD

Attached to the resort of the same name, this small oceanfront dining room is easy to miss as you scoot along the eastern side of the Cabot Trail. There is no menu as such; the chef simply uses available seafood to create a half-dozen dishes (along with at least one vegetarian option), which are written up on a blackboard. I picked a creamy lobster linguini (C$21/US$15), and the lobster was boiled especially for my order. A rather refined-looking couple seated next to me were gleefully tucking into snow crab — complete with bibs (on them, not the crabs).

Seascape Coastal Retreat, 36083 Cabot Trail, Ingonish ☎ *902-285-3003. Reservations recommended. Main courses: C$16–C$22 (US$11.40–US$15.70). MC, V. May–Oct. daily 6–9 p.m.*

Exploring the Cabot Trail

The Cabot Trail, parts of which are covered elsewhere in this chapter, is a 300km (186-mile) route that takes in not just Cape Breton Highlands National Park but also the coastal drive south from the park to St. Anns and on to Baddeck, then through the Margaree Valley to Chéticamp. The spectacular 110km (68-mile) section inside the park is detailed here.

Highlights along the way

Although it's only a little over 100km (62 miles) between Chéticamp and Ingonish, you should allow at least one full day for this stretch of highway, simply due to the number of interesting stops en route. The road is steep and narrow in some sections but is not difficult to drive. Pullouts and viewpoints are spaced along the entire route. Do not use the narrow shoulder as your personal parking space.

My description of the Cabot Trail follows a clockwise direction. It could have gone either way, but by following this course, you'll hit the main information center first up and complete the drive on the east side of peninsula, where most of the recommended accommodations and restaurants can be found.

The most dramatic section of the entire Cabot Trail is the 45km (28-mile) stretch along the west coast. The scenery kicks off in a big way almost immediately, with the road hugging the shoreline, ascending precipitous sea cliffs, and then dropping back down to sea level. Stop at as many overlooks as your time allows, to take in the scenery and read the interpretive boards.

One particularly scenic overlook is the **Veterans Monument,** 18km (11 miles) north of the park entrance. When I last made the stop, a moose and her calf were grazing in the open meadows below, while a whale could be seen in the ocean beyond and a black bear foraged on the high hills behind.

Once you reach the lookout above **Wreck Cove,** the road descends steeply via a series of switchbacks to reach sea level at **Pleasant Bay,** just outside the park boundary. This small village, which was in existence well before road access was possible, now takes full advantage of summer traffic with a variety of tourist services. It tries hard to function primarily as a fishing village, but the harbor is filled with whale-watching boats and sea kayakers. The **Whale Interpretive Centre** (☎ 902-224-1411; open daily 9 a.m. to 6 p.m.) has displays on the various species you may see out on a whale-watching trip. Admission is C\$5 (US\$4) adults, C\$4 (US\$2.90) seniors and children.

From Pleasant Bay, the Cabot Trail begins its ascent to a high plateau, reentering the national park after a few minutes' drive. Just inside the boundary is **Lone Shieling,** the stone replica of a Scottish crofter's hut. It is also the starting point for a short trail leading to a grove of 350-year-old sugar maple trees. Continuing eastward, the road traverses a stunted *taiga* (mostly evergreen) forest before reaching a turnoff to **Cape North.** This side road skirts **Aspy Bay,** where a plaque and statue commemorate John Cabot's 1497 landfall. It then crosses to the northern tip of the island and the picturesque fishing communities of **Bay St. Lawrence, Capstick,** and **Meat Cove,** Cape Breton living in its rawest state.

After a side trip to Cape North, you have no choice but to backtrack before rejoining the Cabot Trail for its final push across the peninsula. Although the landscape on the east coast is less dramatic than the west, it is no less captivating, with long stretches of sand broken by rocky headlands. Highlights include the beach at **Black Brook Cove** and **Lakies Head Lookout.** Continuing south, the Cabot Trail leaves the park again. Along this section, it passes four villages with Ingonish in their names, although in reality, they merge into one long strip broken only by Middle Head, a narrow peninsula that holds one of Canada's finest golf courses and the grand Keltic Lodge. Beyond Ingonish, the Cabot Trail leaves the national park for a final time, making its last grand ascent to **Cape Smokey,** one of the most dramatic lookouts along the entire trail.

Hiking the highlands

You can enjoy the park's spectacular scenery from the inside of your car easily enough, but to really appreciate the place, you need to get out onto the hiking trails. Stray away from the road to experience the park's natural beauty along any of these trails:

- ✔ **Le Buttereau Trail**. Here's an easy one to get you started. This 2km (1.2-mile) loop starts just north of the toll booth, with views across a large lagoon. Plan a dawn walk for the best bird-watching, or wait until dusk to watch the sun set over the Gulf of St. Lawrence.

- ✔ **Skyline Trail.** The Skyline is a high ridge with a long but easy trail leading to a magnificent viewpoint where whales can often be spotted frolicking below. The trailhead is on the left as the Cabot Trail heads inland beyond French Mountain. Allow two to three hours for the return trip.

- ✔ **Benjie's Lake Trail.** This small lake is easily reached in 30 minutes from a parking lot 6km (3.7 miles) beyond the Skyline Trail. As most visitors spend their time along the coastline, this trail is a good way to escape the crowds — and you may even spy moose along the way.

- ✔ **Fishing Cove Trail.** Two trails make the steep descent to this small bay along an otherwise inaccessible stretch of coastline. The first, beginning 3km (1.9 miles) north of Benjie's Lake Trail, is 8km (5 miles) each way. Farther north, another trail is much shorter (4km/2.5-miles) but a lot steeper. Either way, you should pack lunch and something to drink.

- ✔ **Jigging Cove Lake Trail.** On the park's east coast, 4km (2.5 miles) south of Neil's Harbour, this lake lies just out of sight of the highway. It is encircled by a 3km (1.9-mile) trail which can be hiked in well under an hour.

- ✔ **Jack Pine Loop.** Escape the crowds at Black Brook Cove by scrambling through the boulders at the north end of the beach to reach this 3km (1.9-mile) loop which weaves through coastal forest. You'll be back on your beach towel in less than an hour, even if you stop to read the interpretive boards along the way.

✔ **Middle Head Trail.** Drive as far as you can through the grounds of the Keltic Lodge, then walk for 2km (1.2 miles) and you'll find yourself at the very end of a narrow peninsula surrounded by dramatic cliffs. If you're staying at the Keltic Lodge, join a 9:30 a.m. guided walk to learn about the flora and fauna as you go.

✔ **Freshwater Lake Loop.** As the trailhead is Ingonish Beach, one of Canada's finest stretches of sand, you may find that motivating yourself to leave the beach is the hardest part of taking this easy 2km (1.2-mile) loop trail. Walking the path at dusk is a good opportunity to watch beavers hard at work — and you won't feel so bad about not being on the beach.

Other cool reasons to stop along the Cabot Trail

Apart from driving and hiking, consider the following options:

✔ **Whale-watching.** From the village of Pleasant Bay, you can take a tour boat to see whales along the coast. Commonly sighted species are pilot, humpback, and minke whales. The following operators are Coast Guard–certified, have partly-covered vessels, and are run by experienced captains who have a wealth of knowledge: **Captain Mark's Whale & Seal Cruise** (☎ 888-754-5112 or 902-224-1316), **Fiddlin' Whale Tours** (☎ 866-688-2424), and **Highland Coastal Whale Tours** (☎ 866-266-4080 or 902-224-1816). Typically, tours last 90 minutes and cost C$25 (US17.90) per person. Fiddlin' Whale Tours costs a few dollars extra, but Celtic fiddlers keep passengers entertained along the way. Each operator has a booth along the marina at Pleasant Bay, but advance reservations are recommended. All cruises are "weather permitting" — if the captain decides not to go sail because of rough seas, you probably don't want to be out on the water anyway.

The advantage of choosing a whale-watching trip at Pleasant Bay over other locations throughout the Maritimes is that it's only a short ride to where the whales are, so you get to spend more time watching and less time traveling.

✔ **Sea kayaking.** The protected water of St. Ann's Bay, south of Ingonish, is an ideal place to kayak. You're likely to spot eagles and whales while visiting inaccessible-by-foot beaches, sea caves, and tidal pools. Twice daily, **North River Kayak Tours** (☎ 888-865-2925 or 902-929-2628; Internet www.northriverkayak. com) offers a half-day (actually, around 3 hours) trip for C$60 (US$42.90) and a full day for C$100 (US$71.40). I recommend the full-day option. Great for first-timers and families, you'll learn basic paddling techniques and then head off to a sea cave; keep a lookout for eagles and mink along the way. The turnaround point is a remote beach where lunch is prepared. The cost includes kayak rental, instruction, lunch (steamed mussels if you're lucky), and maybe a friendly wave from the lighthouse keeper as you pass his posting. Overnight and multi-day trips explore more remote waters, or opt for the Rough It and Romance overnight excursion, which includes camping gear, all meals, and guidance to a remote beach.

✔ **Beaching it.** The best beaches are on the eastern side of the park. **Black Brook Cove** is somewhat protected from wind and ocean swells, creating a safe swimming spot. This sandy beach is backed by a grassy picnic area. Continuing south, **Ingonish Beach** is a long stretch of sand, well protected by Middle Head. The shallow water is warm, and a short section is patrolled through summer daily from noon.

✔ **Golfing.** A 1939 Stanley Thompson layout, **Highland Links,** near Ingonish (☎ **800-441-1118**; Internet: www.highlandlinks.com), is consistently rated as one of the world's top 100 courses by *Golf Magazine.* Although not overwhelming by today's standards, it is a classic links-style course with a dramatic coastal setting. In keeping with the Scottish theme, each hole has a name with both English and the Gaelic translation signed at the teebox (Hole 6, for example, is Mucklemouth Meg, the nickname for a girl with a big mouth, in reference to a pond that swallows wayward golf balls). Greens fees are C$50 to C$83 (US$35.70 to US$59.30) during peak season, dropping to just C$39 (US$27.90) for twilight golfing during the shoulder season (June and October).

Shopping

Shopping? In a national park? Well, sort of. Cape Breton Island is known for its artists and, with the large number of tourists, many have set up shop in the tiny villages that lie on the edge of the park. Most are open long hours through summer, shorter hours during the shoulder seasons, and then closed completely for winter.

The following are listed in a clockwise direction from Chéticamp: Beyond the top of the park at Dingwell, **Arts North** (☎ **902-383-2911**) showcases the pottery of owners Linda and Dennis Doyan and the jewelry of Johanna Padelt. One of the island's best-known painters is Christopher Corey, whose oil and watercolor landscapes are sold at **Lynn's Craft Shop & Art Gallery,** at Ingonish (☎ **902-285-2845**). **Tartans and Treasures** at South Harbour (☎ **902-383-2005**) claims North America's largest collection of tartan scarves and blankets. Most products come directly from the mother country, so you know you're buying the real thing. **Iron Art & Photography,** south of Ingonish at Tarbot (☎ **902-929-2821**), combines the hand-forged ironwork of Gordon Kennedy with the striking black-and-white photography of his wife, Carol, to make a worthwhile stop on the road back to Baddeck.

Louisbourg

It's been over 250 years since the French were driven from the lonely outpost of Louisbourg, on the remote eastern tip of Cape Breton Island. Today, it is one of the most interesting historical sites in all of the Maritimes, with lodging and other tourist services in an adjacent town of the same name.

Getting there

Louisbourg is 45km (28 miles) southeast of Sydney along Highway 22. No public transportation reaches the town.

Staying in Louisbourg

Even though it's at the end of the road, Louisbourg has several comfortable lodgings within walking distance of the fort, including these two recommendations.

Cranberry Cove Inn
$$–$$$ **Louisbourg**

It's impossible to miss this three-story, cranberry-red inn as you head out to the fortress. Inside, the decor is a little tamer. Each of seven guest rooms has its own theme. The top-floor Captain's Den, for example, has a quirky layout (thanks to the gabled roof), a subtle maritime color scheme, a gas fireplace, and a jetted tub. Not all the rooms have televisions. Downstairs is a parlor, in which three generations of the same family used to spend their evenings during the inn's former life. Breakfast is included in the rates and is served on the sunny side of the house.

12 Wolfe St. ☎ *800-929-0222 or 902-733-2171. Internet:* www.louisbourg.com/ cranberrycove. *Rack rates: C$95–C$160 (US$67.90–US$114.30) double. MC, V. May–Oct.*

Point of View Suites
$$–$$$ **Louisbourg**

This modern oceanfront property hogs the prime spot on a high headland within walking distance of both the town and the fortress. It sprawls over 1.6 hectares (4 acres) of well-maintained grounds, with a private beach at one corner of the property. Inside, the units have a sleek, contemporary styling, hardwood floors, and sliding doors that open to either a balcony or a veranda. The apartments are much larger than the suites and come with a full kitchen.

At the front of the property is a beach house where the owners host a nightly lobster supper. It's a casual gathering of guests, who are served steamed lobster and crab with all the trimmings and entertained with storytelling or a sing-along. Breakfast isn't included in the rates, but is available, eggs, bacon and all, for just C$4 (US$2.90).

15 Commercial St. Extension ☎ ***888-374-8439*** *or 902-733-2080. Internet:* www.louisbourgpointofview.com. *Rack rates: C$125 (US$89.30) suites, C$199 (US$142.10) apartments. MC, V.*

Dining in Louisbourg

Plan on eating lunch at one of the three restaurants at the Fortress of Louisbourg. If you're staying at Point of View Suites, you'll want to reserve a spot at their nightly lobster supper. If not, the single recommendation below is a good one.

Grubstake Restaurant
$$ **Louisbourg** SEAFOOD

It's now been over 30 years since a group of well-traveled friends got together and opened this restaurant that serves local cuisine to visitors from around the world. Not much has changed since, and no one seems to mind. The restaurant is casual and cozy, and the seafood is done without a deep fryer in sight. If you order the seafood linguini with a lobster sauce, plan to give dessert a miss; or, for something lighter, try halibut poached in milk and white wine, a burger, or a delicious seafood wrap. The adjacent cocktail lounge is a popular gathering spot for Fortress workers.

7499 Main St. ☎ ***902-733-2308***. *Main courses: C$10–C$22 (US$7.10–US$15.70). MC, V. Daily noon–8:30 p.m., later in July and Aug.*

Exploring Louisbourg

Even if you don't like history lessons, a little background is necessary to set the scene for a visit to the Fortress of Louisbourg National Historic Site. After the 1713 Treaty of Utrecht, all the French were left with in the Maritimes were Prince Edward Island and Île Royale (Cape Breton Island), the latter a base for a lucrative cod-fishing industry. Wary of an attack on their sovereignty, the French established a massive fortress around the Louisbourg village to repel an attack from the ocean, but in 1745, the British came from behind and took it in a little more than six weeks. After the fortifications changed hands on two more occasions, the British destroyed them and burned the village to the ground in 1760. Two hundred years later, with many Cape Breton coal mines closing, the federal government decided to begin the daunting task of rebuilding the entire village and fort as a make-work project. The result is Canada's largest historical reconstruction — a must-see for anyone traveling around Cape Breton Island.

Fortress of Louisbourg

Plan on spending the better part of a day on the grounds. Start by watching the video at the interpretive center, and then catch the shuttle to the back of the fort to get going on your exploration of the site. Every detail of the original fort and village has been recreated, down to the construction techniques and materials. Even the social structure is historically correct, with ostentatious homes of the rich filled with fine china and French wines while ramshackle working-class abodes have earthen floors and woodstoves for heating. Around 100 costumed interpreters do a wonderful job of playing their parts. Actually, if you ask them, they won't admit they're playing a part at all — a military officer may sternly ask if you're spying for the British, or a carpenter will complain about how much harder it is to get materials in Canada than back in France, while vendors peddle their wares on cobblestone streets.

Traditional menus and costumed servers depict 1700s life at three eateries. **Hotel de la Marine** is where regular folk eat; no meat is served on days of abstinence (Friday and Saturday), and customers eat with only a large spoon. Wealthy citizens (and visitors wanting to live the high life) eat and gossip at **L'Épée Royale**, where fancier European cuisine is served and diners have the privilege of using silver cutlery. If you've arrived at the settlement with limited funds, head to **King's Bakery,** where a loaf of heavy bread and a chunk of cheese cost less than a single appetizer at L'Épée Royale.

Louisbourg. ☎ *902-733-2280. Internet:* www.pc.gc.ca/lhn-nhs/ns/ louisbourg. *Admission: C$13.50 (US$9.60) adults, C$11.50 (US$8.20) seniors, C$6.75 (US$4.80) children. Mid-May–June and Sept.–mid-Oct 9:30 a.m.–5:00 p.m.; July and Aug 9 a.m.–6 p.m.*

Fast Facts: Cape Breton Island

ATMs

ATMs aren't as common as they are elsewhere in Nova Scotia. Most towns have at least one, including Baddeck (Royal Bank) and Ingonish (Scotiabank).

Emergencies

Dial ☎ 911 for all emergencies.

Hospitals

Options include **Cape Breton Regional Hospital**, 1482 George St., Sydney (☎ 902-564-5566), and **Victoria County Memorial Hospital**, Baddeck (☎ 902-295-2112).

Information

Make your first stop over Canso Causeway at the provincial **Visitor Information Centre,** Port Hastings (☎ 902-625-4201). It's open June–Sept daily 9 a.m.–5 p.m. The **Baddeck Welcome Centre** (☎ 902-295-1911) maintains similar hours through the summer season.

Internet Access

You can retrieve your e-mail at **Baddeck Public Library,** 520 Chebucto St., Baddeck (☎ 902-295-2055).

Police

For emergencies, dial ☎ **911;** the non-emergency number in Baddeck is ☎ 902-295-2350.

Post Office

The post office in Baddeck is on Chebucto St.

Weather

Environment Canada maintains a Web site at www.weatheroffice.ec.gc.ca with links to the forecast for major Cape Breton Island towns.

Part IV
New Brunswick

In this part...

New Brunswick is a quiet achiever — though it's the biggest of the Maritimes' provinces, it's the least familiar to outsiders as a tourist destination. Spend any time there and, like me, you will wonder why it's not more popular. Here, I cover New Brunswick's three main cities: Moncton, with its distinct Acadian flavor; historic Saint John, Canada's oldest city; and the stately provincial capital, Fredericton. Follow my lead and you'll be swimming in the warm waters off the Acadian Coast, fishing for lobsters in Northumberland Strait, searching out the "kissing bridges," and marveling at the Fundy tide phenomena.

Chapter 15

Moncton and the Acadian Coast

· ·

In This Chapter

▶ Finding your way to and around Moncton

▶ Deciding where to stay and eat

▶ Hitting the town

▶ Soaking up the sunshine of Shediac

▶ Immersing yourself in Acadian culture

· ·

*M*oncton, which due to its location at the geographic center of the Maritimes serves as a transportation and business hub, began in the 1720s as an Acadian settlement. Today, a third of its 65,000 residents are French-speaking, and it is the only officially bilingual city in Canada. You will see and hear the influence of Acadian culture everywhere you go — all signage is in both English and French, and you'll be greeted in both languages by residents. Moncton University is the largest French university in Canada outside Quebec.

The nearest stretch of coastline is along Northumberland Strait, near the resort town of Shediac, which is renowned for long beaches and warm water. The region north of Shediac is known as the Acadian Coast, for its long association with Acadians who returned to the Maritimes after being expelled from Nova Scotia by the British in 1755. The city itself has two quirky natural attractions: a tidal bore, which moves up the Petitcodiac River twice daily, and a hill with a seemingly magnetic pull.

Getting to Moncton

Moncton is an excellent starting point for a Maritimes vacation. In addition to its location at the geographic center of the region, flights there are often cheaper than they are to Halifax, which is just a three-hour drive to the southeast. You can also roll into the city by rail or bus.

New Brunswick

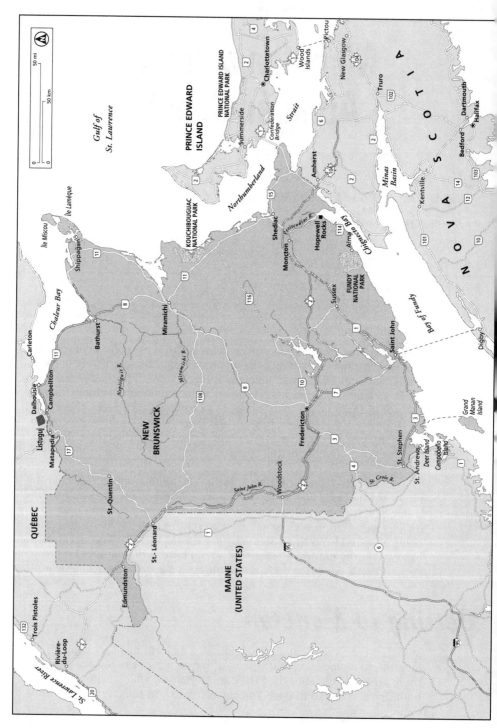

Moncton

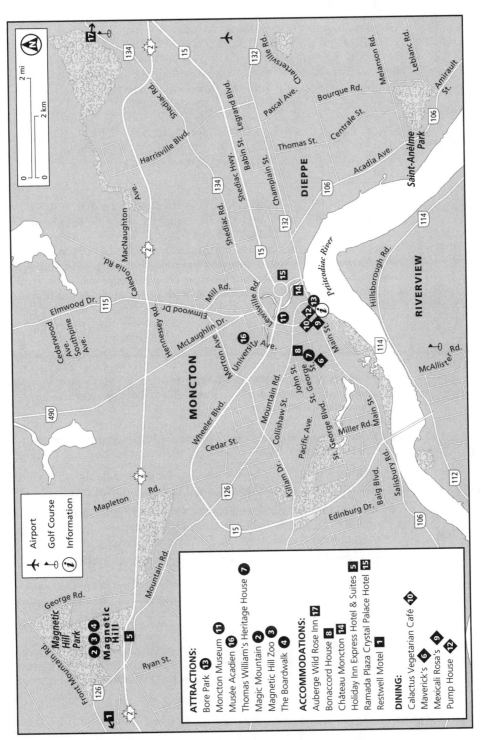

ATTRACTIONS:
Bore Park 13
Moncton Museum 11
Musée Acadien 16
Thomas William's Heritage House 7
Magic Mountain 2
Magnetic Hill Zoo 3
The Boardwalk 4

ACCOMMODATIONS:
Auberge Wild Rose Inn 17
Bonaccord House 8
Château Moncton 14
Holiday Inn Express Hotel & Suites 5
Ramada Plaza Crystal Palace Hotel 15
Restwell Motel 1

DINING:
Calactus Vegetarian Café 10
Maverick's 6
Mexicali Rosa's 9
Pump House 12

By plane

Greater Moncton International Airport (Internet: www.gma.ca) is off Champlain Street (Route 132), about 8km (5 miles) from downtown. It is served by Air Canada, CanJet, and WestJet (see the Appendix for toll-free numbers and Web sites), with direct flights originating in Halifax, Montreal, Ottawa, and Toronto. Fares between airlines are generally competitive, but it pays to check each for specials.

 All passengers departing Greater Moncton International Airport must contribute C$15 (US$10.70) to the Airport Improvement and Reconstruction Fund. Make your payment at a booth inside the main terminal.

Moncton's public bus system, operated by **Codiac Transit** (☎ 506-857-2008), runs between the airport and downtown Monday through Saturday. **Air Cab** (☎ 506-857-2000) is one of many local cab companies. You won't need to call, as taxis always wait out front of the main terminal. The fare to downtown is C$12 (US$8.60). **Avis, Budget, Discount, Hertz,** and **National** have desks at the airport (see the Appendix for the toll-free numbers and Web sites of major car-rental agencies).

By car

If you're driving around the Maritimes, chances are you'll pass through Moncton at some stage of your travels. Here's how to enter the city from a variety of directions:

- ✓ **Route 2 from Nova Scotia:** Take Exit 467 for downtown and Exit 450 for Magnetic Hill.

- ✓ **Route 15 from Shediac and the Confederation Bridge:** Pass under Route 2 and follow the signs right into downtown.

- ✓ **Route 114 from Hopewell Rocks:** Cross the Petitcodiac River via one of two bridges — the first to reach downtown, the second to loop around the western edge of the city to Magnetic Hill.

- ✓ **Route 2 from Fredericton:** Take Exit 466 (Route 128) for downtown or Exit 450 for Magnetic Hill.

By train or bus

VIA Rail's *Ocean* train passes through Moncton on its daily (except Tuesdays) run between Montreal and Halifax. The station is off Main Street, on the southwest side of downtown (☎ 888-842-7245; Internet: www.via.ca).

Acadian Lines (☎ **800-567-5151** or 506-859-5060; Internet: www.acadianbus.com) buses arrive and depart from a centrally located depot at 961 Main Street (corner of Bonaccord Street). The building is open Monday to Friday 7:30 a.m. to 8:30 p.m., weekends 9 a.m. to 8:30 p.m. Some destinations linked to Moncton that are served by Acadian Lines include the Acadian Coast, Prince Edward Island, Halifax, Fredericton, and Saint John.

Getting Around Moncton

Except for morning and evening weekday rush hours, driving around Moncton is easy. The downtown core spreads out around a bend in the Petitcodiac River. Main Street, which runs parallel to the river, is the main thoroughfare. To the east is suburban Dieppe, while south across the Petitcodiac is Riverview. The city's fun sights are 9km (5.6 miles) northwest of downtown at Magnetic Hill, which lies on the north side of Route 2.

Parking

Finding parking in downtown Moncton isn't too difficult if you know where to look. The best bet for a spot is Moncton Market, on Westmorland Street south of Main Street, where parking costs C$1 (US70¢) per hour to a maximum of C$7 (US$5) per day (free on weekends). Metered street parking is C$1 (US70¢) an hour, but it is not monitored after 6 p.m. or on weekends.

Cabbing it

Hailing a cab from the street is possible, but it's easier in front of a major hotel such as the Delta Beausejour, 750 Main Street (at Westmorland Street). From downtown, expect to pay around C$12 (US$8.60) to reach either Magnetic Hill or the airport. Cab companies include:

✔ **Air Cab** (☎ **506-857-2000**)

✔ **Trius Taxi** (☎ **506-858-0000**)

✔ **White Cab** (☎ **506-857-3000**)

Taking transit

Codiac Transit (☎ 506-857-2008) serves Moncton with a bus network running Monday through Saturday 6 a.m. to 7 p.m. (extended to 10:30 p.m. on Thursday and Friday). Buses run east along Main Street to a major interchange at Champlain Place, from where they head out in all directions, including to the airport. Bus fare is C$1.60 (US$1.10) per sector for all passengers aged over 4.

Staying in Moncton

As the hub of the Maritimes, Moncton can meet every lodging need and budget. Accommodations are available all over the city, with the two main concentrations being downtown and out on Route 2 near Magnetic Hill.

As in the rest of the Maritimes, July through August is high season in Moncton — this is when lodging is in most demand and rates are highest.

As always, if you're planning on staying in a chain hotel, check its Web site for discounted weekend and off-season rates.

Auberge Wild Rose Inn
$$–$$$$ **Lakeville**

The Auberge Wild Rose Inn is set on 15 hectares (38 acres) of beautifully landscaped gardens on the north side of Route 2. The inn has a dignified ambience, but is far from formal. The rooms have modern amenities such as cable TV and Internet access, as well as thoughtful touches like bathrobes and plush comforters. Those in the C$135–C$150 (US$96.40 to US$107.10) range, with jetted tubs and either a private entrance or balcony, are the best deal. On the premises is a restaurant that serves full breakfasts (included in the rates) and four-course fixed-price dinners in a French provincial atmosphere.

17 Baseline Rd. (off Route 134) ☎ *888-389-7673 or 506-383-9751. Fax: 506-870-7547. Internet:* www.wildroseinn.com. *Rack rates: C$85–C$250 (US$60.70–US$178.60) double. AE, DC, MC, V.*

Bonaccord House
$ **Downtown**

Centrally located Bonaccord House is halfway between downtown and the university campus. The 100-year-old home has a common lounge area with fireplace, and four guest rooms with private bathrooms.

250 Bonaccord St. (at John St.) ☎ *506-388-1535. Fax: 506-853-7191. Rack rates: C$55 (US$39.30) double. V.*

Château Moncton

$$–$$$$ Downtown

It's difficult to miss this downtown hotel with its bright red roof. The rooms have a vaguely European feel and are comfortably sized. Some have up-close views of the Petitcodiac River, which flows right by the back door. All guests can enjoy views of the river and the tidal bore from Le Galion, a first-floor lounge with a south-facing deck that catches the afternoon sun. A light breakfast is included in the rates, but no other meals are served.

100 Main St. ☎ *506-870-4444. Fax: 506-870-4445. Internet:* www.chateau-moncton.nb.ca. *Parking: free. Rack rates: C$129–C$239 (US$92.10– US$170.70) double.*
AE, MC, V.

Holiday Inn Express Hotel & Suites

$$–$$$ Magnetic Hill

This modern lodging comes exactly as you'd expect from the well-known chain — a handy highway location, an indoor pool, sauna, and hot tub, spacious rooms packed with basic amenities, and a complimentary breakfast bar off the lobby. A few rooms are themed especially for children, and a family-style Italian restaurant is open daily at 4 p.m. From Route 2, take Exit 450; from downtown Moncton, follow Mountain Road northwest for 9km (5.6 miles).

2515 Mountain Rd., Magnetic Hill ☎ *800-595-4656 or 506-384-1050. Fax: 506-859-6070. Internet:* www.hiemoncton.com. *Rack rates: C$110–C$180 (US$78.60–US$128.60) double. AE, DISC, DC, MC, V.*

Ramada Plaza Crystal Palace Hotel

$$$ Dieppe

This modern hotel, which is part of the Crystal Palace Amusement Park complex and a short walk from the largest shopping mall in the Maritimes, is popular with vacationing Maritimers year-round — so don't expect any great off-season bargains. The surroundings are parking-lot plain, but the hotel itself is centered around a tropical atrium with a pool. The business rooms are adequately appointed, while 12 "Fantasy Suites" are devoted to diverse themes ranging from rock 'n' roll to the Victorian era.

499 Paul St., Dieppe ☎ *800-561-7108 or 506-858-8584. Fax: 506-858-5486. Internet:* www.crystalpalacehotel.com. *Parking: free. Rack rates: C$170–C$220 (US$121.40–US$157.10) double. AE, DISC, DC, MC, V.*

Restwell Motel
$–$$ **Magnetic Hill**

This nondescript roadside motel close to Magnetic Hill provides better value than the nearby chain hotel properties. The 12 guest rooms are surprisingly attractive and overlook pleasant grounds with a small outdoor pool and barbecue area. To get there, take Exit 450 (Magnetic Hill) north from Route 2, then go 4km (2.5 miles) west along Ensley Road.

12 McFarlane Rd., Magnetic Hill ☎ *506-857-4884. Internet:* www.restwellmotel.com. *Rack rates: C$70–C$100 (US$50–US$71.40) double. AE, MC, V. May–Oct.*

Dining in Moncton

Moncton bustles with chain restaurants, which can be found along all major arteries and concentrated around Magnetic Hill. For something more original, head to Main Street, the busy thoroughfare that runs through downtown Moncton. You'll find it lined with pubs, cafes, and restaurants, many with tables set out on the sidewalk.

Calactus Vegetarian Cafe
$ **Downtown   VEGETARIAN**

Vegetarian restaurants are scarce in the Maritimes, but this one does everything right. The room is painted in a funky color scheme and has a distinct artsy feel. The food is fresh, sourced mostly from local farms, and presented very simply. Soups and chocolate brownies are highlights.

Corner George and Church sts. ☎ *506-388-4833. Reservations not necessary. Main courses: C$7–C$10 (US$5–US$7.10). V. Daily 10 a.m.–8 p.m.*

Maverick's
$$–$$$$ **Downtown   STEAK**

Finding this lovely restaurant is well worth the effort. Away from the main restaurant strip and a little pricey for the college population, it is mostly the haunt of locals in the know. The winsome menu combines the best cuts of beef with local seafood — lobster-stuffed mushrooms to start, for example, then rib eye with a side of garlic prawns. The wine cellar is one of the best in town, while the weekday lunch buffet gets rave reviews.

40 Weldon St. ☎ *506-855-3346. Reservations recommended. Main courses: C$17–C$29 (US$12.10–US$20.70). AE, MC, V. Mon–Fri 11:30 a.m.–2:00 p.m., daily 5–10 p.m.*

Mexicali Rosa's

$–$$ **Downtown** **MEXICAN**

A central location and inexpensive food make this place hugely popular with the college-aged crowd. The decor is bright and attractive, blending redbrick walls with orange paint and head-high cactuses. The menu is mostly Mexican, with a "California influence" (their words, not mine), and a tip of the hat to Italy (pasta dishes served with tortilla chips). The kitchen prepares a delicious Mexicali dip, as well as combo platters for around C$15 (US$10.70). Save room for the deep-fried ice cream.

683 Main St. ☎ 506-855-7672. Reservations recommended on weekends. Main courses: C$8.50–C$16 (US$6.10–US$11.40). MC, V. Daily 11:30 a.m.–10:30 p.m.

Pump House

$–$$ **Downtown** **PUB FARE**

Locals come to this brewpub for its convivial atmosphere and well-priced food and drink. The menu is mostly pub fare, with the usual westernized Mexican dishes good for sharing and the single-serve pizzas from a wood-fired oven. Explore the pub before settling down at a regular table — choices include booths contained within cut-off wine barrels, a sunny sidewalk deck, and tables in front of the brew tanks.

5 Orange ln. ☎ 506-855-2337. Reservations not necessary. Main courses: C$8–C$17.50 (US$5.70–US$12.50). AE, MC, V. Daily 11 a.m.–10 p.m.

Exploring Moncton

Moncton's location makes it a perfect base from which to explore the region. It's central to the beachy resort town of Shediac, the culturally intriguing Acadian Coast (both covered later in this chapter), and the Bay of Fundy (see Chapter 16, Saint John and the Fundy Coast).

The city itself features two interesting natural phenomena (maybe a little less exciting than the tourist brochures claim, but interesting nevertheless), as well as a mix of museums and cultural pursuits.

Downtown

Bore Park, home to the main visitor information center, is the best starting point for exploring downtown. West of the park, Main Street has been the focus of a rejuvenation program in recent years — redbrick sidewalks, ornate benches, old-fashioned lampposts, and the like.

Bore Park
Downtown

Twice daily, the Petitcodiac River drains dry of water as the huge Fundy tide recedes; then the tide turns, literally, and water rushes up the muddied riverbed, led by a "wave" up to 50 centimeters (20 inches) high. The river takes an hour to fill completely. The phenomenon is interesting rather than exciting, but well worth watching. You can see the bore anywhere along the river (as well as many other places, including Truro in central Nova Scotia), but Bore Park is the most accessible and has interpretive boards describing the how's and why's of the tide. Look for the clock at the park's Main Street entrance to see when the bore is next due.

Bore Park is linked to the **Riverfront Promenade,** a wheelchair-accessible walkway extending east to Hall's Creek and west to the Gunningsville Bridge, a total distance of 2km (1.2 miles). Take the path upstream and you'll quickly leave the city high-rises behind and be rewarded with panoramic views across the river to undeveloped wetlands.

The park is also home to Moncton's main **Visitor Information Centre** (☎ 506-490-5946; June to August daily 9 a.m. to 8 p.m., the rest of the year Monday to Friday 8:30 a.m. to 4:30 p.m.).

Main St. (at Lewis St.). Admission: Free.

Moncton Museum
Downtown

Housed in the former city hall, the Moncton Museum gives a good general overview of local history. Its displays concentrate on the region's first inhabitants, the Mi'kmaq First Nations people, as well as industries such as shipbuilding that have long since disappeared. The museum also hosts several touring exhibits a year.

Beside the museum is the **Free Meeting House,** used by various religious congregations. Dating to 1821, it is Moncton's oldest remaining building.

20 Mountain Rd. (at Belleview St.) ☎ 506-856-4383. Admission: free. July–Aug daily 10 a.m.–8 p.m.; Sept–June Mon–Sat 9 a.m.–4 p.m., Sun 1–5 p.m.

Musée Acadien
North of downtown

Founded by Father Camille Lefebvre in 1886, this museum focuses on historic events and aspects of Acadian life. Over 35,000 pieces are on display, making it Canada's largest collection of Acadian culture. The oldest is an ax dating to 1645, which was recovered from the site of a trading post along the Acadian Coast. Of special historical importance is the original Acadian flag; also of interest are the original register of donated pieces and displays of Acadian art and religious sculptures. The museum is on the sprawling grounds of Moncton University, well worth walking around in summertime for the peaceful student-free setting.

Clément-Cormier Building, Moncton University ☎ *506-858-4088. Admission: C$2 (US$1.40) adults, C$1 (US$.70 cents) children. July–Aug Mon–Fri 10 a.m.–5 p.m., Sat–Sun 1–5 p.m.; Sept–June Tues–Fri 1:00 to 4:30 p.m., Sat–Sun 1–4 p.m.*

Thomas Williams Heritage House
Downtown

Tucked away on a quiet residential street eight blocks from downtown is a grand home built in 1883 for Thomas Williams, treasurer of the Intercolonial Railway. Period furnishings and gardens reflect the Victorian era. The house is worth visiting for afternoon tea alone, which is served on the veranda. It's not particularly traditional (coffee and muffins, by golly!), but the park-like setting and unpretentious ambience offer an enjoyable time out from sightseeing.

103 Park Ave. (at Highfield St.) ☎ *506-856-4383. Admission: free. July–Aug Mon–Fri 9 a.m.–5 p.m., Sat–Sun 1–5 p.m.*

Magnetic Hill

Take Exit 450 from Route 2 or follow Mountain Road northwest from downtown to reach the Magnetic Hill area, a crunch of commercialism that has grown around an optical oddity.

Upon arrival, you must first take care of business and pay C$3 (US$2.10) per vehicle at the toll booth. Continuing a short distance along a rural-type stretch of road, you will be directed by signage to come to a complete stop. Then, when you take your foot off the brake, your vehicle seemingly rolls *uphill*. The illusion is compelling: basically, the entire lower hillside of a larger mountain is tilted at an angle to the surrounding countryside, creating the impression that the top of the hill is lower than the bottom. It has puzzled folks for generations, including early farmers who were forced to pull their wagons "down" the hill to town.

A magnet for commercial attractions

The magnetic appeal of Magnetic Hill extends well beyond one quirky stretch of road. Many local entrepreneurs have set up theme-park style businesses around the bottom (or is that the top?) of the hill. Here are the highlights:

✔ **Magic Mountain** (☎ **506-857-9283**) is the largest waterpark in the Maritimes. Expect wild water rides, a wave pool, kid slides, and an oversized hot tub. Admission is C$21 (US$15) adults, C$15 (US$10.70) children 4 to 11. It's open mid-June through September daily 10 a.m. to 8 p.m.

✔ **Magnetic Hill Zoo** (☎ 506-384-0303) is home to around 90 species of mostly exotic animals. It also has a small petting zoo of farm animals. Admission is C$7 (US$5) adults, C$4 (US$2.90) children. It's open mid-June to September daily 9 a.m. to 8 p.m.

✔ **The Boardwalk** (☎ 506-852-9406) features go-cart rides, batting cages, mini-golf, a golf driving range, and butterflies flying freely in their domed habitats. It's open June through mid-September daily 10 a.m. to 10 p.m.

Nightlife

Despite its outwardly staid appearance, Moncton has a number of happening pubs and clubs. You can find entertainment listings through **Tourism Moncton** (☎ 800-363-4558 or 506-853-3590; Internet: www.gomoncton.com). This organization also publishes a list of annual festivals and events.

Bars and live music

Le Galion, an elegant lounge in the Château Moncton at 100 Main Street (☎ 506-870-4444), is a pleasant place to get away from it all. This bar opens to a deck overlooking the Petitcodiac River.

The stretch of Main Street between Botsford Street and Lutz Street comes alive after dark, with crowds of college-aged drinkers spilling onto sidewalk tables. **Doc Dylan's,** 841 Main Street (☎ 506-382-3627), awaits with one of the best ranges of draught beer in town, and bands on some nights. A half block off Main, the laid-back **Pump House Brewery,** 5 Orange Lane (☎ 506-855-2337), brews a delicious range of beers, which can be enjoyed indoors or out on a small porch with parking lot views. For something a little different, try the Blueberry Ale, which comes complete with floating blueberries. The **Rattlesnake Saloon,** in the back of the Lone Star Café at 644 Main Street (☎ 506-384-7772), is a Texas-themed bar that is generally quieter than those facing the main street.

Kramer's Corner, 702 Main Street (☎ 506-857-9118), is busiest on Saturdays, when bands play. In the same building, the **Cosmopolitan Club,** 700 Main Street (☎ 506-857-9117), with Moncton's largest dance floor, attracts the under-25 crowd. The music is as hip as it gets in New Brunswick, with a crowd to match. Open Wednesday through Sunday only. **Ziggy's,** 730 Main Street (☎ 506-858-8844), is another place that beckons you with live music, stand-up comedy, and pool tables.

The arts

The **Capitol Theatre,** at 811 Main St. (☎ **506-856-4379**), is an old vaudeville house that has been devotedly restored to its 1920s grandeur, right down to gold leaf stenciling and renovated opera boxes. It provides a home for Theatre New Brunswick and the New Brunswick Symphony, as well as a stage for a wide range of touring acts.

Acadian Coast

The French-flavored Acadian Coast stretches north from Moncton along Northumberland Strait. Separating Prince Edward Island from the mainland, this narrow waterway is lined along the New Brunswick side by beaches galore, where shallow water warms quickly under the summer sun. The center of beach culture is Shediac, while the place to get away from the crowds is to the north, in Kouchibouguac National Park.

Expulsion, then a cultural explosion

Most of the French-speaking population in the Maritimes today is Acadian, a culture that differs from that of its better-known francophone cousin, Quebec, not only in history but in dialect, cuisine, and customs.

When the French began colonizing the Maritimes in the 1630s, most settled in the Annapolis Valley, which came to be known as Acadia (and its settlers, hence, as Acadians). In 1713, the British claimed sovereignty to Nova Scotia, and the Acadians were encouraged to swear an oath of allegiance to England. Most refused, and in 1755 the British reacted by confiscating their property and expelling them. With no place to call home, the Acadians scattered — some returned to France, others moved west to Quebec, and some settled in Louisiana (where they became known as Cajuns); a small percentage escaped into the remote forests of what is now New Brunswick and the far corners of Prince Edward Island.

A decade after their expulsion, many who had been exiled came out of hiding and returned to the region. They resettled and built new communities as far from the British as possible. In 1884, at an Acadian convention held in Miscouche, Prince Edward Island, these once-displaced people officially adopted their own flag and anthem ("Ave Maris Stella"), the seeds of a distinct and unique culture that thrives to this day.

New Brunswick, Canada's only bilingual province, has a large Acadian population centered in Moncton and stretching up the coast. Acadian heritage and traditions remain strong, and visitors are offered many opportunities to experience it first-hand through museums, historical re-enactments, and, of course, the food!

Shediac

Beach lovers will feel right at home in laid-back Shediac. The coast here borders Northumberland Strait, a shallow stretch of water between the mainland and Prince Edward Island where the water reaches a pleasant 22°C (72°F) in summer. So even when it's foggy around the Bay of Fundy, or the water along the Nova Scotia coast is too cold for swimming, this beach sparkles in the sun. But don't expect to have the place to yourself through the warmest months of the year — the town gets packed with college students on summer break and retirees who can afford to kick back for a few months.

Getting there

From Moncton, follow Route 15 in a northeasterly direction for 20km (12 miles) to Exit 31B. Head north along Route 11 for a few hundred meters (yards), and then take Exit 1. This road leads past the main information center and Shediac Harbour, then along the long main street. The turn-off to Parlee Beach is through the town to the east.

Staying in Shediac

Many of the accommodations near the water are rented by the week or the month, making them impractical for the casual visitor. If hanging out at the beach for a week fits into your schedule, **Domaine Parlee Beach Chalets & Suites**, a short walk from the water at 642 Main Street (☎ 800-786-5550 or 506-532-5339; Internet: www.domaineparleebeach.ca) is the place to do it. Chalets rent for C$1,100 (US$785.70) per week, cottages are C$1,400 (US$1,000), with rates discounted 50 percent September through June.

Auberge Belcourt Inn
$$ **Shediac**

This stately residence was built in 1911 for a local doctor, and was the home of a former New Brunswick premier for a time. Today, it provides a refined and relaxing retreat from the sun and sand (spend some time on the covered veranda for the full effect). The seven guest rooms are filled with Victorian charm and period antiques. All have en suite bathrooms. The rate includes a full breakfast.

310 Main St. ☎ *506-532-6098. Rack rates: C$85–C$125 (US$60.70–US$89.30) double. AE, DC, MC, V. Feb–Dec.*

Dining in Shediac

Lobsters can be enjoyed at most restaurants along the main street, or buy them live or cooked from **Shediac Lobster Shop,** a seafood market at 261 Main Street (☎ **506-532-4302**). Expect to pay around C$10 (US$7.10) per pound.

Captain Dan's

$–$$ Shediac SEAFOOD

This boisterous restaurant/bar is away from the best beaches but attracts hordes of tanned bods for fresh seafood, cold beer, and live music nightly throughout the summer (Sunday from 2 p.m.). The food is exactly what you'd expect from a seafood house, with prices that may pleasantly surprise you: for example, the substantial three-piece fish-and-chips entree comes with freshly made tartare sauce for under C$9.50 (US$6.80). The lobster bisque and maritime chowder are also both under C$10 (US$7.10). Take a table either downstairs, upstairs on the tiered deck — with views across to the marina — or in the Lobster Hut, where you can order full lobster, chowder, coleslaw, and dessert for just C$25 (US$17.90).

Pointe-du-Chêne Wharf ☎ *506-533-2855. Main courses: C$8–C$17.50 (US$5.70–US$12.50). AE, MC, V. Daily 11 a.m.–10 p.m.*

Cool things to do in and around Shediac

Don't come to Shediac looking for cultural stimulation. This is a place to lie on the beach, swim in the warmest ocean water north of Virginia, and feast on lobster.

The swimming season is short — July and August only. **Parlee Beach,** accessed from the east side of town, is by far the most popular spot for sunning and swimming. A large complex behind the dunes holds change rooms, a concession, and a lively bar/restaurant with a huge deck. Mid-May through mid-September, beach access costs C$5 per vehicle (it's free the rest of the year). Further east, **Ocean View Beach** and **Gagnon Beach** are quieter and just as pleasant.

When you've had enough sun, sand, and salt, consider the following:

> ✔ **Visit Shediac Island.** Lying just offshore, this forested island is laced with nature trails, including a boardwalk over fragile marshland and a walking path through a mixed forest of spruce, fir, and maple. The island is ringed by some appealing beaches. Get there by boat from the **Shediac Island Interpretation Centre,** at the foot of Pleasant Street (☎ 506-532-7000). The hourly shuttle to the island costs just C$3 (US$2.10) per person.

✔ **Go lobster fishing.** With Eric LeBlanc at the helm, **Shediac Bay Cruises** (☎ **888-894-2002** or 506-532-2175; Internet: www.lobstertales.ca) takes visitors on a 2.5-hour fishing trip that culminates in an onboard lobster feast. The cost is C$65 (US$46.40) adults, C$32 (US$22.90) children. Call for times and directions.

✔ **Drive to Cape Jourimain.** The easternmost point of New Brunswick, 80km (50 miles) east of Shediac, is protected by a national wildlife area that is home to 170 species of birds. A system of hiking trails branches out from a large nature center (☎ **506-538-2220**; open mid-June through August daily 8 a.m. to 8 p.m.). One trail ends at the cape itself, where views extend north along the Confederation Bridge.

✔ **Climb on the world's largest lobster.** This 10-meter-long (33-foot) cast-iron crustacean stands guard at the mouth of the Scoudouc River, at the west entrance to town. Kids will love clambering over its massive claws, while adults are usually content with a photograph.

Bouctouche and beyond

Imagine spending the morning exploring a seemingly endless sand dune, followed by an afternoon immersing yourself in Acadian culture in a make-believe island village. You can do this at Bouctouche, a small coastal town 20km (12 miles) north of Shediac along Route 11.

Staying in Bouctouche

Accommodation in Bouctouche is limited. If the recommendation below doesn't sound like your scene, continue north to the Acadian Peninsula, or plan on visiting the region as a day trip from Moncton.

Inn By The Dune
$$ Bouctouche

A small inn catering to guests who value a homey atmosphere over a room full of fancy amenities, this historic property is a five-minute drive from La Dune de Bouctouche, so you can rise early and enjoy the spit before the crowds arrive, or walk to Le Pays de la Sagouine. The six guest rooms are on the small side, but each has an en suite bathroom and television. Rates include breakfast, and German-style dinners are available with advance notice.

House #589, Route 475 ☎ *877-743-8182 or 506-743-8182. Fax: 506-743-8896. Internet:* www.innbythedune.nb.ca. *Rack rates: C$109–C$119 (US$77.90–US$85) double. MC, V.*

Exploring Bouctouche

It may not be much more than a lot of sand, but **La Dune de Bouctouche** is one of the natural highlights of New Brunswick. It is an extremely narrow spit of sand, extending 12km (7.5 miles) into Northumberland Strait. Plant life, such as beach heather, has a stabilizing effect, but tidal action and wind still manage to move the sand around, ever so slowly extending the spit while also making it more narrow. To learn more about the unique ecosystem, stop by **Irving Eco Centre,** along Route 475 at the start of the spit (☎ **506-743-2600;** open July to August 10 a.m. to 8 p.m.). To protect the fragile environment from over use in the busiest months (July and August), only the first 2,000 visitors to arrive each day after 10 a.m. are allowed access. A boardwalk extends for the first 2km (1.2 miles); to continue farther, walk along the high tide mark.

Located on a small island in the Bouctouche River, **Le Pays de la Sagouine,** accessed by footbridge from Acadie Street (☎ **506-561-9188**), is a fun place to immerse yourself in the rich culture of Acadia. Part theme park, part learning experience, it is centered on a fictional Acadian village created by writer Antonine Maillet. Costumed performers put on musical and theatrical presentations throughout the day. Storytelling neighbors, young pranksters, and Acadian bands encouraging singalongs are just a taste of what you can expect. Admission is C$13 (US$9.30) adults, C$12 (US$8.60) seniors, C$7 (US$5) children. Nightly (except Monday) there's a dinner theater for C$42 (US$30).

Kouchibouguac National Park

Although the entire Acadian Coast offers similar coastal scenery, the section between Bouctouche and Miramichi is particularly appealing because it is protected as a national park and therefore remains in its natural state. Kouchibouguac (pronounced Koo-she-boo-gwack), meaning "river of long tides," is dominated by a ribbon of barrier islands composed entirely of sand. Extending for 25km (15.5 miles), these islands have formed lagoons that attract a wide variety of bird life (over 200 bird species have been recorded in the park). The rest of the park is a mix of forest, slow-flowing rivers, peat bogs, and marshland. Deer, moose, black bears, and beavers are all resident, while seals are often spotted in the surrounding waters.

To experience the best of Kouchibouguac, you will want to explore beyond the paved roads. Here's how:

> ✔ **Hiking.** This isn't the place for grueling all-day hikes. Instead, visitors have a choice of short trails, many lined with interpretive panels describing the surroundings. If you take just one trail, make it **Kelly's Beach Boardwalk,** which crosses a lagoon to sand dunes and open water. Don't be perturbed by the name of the Bog Trail — a boardwalk leads through the marshland.

✔ **Biking.** You'll find a 60km (37-mile) system of crushed-gravel bike trails. The main loop — taking in the river, the forested interior, and the coast — is 23km (14.3 miles). Complete the circuit in two hours, or spend all day stopping at its points of interest. Bikes can be rented at **Ryan's Rental Centre,** based at Ryan's day-use area (☎ 506-876-8918), for C$6 (US$4.30) per hour or C$30 (US$21.40) per day.

✔ **Canoeing.** If you are comfortable out on the water on your own, canoes can be rented from Ryan's day-use area (see above), which is beside the calm waters of the Kouchibouguac River. Just as enjoyable is joining park staff on a three-hour guided paddle in a large voyageur canoe, which seats up to nine people. The cost is C$30 (US$21.40) adults, C$15 (US$10.70) children. Reserve a ticket at the visitor center (☎ 506-876-2443).

✔ **Swimming.** The water on the ocean side of dunes at Kelly's Beach is supervised through summer. Although the water temperature is comfortable, it's even warmer to the south at Callender's Beach along a tidal lagoon.

Get to the park by taking Exit 75 from Route 11, 35km (21.7 miles) north of Bouctouche. Just inside the park boundary is the **Visitor Reception Centre** (☎ 506-876-2443), holding displays on the park ecosystem, a small theater, a gift shop, and an information desk. This is also the place to pick up a park **day pass,** which costs C$5 (US$3.60) adults, C$4.25 (US$3) seniors, C$2.50 (US$1.80) youths, to a maximum of C$12.50 (US$8.90) per vehicle. The center is open mid-May through mid-October daily 9 a.m. to 5 p.m., with extended hours in July and August daily 8 a.m. to 8 p.m. Access to the park is possible year-round, but everything closes down in mid-October, and the entry fee isn't collected out of season.

Check the bulletin board at the visitor center for a schedule of events, which may include interpretive hikes, guided canoe outings, campfire talks, slide presentations, and a puppet theater.

Acadian Peninsula

Extending northeast from Miramichi along Baie des Chaleurs, the Acadian peninsula is a hotbed of Acadian culture. You can experience this unique culture by exploring local museums, sampling the cuisine, or simply taking a drive through the many small villages where traditions run deep.

At Miramichi, you are presented with two options for onward travel: either cut south through the heartland of New Brunswick to Fredericton, or follow Route 11 around the Acadian Peninsula, which is dotted with farms and fishing villages.

Staying on the Acadian Peninsula

Use Miramichi as a base for a day-trip around the Acadian Peninsula, or push on and spend the night at the recommended accommodations in Caraquet (the region's largest town) or Miscou Centre.

Governor's Mansion Inn

$–$$ **Miramichi (Nelson)**

The lovely location and budget-priced rooms alone would make this lodging a good choice. But best of all is the historic atmosphere — pull up a chair on the covered veranda, look across to the river, and imagine yourself transported back in time. Formerly the home of a provincial lieutenant governor, this stately 1860 mansion has been given a bright yellow coat of paint on the outside and undergone a rigorous restoration inside. Rooms are divided between the main home and the adjacent Beaubear Manor. Antiques and convivial hosts make up for slightly threadbare furnishings. Some rooms share bathrooms (the Eagles Eyrie, with water views, is the pick of these), but at just C$85 (U$60.70) for the most expensive (the Lord Beaverbrook Room, which comes complete with a four-piece bath and fireplace), you can afford to splurge. Within sight of the inn is Beaubears Island; tours depart the nearby dock Tuesday and Thursday at 6:30 p.m. and Sunday at 1:30 p.m.

62 St. Patrick's Dr. ☎ *877-647-2642 or 506-622-3036. Fax: 506-622-3035. Internet:* www.governorsmansion.ca. *Rack rates: C$60–C$85 (US$42.90–US$60.70) double. AE, MC, V.*

Hotel Paulin

$$–$$$ **Caraquet**

Modern development has encroached on the water views at this 1891 hotel, but it still offers a level of intimacy you just can't get at a similarly priced motel. Operated for three generations by the same family, the Paulin has a Christmasy red and green exterior and a cheerful interior to match. The eight guest rooms are nothing fancy, but each has a comfortable bed and an en suite bathroom.

143 St-Pierre Blvd., Caraquet ☎ *866-727-9981 or 506-727-9981. Internet:* www.hotelpaulin.com. *Rack rates: C$115–C$160 (US$82.10–US$114.30) double. MC, V.*

Plage Miscou Chalets
$ **Miscou Centre**

Situated on Miscou Island, which is linked to the mainland by a bridge, this complex is part cottages, part campground, and all fun. It lies behind a long sandy beach, with water warm enough for swimming. There are plenty of other things to keep everyone busy — fishing trips, canoeing (rentals available), volleyball, mini-golf, horseshoes, and more. The six cabins each have two bedrooms and a fully equipped kitchen, making them excellent value.

22 Alphonse Lane ☎ *506-344-1015. Fax: 506-344-7444. Rack rates: C$73 (US$52.10) double. MC, V. Mid-June–mid-Sept.*

Rodd Miramichi River
$$–$$$ **Miramichi (Chatham)**

Located right on the Miramichi River, this modern motel has a distinctive lodge feeling to its rooms, which are decorated in earthy tones and have fish prints on the walls. The specialty at the in-house Angler's Reel Restaurant is salmon, while the adjacent lounge spreads onto a riverside deck. You'll want to request a room with a river view when booking.

1809 Water St., Chatham ☎ *800-565-7633 or 506-773-3111. Fax: 506-773-3110. Internet:* www.rodd-hotels.ca. *Rack rates: C$145–C$190 (US$103.60–US$135.70) double. AE, DC, MC, V.*

Dining on the Acadian Peninsula

Most villages have a choice of cafes or restaurants, and you may consider taking a chance at any of them. I recommend two very different restaurants that both showcase the charm of the region in their own unique ways. As alternatives, the Hotel Paulin or Rodd Miramichi River, both recommended above as places to stay, have dining rooms worthy of a visit.

La Fine Grobe Sur Mer
$$–$$$ **Nigadoo   FRENCH**

Translating to "fine grub by the sea," this fine restaurant provides some of the best cooking in New Brunswick, with spectacular views of Baie des Chaleurs. The seasonal menu offers a great variety of traditional French dishes, relying on local seafood and produce from the garden to create a memorable meal. The chateaubriand and herb-crusted leg of lamb are both noteworthy. For dessert, the cheese plate will tempt you, but seriously, can you choose anything but the chocolate cake?

289 Main St., Nigadoo (north of Bathurst) ☎ *506-783-3138. Main courses: C$14–C$23 (US$10–US$16.40). AE, DC, MC, V. Daily 5–9 p.m.*

Old Town Diner
$ Miramichi (Chatham)   DINER

Chances are you'll be the only out-of-towner at this small-town, super-friendly diner on the south side of the Miramichi River in Chatham. The menu is exactly what you might expect — breakfast served all day, deep-fried seafood, and a couple of token salads. A full cooked breakfast costs just C$5 (US$3.60), including bottomless coffee.

1724 Water St., Chatham ☎ 506-773-7817. Main courses: C$6–C$9.50 (US$4.30–US$6.80). Daily 7 a.m.–7 p.m.

Exploring the Acadian Peninsula

To fully appreciate the peninsula's natural and cultural appeal, plan on spending at least a day in the region. Visiting the two top Acadian attractions detailed below alone will fill the better part of a day.

Route 11 parallels the Gulf of St. Lawrence all the way from Miramichi to Bathurst, a total distance of 170km (106 miles). From Bathurst, it's a short hop back across the peninsula to Miramichi.

Village Historique Acadien
Route 11 west of Caraquet

Definitely a highlight of the Acadian Coast, this park re-creates Acadian life between 1770 and 1890. The 40 restored buildings include simple homes, a chapel, a farmyard, a schoolhouse, various workshops, a lobster hatchery, and a tavern. The village is brought to life by costumed staff who go about their daily business — tending to their animals, overseeing auctions, spreading gossip, attending marriages, and more. Visitors can also watch as artists ply their trade, or dine on Acadian food in one of two restaurants.

Route 11 between Caraquet and Grand-Anse ☎ 506-726-2600. Admission: C$14 (US$10) adults, C$12 (US$8.60) seniors, C$9 (US$6.40) children. June to early Sept daily 10 a.m.–6 p.m.

Acadian Museum
Caraquet

Founded by Acadians fleeing the British in 1755, the village of Caraquet has evolved into the unofficial center of the peninsula's French-speaking community. This small museum does a wonderful job of representing the town and its residents, many of whom have donated items to display. It's also worth taking in the water view from the second-floor balcony.

15 St-Pierre Blvd., Caraquet ☎ 506-726-2682. Admission: C$3 (US$2.10) adults, C$1 (US70¢) children. Open: June–mid-Sept Mon–Sat 10 a.m.–6 p.m., Sun 1–6 p.m.

Newcastle

Now incorporated as part of Miramichi, this bustling river town is more attractive than at first glance. Make your way down to Ritchie Wharf (Leddon Street) and let the children go wild on the Maritime-themed playground; take lunch at one of the cafes; and learn more about the region at the local information center.

In the heart of downtown is a memorial to Lord Beaverbrook (1879–1964), a British press baron who spent his childhood in west of the memorial (☎ 506-624-5474). It's open to the public mid-June to August Monday to Friday 9 a.m. to 5 p.m. Admission is free.

Take King George Highway south from Route 8 after it crosses the Miramichi River.

Fast Facts: Moncton

ATMs

Most banks have ATMs, including the Bank of Montreal, at 633 Main St., CIBC; at Church and Main sts; and Scotiabank; at 780 Main St.

Emergencies

Dial ☎ **911** for all emergencies.

Hospital

Moncton Hospital is at 135 MacBeath Ave. (☎ **506-857-4150**).

Information

Tourism Moncton (☎ **800-363-4558** or 506-853-3590; Internet: www.gomoncton. com) operates an information center at Bore Park, Main St. It's open June–Aug. daily 9 a.m.–8 p.m., the rest of the year Mon–Fri 8:30 a.m.–4:30 p.m.

Internet Access

Moncton Public Library, 644 Main St. (☎ **506-869-6000**), has free public Internet access.

Pharmacy

Drugstore Pharmacy is at 165 Main St. (☎ **506-857-7240**).

Police

For emergencies, dial ☎ **911**. For other police matters, call ☎ **506-857-2400**.

Post Office

The main post office is at 281 St. George St. (at Highfield St.).

Restrooms

The main Visitor Information Centre, in Bore Park, has public restrooms.

Taxis

Reliable cab companies include **Trius Taxi** (☎ **506-858-0000**) and **White Cab** (☎ **506-857-3000**).

Transit Info

Public buses are operated by **Codiac Transit** (☎ **506-857-2008**) daily except Sunday.

Weather

For the local weather forecast, call **Environment Canada** at ☎ **506-851-6610** or check the Web site www.weather office.ec.gc.ca.

Chapter 16

Saint John and the Fundy Coast

● ●

In This Chapter

▶ Getting to Saint John and finding your way around the city

▶ Deciding where to stay and dine

▶ Seeing the sights and spending a night on the town

▶ Visiting St. Andrews and exploring Fundy National Park

● ●

*S*aint John is a gritty industrial city with a striking waterfront
enhanced by the Harbour Passage, a municipal beautification project. With a population of 75,000, it is New Brunswick's largest city, and
offers all the benefits of big-city life — like upscale accommodations
and creative dining — at affordable small-town prices.

Established in 1785 by Loyalists (American colonists who wished to
remain loyal to the British crown after the birth of the United States),
Saint John was Canada's first incorporated city, prospering as a port
and shipbuilding center. In 1877, a fire destroyed almost the entire
downtown, which was then rebuilt with fine brick and stone buildings,
most of which remain today.

Saint John is always spelled out. It is never abbreviated to "St. John,"
thereby avoiding confusion with St. John's, Newfoundland.

Saint John may be the biggest name on the map, but there are plenty of
reasons to explore the rest of the Fundy Coast. Take Route 1 west from
Saint John to reach St. Andrews, a one-time retreat for the wealthy that
now welcomes everyone. Up the Bay of Fundy from Saint John, a rugged
section of the coast is protected by Fundy National Park. Beyond the
park is Hopewell Rocks, intriguing towers of sandstone that have become
separated from the mainland.

Saint John

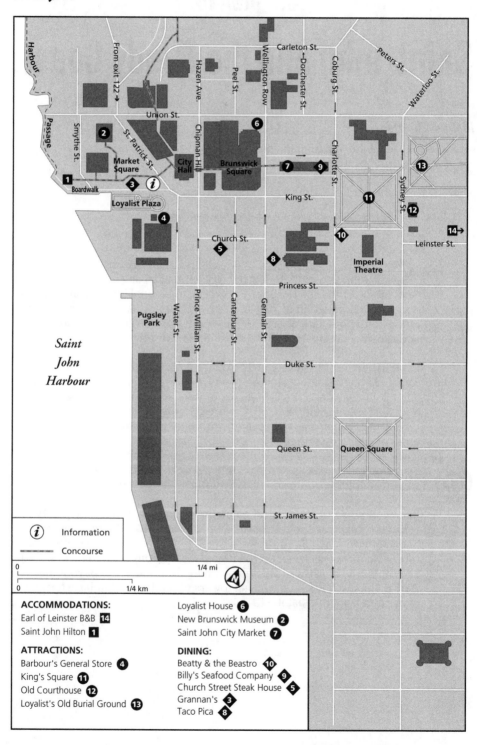

ACCOMMODATIONS:
Earl of Leinster B&B **14**
Saint John Hilton **1**

ATTRACTIONS:
Barbour's General Store **4**
King's Square **11**
Old Courthouse **12**
Loyalist's Old Burial Ground **13**

Loyalist House **6**
New Brunswick Museum **2**
Saint John City Market **7**

DINING:
Beatty & the Beastro **10**
Billy's Seafood Company **9**
Church Street Steak House **5**
Grannan's **3**
Taco Pica **8**

Getting to Saint John

You'll probably arrive in Saint John by road, but options include flying in or coming from Nova Scotia by ferry.

By plane

Saint John Airport (Internet: www.saintjohnairport.com) is along Route 111 toward St. Martins, 16km (10 miles) east of downtown. Air Canada and its regional carriers fly into Saint John from Halifax, Toronto, and Montreal. Rental-car companies with desks at the airport are Avis, Budget, Hertz, and National.

The least expensive way to travel between the airport and downtown is on a **Saint John Transit** bus (☎ 506-658-4700). The service costs C$1.75 (US$1.25), exact change only. A more expensive option is the airport shuttle operated by **Diamond Taxi** (☎ 506-648-0666). The drivers pick up at major downtown hotels around 90 minutes before flight departures. Cost for the trip is C$10 (US$7.10). The cab fare between the airport and downtown is C$25 (US$17.90) for the first person, C$2 (US$1.40) for each additional person.

All passengers departing Saint John Airport are required to pay a **Passenger Facility Charge** of C$15 (US$10.70). The fee is payable by cash, credit card, or debit card at a booth near the entrance to the departure lounge.

By car

The most direct route between Moncton and Saint John is Route 1, a distance of 155km (96 miles) that should take you about 90 minutes to drive. A more scenic option is Route 114 along the Bay of Fundy, which passes two of New Brunswick's most appealing natural attractions — Hopewell Rocks and Fundy National Park. Taking this route doubles the driving time.

The provincial capital of New Brunswick, Fredericton, is 105km (65 miles) north of Saint John via Route 7. If you are willing to do a longer course with scenic appeal, take Route 102 via Gagetown.

By ferry

If you're planning on visiting both southwestern Nova Scotia and New Brunswick, it makes sense to take advantage of the ferry service between Digby and Saint John. **Bay Ferries** (☎ 888-249-7245 or 902-245-2116; Internet: www.nfl-bay.com) runs this passage year-round, up to three times daily in each direction. The fare is C$20 to C$35 (US$14.30 to US$25) for adults, C$17.50 to C$25 (US$12.50 to US$17.90) for seniors, C$10 to C$15 (US$7.10 to US$10.70) for children 5 to 17, and C$70 to C$75 (US$50 to US$53.60) for vehicles under 6.4 meters (21 feet) long. Reservations for the two- to three-hour trip are highly recommended in summer.

Getting Around Saint John

Saint John is very spread out, with downtown (and the best attractions) centered on a peninsula at the mouth of the Saint John River. Exit 122 from Route 1 leads right into the heart of downtown. Immediately west, Route 1 crosses the Saint John River via the Harbour Bridge (C25¢ toll) and heads out toward Irving Nature Park.

Ferries from Digby arrive in Saint John West, from where signage directs you to Exit 120 of Route 1. From this point, head east over the Harbour Bridge to downtown.

Note that many streets of Saint John West have the same names as those downtown. To avoid confusion, they are designated as "West," as in Church Street West.

Parking

To park downtown, take Exit 122 from Route 1 and then turn down the first street to the right to have a choice of outside parking for C$1 (US70¢) per hour, or slightly more for underground parking.

Grabbing a cab

You can hail a cab anywhere downtown, but if you're having trouble, walk through the Market Square and wait for one at the Saint John Hilton. Local companies include:

- ✔ **Century Taxi** (☎ 506-696-6969)
- ✔ **Coastal Taxi** (☎ 506-635-1144)
- ✔ **Diamond Taxi** (☎ 506-648-8888)
- ✔ **Royal Taxi** (☎ 506-652-5050)

Taking transit

Saint John Transit (☎ **506-658-4700**) is a highly efficient bus system that operates along 30 routes to all corners of the city, including out to the airport. Many buses run at 10-minute intervals from the main downtown pick-up point at King's Square. The fare is C$1.75 (US$1.25), exact change only.

Staying in Saint John

Saint John has a number of historic inns, the best of which are within walking distance of downtown. Concentrations of mid-priced chain motels lie along Route 1 east and west of the city.

A string of cheap motels is spread along Manawagonish Road, west of downtown. Among the least expensive is the **Anchor Light Motel,** at 1989 Manawagonish Road (☎ **506-674-9972**), which charges just C$42 (US$30) double. Or dig deeper for a room with a view across the Bay of Fundy at the **Island View Motel,** 1726 Manawagonish Road. (☎ **888-674-6717** or 506-672-1381), C$65 (US$46.40) double. Both these places are in the $ price category.

Coastal Inn Saint John
$$ **Downtown**

Across Route 1 from the heart of downtown, the Coastal Inn is a good choice for families — more appropriate for children than a bed-and-breakfast, within walking distance of most attractions, and free for children under 18. The property itself is large and blockish, but that is of little consequence if you're looking *outward* from a harbor-view room. Amenities include an indoor pool and a sauna, while a downstairs cafe and a top-floor restaurant are other worthy options. Coming from the west, take Exit 121 and turn right onto Chelsey Drive, then right again onto Main Street. From the east, take Exit 123 and follow Paradise Row onto Main.

10 Portland St. (at Main St.) ☎ *800-943-0033 or 506-657-7320. Fax: 506-693-1146. Internet:* www.coastalinns.com. *Rack rates: C$95–C$125 (US$67.90–US$89.30) double. AE, DC, MC, V.*

Earl of Leinster B&B

$–$$ Downtown

Inside this redbrick downtown building, you will find seven inviting guest rooms, each with a smallish en suite bathroom, phone, fridge, and television. Those out back in a converted coach house have kitchenettes. A cooked breakfast, as well as access to a games room and laundry, is included in the very reasonable rates.

96 Leinster St. ☎ **506-652-3275**. *Parking: on the street. Rack rates: C$65–C$95 (US$46.40–US$67.90) double. AE, DC, MC, V.*

Homeport Historic Bed & Breakfast

$$–$$$ West of downtown

This large and luxurious bed-and-breakfast lies on a high ridge overlooking the harbor and is within walking distance of downtown via the Harbour Passage promenade. The creation of the inn, a subtle amalgamation of two side-by-side mansions built for shipbuilding brothers, was a labor of love for owners Ralph and Karen Holyoke. The inn is full of appropriate antiques sourced by Ralph throughout the Maritimes; big windows, high ceilings, and ornate furnishings add to the grandeur. The ten guest rooms are all very different, but each is outfitted with a large bathroom. The Veranda Room (C$125/US$89.30) is my favorite. The centerpiece of this unit is an 1850s walnut bed, while the adjacent sitting area has views across to Saint John Harbour. The parlor is a popular place to relax, especially in the afternoon when refreshments are laid out. A big breakfast will get you going each morning.

60–80 Douglas Ave. ☎ **888-678-7678** *or 506-672-7255. Fax: 506-672-7250. Internet:* www.homeport.nb.ca. *Rack rates: C$90–C$165 (US$64.30–US$117.90) double. AE, MC, V.*

Inn on the Cove & Day Spa

$$$ Irving Nature Park

This sprawling property well away from the bustle of the city has 11 stylish guest rooms, all with stunning ocean views and some with private balconies. Centered on a 1907 mansion that has been thoroughly modernized, the place is sophisticated, but has a wonderfully carefree feeling about it. The perfect way to follow up a walk in the adjacent Irving Nature Park (which was once part of the estate) is with time spent in the inn's day spa. Ross and Willa Mavis, the hosts, are extremely welcoming, juggling the needs of their guests with the taping of a local cooking show in their kitchen. A gourmet breakfast is included in the rates, while dinner, available three nights a week, revolves around seafood and seasonal produce.

1371 Sand Cove Rd. (take Exit 119 from Route 1) ☎ **877-257-8080** *or 506-672-7799. Fax: 506-635-5455. Internet:* www.innonthecove.com. *Rack rates: C$165–C$195 (US$117.90–US$139.30) double. MC, V.*

Saint John Hilton
$$$–$$$$ **Downtown**

Located right on the water and linked by a covered walkway to Market Square, this hotel has the best location of any downtown Saint John accommodation. The 197 rooms are spacious and comfortable, and most have water views. You won't find any surprises on the menu at the Turn of the Tide Restaurant, but it offers good solid contemporary Canadian cooking, while the Brigantine Lounge is one of the best places in town to enjoy a quiet drink. Both the restaurant and lounge have water views. The hotel also has a swimming pool and exercise room.

1 Market Square ☎ *800-561-8282 or 506-693-8484. Fax: 506-657-6610. Internet:* www.hilton.com. *Parking: C$14 (US$10) weekdays, free on weekends. Rack rates: C$210–C$280 (US$150–US$200) double. AE, DC, DISC, MC, V.*

Dining in Saint John

In Saint John, many of the better restaurants are tucked away and easy to overlook. One place you can't miss is Market Square, down on the waterfront, where a string of restaurants take full advantage of summer warmth by setting out tables along a cobbled plaza.

Beatty & the Beastro
$$–$$$ **Downtown** **EUROPEAN**

This restaurant overlooks King's Square from beside the historic Imperial Theatre. Lunch is extremely popular — mussels steamed open in white wine, "Beast of the Day" soup, Caesar salad, and a curried chicken wrap are all good. In the evening, the curry of the day is a local favorite (as is the accompanying freshly made mango chutney), but my last visit coincided with a delivery of spring lamb from a local farm, so choosing anything else wasn't even an issue.

60 Charlotte St. ☎ *506-652-3888. Reservations recommended. Main courses: C$21–C$25 (US$15–US$17.90). AE, DC, MC, V. Mon–Fri 11:30 a.m.–3:00 p.m. and 5–9 p.m., Sat 5–10 p.m.*

Billy's Seafood Company
$$–$$$$ **Downtown   SEAFOOD**

Tucked away at the back of the Saint John City Market, Billy's enjoys a stellar reputation for fresher-than-fresh seafood, which can also be bought market-style at the front counter. The restaurant itself is a sleek, old-fashioned room with comfortable booths, dim lighting, and lots of dark polished wood. You could start by sharing steamed mussels and lightly battered calamari, then move on to cedar plank salmon, broiled halibut, or a full lobster. The wine list complements the food well but is a bit on the expensive side. A lunchtime visit would be a good time to try the lobster roll, packed with a combination of the delicious meat and mayonnaise.

49 Charlotte St. (Old Market Square) ☎ *506-672-3474. Reservations recommended. Main courses: C$17–C$26 (US$5.70–US$12.10). AE, DC, MC, V. Mon–Thurs 11 a.m.–10 p.m., Fri–Sat 11 a.m.–11 p.m.*

Church Street Steak House
$$–$$$$ **Downtown   STEAK**

Saint John is a long way from the rangelands of Alberta, but this popular steakhouse does an excellent job of sourcing the best cuts of beef and cooking them exactly as you ordered them. The appetizers are mostly seafood-oriented, a perfect complement to a beef entree. The setting is an historic redbrick building which remains virtually unchanged in appearance since it was built following the 1877 fire that destroyed most of downtown.

10 Church St. ☎ *506-672-3463. Reservations recommended. Main courses: C$14–C$30 (US$10–US$21.40). AE, MC, V. Mon–Sat 11:30 a.m.–midnight, Sun 4 p.m. to midnight.*

Grannan's
$$–$$$$ **Downtown   SEAFOOD**

My favorite of the many Market Square restaurants. Grannan's has lots of outdoor seating, but the interior is also appealing, with a stylish mix of Maritime-themed artifacts, including brass ship lamps and an antique diving suit. A blackboard menu is the place to search out seasonal seafood, but you won't go wrong with a pick from the Captain's Choices section of the regular menu (my blackened salmon was delicious). For a splurge, consider the Seafood Brochette, a lobster tail with skewered scallops and shrimp sautéed at your table.

Market Square ☎ *506-634-1555. Reservations recommended for dinner. Main courses: C$17–C$34 (US$12.10–US$24.30). AE, DC, MC, V. Mon–Sat 11:30 a.m.–11:00 p.m., Sun noon–10 p.m.*

Taco Pica

$–$$ Downtown   GUATEMALAN/MEXICAN

Look no farther than Taco Pica for a unique and inexpensive meal in cheerful surroundings. You'll be impressed by the flavor of such dishes as *pepian*, a spicy beef stew, and *chimichanga*, a minty flavored pork tortilla. Seafood offerings include a Spanish-style *paella* and a garlic shrimp dish. The dessert menu goes beyond the confines of Central America to include Pavlova, an Australian meringue cake topped with cream and fruit.

96 Germain St. ☎ 506-633-8492. Reservations recommended. Main courses: C$8–C$17 (US$5.70–US$12.10). AE, DC, MC, V. Mon–Sat 10 a.m.–10 p.m.

Exploring Saint John

Now that you've chosen somewhere to stay and have an idea of dining options, it's on to the real reason you will want to spend time in Saint John — to soak up the sights, sounds, and smells of a port city that has changed little in appearance in over 100 years.

All of the attractions discussed in this section (except Carleton Martello Tower) are within walking distance of each other. Pick up the Three Historic Walking Tours brochure (free) from the information center to learn more about the most notable buildings as you explore downtown.

Barbour's General Store

Downtown

This 19th-century shop is preserved as a museum, its shelves stocked with merchandise sold a century ago, like candy, tobacco, and smoked fish. Some items are for sale, including *dulse*, an edible seaweed snack.

Market Square ☎ 506-658-2939. Admission: free. Mid-June–early Sept daily 9 a.m.–6 p.m.

Walking the walk

Harbour Passage, along Saint John's downtown foreshore, is an ambitious project that will eventually see the entire waterfront area linked by pathways and dotted with green space, benches, and interpretive panels that extend all the way to Reversing Falls. At this stage, the paved trail extends to Chesley Drive. Along the way it passes by the Gathering Garden, planted with species used by natives; the site of a 1600s Acadian fort; and a power substation with audio push-button stations to tell you what goes on behind the wires.

Carleton Martello Tower
Saint John West

Built in 1812 to protect the then-fledgling Loyalist city of Saint John from attack, the tower is similar in design to circular towers built along the British coastline during the Napoleonic Wars. Over the years this solid stone structure has also been used for ammunition storage, as a soldiers' barracks, as a detention center for deserters, and as an anti-aircraft position. Today, protected as a National Historic Site, it's all tourist attraction.

545 Whipple Dr. (at Fundy Dr.; take Exit 120 from Route 1) ☎ **506-636-4011**. *Admission: C$3.50 (US$2.50) adults, C$3 (US$2.10) seniors, C$1.75 (US$1.25) children. June–Sept daily 10 a.m.–6 p.m.*

Fort Howe Lookout
North of Downtown

The best place to get a feel for the layout of Saint John is Fort Howe Lookout, a two-minute drive north of downtown, off Main Street. The Loyalists established a fort here in 1778 to defend their new settlement against attack by Americans. Looking out to the mouth of the harbor, which affords unobstructed views of incoming vessels, it's clear why they chose this lofty location.

Magazine St. off Main St.

King's Square
Downtown

From the waterfront, it's a steep walk up King Street to reach King's Square, which was laid out in the shape of a Union Jack to reflect the loyalty to the British monarchy held by those who escaped the American Revolution to settle in Saint John. The most intriguing of numerous monuments is a lump of melted metal salvaged from a hardware store destroyed by the fire that raced through downtown in 1877.

Across Sydney Street from King's Square are a couple of other historic diversions. Inside the 1829 **Old Courthouse,** at King and Sydney streets, is a massive spiral staircase built of unsupported stones. Across King Street is the **Loyalist's Old Burial Ground,** the final resting place of the city's founding fathers.

At King and Charlotte streets.

Loyalist House
Downtown

Dating to 1810, this Georgian-style Loyalist House is Saint John's oldest building and well worth visiting. Lived in by six generations of the same family, it is furnished with authentic Georgian antiques and has a total of eight fireplaces, an indication of the wealth of its original owner, David Daniel Merritt.

120 Union St. ☎ 506-652-3590. Admission: C$3 (US$2.10) adults. June Mon–Fri 10 a.m.–5 p.m., July–early Sept daily 9 a.m.–5 p.m.

New Brunswick Museum
Downtown

One of the largest museums in the Maritimes, this modern facility is part of the Market Square complex, down on the harborfront. Every gallery has something different and interesting: the Shipbuilding Gallery catalog the city's first industry, the Hall of Great Whales is dominated by a full-size right whale skeleton, the Birds of New Brunswick Gallery features displays describing some of the province's 370 recorded species, and the Discovery Gallery is filled with kid-friendly learning experiences.

Market Square ☎ 506-643-2300. Admission: C$6 (US$4.30) adults, C$4.75 (US$3.40) seniors, C$3.25 (US$2.30) children. Mon–Fri 9 a.m.–5 p.m. (Thurs until 9 p.m.), Sat–Sun noon–5 p.m.

Saint John City Market
Downtown

The 1876 City Market, the oldest in Canada, occupies a full block between Charlotte and Germain streets. The handsome building was designed by local shipbuilders, whose influence is obvious when you look up at the inverted-keel ceiling. The collection of stalls is varied — an old-fashioned butcher, fruit produce, fresh seafood, and touristy knickknacks. Instead of eating at the unappealing food court along one side, choose some cheeses from the dairy bar, some smoked salmon and a cooked lobster from the seafood counter, and some crusty rolls from the bakery, and head out to Irving Nature Park for a picnic lunch.

47 Charlotte St. ☎ 506-658-2820. Admission: free. Mon–Thurs 7:30 a.m.–6:00 p.m., Fri 7:30 a.m.–7:00 p.m., Sat 10 a.m.–5 p.m.

Other cool things to see and do

Once you've finished exploring downtown, expand your horizons and consider the following attractions.

Reversing Falls

Another Fundy phenomenon, this is Saint John's most hyped natural attraction. As the massive Fundy tide rises, the flow of the Saint John River reverses as ocean water pushes upstream. When the tide recedes, the water flows in the opposite direction. The "falls" are a series of rock ledges at the base of a narrow gorge, which form rapids where the water tumbles in each direction either side of low tide. You really need to visit at both high and low tides to appreciate the difference in water level — 4.4 meters (14.5 feet).

To get to Reversing Falls from downtown, cross Route 1 via Main Street and take Chesley Drive off to the left. You can also get there by taking Exit 119 from Route 1 and turning right onto Bridge Road.

Overlooking the gorge is the **Reversing Falls Visitor Centre,** 200 Bridge Rd. (☎ **506-658-2937**), which has tide tables and shows a film about the falls. Entry to the adjacent observation deck is C$2 (US$1.40). The center is open mid-May through early October, daily 8 a.m. to 7 p.m. Or cross to **Fallsview Park,** on the east side of the gorge. Access is via Douglas Avenue.

Only when the tide reaches a certain level and the current slows are boats able to safely navigate the gorge. The only people who avoid this "slack" tide are folks at **F1 Reversing Falls Jet Boat Tours** (☎ **506-634-8987**), who wait until the rapids are at their roughest to take you out for an exhilarating ride through the churning water. The cost is C$32 (US$22.90) adults, C$25 (US$17.90) children. The departure point is Fallsview Park. The same company runs a regular one-hour boat tour through the gorge and around the harbor for C$32 (US$22.90) adults, C$25 (US$17.90) children. These trips depart from downtown's Market Square to coincide with calm, slack tide.

Rockwood Park

Canada's largest urban park (810 hectares/2,000 acres) encompasses native forests and numerous lakes northeast of downtown Saint John. There's plenty for everyone to do, including:

- ✔ **Monkey around,** at **Cherry Bank Zoo,** Sandy Point Rd. (☎ **506-634-1440**), where you can see lions, tigers, and over 30 other exotic species.

- ✔ **Take a hike,** along 25km (15.5 miles) of pathways. One trail begins from Lake Drive South and encircles pretty Crystal Lake.

- ✔ **Aim for the water hazard,** at **Rockwood Park Golf Course,** on Sandy Point Road (☎ **506-634-0090**), which has the Maritimes' only aquatic driving range.

- ✔ **Swim and splash,** in one of the park's 12 lakes. **Fisher Lakes,** off Lake Drive South, has supervised swimming, canoe rentals, and a sandy stretch of beach.

The easiest way to get to Rockwood Park is to take Foster Thurston Drive north from Exit 128 off Route 1, 3km (1.9 miles) east of downtown. This road leads all the way around the park. If you're feeling confident in your route-finding ability, cross Route 1 via Somerset Street and hook a right on Churchill Boulevard. For park information, dial ☎ **506-658-2883.**

Irving Nature Park

A rocky peninsula jutting into busy Saint John Harbour has escaped development and is protected as Irving Nature Park. This 240-hectare (600-acre) park has a sandy stretch of beach near the entrance, rocky coves, pleasant hiking trails, and tidal pools filled with colorful critters. Along the **Squirrel Trail,** near the information booth, an observation tower offers sweeping views back across the mudflats linking the peninsula to the mainland. Between late June and early October the park becomes home to hundreds of seals which haul themselves out of the water and onto the rocky shoreline. Bird life is prolific year-round — over 200 species have been recorded in the park.

Irving Nature Park is west of downtown. To get there, take Exit 119 from Route 1 and follow Bleury Street, then Sand Cove Road into the park. Cross the mudflats to reach an information booth which is staffed late May through October. For park information, call ☎ **506-653-7367.** Admission is free.

Nightlife

If you feel like a tipple and some local music but want to avoid the hard-drinking, dimly lit downtown bars, there are plenty of options. Stop by either of the city information centers for a schedule of what's on, or check with **Tourism Saint John** (☎ **866-463-8639** or 506-658-2855; Internet: www.tourismsaintjohn.com) directly.

Pubs and clubs

All the restaurants in Market Square, including **Grannan's** (☎ **506-634-1555**), have a section of the public walkway cordoned off for outdoor seating. You're welcome to stop by for just a refreshing drink in the sun at any of these places. In the vicinity, the **Brigantine Lounge,** in the Saint John Hilton, at 1 Market Square (☎ **506-693-8484**), has unobstructed harbor views.

The Trinity Royal area, up King and Princess streets, is a good place to look for local color and live music. **D'Arcy Farrow's Pub,** at 43 Princess Street (☎ 506-657-8939), is a large pub with many rooms. Celtic and Irish bands are a feature most nights. **O'Leary's Pub,** across the road at 46 Princess Street (☎ 506-634-7135), has more of the same. **Tapps Brew Pub,** 78 King Street (☎ 506-634-1957), attracts an older crowd.

The arts

The **Imperial Theatre,** on King's Square (☎ 506-633-9494), is a meticulously restored 1913 vaudeville theater. It is home to local theater, opera, ballet, and music productions, with programs that usually run through the winter months. Theater tours are available in summer Monday through Saturday 10 a.m. to 6 p.m.

The city sponsors a schedule of **summer concerts** in King's Square. Expect everything from country to Celtic. Call ☎ 506-658-2893 for details.

Fundy Coast

Beyond Saint John, you can head west to the resort town of St. Andrews, back toward Moncton via Fundy National Park, or inland to the provincial capital of Fredericton. The following sections detail the first two options, while Fredericton is covered in the next chapter.

Fundy National Park

The massive Fundy tides are the most dramatic aspect of this popular coastal park northeast of Saint John, but it's the rugged interior dotted with lakes along with the network of hiking trails that brings in the summertime crowds. The park even has a covered bridge, which lies near the end of Point Wolfe Road.

Wildlife is prolific on the land, in the air, and out in the Bay of Fundy. At dawn or dusk you have an excellent chance of spying moose, beavers, and black bears, while birdwatchers delight in spotting peregrine falcons.

Getting there

You'll need a vehicle to reach Fundy National Park. It is bisected by Route 114, which branches off Route 1, 84km (51 miles) northeast of Saint John. From this junction, it's 25km (15.5 miles) to the park gate and a further 17km (10.6 miles) to the main facility area.

Park entry fees

The daily entry fee to Fundy National Park is C$5 (US$4) adults, C$4.25 (US$3) seniors, C$2.50 (US$1.80) children, to a maximum of C$12.50 (US$8.90) per vehicle. A season pass pays for itself in 5 days, so it's worth considering if you're planning an extended stay in the park. Fees are collected at booths located at both park entrances.

Gathering more information

The main **Visitor Centre** (☎ **506-887-6000;** Internet: www.pc.gc.ca) is just inside the east park gate. It's open mid-June through August daily 8 a.m. to 10 p.m., and mid-May through mid-June and September to mid-October daily 8 a.m. to 4 p.m.

If you're coming in from the west, make a stop at the **Wolfe Lake Visitor Centre,** open mid-June through September, daily 10 a.m. to 6 p.m.

Staying in Fundy National Park

Most people staying in Fundy camp out in one of four park campgrounds. Indoor accommodations are limited, so you will want to reserve a room as far in advance as possible.

Fundy Highlands Inn & Chalets
$–$$ **Fundy National Park**

Perched on a grassy slope within walking distance of the main facility area, this comfortable lodging offers views across the Bay of Fundy that make it worth every cent of the already reasonable rates. Units within the main complex are slightly dated, but each comes with cooking facilities and opens to a large patio with ocean views. The chalets are smaller, but have kitchenettes as well as a little more character.

Route 114, Fundy National Park ☎ *888-883-8639 or 506-887-2930. Fax: 506-887-2453. Internet:* www.fundyhighlandchalets.com. *Rack rates: C$85–C$90 (US$60.70–US$64.30) double. MC, V. May–Oct.*

Fundy Park Chalets
$$ Fundy National Park

These fresh little cottages lie in a grove of trees adjacent to hiking trails, the swimming pool, the golf course, a restaurant, and the main information center. Each has basic cooking facilities and a bathroom. In the shoulder seasons, you can enjoy accommodations, a round of golf, and a lobster dinner for just C$70 (US$50) per person. Book well ahead for July and August.

Route 114, Fundy National Park ☎ **506-887-2808**. *Fax: 506-887-2282. Internet:* www.fundyparkchalets.com. *Rack rates: C$80 (US$57.10) double. MC, V. May–Oct.*

Dining in Fundy National Park

The park has just one restaurant, but as both accommodations have cooking facilities, preparing your own meal is an easy option. In adjacent Alma, **Butland's Seafood,** on Main Street (☎ **506-887-2190**), sells cooked lobsters for around C$10 (US$7.10) per pound, with the price clearly displayed in black marker on their claws. You can also buy fresh shrimp, mussels, scallops, and a variety of fish.

Seawinds Dining Room
$$–$$$ Fundy National Park   SEAFOOD

This restaurant is exactly what you'd expect in the popular park — family-friendly and informal, with well-priced, unfussy food. Three massive chandeliers, a large stone fireplace, and a 6-kilogram (13.5-pound) lobster shell dominate the main dining room. The menu is short and simple, ranging from a traditional roast beef dinner to sautéed scallops. All children's dishes are under C$6 (US$4.30).

Route 114, Fundy National Park ☎ **506-887-2098**. *Reservations not necessary. Main courses: C$12–C$21 (US$8.60–US$15). MC, V. May–Oct daily 11:00 a.m.–9:30 p.m.*

Exploring Fundy National Park

The main facility area, just inside the east gate, is a good place to get oriented. Stop by the visitor center for a park map and hiking trail description brochure, then wander down to the water's edge for panoramic views across the Bay of Fundy.

Hiking
Within the park are 120km (74.6 miles) of hiking trails designed for all fitness levels. Head to either visitor center for a trail map and to ask advice about which trails would suit your fitness level and interests.

At low tide, you can walk along the beach below the main visitor center, but don't expect to have it to yourself.To escape the crowds, drive west along Point Wolfe Road. From the end of this road, a 0.6km (0.4-mile) path leads through a lush spruce forest to **Point Wolfe Beach,** at the braided mouth of the Point Wolfe River. From the same trailhead, the **Coppermine Trail** leads 2.3km (1.4 miles) farther west along the coast to the site of an abandoned mine. Allow two hours for the round-trip. Backtrack along Point Wolfe Road and take Herring Cove Road to reach **Herring Cove Trail,** a 15-minute jaunt down to a rocky cove with a tidal cave off to one side. From the cove, the **Matthews Head Trail** leads off to the south, traversing to a high headland with stunning ocean views. Allow 90 minutes for this 4.5km (2.8-mile) circuit.

An easy introduction to the park's interior forest is the **Caribou Plain Trail,** a 3.4km (2.1-mile) circuit that loops around a beaver pond. The trailhead is just east of Bennett Lake. **Third Vault Falls** tumbles over a 16-meter-high (52.5-foot-high) ledge in the eastern portion of the park. The falls are reached via a 3.7km (2.3-mile) trail that branches off Laverty Road. Allow 60 to 70 minutes each way.

Other things to do and see in Fundy National Park

Hiking is the major attention-getter in the park, but you can also do the following:

- ✔ **Swim.** A unique **saltwater pool** is filled with water pumped up from the Bay of Fundy, then heated to a comfortable temperature. Entry is C$3 (US$2.10) adults, C$2.50 (US$1.80) seniors, C$1.50 (US$1.07) children. It's open July through August, 11 a.m. to 6:30 p.m.

- ✔ **Golf.** The fairways of a short nine-hole golf course wind their way along Dickson Brook, beside the main facility area. A pro shop (☎ **506-887-2970**) rents clubs and collects greens fees of C$16 (US$11.40).

- ✔ **Paddle.** Rent a canoe (C$8/US$5.70 per hour) at **Bennett Lake,** halfway along the park road, to explore the shoreline of this tranquil body of water.

- ✔ **Watch the tide.** Okay, it's not very exciting watching tidal movements, but at low tide, **Alma Harbor** is devoid of water, leaving fishing boats high and dry on the ocean floor.

Hopewell Rocks

Hopewell Rocks, along Route 114 halfway between Fundy National Park and Moncton, is a cluster of rock towers that were once part of the mainland but became separated by erosion caused by the tides. Known as "flower pots" (many have trees and shrubbery growing on top), they are partly covered at high tide, but when the massive Fundy tide recedes, they rise starkly from the muddy shoreline.

Plan on arriving 1 to 3 hours before low tide. Tidal charts are published in all local newspapers and are available at information centers. The visitor's guide to Fundy National Park (you'll be given one at the park entrance) has a tide chart on the center page.

Staying and dining at Hopewell Rocks

Most visitors to Hopewell Rocks spend two to four hours poking around, and then move on to Moncton or Fundy National Park. Alternatively, you can stay overnight at the Hopewell Rocks Motel & Country Inn, within walking distance of the attraction.

Hopewell Rocks Motel & Country Inn

$–$$ **Hopewell Cape**

Located at the entrance to Hopewell Rocks, this adequate motel has large air-conditioned rooms and a small outdoor pool. The hanging baskets of colorful flowers out front are a nice touch. Rooms 11 through 20 face away from the road and are quieter.

Ignore your hunger pangs down at Hopewell Rocks and plan on taking a meal back out on the highway at this motel's **Log Cabin Restaurant.** The lobster dinner is well priced, or choose one of the daily specials, which are discounted from the main menu. The dining room is open May through October, daily 8 a.m. to 9 p.m.

Route 114 ☎ *888-759-7070 or 506-734-2975. Fax: 506-734-2252. Internet:* www. hopewellrocksmotel.com. *Rack rates: C$65–C$85 (US$46.40–US$60.70) double. AE, MC, V. May–Oct.*

Exploring Hopewell Rocks

At the end of the access road off Route 114 is a massive parking lot and a fee station, where the entry charge is collected. Admission is C$6 (US$4.30) adults, C$5 (US$3.60) seniors, C$4 (US$2.90) children.

The gates are open mid-May to mid-June 9 a.m. to 5 p.m., mid-June to late June 8 a.m. to 7 p.m., July to mid-August 8 a.m. to 8 p.m., mid-August to late August 8 a.m. to 7 p.m., September to mid-October 9 a.m. to 5 p.m., closed the rest of the year.

Beyond the fee station, make your way down to the large **interpretive center.** This is a good place to get an overview of these geological oddities, as well as to learn more about the Fundy tides.

The rock towers are scattered along a 2km (1.2-mile) stretch starting immediately below the interpretive center, but the most impressive concentration is a 30-minute walk away along a wooded trail. The alternative to walking is to catch a ride in an oversized golf cart. This costs just C$1 (US$.70) each way; buy tickets at the main entrance or at the cart turn-around point.

At the end of the trail/cart path, a steep metal stairway descends to the muddy shoreline and the **Flower Pot Rocks.** To escape the summer crowds, walk west along the beach (to the right from the bottom of the stairs). Hoses are provided back at the top to clean the sticky red mud from the soles of your shoes.

The time of day you visit is restricted by the tide, but early morning is best if you want to avoid the crowds. For shutterbugs, an early-morning visit also offers more favorable light for photography.

St. Andrews

On the Fundy Coast west of Saint John, St. Andrews is New Brunswick's most famous resort town. Laid out by Loyalists in 1783, the oldest part of town has remained remarkably untouched by modern encroachment, and is protected as a National Historic Site.

St. Andrews was mainly a port city until it was discovered in the late 1880s by wealthy Americans looking to escape the summer heat of the Eastern Seaboard. They stayed in grand resorts like the Algonquin or in their own private retreats, and St. Andrews was transformed.

Today, St. Andrews is popular not only with vacationing New Englanders but also with Canadians, who come to celebrate special occasions, spend time out on the water, or simply stroll the streets browsing through the many galleries and boutiques.

Getting there

Although St. Andrews is across the St. Croix River from Maine, access from the United States is via the Calais/St. Stephen border crossing, 24km (15 miles) northwest.

From elsewhere in New Brunswick, the most direct access to St. Andrews is Route 1 west along the Bay of Fundy from Saint John, a distance of 100km (62 miles). From Fredericton, 133km (82.6 miles) away, the most direct way is Route 3 via St. Stephen.

Just before entering the town proper, make a stop at the **St. Andrews Welcome Centre,** in a converted residence at 46 Reed Avenue (☎ **506-529-3556**). It's open May through September daily 9 a.m. to 6 p.m. (July and August until 8 p.m.).

Staying in St. Andrews

Many of St. Andrews' lodgings are upscale inns and bed-and-breakfasts, priced higher than elsewhere in the Maritimes. I've included the best of these, and dug out a cheapie and a family favorite to keep everyone happy.

Kennedy House

$ **Downtown**

Built in 1881, Kennedy House was one of the town's first hotels catering specifically to summer guests. Six very basic guest rooms are available, and rates include a light breakfast. Kick back on a wicker chair along the veranda and watch the world go by.

218 Water St. ☎ *506-529-8844. Rack rates: C$75 (US$53.60) double. MC, V.*

Kingsbrae Arms

$$$$ **Downtown**

Staying at this country estate, the only Relais & Châteaux property in the Maritimes, is an unforgettable experience. Set on 11 hectares (27 acres) of beautifully landscaped grounds, the Kingsbrae was built in 1897 and has been converted to an inn with impeccable pedigree. The seven rooms have marble bathrooms, gas fireplaces, and canopy beds topped with luxurious linens. Rates include a gourmet breakfast, picnic lunch, and four-course table d'hôte dinner inclusive of wine. A three-night minimum stay is in effect July through August.

219 King St. ☎ *800-470-4088 or 506-529-4210. Fax: 506-529-4311. Internet: www.kingsbrae.com. Rack rates: US$690–US$1175 double inclusive of meals. AE, MC, V. May–Oct.*

Picket Fence Motel

$ **North of Downtown**

If all you want is a regular motel room, consider this hotel on the edge of town.

102 Reed St. ☎ *506-529-8985. Rates: C$75 (US$53.60) double.*

Seaside Beach Resort

$$ Downtown

Located at the end of the main street, this is a good choice for families if you're looking for a waterfront setting at a reasonable price. Each unit in this miscellany of cottages and apartments is different, but most have cooking facilities and bright, practical furnishings. The Seagull apartment is right on the water and opens to a boardwalk dotted with Adirondack chairs, while the Sandpiper cottage is a cozy space set back from the water. Barbecues and picnic tables dot the grounds.

*339 Water St. ☎ **800-506-8677** or 506-529-3846. Fax: 506-529-4479. Internet:* www.seaside.nb.ca. *Rack rates: C$90–C$110 (US$64.30–US$78.60) double. AE, MC, V. April–Dec.*

Treadwell Inn

$$–$$$$ Downtown

The seven-room olive-and-burgundy colored lodge, built in the 1820s for a ship chandler, combines a waterfront setting with comfortable rooms to make it one of the nicest places to stay in St. Andrews. The current owner's faultless taste shines through without taking away from the historic charm. Of the well-furnished rooms, only two don't have ocean views. My fave? Room 7 (C$185/US$132.10), with a king-sized bed, a bathroom with a soaker tub, and wide doors that open to a private balcony with sweeping views across Passamaquoddy Bay.

*129 Water St. ☎ **800-529-1011** or 506-529-1011. Fax: 506-529-4826. Rack rates: C$145–C$250 (US$103.60–US$178.60) double. MC, V.*

Dining in St. Andrews

Dining in St. Andrews compares favorably with that in much larger centers across the Maritimes — a combination of an abundance of seafood and a century of demand from well-heeled visitors.

The Gables

$$–$$$ Downtown   SEAFOOD

This restaurant lies down a narrow alley, beyond a giant wood carving of a lobster. It is a casual affair liberally decorated with netting and the like, all salvaged from the sea. Seating is inside or out on a deck that extends to above the high tide mark. The cooking is simple but tasty. Plan on starting with a plate piled high with steamed mussels. For mains, peruse the blackboard offerings, which feature whatever seafood is in season — lobster, scallops, halibut, and haddock are all staples. The Gables opens for breakfast in summer, with full cooked breakfasts costing a reasonable C$6 (US$4.30).

143 Water St. ☎ 506-529-3440. Reservations recommended for dinner. Main courses: C$14–C$20 (US$10–US$14.30). AE, MC, V. July–Aug daily 9 a.m.–11 p.m., Sept–June daily 11 a.m.–9 p.m.

Niger Reef Tea House

$$–$$$ **Downtown** **CANADIAN**

This historic teahouse is my favorite spot in St. Andrews for lunch, although I have dropped by just for a piece of the melt-in-your-mouth strawberry shortcake. Choose to dine in a cozy room and enjoy the wonderful aromas that waft in from the kitchen, or sit out on the weathered deck and take in the view across Passamaquoddy Bay. In the evening, you can indulge in the rich seafood chowder or skewered scallops, grilled with a ginger and curry glaze. If you weren't here at lunch, end your meal with the shortcake; otherwise, go for the triple chocolate brownie sundae. The salmon Eggs Benedict (C$12.50/US$8.90), served at Sunday brunch, is to die for.

1 Joe's Point Rd. ☎ 506-529-8007. Reservations recommended for dinner. Lunch: C$5–C$13 (US$3.60–US$9.30). Dinner: C$17–C$20 (US$12.10–US$14.30). MC, V. Mid-June–mid-Sept daily 11:30 a.m.-4:30 p.m. and 6–9 p.m.

Windsor House

$$–$$$ **St. Andrews** **CONTINENTAL**

The cooking at this upscale establishment in a 1798 Georgian-era home is among the best in St. Andrews. Starters include pâté, made in-house, and a salad of greens harvested from the garden. The mains vary, depending on what's in season, but may include a creamy seafood fettuccini or beef tenderloin stuffed with Stilton cheese and doused in a red wine demi-glaze. You can dine in one of two elegant rooms, both with fireplaces, or in the walled courtyard. If you want to stay here, there are six beautiful rooms for C$225 to C$300 (US$160.70 to US$214.30).

132 Water St. ☎ 506-529-3330. Reservations essential. Main courses: C$24–C$38 (US$17.10–US$27.10). AE, DC, DISC, MC, V. May–Dec Mon–Fri 5:30–9:30 p.m., Sat–Sun 11:30 a.m.–2:00 p.m. and 5:00–9:30 p.m. (closed Mon and Tues in spring and fall).

Exploring St. Andrews

If you'd like to take a self-guided walking tour of St. Andrews, pick up a map highlighting points of interest from the Welcome Centre. Another option is to join a **Heritage Discovery Tour** (☎ 506-529-4011), led by a costumed guide. If you're heading out on your own, here are some sights you won't want to miss.

Atlantic Salmon Interpretive Centre

Very different from St. Andrews' historic attractions, this is the public portion of a research station that studies one of Canada's most important fishing exports. The modern interpretive center nestles in a lush forest, right over a stream where salmon spawn. Inside the timber-frame building are displays on the life cycle of the salmon and the ongoing fight to save its habitat, as well as some old fly-fishing equipment. A trail leads downstream to Chamcook Harbour, and upstream to shallow gravel beds where the fish spawn.

Route 127 (6 km/3.7 miles toward Saint John) ☎ **506-529-1384**. *Internet:* www.asf.ca. *Admission C$4 (US$2.90) adults, C$2.50 (US$1.80) children. Mid-May–mid-Oct daily 9 a.m.–5 p.m.*

Kingsbrae Garden

Once part of the sprawling Kingsbrae Arms Estate, this 11-hectare (27-acre) plot is generally regarded as one of the top ten gardens in Canada. The Rose Garden, filled with fragrant old varieties, is from the original estate; the White Garden is composed entirely of white and silver blossoms; and the Scents and Sensitivity Garden allows visually impaired visitors to experience distinct smells and textures up close. And new gardens are always being added — the Gravel Garden addresses modern environmental concerns by using a minimum of water. In other parts of the grounds, you'll find a scaled-down windmill, a wooden maze, and fish-filled ponds. Complement your visit with a bowl of steaming seafood chowder in the Garden Café. Kingsbrae is an easy walk up King Street from the waterfront.

220 King St. ☎ **506-529-3335**. *Admission C$8 (US$5.70) adults, C$6.50 (US$4.60) seniors and children. Mid-May–mid-Oct daily 9 a.m.–6 p.m.*

Ministers Island

Once the summer retreat of William Van Horne, the driving force behind the completion of Canada's transcontinental railway, this small island holds one of the finest private residences you are likely to come across in Canada. Built of locally quarried sandstone, the mansion is notable for its 50 rooms, including a massive drawing room and a billiard room with the original table. On the grounds is a sandstone bathhouse with a tidal swimming pool.

Getting to the island is an adventure in itself. The only access is at low tide (dial ☎ **506-529-5081** to hear a recorded message with exact tide and tour times), at which time everyone meets at the end of Bar Road. from where an escort is provided across the dry sea floor to the island. You must have your own vehicle.

Bar Rd. (off Mowat Dr.) ☎ **506-529-5081**. *Admission C$5 (US$3.60) adults, C$2.50 (US$1.80) children. June–mid-Oct daily sunrise to sunset.*

Ross Memorial Museum

Formerly the summer retreat of a wealthy American family named Ross, this 1824 home was deeded to the town to help preserve local history. It offers a glimpse into the life of the Rosses, with rooms that remain much as they left them, filled with fine furnishings and original paintings.

188 Montague St. ☎ *506-529-5124. Admission: donation.July–Aug Mon–Sat 10 a.m.–4:30 p.m.; Sept–mid-Oct Tues–Sat 10:00 a.m.–4:30 p.m.*

Other cool things to do in and around St. Andrews

Several companies run sightseeing trips on Passamaquoddy Bay, or you can go whale-watching or kayaking. The **Day Adventure Centre**, beside Market Wharf (☎ **506-529-2600**), represents various operators, or choose from one of these options:

- ✔ **Whale-watching. Fundy Tide Runners,** Market Wharf (☎ **506-529-4481**), uses a stable Zodiac to reach whale-watching grounds out in the Bay of Fundy. Tours last two hours and cost C$50 (US$35.70) adults, C$35 (US$25) children. The whale-watching season is June through September.

- ✔ **Sea kayaking.** Even if you've never kayaked before, the guides at **Eastern Outdoors,** 165 Water Street (☎ **506-529-4662**), will make you feel at ease on a two-hour introductory paddle from their seafront headquarters; C$45 (US$32.10) per person.

- ✔ **Sailing.** The **SV** *Cory* is an elegant tall ship that departs Market Wharf (☎ **506-529-8116**) up to four times daily for a harbor sailing trip. The fare of C$55 (US$39.30) adults, C$50 (US$35.70) seniors, C$35 (US$25) children, includes snacks and drinks and the use of binoculars to search out birds and seals.

- ✔ **Golfing.** It will *feel* like you're out at sea as you stand on the 12th tee at **Algonquin Golf Club,** Brandy Cove Road (☎ **506-529-7142**), aiming for a tiny patch of green perched on a nub of land surrounded by water. Greens fees are C$125 (US$89.30).

Shopping

Artisans will say they're attracted to St. Andrews for the inspiration of its scenic setting, and there's no denying the area is beautiful, but the more cynical may say it's because of affluent U.S. residents and visitors with pockets full of greenbacks. Regardless, the result is a street lined with galleries and boutiques, including the following:

- ✔ **Jarea Art Studio,** 157 Water St. (☎ **506-529-4936**), displays the unusual art of Geoffrey David-Slater, whose paintings feature a single line that changes color but remains unbroken.

- ✔ **Serendipin' Art,** 168 Water St. (☎ **506-529-3327**), features colorful hand-blown glass fish.

✔ The **Whale Store,** 173 Water St. (☎ **506-529-3926**), is highlighted by stylish whale woodcarvings.

✔ If you want to find that perfect nautical-themed painting, start your search at the **Seacoast Gallery,** 174 Water St. (☎ **506-529-0005**).

✔ **Gumushel's Tartan Shop,** 183 Water St. (☎ **506-529-3859**), sells tartan ties, berets, and jackets — but you guessed that from the name, didn't you?

✔ **St. Andrews Hardware,** 189 Water St. (☎ **506-529-3158**), is filled to the rafters with a hodgepodge of hardware and nautical-themed knickknacks.

✔ Since 1915, local knitters have sold their hats, blankets, sweaters, and dolls at **Cottage Crafts,** in Market Square (☎ **902-368-2663**). You can also buy a great variety of yarns.

Fundy Isles

Time spent on one or more of the Fundy Isles is a unique and memorable addition to your travels along the Fundy Coast. The three main islands, Deer, Campobello, and Grand Manan, are all linked to the mainland by ferry and easily visited in a day. You can explore the islands or, if you prefer, head out to the water to marvel at marine life or try your hand at some of the area's popular water sports.

Deer Island

It may be named for a land mammal, but life on this small island revolves around the ocean. The importance of the lobster industry is clear — you'll see the pounds used to hold live lobsters scattered around the shoreline. To get to the island, catch the free ferry (departures year-round, every 30 minutes) from Letete, south of St. George. You can explore the island in just a few hours, but allow two extra hours to take a whale-watching trip with **Cline Marine Tours** (☎ **800-567-5880** or 506-529-2287). **Sunset Beach Cottage & Suites,** on the west side of the island (☎ **888-576-9990** or 506-747-2972), is right on the beach and has an outdoor pool; rates are C$70 to C$100 (US$50 to US$71.40) double, which is in the $ to $$ range.

Campobello Island

A summer-only ferry links Deer and Campobello islands, but most visitors cross to the island by bridge from Lubec, Maine — even those visiting from New Brunswick, as St. Stephen is just 70km (43 miles) away by road. Franklin Roosevelt's family were perhaps the most notable of the many wealthy people who have spent their summers here. His 34-room cottage is protected as part of **Roosevelt Campobello International Park** (☎ 506-752-2922) and is open for inspection late May through mid-October daily 10 a.m. to 6 p.m. Admission is free.

An adjacent property, once owned by Roosevelt's cousin, has been converted to **Lupine Lodge** (☎ 888-912-8880 or 506-752-2555; Internet www.lupinelodge.com), with 11 basic rooms in two log cottages. Rates are C$75 to C$100 (US$53.60 to US$71.40) per unit ($ to $$). The restaurant here is recommended. A good source of island information is the Web site www.campobello.com.

Grand Manan Island

Grand Manan is larger than the other Fundy Isles and much farther from the mainland. Birdwatchers in particular are drawn to the island — famed naturalist John James Audubon spent time here painting. Other draws are whale- and seal-watching, biking, hiking, and a string of sandy beaches.

Coastal Transport (☎ 506-662-3724) operates ferries year-round, four to seven times daily between Blacks Harbour (take Exit 60 from Route 1) and the island. The crossing takes two hours. The round-trip fare is C$9 (US$6.40) adults, C$4.50 (US$3.20) children, C$27.50 (US$19.60) vehicles. No reservations are taken.

Don't look farther than the **Swallowtail Inn,** on North Head Rd. near the ferry dock (☎ 866-563-1100 or 506-662-1100; Internet: www.swallowtailinn.com), for a gorgeous setting high atop a rocky bluff. Formerly a lighthouse keeper's residence, the guest rooms (C$85 to C$125/US$60.70 to US$89.30; $ to $$) have en suites and ocean views.

Island Coast Whale Watching (☎ 877-662-9393 or 506-662-8181) takes visitors on five-hour boat tours searching out humpback, finback, and minke whales. Whale sightings are guaranteed through the July to mid-September season. The cost is C$45 (US$32.10) adults, C$22.50 (US$16.10) children. **Sea Watch Tours** (☎ 877-662-8552 or 506-662-1081) have onboard naturalists who are especially knowledgeable about local bird life. **Adventure High,** based near the ferry dock (☎ 506-662-3563), takes visitors kayaking (C$55/US$39.30 per half day) and rents bikes (C$20/US$14.30 per day). In addition to being a wonderful way to explore the island, using a bike means you don't need to bring a vehicle across on the ferry, saving both the expense and, more importantly, a possible long wait in line to board.

Fast Facts: Saint John

ATMs

All banks along King St. have ATMs accessible 24 hours daily.

Emergencies

Dial ☎ 911 for all emergencies.

Hospital

Saint John Regional Hospital is at 400 University Ave. (☎ 506-648-5000).

Information

Tourism Saint John (☎ 866-463-8639 or 506-658-2855; Internet: www. tourismsaintjohn.com) operates an information center downtown in Market Square (open daily 9 a.m.–6 p.m., July–Aug until 8 p.m.) and along Route 1 as you approach the city from the west (open mid-May–mid-Oct daily 9 a.m.

Internet Access

Internet access is free at **Saint John Public Library, in Market Square** (☎ 506-643-7220); closed Sunday.

Police

For emergencies, dial ☎ 911. For other police matters, call ☎ 506-757-1020.

Post Office

Downtown drugstores such as the one in Brunswick Square have postal services. The main post office is at 41 Church Ave. W. West Saint John.

Restrooms

Public restrooms are located at street level in Market Square.

Taxis

Local cab companies include Diamond Taxi (☎ 506-648-8888) and Royal Taxi (☎ 506-652-5050).

Transit Info

Saint John Transit (☎ 506-658-4700) is discussed earlier in this chapter under "Getting Around Saint John."

Weather

The Environment Canada Web site (www.weatheroffice.ec.gc.ca) has links to the Saint John forecast.

Chapter 17

Fredericton

∙ ∙

In This Chapter

▶ Getting to Fredericton

▶ Finding your way around the city

▶ Deciding on the best places to stay and dine

▶ Seeing the downtown sights and exploring the Saint John River Valley

∙ ∙

*F*redericton, the capital of New Brunswick, is an appealing and practical stopping place with classic Victorian architecture, interesting museums, riverfront pathways, and an excellent range of lodging and dining options.

In 1793, at the end of the American Revolution, around 2,000 Americans loyal to the British Crown made their way north into the Saint John River Valley and set up camp at a site that had been the one-time capital of Acadia. These Loyalists set out to create a gracious town, and this sense of style remains today.

Getting to Fredericton

Fredericton is accessible by plane and bus, but most people arrive by automobile, driving in via an excellent provincial highway system.

By plane

Greater Fredericton Airport (Internet: www.frederictonairport.ca) is 14km (8.7 miles) southeast of downtown via Route 102. Air Canada and its subsidiary Air Canada Jazz fly in daily from Halifax, Toronto, Montreal, and Ottawa. Delta Air Lines links Fredericton with Boston.

Taxis line up out front of the main terminal and charge around C$18 (US$12.90) to take you downtown. Rental-car companies that maintain desks at the airport are Avis, Budget, Hertz, and National.

Fredericton

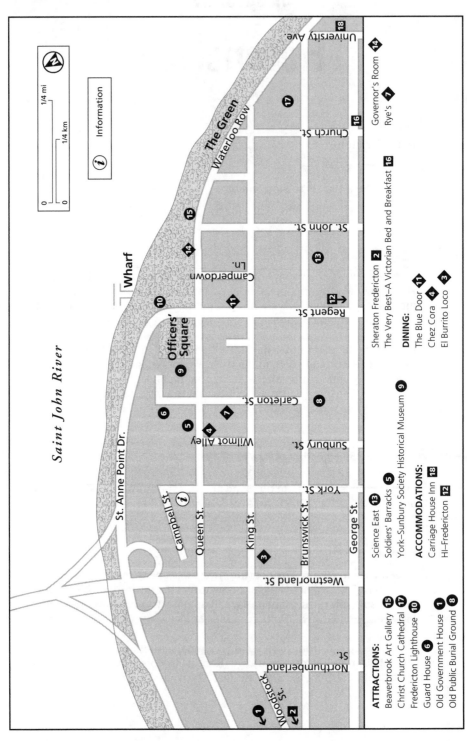

ATTRACTIONS:
Beaverbrook Art Gallery **15**
Christ Church Cathedral **17**
Fredericton Lighthouse **10**
Guard House **6**
Old Government House **1**
Old Public Burial Ground **8**
Science East **13**
Soldiers' Barracks **5**
York–Sunbury Society Historical Museum **9**

ACCOMMODATIONS:
Carriage House Inn **18**
HI-Fredericton **12**
Sheraton Fredericton **2**
The Very Best–A Victorian Bed and Breakfast **16**

DINING:
The Blue Door **11**
Chez Cora **4**
El Burrito Loco **3**
Governor's Room **14**
Rye's **7**

By car

Route 2 (the Trans-Canada Highway) is the main highway from Moncton and all points east, including Halifax. The drive from Moncton is 174km (108 miles), or a little under two hours.

Entering New Brunswick near Edmundston, **Route 2** follows the winding Saint John River all the way to Fredericton for 290km (180 miles), which means you should allow at least four hours.

If you're traveling up the Acadian Coast from Moncton, take **Route 8** from Miramichi south through the heart of New Brunswick to reach Fredericton in two hours.

Route 7 is the most direct road between Saint John and Fredericton (105km/65 miles), but **Route 102** along the Saint John River is a more scenic alternative.

By bus

Acadian Lines (☎ **506-458-6007**) buses arrive at 101 Regent Street (at Brunswick Street), on the same block as a Discount car rental agency (☎ **506-458-1118**) and within walking distance of many downtown hotels.

Getting Around Fredericton

Downtown Fredericton lies on the inside of a bend in the Saint John River. King and Queen streets, running parallel to the river, are the main thoroughfares. North Fredericton, on the north side of the river, is mostly residential. It is linked to downtown by the Westmorland Street Bridge. Farther east, the Trail Bridge, starting at the corner of Brunswick Street and University Avenue, is for pedestrians only. Even if you don't need to get to the other side, it's worth crossing the bridge just for the views that extend back across downtown, where you can see the higher buildings rising above the tree-lined riverbank.

Parking

You've gotta love a city that welcomes visitors with free parking. At the visitor center at the corner of Queen and York streets, show proof that you are from out of province — such as a driver's license — and the staff will issue you a two-day parking permit valid at all parking meters and at the lot at the north end of York Street, immediately behind the visitor center.

Catching cabs

Hailing a taxi is easy along Queen and King streets. If you're really stuck, you can always go to the Lord Beaverbrook Hotel and have the front desk attendant call one for you. Among the local companies are **Checker Cabs** (☎ **506-450-8294**), **Standard Taxi** (☎ **506-450-4444**), and **Loyal Taxi** (☎ **506-455-6789**).

Transit tips

Fredericton Transit (☎ **506-460-2200**) operates city buses along seven routes, Monday through Saturday 6:30 a.m. to 11:00 p.m. The fare is C$1.60 (US$1.10) per sector (children 6 and under ride free). Exact change is required.

Staying in Fredericton

The following recommendations are my preferences in various price categories. Downtown accommodations are within walking distance of the riverfront and most major attractions.

Room rates here don't tend to fluctuate as much as elsewhere, but offer good value year-round. If you're just looking for a regular motel room, consult the provincial tourism guide, or cruise the arterial roads for posted vacancies (start along Route 105, across the river from downtown). The friendly staff at the City Hall visitor center will be more than happy to help you find a last-minute room.

Carriage House Inn
$$ **Downtown**

Built in 1875 for a one-time mayor of Fredericton, this three-story mansion lies one block from a riverfront pathway leading right to downtown. The medium-sized rooms are decorated in a subtle Victorian theme and filled with antiques. A cooked breakfast, served in a sunny side room, is included in the rates.

230 University Ave. ☎ ***800-267-6068*** *or 506-452-9924. Fax: 506-452-2770. Internet:* www.carriagehouse-inn.net. *Rack rates: C$90–C$100 (US$64.30–US$71.40). AE, MC, V.*

Fort Nashwaak Motel

$ **North Fredericton**

This motel is situated beside a restored fort, where the Nashwaak and Saint John rivers meet. The rooms are fairly large but plainly furnished; what makes this place stand out from the 30-odd other roadside motels scattered around the city is its location, a pleasant 15-minute walk from downtown via the pedestrian-only Trail Bridge.

15 Riverside Dr. (at Route 10) ☎ ***800-684-8999*** *or 506-472-4411. Fax: 506-450-8586. Parking: Free. Rack rates: C$60–C$75 (US$42.90–US$53.60) double. AE, MC, V.*

HI–Fredericton

$ **Downtown**

Nestled on a peaceful tree-lined street six blocks up Regent Street from the river, this hostel is in a converted residence hall. Thoughtful renovations have created more atmosphere than you may imagine a hostel would offer. All the expected amenities are available, including a communal kitchen, laundry, and lockers. Beds are available in both dormitories and private rooms, but outside of summer, you could find yourself a private room for the price of a dorm. Check-in is 7 a.m. to noon and 6 to 10 p.m.

620 Churchill Row ☎ ***506-450-4417***. *Fax: 506-462-9692. Internet:* www. hihostels.ca. *Parking: Free. Rack rates: C$16 (US$11.40) members of Hostelling International, C$20 (US$14.30) nonmembers. MC, V.*

On the Pond

$$ **Mactaquac**

Set on a forested waterfront property well beyond city limits, this European-style country lodge is inviting and relaxing rather than luxurious. Stress-reducing facilities include a wide range of spa services and on-site masseuses, or grab a bike or canoe and pedal or paddle to your heart's content. The eight spacious guest rooms are richly handsome in an old-fashioned kind of way. Breakfast and dinner are served in the dining room.

Route 615 (off Route 105, 21km/13 miles west of Fredericton) ☎ ***800-984-2555*** *or 506-363-3420. Fax: 506-363-3479. Internet:* www.onthepond.com. *Rack rates: C$125–C$145 (US$89.30–US$103.60). MC, V.*

Ramada Fredericton

$$ North Fredericton

Yes, it's part of a chain, but the Ramada Fredericton is excellent value. It's also right by the river and adjacent to a par-3 golf course and a complex of tennis courts. The 116 rooms are set around a tropical atrium that contains a swimming pool, hot tub, and poolside bar. The standard guest rooms face the atrium and have small balconies. They are tastefully decorated, and you'll find coffeemakers, irons, and comfortable couches in all units. Executive rooms are larger and overlook the golf course. The on-premises restaurant serves typical hotel fare in a Mediterranean setting.

480 Riverside Dr. (Route 105). ☎ **800-596-4656** *or 506-460-5500. Fax: 506-472-0170. Internet:* www.ramadafredericton.com. *Rack rates: C$85–C$105 (US$60.70–US$75) double. AE, DC, MC, V.*

Sheraton Fredericton

$$ Downtown

This 206-room property, Fredericton's largest, rises above the Saint John River on the west side of downtown (about a ten minute walk to City Hall). All the amenities of a full-service hotel are available — room service, business services, a lounge/restaurant, and so on — as well as a few bonuses: free parking, indoor and outdoor pools, and a summer-only poolside grill. The rooms aren't particularly large but are smartly designed. Request one with a river view when booking.

225 Woodstock Rd. ☎ **800-325-3535** *or 506-457-7000. Fax: 506-457-4000. Internet:* www.sheraton.com. *Rack rates: C$159–C$249 (US$113.60–US$177.90) double. AE, DC, MC, V.*

The Very Best — A Victorian Bed-and-Breakfast

$$ Downtown

On a quiet street at the eastern edge of downtown, this elegant 1840 home, run by friendly owners Yolande and Sam Rubenstein, is a wonderful retreat from the surrounding city. Inside, welcoming public areas open onto guest rooms that mix modern conveniences like air-conditioning and super-comfy beds with antiques and historic charm. The sunny rear garden has a heated pool and plenty of space to stretch out and relax. You can have your breakfast in the formal dining room or outdoors under a gazebo.

806 George St. (at Church St.) ☎ **506-451-1499**. *Fax: 506-454-1454. Rack rates: C$109 (US$77.90). AE, MC, V.*

Dining in Fredericton

You can indulge in a surprising range of cuisine in this outwardly staid city, thanks in part to the population of worldly university students. Outdoor dining is a treat that locals take full advantage of throughout the summer.

The Blue Door
$–$$$ Downtown FUSION

It's difficult to miss this casual and colorful downtown restaurant — just look for the historic brick building with bright red shutters, distinctive white trim and, yes, a blue door. In good weather, enjoy your meal (or just a martini) on the large patio. The young owners have brought their West Coast experiences to Fredericton, offering dishes that combine Canadian produce with spices and cooking styles from around the Pacific Rim. You'll be hooked on the flavorful jambalaya, which is full of shrimp, mussels, chicken, and sausage. Other choices are varied: Try the maple Dijon salmon or a Mexi burger topped with tangy blackened corn and tomato salsa. Non-meat eaters (as well as meat-eaters) will love the pad Thai, a filling noodle dish.

100 Regent St. ☎ 506-455-2583. Reservations recommended for dinner. Main courses: C$8–C$18 (US$5.70–US$12.90). AE, MC, V. Mon–Sat 11:30–10:00 p.m., Sun 5:30–9:30 p.m.

Chez Cora
$–$$ Downtown BREAKFAST

The story sounds good — a Quebec woman makes good with a local cafe that serves up healthy breakfasts in a cheery environment, then franchises the concept across eastern Canada. In reality, you get a Denny's-style breakfast with a couple of slices of fruit on the side. Your best bet is the crepes, which are as adventurous as a spinach/cheddar combo or as sweet and creamy as the Strawberry Satisfaction. This place stands out because of its bright color scheme, fun-loving furnishings (lots of stuffed chickens), and walls graffitied with the names of dishes. Kids will love the fun atmosphere, and parents will fall for the reasonable prices. Breakfast is served all day; lunch is from 11 a.m. until the mid-afternoon closing.

476 Queen St. ☎ 506-472-2672. Reservations not taken. Main courses: C$6–C$12 (US$4.30–US$8.60). AE, MC, V. Mon–Sat 6 a.m.–3 p.m., Sun 7 a.m.–3 p.m.

El Burrito Loco

$-$$ **Downtown**   **MEXICAN**

Locals are drawn in droves to this smallish restaurant for one reason: the authentic Mexican cooking of owner Perez Huerta. Everything from the guacamole to the taco shells is created in-house. In warmer weather, you'll need to reserve ahead to snag a table on the patio. Occasional live entertainment creates a fun vibe.

304 King St. ☎ 506-459-5626. Reservations recommended. Main courses: C$8–C$14.50 (US$5.70–US$10.40). AE, MC, V. Daily 9:30 a.m.–10:30 p.m.

Governor's Room

$$-$$$$ **Downtown**   **CONTINENTAL**

The intimate setting and consistently high quality of food make the Governor's Room popular with locals celebrating a special occasion and business travelers on expense accounts (it's ensconced in a bustling business hotel). The kitchen concentrates on classic European cooking. For starters, try the brie in filo, infused with a cranberry and roasted garlic sauce. Then move on to pheasant, pan-seared in a caramelized crust, or roasted crown rack of lamb smothered with mint paste. End the meal with a rum-based, nut-topped ice cream Bananas Foster.

Also in the hotel is the informal **Terrace Dining Room,** with a wide-ranging hotel menu and a large deck overlooking the river. The hotel's **James Joyce Irish Pub** is the place to tuck into a hearty bowl of Irish stew or a generous piece of cottage pie.

Lord Beaverbrook Hotel, 659 Queen St. ☎ 506-455-3371. Reservations essential. Main courses: C$16–C$30 (US$11.40–US$21.40). AE, DC, MC, V. Daily 6:00–9:30 p.m.

Rye's

$-$$ **Downtown**   **DELI/PUB FARE**

The combination of healthy deli food and traditional pub fare may seem a little strange, but Rye's does it well. The interior is pub-like, but if the weather is warm, you'll want to be outside on the trellised patio. The specialty is smoked meat on rye or in a wrap (all under C$10/US$7.10), a perfect lunchtime meal, although the portions are huge and could pass for dinner. Other notable offerings include Cajun-spiced chicken nachos and a tangy Thai chicken-and-bacon burger. The most popular breakfast dish — with good reason, as I found out after dining here — is huevos rancheros.

73 Carleton St. ☎ 506-472-7937. Reservations not necessary. Main courses: C$7.50–C$15 (US$5.40–US$10.70). AE, MC, V. Mon–Fri 8 a.m.–11 p.m., Sat from 9 a.m., Sun from 10 a.m.

Exploring Fredericton

Queen Street, one block from and running parallel to the Saint John River, is lined with historic sights and attractions. Most major sights are within walking distance of the City Hall at 397 Queen Street, which houses the **Visitor Information Centre** (☎ **506-460-2129**), open mid-May through mid-October daily 8 a.m. to 5 p.m. (July and August until 8 p.m.).

Historic Garrison District

Due to its status as the capital of New Brunswick and to the proximity of the United States border, Fredericton was the headquarters to a large contingent of British military personnel. After Confederation in 1867, the military moved on, but much of the character remains within the walls of the old military compound, now protected as the Historic Garrison District National Historic Site, located right downtown.

Guard House
Downtown

The interior of this solid stone building looks much as it did when occupied by garrison guards in the mid-1800s, complete with muskets at the ready and uniforms hanging along one wall. The adjacent windowless cellblock is also open for inspection. Try to time your visit with the outdoor musical presentations, which take place on the veranda through summer on Wednesdays at 12:30 p.m.

Carleton St. ☎ *506-460-2129. Admission: free. July–Aug daily 10 a.m.–6 p.m.*

Soldiers' Barracks
Downtown

Facing away from Queen Street at Carleton Street, the three-story Soldiers' Barracks was built in 1827 as living quarters for British soldiers. One room is open to the public, set up as it would have looked almost 200 years ago. Along the lower level, low-roofed rooms once used for ammunition storage are now occupied by vendors selling local crafts.

Queen St. (at Carleton St.) ☎ *506-460-2129. Admission: free. July–Aug daily 10 a.m.–6 p.m.*

York–Sunbury Society Historical Museum
Downtown

Displays in this museum give an insight into military and civilian life in Fredericton from the late 1800s through to the early part of last century. The much-touted highlight is the super-sized Coleman Frog. He was handfed cornmeal and whisky for much of his life and at the time of his death in 1893, he weighed in at a whooping 18 kilograms (42 pounds), or so the story goes. The frog now sits in a glass display case on the upper floor surrounded by tattered newspaper articles linked to his death and unlikely size. For me, the actual building holding the museum is of as much interest as the displays. Built in 1839 to house military officers, it is a rabbit warren of rooms, separated by solid stone walls and lined with original hand-hewn timbers.

The museum overlooks **Officers' Square**, where you can watch the **Changing of the Guard** July through August Tues.–Sat. at 11 a.m. and 7 p.m.

Queen St. and Regent St. ☎ *506-455-6041. Admission: C$3 (US$2.10) adults, C$1 (US70¢) children. July–Aug daily 10 a.m.–5 p.m., April–June and Sept to mid Dec Tues–Sat 1–4 p.m.*

Other Fredericton sights

Beaverbrook Art Gallery
Downtown

A gift to the city from the late press baron Lord Beaverbrook, this is one of Canada's premier art galleries. The building's rather dour exterior belies the treasures inside, most notably Salvador Dali's *Santiago el Grande*. The gallery is also home to an impressive collection of works by other European masters — J.M.W. Turner, John Constable, and Augustus John, as well as works of Canada's best-known artists from all eras, including Emily Carr.

Kids are encouraged to try their hand at painting and drawing in a special summer program operated by the gallery. Children aged 5 to 8 are invited to the 10 a.m. session, while those aged 9 to 12 attend the 2 p.m. sitting. Classes last around two hours and cost C$12 (US$8.60) per child.

703 Queen St. ☎ *506-458-8545. Internet:* www.beaverbrookartgallery.org. *Admission: C$5 (US$3.60) adults, C$4 (US$2.90) seniors, C$2 (US$1.40) children. June–Sept Mon–Fri 9 a.m.–6 p.m., Sat–Sun 10 a.m.–5 p.m.; Oct–May Tues–Fri 9 a.m.–5 p.m., Sat 10 a.m.–5 p.m., Sun noon to 5 p.m.*

Christ Church Cathedral
Downtown

For over 150 years, the single spire of this compact Gothic Revival church has dominated the Fredericton skyline. Rising regally from the surrounding residences and the tree-lined riverbank, the building was modeled on the 1340 St. Mary's Church in the village of Snettisham, Norfolk.

The most beautiful of many stained-glass windows is on the east side and is best viewed from the nave. From this central location, the morning sun illuminates a seven-paneled scene depicting Christ on the cross, flanked by three apostles on either side. Facing the nave from the northern transept is a massive organ comprising 1,500 pipes.

168 Brunswick St. ☎ ***506-450-8500;*** *Internet:* www.christchurchcathedral. com. *Church tours (free) are offered mid-June through August Mon.–Fri. 9 a.m.–6 p.m., Saturday 10 a.m.–5 p.m., and Sunday 1–5 p.m. July through August chamber music recitals are held every Friday at 12:10 p.m.*

Old Government House
Downtown

An impressive stone structure set on the banks of the Saint John River, this mansion was built in 1826 as the official residence of the governor, and served as such until 1892. In the ensuing years, it housed a school for the deaf, functioned as a hospital, and was the headquarters of the RCMP in New Brunswick. In the late 1990s, a massive overhaul of the grand old building saw it return to its original use as the home of the lieutenant governor, the representative of Queen Elizabeth II in New Brunswick. Great care was taken in the restoration work to properly replicate the original look, right down to the carpet and draperies. The governor's living quarters are on the top floor, away from the eyes of the public, but the rest of the building is open for tours throughout the year. Rooms restored to their former look include the library, formal dining room, and drawing room.

51 Woodstock Rd. ☎ ***506-453-2505.*** *Admission: free. Mid-June–mid-Sept daily 10 a.m.–5 p.m., mid-Sept–mid-June Mon–Fri 10 a.m.–4 p.m.*

Science East
Downtown

Set in a stone jail that dates to 1840 and was used as a prison until 1996, this fun attraction will keep enquiring minds occupied for at least a few hours. Everywhere you turn are interesting displays and interactive activities — an oversized kaleidoscope, an insectarium, and the chance to create a mini-tornado are the more popular ones. Outdoor amusements center on a large playground. The building's former life has been preserved in the grim dungeon, where displays describe the most notorious inmates and tell the story of the last hanging.

668 Brunswick St. ☎ ***506-457-2340.*** *Internet:* www.scienceeast.nb.ca. *Admission: C$5 (US$3.60) adults, C$3 (US$2.10) children. Mon–Sat 10 a.m.–6 p.m., Sun 1–5 p.m.*

Other cool things to see and do in Fredericton

Fredericton has a well-marked trail system, good for walking or biking. The downtown section extends east from the front of the Fredericton Sheraton to the Princess Margaret Bridge. Along the way is the Trail Bridge, originally built for trains but which now provides a pleasant link to North Fredericton for cyclists and pedestrians.

You can also take a break from sightseeing to:

- **Climb a lighthouse.** The nationalistic red and white **Fredericton Lighthouse,** at the foot of Regent Street (☎ **506-460-2939**), was built as a tourist attraction. To climb to the top costs C$2 (US$1.40) adults, C$1.50 (US$1.10) seniors and children. At street level is a booking desk for attractions throughout the region. You can also rent bikes and canoes here. It's open July to August daily 10 a.m. to 9 p.m., September daily noon to 7 p.m.

- **Take a river cruise.** The *Carleton II* takes up to 100 passengers on one-hour cruises along the downtown shoreline. The cost is a very reasonable C$8 (US$5.70) adults, C$4 (US$2.90) children. The departure point is the wharf near the foot of Regent Street (☎ **506-454-2628**). Tours run June through August, up to five times daily.

- **Explore an urban forest.** At 175-hectare (430-acre) **Odell Park,** ducks frolic on a small pond, trails lead through various forest environments, and large grassy areas are perfect for stretching out and doing absolutely nothing. In the southern section (access from Waggoner's Road) is an arboretum containing all of New Brunswick's native tree species.

- **Wander among headstones.** Walk up Carleton Street to Brunswick Street to reach the **Old Public Burial Ground,** the final resting place of the city's earliest residents.

- **Head back to school.** Founded in 1785, the **University of New Brunswick,** Bailey Drive (☎ **506-453-4666**), is North America's oldest public university. Feel free to walk the grounds.

- **Go golfing.** Picturesque **Lynx at Kingswood Park,** south of downtown along Hanwell Road (☎ **800-423-5969** or 506-443-3333), stretches over 2,100 meters (7,000 yards) from the back markers. Big bunkers, rolling fairways, and a 10-meter (33-foot) waterfall on the signature 14th hole define the layout. Greens fees are C$70 (US$50).

- **Get hooked on fishing. Kingsclear Freshwater Fishing,** based in Kingsclear, 15km (9.3 miles) west of Fredericton (☎ **506-363-5558**), charges around C$200 (US$142.90) for a guided river trip chasing smallmouth bass.

Shopping

You may be surprised at the diversity of shops in the downtown area, especially along the lower end of York Street, where an old-fashioned drug store, trendy import stores, and secondhand clothing shops sit side by side.

Fredericton has mall shopping along Prospect Street, including the **Fredericton Mall,** at 1150 Prospect Street (☎ **506-458-9226**).

Antiques

Old Tyme Collectibles, 152 King Street (☎ **506-451-9218**), is the largest of Fredericton's antique shops. Across the road is **This Old Thing Antiques,** at 173 King Street (☎ **506-454-4317**). Both have solid collections of Maritimes furniture and knickknacks from the late 1800s and early 1900s.

Arts and crafts

The centrally located **Gallery Connexion,** Justice Building on Queen Street at York Street (☎ **506-454-1433**), is an artist-operated, not-for-profit outlet where artists work in-situ. Also within the Garrison Historic District is **River Valley Fine Crafts,** a string of vendors with summer-only outlets on the lower level of the Soldier's Barracks (☎ **506-460-2837**). Look for handmade soaps and candles, jewelry, knitted clothing, and more. **Aitkens Pewter** has a more traditional setting, at 408 Queen Street (☎ **506-453-9474**). The **New Brunswick Crafts Council** displays an eclectic range of its members' work at a gallery on 87 Regent Street (☎ **506-450-8989**).

Gallery 78, at 796 Queen Street (☎ **506-450-8989**), housed in a converted century-old residence just a few blocks east of the main downtown core, is worth visiting to view the building itself . But the art is worth a peek too — the gallery sells mostly contemporary Canadian work at prices that aren't as high as you might expect.

Books

Westminster Books, 445 King Street (☎ **800-561-7323** or 506-454-1442), is Fredericton's premier independent bookstore. You can pick up everything from the latest bestsellers to local fiction, along with maps and specialty guidebooks.

Market

The **W.W. Boyce Farmer's Market,** 665 George Street at Regent Street (☎ 506-451-1815), is open year-round, Saturday 6 a.m. to 1 p.m. It attracts hordes of locals for fresh produce, meats, and cheeses, as well as local arts and crafts.

Nightlife

Fredericton isn't particularly known for its nightlife, but warm summer nights keep numerous decks and patios busy, while the populations of two universities keep the downtown spots busy the rest of the year.

Pubs and clubs

Most pubs and clubs are within walking distance of each other in the downtown core. Here are a few options:

- ✔ The **Lunar Rogue,** 625 King Street (☎ 506-450-2065), is an English-style pub with lots of draught beer choices. The patio hops on hot nights.

- ✔ **Rye's,** 73 Carleton Street (☎ 506-472-7937), has a small outdoor patio, and books jazz and blues music acts on weekends.

- ✔ Head to **Dolan's Pub,** 349 King Street (☎ 506-454-7474), for a traditional pub atmosphere and live East Coast music.

- ✔ Set beside an outdoor swimming pool, the **Dip Pool Bar,** in the Sheraton Fredericton at 225 Woodstock Road (☎ 506-457-7000), offers a resort atmosphere.

- ✔ **Upper Deck,** 1475 Piper's Lane (☎ 506-457-1475), is your typical sports bar, with big-screen televisions, pool tables, nightly drink specials, and bands on weekends.

- ✔ **Liquid,** 375 King Street (☎ 506-457-1475), is one of the city's hottest nightclubs.

- ✔ Fredericton's only gay nightspot is **G Club,** 377 King Street (☎ 506-455-7768), open Wednesday through Sunday from 8 p.m.

The arts

The Playhouse, at 686 Queen Street (☎ 506-458-8344), is Fredericton's main venue for performing arts and live music. Symphony New Brunswick and Theatre New Brunswick regularly perform here.

Time Travellers (☎ 506-460-2129) is a troupe of costumed performers who lead theatrical walking tours of the historic precinct. The meeting point is the Soldiers' Barracks, at Queen and Carleton streets. Times are Monday through Friday at 2:30 p.m.

Side Trips from Fredericton

The Saint John River flows past Fredericton, draining into the Bay of Fundy at Saint John. If you're traveling between these two cities, the detour to pretty Gagetown is well worthwhile.

Upstream of Fredericton are a string of historic riverside towns, along with King's Landing Historical Settlement, which recreates a Loyalist village from 200 years ago.

Gagetown

Historic Gagetown is regarded by many as one of the most picturesque villages in all of the Maritimes. Laid out by Loyalists in 1783, the streets lie parallel to Gagetown Creek and are lined with stately trees and carefully restored buildings, some over 200 years old. The surrounding countryside is equally appealing — think apple orchards, grazing cattle, and the wide Saint John River dotted with islands.

To get to Gagetown from Fredericton, follow Route 2 (Trans-Canada Highway) east for 50km (31 miles) and take Exit 330 to the south. Following Route 102 from the capital takes a little longer, but the scenery is more eye-catching.

Gagetown is a fertile ground for shopping. **Jugglers Cove Fine Arts & Crafts,** 32 Tilley Road (☎ 506-488-2574), displays a colorful range of pottery and paintings; **Gran-An's Charmers,** 44 Front Street (☎ 506-488-2074), sells traditional arts and crafts; and **Loomcrafters,** 23 Loomcraft Lane (☎ 506-488-2400), located in a structure dating to 1761 at the east end of Tilley Road, is the place to pickup handmade woven items.

Steamers Stop Inn, 74 Front Street (☎ 877-991-9922 or 506-488-2903), has perks that include a screened-in veranda overlooking Gagetown Creek, comfortable rooms with en suites (Room 6 has the nicest views), canoes and kayaks for guest use, and an in-house art gallery. Rates of C$95 (US$67.90) double include a full breakfast. The inn is open May through September.

Kissing bridges

If your travels include driving around New Brunswick, you'll no doubt notice that an abundance of covered wooden bridges dot the province. Now a symbol of New Brunswick, the enclosures, affectionately referred to as "kissing bridges," were originally created to protect the wood from weathering by sun and rain — not to provide an opportunity for a romantic rendezvous. It was estimated that uncovered bridges lasted around 10 years, while those that were covered would last many times longer. The fact that around 70 covered bridges remain is a testament to their durability.

Some of the easiest bridges to find are along the upper Saint John River Valley. Heading north from King's Landing, the **Nackawic Siding Covered Bridge** straddles Route 585 west of Millville, while in Benton, west of Meductic, the **Benton Village Covered Bridge** is in a particularly scenic locale. Further north, the **Hartland Covered Bridge,** in the town of Hartland, stretches for 390 meters (1,280 feet), making it the world's longest covered bridge.

East of Fredericton, along Route 890 between Sussex and Petitcodiac (take Exit 365 from Route 2), you'll find a string of covered bridges. Along this road, the village of Newtown is home to the world's only **covered bridge gift shop** (☎ 506-433-4813).

Mactaquac and area

The highlight of the Mactaquac area, west of Fredericton, is King's Landing Historical Settlement, but **Mactaquac Provincial Park** is also worth exploring. Protecting the shoreline of a reservoir formed by the Mactaquac Dam, which spans the Saint John River, activities on offer include canoeing (rentals available), golfing, and hiking. To get to the park, cross the Saint John River via Fredericton's Westmorland Street Bridge and follow Route 105 west for 24km (15 miles). Access to the park costs C$5 (US$3.60) per vehicle per day.

From the park, retrace your path and drive south across the Mactaquac Dam to reach Route 2.

King's Landing Historical Settlement
King's Landing

Fleeing the American Revolution in 1783, around 15,000 people loyal to Britain headed north to New Brunswick. They established settlements throughout the region, including Saint-Anne, on the site of present-day Fredericton. King's Landing is a re-creation of one of these villages, historically accurate down to the last detail and fun for the whole family. Over 100 costumed staff "live" here, transporting visitors along dirt roads in horse-drawn carts, tending to crops, crafting horseshoes in the black-smith shop, and cooking simple meals for visitors in the King's Head Inn. Children will love the outdoor theater program, while all ages will enjoy the ice cream shop.

King's Landing (Exit 253 from Route 2) ☎ *506-363-4959. Internet:* www. kingslanding.nb.ca. *Admission C$14 (US$10) adults, C$12 (US$8.60) seniors, C$9 (US$6.40) children. June–mid-Oct daily 10 a.m.–6 p.m.*

Fast Facts: Fredericton

ATMs

Look for ATMs at all downtown banks. Try **CIBC,** at 448 Queen St., and **Bank of Montreal,** at 505 King St.

Emergencies

Dial ☎ **911** for all emergencies.

Hospital

Dr. Everett Chambers Hospital is at 700 Priestman St. (☎ **506-452-5400**).

Information

Contact **Fredericton Tourism** at ☎ **506-460-2041;** Internet: www. fredericton.ca. The main visitor center is in **City Hall,** at 397 Queen St. It's open mid-May–mid-Oct daily 8 a.m.–5 p.m., extended hours July–Aug until 8 p.m.

Internet Access

Fredericton Public Library, at 4 Carleton St. (☎ **506-460-2800**), has free Internet access on a first-come, first-served basis.

Police

Dial ☎ **911** in an emergency. For non-emergencies, dial ☎ **506-452-3400.**

Post Office

The main downtown post office is at 570 Queen St.

Restrooms

Militia Arms Store, Historic Garrison District, Carleton St.

Taxis

Call **Checker Cab** (☎ **506-450-8294**), **Loyal Taxi** (☎ **506-455-6789**), or **Standard Taxi** (☎ **506-450-4444**).

Transit Info

The information line for **Fredericton Transit** is ☎ **506-460-2200.**

Weather

Click through the links at the **Environment Canada** Web site (www.weatheroffice. ec.gc.ca) for local forecasts, or call ☎ **506-446-6244** for a recorded message.

Part V
Prince Edward Island

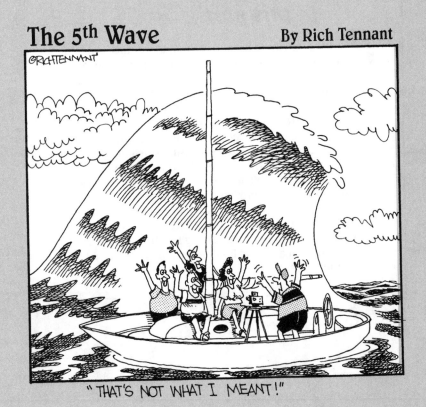

The 5th Wave   By Rich Tennant

@RICHTENNANT

"THAT'S NOT WHAT I MEANT!"

In this part...

*P*otatoes, lobsters, and an orphan girl named Anne are the best-known exports from Prince Edward Island, a serene oasis unlike anywhere else in the Canada. Usually referred to simply as "PEI," it may be the country's smallest province, but for many visitors it is the most memorable. Beyond the historic capital of Charlottetown, a patchwork of fields extends in all directions, ringed by red cliffs that descend to calm ocean waters. Dotting this landscape are painted farmhouses, quaint towns, and fishing villages. PEI became more accessible in 1997 with the completion of the Confederation Bridge linking it to the mainland, yet the atmosphere on the island remains mellow. The short summer visiting season attracts visitors from around the world to Cavendish, the setting for *Anne of Green Gables,* while vacationing families are drawn to surrounding beaches.

Chapter 18

Charlottetown

● ●

In This Chapter

▶ Making your way to Charlottetown

▶ Getting to know the city

▶ Learning about the top places to stay and eat

▶ Checking out the prime attractions and activities

● ●

*W*ith a population of 35,000, Charlottetown is Canada's smallest provincial capital and like no other city in the country. A distinct lack of pretense and an unhurried feel make it decidedly un-capital–like, while its tree-lined downtown streets and incredibly rich history only add to the charm.

In summer, the streets of Charlottetown bustle with activity. Its central location makes it a natural draw for visitors and its well-priced lodgings and cultural events make the city a perfect base for day-trips to other island destinations (Cavendish, for example, less than an hour's drive away).

Getting to Charlottetown

Sitting in the central portion of Queens County, Charlottetown is at the hub of a varied road system that includes everything from the major thoroughfares to narrow back roads. Most important of these roads is the Trans-Canada Highway, which links Charlottetown to the mainland by bridge and ferry.

By plane

Air Canada and its connectors have direct flights to Charlottetown from Halifax, Montreal, and Toronto. **Charlottetown Airport** is 8km (5 miles) north of downtown. Charlottetown has no airport service, but you'll find a row of taxis waiting out front of the arrivals terminal, charging C$12 (US$8.60) for the ride downtown.

Prince Edward Island

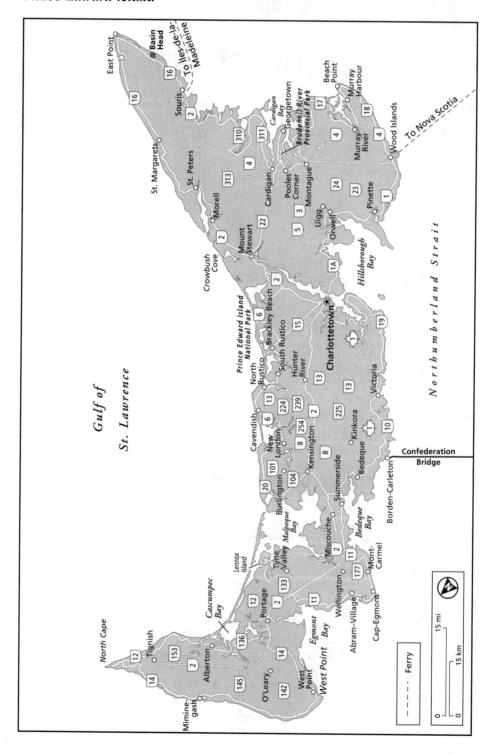

Charlottetown

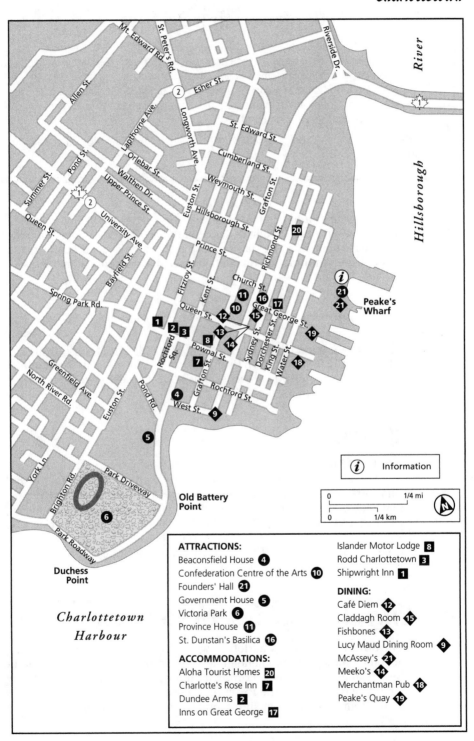

Old Battery Point

Duchess Point

Charlottetown Harbour

Peake's Wharf

i Information

| 0 | | 1/4 mi |
| 0 | | 1/4 km |

ATTRACTIONS:
Beaconsfield House **4**
Confederation Centre of the Arts **10**
Founders' Hall **21**
Government House **5**
Victoria Park **6**
Province House **11**
St. Dunstan's Basilica **16**

ACCOMMODATIONS:
Aloha Tourist Homes **20**
Charlotte's Rose Inn **7**
Dundee Arms **2**
Inns on Great George **17**

Islander Motor Lodge **8**
Rodd Charlottetown **3**
Shipwright Inn **1**

DINING:
Café Diem **12**
Claddagh Room **15**
Fishbones **13**
Lucy Maud Dining Room **9**
McAssey's **21**
Meeko's **14**
Merchantman Pub **18**
Peake's Quay **19**

Confederation Bridge

Completed in 1997, the Confederation Bridge links Prince Edward Island to the rest of Canada. It's the world's longest bridge over ice-covered water — 13km (8 miles) from Cape Jourimain, New Brunswick, to Borden-Carleton, just an hour west of Charlottetown in PEI. Built at a cost of almost C$1 billion (US$700 million), it comprises 44 spans, each as long as a city block, and extends up to 20 meters (66 feet) above Northumberland Strait.

Driving to the island is free. The toll (C$38.50/US$27.50) is only collected on the return journey.

All major **car-rental** companies have airport desks and vehicles are parked within easy walking distance of the arrivals area. The number of vehicles is limited, so be sure to make reservations as far in advance as possible. For information on contacting major car-rental companies, see the Appendix.

By car

The **Trans-Canada Highway** (Highway 1) crosses to Prince Edward Island via the Confederation Bridge, 60km (37 miles) from the capital. If you cross to the island via the ferry, it's a similar distance from the dock to downtown.

By bus

Acadian Lines (☎ **800-567-5151** or 902-628-6432; Internet: www. acadianbus.com) has service three times daily between Moncton and Charlottetown, with connections in Moncton from throughout the Maritimes. The Charlottetown bus depot is at 156 Belvedere Avenue. **PEI Express Shuttle** (☎ **877-877-1771** or 902-462-8177; Internet www.peishuttle.com) offers van service between Halifax and Charlottetown for C$50 (US$35.70) each way, stopping at hotels and bed-and-breakfasts upon request.

Getting Around Charlottetown

The downtown core of Charlottetown is very compact. Almost all the accommodations recommended here are within walking distance of the best restaurants. Scattered throughout are the main city attractions, including the very central **Province House,** with other buildings of historic interest, the best shops, and the harbor all within six blocks.

Downtown streets are laid out in a grid pattern. Those running north-west to southeast end at Water Street, which runs along the harborfront. At its north end, Water Street merges with the eastbound Trans-Canada Highway. University Avenue is the major northbound artery. North of the university, you can take Malpeque Road to Route 2 towards Cavendish and the North Shore, or head west along the Trans-Canada Highway to the Confederation Bridge.

Parking

Public parking is spread along Water Street. Parking meters and pay lots cost C$.50 (US$.35) per hour on weekdays. Look for free street parking on the outskirts of downtown (try northeast of Prince Street). Parking is free everywhere on weekends.

The main information center is along Water Street at Hillsborough Street. It's the best place to park and start your exploration of the city. Don't forget to pick up a voucher for one hour's free parking at the information center.

Transit and tours

Charlottetown Transit (☎ **902-566-5664**) serves mostly residential areas along four routes Monday through Friday only. The fare is C$1.50 (US$1.07) per sector.

Jump aboard the red double-decker bus operated by **Abegweit Tours** (☎ **902-894-9966**) to see all the downtown highlights as well as outlying attractions, such as the Lieutenant Governor's mansion, the University of Prince Edward Island campus, and Victoria Park. The tour takes one hour and is bargain-priced at just C$9 (US$6.40). The bus departs June through mid-September up to seven times daily, with pickup points in front of the Rodd Charlottetown and the Queen Street side of the Confederation Centre of the Arts.

Staying in Charlottetown

Accommodations in Charlottetown are generally well priced and fall within one of two categories: hotels or historic inns. Don't associate the city's lower rates with a lack of services or charm — you get excellent value for your money in Charlottetown, especially during non-summer months.

Because the city is compact, you can plan on walking to all the top attractions and restaurants from your room.

Aloha Tourist Homes

$ Downtown

Lifetime local Maynard MacMillan has converted two adjacent historic homes into accommodation for travelers on a budget. Each house has a shared bathroom, lounge with cable TV, and fully equipped kitchen. The five guest rooms are brightened by a coat of colorful paint and all are clean and well-maintained. The property is open year round, with discounts outside the summer months.

234 Sydney St. ☎ *902-892-9944. Internet:* www.alohaamigo.com. *Rack rates: C$50 (US$35.70) double.*

Charlotte's Rose Inn

$$ Downtown

This cozy 1884 Victorian residence is on a quiet, tree-lined street close to everything. The four guest rooms are decorated with period antiques and lots of frilly fabrics. Each has an ensuite bathroom, a TV/VCR combo, original artwork on the walls, and comfortable wingback chairs. The top floor loft apartment has a small kitchen and opens to a private rooftop deck. Downstairs you'll find a parlor stocked with cookies and coffee and a richly decorated breakfast room. Rates include a full breakfast.

11 Grafton St. ☎ *888-237-3699 or 902-892-3699. Fax: 902-894-3699. Internet:* www.peisland.com/charlottesinn. *Rack rates: C$135–C$175 (US$96.40–US$125) double. MC, V.*

Dundee Arms

$$–$$$ Downtown

Built in 1906 as the home of a local entrepreneur, this elaborate Queen Anne Revival building has housed an inn since 1972. It has gone through many changes over the years, including the additions of an English-style pub, a dining room, and a wing of motel rooms. Through it all, the Dundee Arms remains a charming choice for your stay in Charlottetown. Guest rooms in the original building range from cutesy (Anne's Room) to staid (Chandler Suite), but all come packed with niceties, such as bathrobes and Internet access.

200 Pownal St. ☎ *877-638-6333 or 902-892-2496. Fax: 902-368-8532. Internet:* www.dundeearms.com. *Rack rates: C$130–C$220 (US$92.90–US$157.10) double. MC, V.*

Inns on Great George
$$$–$$$$ Downtown

Dating to 1811, three adjoining townhouses bookended by two hotels and a smattering of surrounding buildings make up this grand lodging complex one block from Province House. In its heyday, the Pavilion Hotel at Dorchester Street was the fashionable social center of the city and the accommodation of choice for delegates attending the 1864 Charlottetown Conference. This property now holds the most rooms (24) along with the reception area and a sofa lounge — a comfortable gathering spot where a light breakfast is served each morning. The layout and decor of the guest rooms varies greatly, but all are thoroughly modern (ensuites, air-conditioning, high-speed Internet access, and so on.). For a splurge, consider one of the four suites in the Stable House, especially room 222, which features a kitchen, luxurious bathroom, separate bedroom, and lounge area with leather furniture and a fireplace. My favorite rooms can be found in the Wellington Hotel, which combines historic charm with modern styling at a reasonable price.

58 Great George St. ☎ 800-361-1118 or 902-892-0606. Fax: 902-628-2079. Internet: www.innsongreatgeorge.com. Rack Rates: C$180–C$340 (US$128.60–US$242.90) double. AE, DC, MC, V.

Islander Motor Lodge
$$ Downtown

Don't expect anything too fancy at the Islander. It's simply an inexpensive downtown motel that is a better choice for families than the many similarly priced bed-and-breakfasts. Rooms are spacious, air-conditioned, and regularly renovated, although basic. The motel has a coffee shop and dining room, but everything is so close that your best dining bet is one of the recommendations below.

146–148 Pownal St. ☎ 800-268-6261 or 902-892-1217. Fax: 902-566-1623. Internet: www.islandermotorlodge.com. Parking: Free. Rack rates: C$120 (US$85.70) double. AE, MC, V. Wheelchair-accessible rooms.

Rodd Charlottetown
$$ Downtown

A distinctive redbrick building with grand colonnades flanking its entry, this downtown hotel is perfectly located for the tour group crowd. The marble-floored lobby gives way to elegant rooms decorated with period reproductions. Amenities include a largish indoor pool, a fitness room, and a sauna. You can take a break from seafood with the finest cuts of beef in the Carvery Dining Room, or relax with a cocktail in The Provinces lounge before searching out dinner at one of the many nearby restaurants. Weekend discounts are standard year-round, but the best deals are packages advertised on the Rodd Web site.

75 Kent St. ☎ *800-565-7633 or 902-894-7371. Fax: 902-368-2178. Internet:* www.rodd-hotels.ca. *Parking: Free. Rack rates: C$119 (US$85) double. AE, DISC, DC, MC, V.*

Royalty Maples Cottages and Motel
$$ North of Downtown

On the north side of downtown, close to the airport and perfect for getting an early morning start to Cavendish, this lodging is about as un-city-like as you'll ever find. It comprises a collection of neat cottages set around a sprawling greenspace — perfect for children. The cottages come with one or two bedrooms and each has a kitchen and cable TV.

Malpeque Rd. (north of the Trans-Canada Hwy.) ☎ *800-381-7829 or 902-368-1030. Rack rates: motel rooms C$79 (US$56.40) double, cottages C$95–C$105 (US$67.90–US$75) double. AE, MC, V. May–Dec.*

Shipwright Inn
$$–$$$$ Downtown

The water views that the original owner, a local shipbuilder, enjoyed from this 1860s home are long gone, but the building's solid timber construction — including the original hardwood floors — remains through extensive restoration work. The result is one of Charlottetown's premier accommodations. Each of the nine guest rooms has its own character and configuration — about all they have in common is a distinct historic charm and a subtle maritime theme. The rooms have amenities you'd expect in a hotel — TV, air-conditioning, telephone — as well as many you wouldn't, like goose-down duvets and nautical-themed antiques. Even the smallest unit, the Chart Room (which really isn't that small), has a fireplace, a walnut four-poster bed, an antique writing desk, and, of course, nautical charts on the walls. Breakfast is taken in a communal dining area, although I found myself sneaking back through the day for the complimentary homemade goodies and freshly squeezed lemonade.

51 Fitzroy St. ☎ *888-306-9966 or 902-368-1905. Fax: 902-628-1905. Internet:* www.shipwrightinn.com. *Rack rates: C$135–C$280 (US$96.40–US$200) double. MC, V.*

Dining in Charlottetown

Charlottetown's local dining scene is surprisingly vibrant, thanks to a healthy student population and thriving tourism industry.

Café Diem

$ **Downtown**   CAFE

Of Charlottetown's small selection of cafes, this is the best. You can take advantage of the tree-shaded tables out front or check your e-mail on computer terminals along the narrow indoor loft. The blackboard menu is crammed with healthy choices — salads, soups, curries, and more — all under C$10 (US$7.10).

128 Richmond St. ☎ *902-892-0494. Lunches: C$6–C$10 (US$4.30–US$7.10). MC, V. Daily 9 a.m. to midnight.*

Claddagh Room

$$$–$$$$ **Downtown**   SEAFOOD

Owner/chef Liam Dolan named this restaurant for a fishing village in his Irish homeland, and naturally the menu features mostly seafood with a small selection of other dishes. Choose between lobster-stuffed mushrooms and orange salad with almonds to start, or dive right into typical mains like jumbo shrimp Creole or herb-crusted honey-mustard lamb chops. A handsome, old-fashioned dining room, sharp service, and a delicious dessert selection round out what many consider to be Charlottetown's finest restaurant.

131 Sydney St. ☎ *902-892-9661. Main courses: C$18–C$30 (US$12.90–US$21.40). AE, DC MC, V. Mon–Fri 11:30 a.m.–2:00 p.m., daily 5–10 p.m.*

A moolicious treat

Wowie Cowie. Deja Moo. Gooey Mooey. These are 3 of over 30 flavors you'll be confronted with at COWS, an island institution whose ice cream holds up against the best Ben & Jerry's can offer (I've "researched" both). COWS uses handmade waffle cones and an old-fashioned recipe that calls for the freshest island cream. Started from a single outlet in Cavendish, the company now has 13 stores, including two in Charlottetown (one at Queen and Grafton streets and another at Peake's Wharf), one in Gateway Village (at the north end of Confederation Bridge), and another onboard the Caribou–Wood Islands ferry.

The ice cream may be traditional, but the associated COWS fashion line is anything but — the distinctive and colorful T-shirts make a wonderful souvenir. Look for them in all COWS stores or purchase online at www.cows.ca.

Fishbones

$$-$$$ **Downtown   SEAFOOD**

This glorified oyster bar is on Victoria Row, a short section of Richmond Street that is designated pedestrian-only throughout the summer months. Choose to dine at tables out on the sidewalk, or inside at regular tables and in very private booths. Malpeque Bay oysters are a natural starter. They sit on a massive bed of ice, accompanied by your choice of sauces for C$2 (US$1.40) each. Other sample starters are Cajun calamari salad and steamed mussels broiled in a garlic broth; mains include seafood stir-fry and red snapper pan-seared in a chili glaze. Lunches are mostly under $12, including tangy lemon-peppered haddock.

136 Richmond St. ☎ *902-628-6569. Reservations not necessary. Main courses: C$14–C$23 (US$10–US$16.40). MC, V. Daily 11 a.m.–11 p.m.*

Lucy Maud Dining Room

$$-$$$ **Downtown   MODERN CANADIAN**

Students at the highly regarded Culinary Institute of Canada prepare lunch and dinner, then enthusiastically serve it to the public as part of their training at this large restaurant. Dining here is a wonderful opportunity to enjoy fine food at reasonable prices. Be sure to snag a window seat to enjoy views that extend over Charlottetown Harbour. The menu changes each semester and is based on seasonal specialties, such as Cornish game hen in the fall. You'll be thankful seafood chowder is a staple. End your meal with one of the extravagant desserts.

4 Sydney St. ☎ *902-894-6868. Reservations recommended. Main courses: C$16–C$27 (US$11.40–US$19.30). AE, MC, V. Tues–Fri 11:30 a.m.–1:30 p.m., Tues–Sat 6–8 p.m.*

McAssey's

$$-$$$ **Downtown   SEAFOOD/CONTEMPORARY**

In the upstairs section of Founders' Hall, Charlottetown's premier attraction, McAssey's is a stylish space and surprisingly untouristy. The menu emphasizes local produce and Atlantic seafood, all prepared with a creative twist — Digby scallops with asparagus and grilled halibut with a hint of curry are examples. The lamb is from Australia, but the accompanying potatoes are island-grown. The location makes McAssey's an ideal lunch spot — offerings such as spinach and mango salad are a sensible alternative to a full meal. Diners enjoy live music on Tuesday and Thursday evenings.

6 Prince St. ☎ *902-892-1223. Reservations recommended. Main courses: C$14–C$23 (US$10–US$16.40). AE, MC, V. July–Sept Mon–Sat 11:30 a.m.– 11:30 p.m.; May–June and Oct–Dec Thurs–Sat 11:30 a.m.–11:30 p.m.*

Meeko's

$–$$ **Downtown   GREEK**

At Meeko's you'll find the best Greek food on Prince Edward Island, served in a nationalistic blue and white room with murals on the walls and mellow Greek music in the background. You can take a break from seafood by choosing a tzatziki and moussaka combo for two, which will set you back just $20. The same menu is offered all day, with well-priced salad and sandwich choices at lunchtime.

146 Richmond St. ☎ *902-892-9800. Main courses: C$8.75–C$17 (US$6.25–US$12.10). MC, V. Daily 11 a.m.–10 p.m.*

Merchantman Pub

$$ **Downtown   PUB FARE**

Across from Confederation Landing Park, the Merchantman is a typical British-style pub — think dim lighting, exposed beams, and redbrick walls — with an ambitious selection of food that goes well beyond the traditional bangers and mash. You can order all sorts of fresh seafood, chicken, and steaks, some prepared with Cajun or Asian influences.

23 Queen St. (at Water St.) ☎ *902-892-9150. Main courses: C$11–C$20 (US$7.90–US$14.30). AE, MC, V. Mon–Sat 11:30 a.m.–11:30 p.m.*

Peake's Quay

$–$$ **Downtown   PUB FARE/SEAFOOD**

Peake's Quay offers a wonderful waterfront location and well-priced food, though the service is not exactly stellar. This restaurant-cum-bar takes full advantage of its upstairs location with garage-style doors opening to a huge deck overlooking the marina. The menu mixes regular pub food with Maritimes staples like seafood chowder served in a bread bowl, lobster rolls, and a boiled lobster that comes with all the usual trimmings. Desserts are all around C$5 (US$3.60), or head to the COWS ice cream shop directly below for a scoop to go.

1 Great George St. (at Water St.) ☎ *902-368-1330. Main courses: C$9–C$18 (US$6.40–US$12.90). AE, DISC, DC, MC, V. Daily 11 a.m.–10 p.m.*

Exploring Charlottetown

As the provincial capital, Charlottetown has a number of major attractions. Most notable among them are Founders' Hall and Province House, both of particular interest to Canadians. One thing that everyone should do in Charlottetown is stroll through the narrow streets between Province House and the waterfront, where the mix of residential and commercial architecture has remained unchanged for over a century.

Beaconsfield House
Downtown

Built in 1877 for local shipbuilder James Peake Junior, this gracious home is one of the finest pre-1900 residences on the island. From the street, it's the sharp yellow exterior and gingerbread trim that will catch your eye. Inside, you'll find an impressive 25 rooms and 8 fireplaces. The first two of three floors are furnished, while a narrow stairway leads to the belvedere, a turret with water views. Special events include musical performances and a weekday children's program in the adjacent carriage house. The on-site bookstore has a solid collection of island literature.

2 Kent St. (at West St.) ☎ *902-368-6603. Admission: C$3.50 (US$2.50) adults. June–Sept daily 10 a.m.–5 p.m.*

Confederation Centre of the Arts
Downtown

This large, boxy structure in the heart of downtown is at odds with surrounding historic buildings, but once inside, you'll find many redeeming features, including the largest art gallery east of Montreal. The Confederation Centre Art Gallery is highlighted by the luminaries of Canadian art through the last 200 years. Many of the names won't be familiar (even to most Canadians), but Gordon Smith sculptures, paintings by the husband-and-wife team of Christopher and Mary Pratt, and works by Robert Harris are standouts. The center also has three theaters (see "Nightlife" later in this chapter), a large library with first editions of *Anne of Green Gables,* a craft shop, a memorial hall, and a cafe. Through summer, it hosts the Charlottetown Festival, which includes daily lunchtime entertainment at an amphitheater by the main entrance.

145 Richmond St. ☎ *902-566-1267. Internet:* www.confederationcentre. com. *Gallery admission: free. Gallery hours: Daily 9 a.m.–5 p.m.*

Walk the walk

Joining a walking tour with the **Confederation Players** (☎ 800-955-1864 or 902-368-1864), a group of eager locals dressed in Confederation-era garb, is a great way to learn a little about Charlottetown while taking advantage of warm summer temperatures. Choose from three tours: a trip back in time along Great George Street, storytelling along the waterfront, or the Merchants and Mansions walk. All depart Founders' Hall June through late September hourly 10 a.m. to 4 p.m. and cost C$4.50 (US$3.20). Historical reenactments on the steps of Province House (daily at 11 a.m. and 4 p.m.; free) and old-fashioned games on the grounds of Founders' Hall (Sunday at 1:30 p.m.; free) are part of the same program.

Founders' Hall
Downtown

Using innovative state-of-the-art displays, this waterfront attraction transports visitors back in time to the 1864 Charlottetown Conference. It is contained within a historic railway building just steps from where the Fathers of Confederation came ashore. You begin your journey by entering the Time Tunnel, which takes back to life in the 1860s. The tunnel opens to the octagonal Hall of the Fathers, which describes the men who met to discuss the formation of the country. Beyond this exhibit is a string of rooms, each dedicated to a province or territory, linking up in the order they joined the Dominion of Canada. Along the way, televisions, computer terminals, headsets, trivia games, and dynamic audiovisual displays enhance the story.

6 Prince St. ☎ *902-368-1864. Internet:* www.foundershall.ca. *Admission: C$7 (US$5) adults, C$5.50 (US$3.90) seniors, C$3.75 (US$2.70) children. Mid-May–mid-Oct Mon–Sat 9 a.m.–5 p.m., Sun 9 a.m.–4 p.m. (July–Aug Mon–Sat until 8 p.m.)*

Government House and Victoria Park
Downtown

Perched on a slight rise at the edge of downtown, the 1835 Government House is the official residence of the lieutenant governor. The grounds are not open to the public, but the grand mansion is clearly visible through stands of mature white birch.

Beyond Government House, Kent Street passes through Victoria Park, a pleasant green space that ends at the shoreline of Charlottetown Harbour. The best way to enjoy the park is on foot (although you'll be passed by a stream of jogging, skating, and biking locals). Near the entrance to the park, a row of six antique cannons points to the harbor entrance.

Take Kent St. southwest through downtown.

Province House
Downtown

Still the seat of the provincial legislature, Province House is where the Fathers of Confederation met in 1864 to discuss the formation of the Dominion of Canada. This landmark meeting took place in the second-floor chamber, which has been restored to the way it looked back then, right down to the original furniture, and has an adjacent clerk's office and library. Also on the second floor is the current Legislative Chamber, a smallish room that looks to have changed little in well over a century.

Traditions are well entrenched here — the premier gets a small flag on his desk and the ruling party is always seated on the south side of the room, a throwback to the days before central heating when the afternoon sun warmed only this part of the chamber.

165 Richmond St. (at St. George St.) ☎ *902-566-7626. Admission: free. June–Sept daily 9 a.m.–5 p.m., Oct–May Mon–Fri 9 a.m.–5 p.m.*

St. Dunstan's Basilica
Downtown

Distinctive for its twin Gothic spires, St. Dunstan's Basilica is one of Canada's largest churches. The interior is notable for its intricate vaulted ceiling, ornate Italian carvings, and polished marble columns.

45 Great George St. ☎ *902-894-3486. Admission: free. Daily 8 a.m.–5 p.m.*

Other cool things to see and do

When you've had your fill of downtown attractions, and are ready for other diversions or sights lying beyond city limits, here are a few possibilities:

- ✔ **Peake's Wharf Boat Cruises** (☎ 902-566-4458), departing from Peake's Quay on Water Street June through September. Choose from harbor tours with full commentaries (1:00, 6:30, and 8:00 p.m.; C$16/ US$11.40) or a seal-watching excursion (2:30 p.m.; C$22/US$15.70).

- ✔ The **Farmer's Market**, on Belvedere Avenue, opposite the university. Vendors at this indoor market sell everything from fresh seafood to island-made crafts. It operates year-round Saturday 9 a.m. to 2 p.m., and in July and August also Wednesday 10 a.m. to 5 p.m.

- ✔ **Orwell Corner Historical Village,** 30km/18.6 miles east of Charlottetown (☎ 902-651-8510). Experience life in the 1850s at this restored farming community. The village is open late May through mid-October Monday to Friday 9 a.m. to 5 p.m. and admission is C$5 (US$3.60) adults, C$1.50 (US$1.07) children.

- ✔ **Fort Amherst/Port-la-Joye National Historic Site,** a pleasant 35-minute drive west, then south, from downtown (☎ 902-566-7626). Not much remains of the island's first European settlement, which was established in 1720, but a visitor center (mid-June through August daily 9 a.m. to 5 p.m.) at the site tells its story. The surrounding grounds are a great place for a picnic.

Shopping

As the hub of Prince Edward Island, Charlottetown shops cater well to the needs of islanders, with a nod to the tourists down on the waterfront along Water Street. For mall shopping, head north from downtown along University Avenue. Here are some of my favorite shops in Charlottetown (in no particular order):

- **Anne of Green Gables Store** 102 Queen St. (☎ 902-368-2663) is the place to pick up kitschy Green Gables souvenirs.

- **Island Crafts Shop** 156 Richmond St. (☎ 902-892-5152) is crammed with arts and crafts, including woodwork and weaved items.

- **Details** 166 Richmond St. (☎ 902-892-2233) displays fine art in the front and an eclectic range of antiques out back.

- **Pilar Shephard Art Gallery** 82 Great George St. (☎ 902-892-1953) is another fine art gallery. It features island landscapes.

- **Gallery 18** 41 Grafton St. (☎ 902-628-8869) holds an impressive collection of antiquarian books, maps, and charts.

- **Moonsnail Soapworks:** 87 Water St. (☎ 902-892-7627) specializes in handmade soaps and other body treats.

- **PEI Specialty Chip Co.** is based in Marshfield, northeast of Charlottetown (☎ 902-629-1818), but look for their lobster-flavored potato chips at retail outlets throughout the city.

- **Canada Eh?,** in Founders' Hall, 6 Prince St., (☎ 902-368-1864), is crammed with Canadian souvenirs — maple syrup, smoked salmon, wooden fishermen, Canadian flag kites, and more.

Nightlife

No one could ever describe Charlottetown as a hotbed of after-dark action, but still, there's usually something going on somewhere.

The Buzz is a free publication with listings of what's happening throughout Charlottetown. It comes out monthly, or check the online version at www.isn.net/buzzon. The Web site www.visitcharlottetown.com lists festivals and events, including all performing arts.

Of course, you can also drop by the Visitor Information Centre on Water Street (☎ 902-368-7795) to find out what's on when you're in town.

Pubs and clubs

Victoria Row, a short section of Richmond Street between Queen and Great George streets, is designated as pedestrian-only through summer. The local restaurants and bars set tables out across the sidewalk and some have live music.

Most pubs open at 11 a.m., and close at midnight through the week and at 1 a.m. on weekends.

Around the corner from Victoria Row, the **Olde Dublin Pub**, 131 Sydney Street (☎ 902-892-6992), is a lively Celtic-style bar, often with live Maritime music and always with pints of Guinness. In the same vicinity, **Gahan House,** 126 Sydney Street (☎ 902-626-2337), is PEI's only brewpub — and it's a good one. Six ales are brewed in-house, including a stout that gets rave reviews. The food is also a cut above pub grub (the beer-battered haddock and chips are delicious). Named for one of the delegates at the Charlottetown Conference, **D'Arcy McGee's** sits in the heart of the city at the corner of Prince and Kent streets (☎ 902-894-3627). Inside is a fun and fittingly British atmosphere, with visitors and regulars mixing easily. Overlooking the harbor, **Peake's Quay,** 1 Great George St. at Water Street (☎ 902-368-1330), has a slightly hipper feel than the other places.

The club scene in Charlottetown is dominated by **Myron's,** at 151 Kent Street (☎ 902-892-4375), a two-story complex that books bands ranging from rock to country Wednesday to Saturday for the downstairs stage. The upstairs crowd is equally diverse, dancing to everything from hip hop to disco, Thursday through Saturday.

The arts

The **Confederation Centre of the Arts,** at 145 Richmond Street (☎ 800-565-0278 or 902-628-1864; Internet: www.confederation centre.com), hosts the Charlottetown Festival late May through early October. This theatrical event combines outdoor performances, a children's theater, and two or three musical productions. The star of the show is *Anne of Green Gables–The Musical*, a family-oriented production that brings Lucy Maud Montgomery's most famous character to life. Showtime is Monday to Saturday at 8 p.m. with additional 2 p.m. matinees in July and August on Monday, Wednesday, and Saturday. Expect to pay C$22 to C$40 (US$15.70 to US$28.60) adults, half price for children.

Harness racing

Locals who attend harness racing meets at **Charlottetown Driving Park,** 46 Kensington Road (☎ **902-892-6823**), do so to gamble, so the operators welcome them with open arms — letting everyone in for free. Races are held on Saturdays May through January as well as Thursdays in summer; race time is 7:30 p.m. (call to confirm the schedule).

Fast Facts: Charlottetown

ATMs

Look for ATMs at most banks, including the CIBC at Queen and Grafton streets. A growing number of grocery stores and gas stations also have ATMs, but beware of additional charges.

Emergencies

Dial ☎ **911** for all emergencies.

Hospital

Queen Elizabeth Hospital is at 60 Riverside Dr. (☎ **902-894-2095**).

Pharmacy

Murphy's Pharmacy, at 24 St. Peters Rd. (☎ **902-894-4449**), is open Mon–Fri 8 a.m.–10 p.m., Sat–Sun 9 a.m.–10 p.m.

Information

The **Visitor Information Centre** is at 178 Water St. (☎ **902-368-7795**; Internet: www.visitcharlottetown.com). It's open July–Aug daily 8 a.m.–10 p.m.; Sept–June Mon–Fri 9:00 a.m.–4:30 p.m.

Internet Access

Café Diem, at 128 Richmond St. (☎ **902-892-0494**), has public computers with a high-speed Internet connection.

Police

For emergencies, dial ☎ **911;** for general **RCMP** matters, call ☎ **902-368-9300.**

Post Office

The main post office is at 135 Kent St.

Restrooms

Public restrooms can be found in Founders' Hall on Water St.

Taxis

Recommended companies include **City Taxi** (☎ **902-892-6567**), **Co-op Taxi Line** (☎ **902-628-8200**), and **Yellow Cab** (☎ **902-566-6666**).

Transit Info

Local bus service is provided by **Charlottetown Transit** (☎ **902-566-5664**). See "Getting Around Charlottetown," earlier in this chapter, for details.

Weather

Environment Canada maintains a Web site at www.weatheroffice.ec.gc.ca with links to the forecast in Charlottetown, as well as locations around Prince Edward Island.

Chapter 19

Cavendish

In This Chapter

▶ Finding your way to Cavendish

▶ Picking the best places to stay and eat

▶ Making the most of "Anne's Land"

▶ Exploring the coast

Cavendish is known worldwide through the writing of Lucy Maud Montgomery, who used her childhood in the idyllic island setting as inspiration for her timeless tale, *Anne of Green Gables*. The setting for the book was Green Gables, a farmhouse now protected as a National Historic Site, which, along with other spots related to the author and her writing, will keep fans of Anne occupied for at least a full day.

The tranquility of the "Avonlea" that Montgomery wrote about so floridly has mostly gone, thanks somewhat ironically to the popularity of the book. Cavendish's main thoroughfare is lined with theme parks, accommodations, and other touristy offerings. The only thing stopping commercial sprawl from spreading to the adjacent coastline is Prince Edward Island National Park, which protects long stretches of red-sand beach and provides prime habitat for over 100 species of birds.

 Cavendish has served as a summer retreat for decades. You need only take a drive through the rolling rural landscape, spend time down on the beach, or walk the wooded trails to see why families return year after year. The off-season, however, really does mean lights off. November through April almost everything is closed, including most accommodations and all the attractions and restaurants.

Getting There

Cavendish is 40km (25 miles) northwest of Charlottetown. To get there from the capital, take Route 15 to Brackley Beach, then head west on Route 6; or take Route 2 west to Hunter River, followed by Route 13 north through New Glasgow.

Cavendish

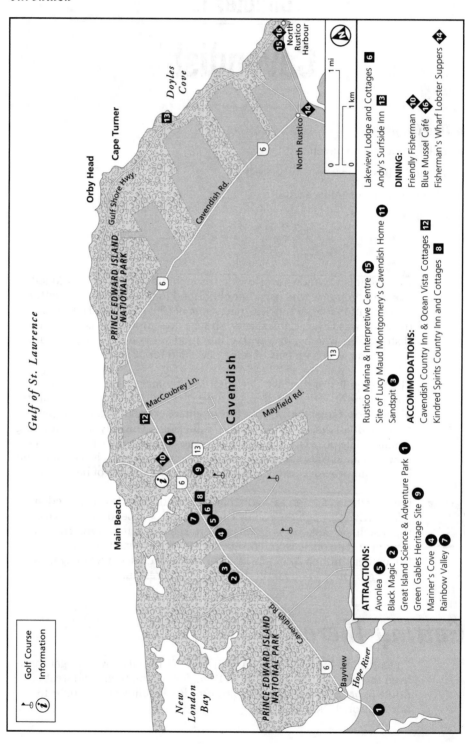

ATTRACTIONS:
Avonlea **5**
Black Magic **2**
Great Island Science & Adventure Park **1**
Green Gables Heritage Site **9**
Mariner's Cove **4**
Rainbow Valley **7**

Rustico Marina & Interpretive Centre **15**
Site of Lucy Maud Montgomery's Cavendish Home **11**
Sandspit **3**

ACCOMMODATIONS:
Cavendish Country Inn & Ocean Vista Cottages **12**
Kindred Spirits Country Inn and Cottages **8**

Lakeview Lodge and Cottages **6**
Andy's Surfside Inn **13**

DINING:
Friendly Fisherman **10**
Blue Mussel Café **16**
Fisherman's Wharf Lobster Suppers **14**

Golf Course
i Information

Staying in Cavendish

As well as being inundated with visitors from around the world, Cavendish is very popular with families on summer vacation. For travel in July and August, you should reserve accommodations as far in advance as possible. Discounted rooms and a lack of crowds make June and September a fine time to visit Cavendish; in early September, it's still warm enough to swim in the ocean, yet you will find rooms discounted up to 50%.

Cavendish Country Inn & Ocean Vista Cottages
$$ Cavendish

Choose between motel units, bed-and-breakfast rooms, or lovely wooden cottages at this modern resort within walking distance of both the national park and Cavendish. The cottages (from C$140/US$100) are the best value. Each has a deck with outdoor furniture and a barbecue, while inside, lots of polished wood and comfortable furnishings create an inviting atmosphere. Also on the property is a playground and outdoor heated pool.

Route 6, 1km (0.6 miles) east of Route 13, Cavendish ☎ **800-454-4853** *or 902-963-2181. Fax: 902-963-3213. Internet:* www.cavendishpei.com. *Rack rates: C$95–C$350 (US$67.90–US$217.50) double. AE, MC, V. May–mid-Oct.*

Kindred Spirits Country Inn and Cottages
$$–$$$$ Cavendish

In the heart of Cavendish, but set well away from the busy main road, this delightful country estate is a world away from the rest of the bustling village. Green Gables Heritage Site is reached along Lover's Lane, a walking trail that remains exactly as described by Montgomery in *Anne of Green Gables*. The local golf course is even closer. Guest rooms in the inn are country cozy and loaded with local antiques. Three price levels are offered: the lower-priced rooms include all the basics, while more expensive rooms add a balcony and a fireplace. Surrounding the inn are 14 luxurious cottages, with kitchens, color TV, and a deck with a barbecue. The most expensive cottages have a king-size bed, air-conditioning, fireplace, and hot tub. Regardless of the type of accommodation chosen, all guests can enjoy the playground area and outdoor heated pool.

Memory Lane, off Route 6, Cavendish ☎ **902-963-2434**. *Fax: 902-963-2619. Internet:* www.kindredspirits.ca. *Rack rates: inn rooms C$120–C$245 (US$85.70–US$175) double, cottages C$185–C$350 (US$132.10–US$250). MC, V. Mid-May–mid-Oct.*

Lakeview Lodge and Cottages
$$ Cavendish

Close to everything, this large property features a heated outdoor pool, a barbecue area, a playground, and a variety of room choices. Basic motel rooms can be had for under C$110 (US$78.60). From June to September, the kitchen-equipped duplex cottages offer the best value for larger groups. Freestanding executive cottages, each with a kitchen and private deck, are a step up in quality (and price) while two modern suites in the main lodge are also well priced. In June and September, Lakeview has great off-season specials with rates reduced up to 50%.

Route 6, Cavendish ☎ **800-565-7550** *or 902-963-2436. Fax: 902-963-2493. Internet:* www.lakeviewlodge.cc. *Rack rates: C$90–C$170 (US$64.30–US$121.40) double. MC, V. Late May–early Oct.*

Andy's Surfside Inn
$ North Rustico

This rambling whitewashed, red-roofed home sits above a pebbly beach 3km (1.9 miles) east of Cavendish. The nine rooms are basic and share bathrooms, but the seaside setting is gorgeous. Guests have use of a kitchen, barbecues, and bikes.

Gulf Shore Hwy., between North Rustico and Cavendish ☎ **902-963-2405**. *Rack rates: C$50–C$75 (US$35.70–US$53.60) double. MC, V. June–Nov.*

Dining in Cavendish

The Cavendish dining scene reflects the characteristics of local accommodations — touristy, mostly overpriced, and always busy. Thankfully, a number of alternatives lie in surrounding villages.

Blue Mussel Café
$$ North Rustico Harbour SEAFOOD

My favorite dining spot on all of Prince Edward Island is the Blue Mussel Café. The cafe is terribly small, but that's a good thing if you manage to get a table. Most of the seating is outside, on an old dock that catches the evening sun and has views extending back down the harbor. You can't go wrong with any of the seafood, like creamy chowder or lobster pâté to start, followed by a full lobster or poached fish, such as haddock or salmon. Best of all, the Blue Mussel must be one of the few seafood restaurants anywhere in the Maritimes without a deep fryer.

Harbourview Dr., North Rustico Harbour ☎ **902-963-2152**. *Main courses: C$11.50–C$17 (US$7.90–US$12.10). Late June–Sept daily 11:30 a.m.–8:00 p.m.*

Lovin' lobster

Believe it or not, it wasn't that long ago that the supply of lobster exceeded demand so much that islanders used it as fertilizer. Things have changed, though; lobster is now promoted as a delicacy across the Maritimes. The trapping season for lobsters is short, but the lobsters are held live in holding tanks so they can be offered fresh year-round.

Lobsters served in restaurants and at lobster suppers usually weigh around one pound, which provides enough of the rich meat for most people. They are generally served whole, challenging diners to extract as much of the meat as they can using fingers, lobster crackers, and skewers. It can be a messy process, so most places — even upscale restaurants — supply a bib.

One of the best things about lobster is that it tastes best simply boiled, which means you can do the cooking yourself (many accommodations provide big pots especially for this purpose). **Doiron Fisheries,** on the dock at North Rustico (☎ 902-963-2442), is the best place around Cavendish to buy lobster. Expect to pay around C$10 (US$7.10) per pound, live or precooked. This seafood market is also the place to pick up Malpeque Bay oysters, mussels, clams, and fresh fish. It's open May to early October daily 8 a.m. to 8 p.m.

Fisherman's Wharf Lobster Suppers
$$ North Rustico SEAFOOD

A little more commercialized than the New Glasgow Lobster Supper (see below), the North Rustico version is otherwise very similar. Over 400 diners can be seated at once in the cavernous restaurant, which is lined on one side by a long buffet of hot and cold appetizers and desserts. Tables feature paper place mats that describe how lobsters are caught and, more importantly, the best way to eat them.

Route 6, North Rustico ☎ 902-963-2669. Lobster supper: from C$27 (US$19.30). AE, MC, V. Mid-June–mid-Oct daily noon–9 p.m.

Friendly Fisherman
$ Cavendish BUFFET

I thought I should include at least one restaurant in Cavendish, so I joined the throngs of families and entered the fray to research the Friendly Fisherman, right at the town's main intersection. (It was friendly enough, but there wasn't a fisherman in sight.) Because this buffet restaurant is perpetually busy, the turnover of food is fast, which keeps the salads fresh and the hot food hot. Seafood is limited to a lasagna and a couple of baked fish dishes, but there are plenty of other choices. Beer and wine is extra, but well priced. Pay for a ticket at the front door and wait your turn for a table. Children pay C$1 (US$.70 cents) for every year of age. Breakfast and lunch are served cafeteria-style.

Route 6, Cavendish ☎ **902-963-2234.** *Buffet dinner: C$14 (US$10). AE, DC MC, V. Mid-June–mid-Oct daily 8 a.m.–9 p.m.*

New Glasgow Lobster Supper
$$ New Glasgow   SEAFOOD

Held in community halls and restaurants throughout the province, lobster suppers are informal, fun, and good value. The one at New Glasgow is the oldest, having been in operation since 1958. Here, up to 500 diners can be seated at once in a two-level riverside building with its own lobster holding pond. Choose the size of lobster you want 0.5 to 1 kilogram (1–2 pounds) and enjoy all-you-can-eat chowder, mussels, salad, breads, desserts, and non-alcoholic beverages for a set price. If you want to pass on the lobster as a main, breaded scallops, haddock, and roast beef are offered as alternatives. Children under 12 get their own menu, which includes a lobster supper for C$12 (US$8.60), and kids 3 and under eat for free. To get to New Glasgow, take Route 13 southeast from Cavendish. The big building is impossible to miss across the river in New Glasgow.

Route 258, New Glasgow ☎ **902-964-2870.** *Lobster supper: from C$26 (US$18.60). AE, MC, V. June–mid-Oct daily 4:00–8:30 p.m.*

Exploring Cavendish

The sights associated with *Anne of Green Gables* are somewhat over-shadowed by amusement parks and tacky tourist traps (although you won't hear any complaints from children). I've divided this section up accordingly, with some suggestions for touring beyond Cavendish to round out the chapter

Anne attractions

Separating fact from fiction is somewhat difficult when it comes to visiting the childhood haunts of Lucy Maud Montgomery, many of which ended up in her famous novels and are now shrines open to fans from around the world.

Anne's land

Anne of Green Gables chronicled the life of Anne Shirley, a lovable character created by Canada's best-known author, Lucy Maud Montgomery (1874–1942). Although the enduring tale of the red-haired orphan girl and her life at Avonlea was fictional, it drew on Montgomery's own experiences growing up in her grandparents' Cavendish home and spending her younger days exploring the rural surroundings.

On the island, the tale has spawned an entire industry. *Anne of Green Gables* has been translated into dozens of languages and has been reprinted over 100 times. The character of Anne has been recreated in a musical and television drama. Half a world away, it is even part of the official curriculum in Japanese schools — and hence Cavendish receives large numbers of Japanese visitors.

If you're an Anne fan, it's worth planning your time in Cavendish to coincide with the **L.M. Montgomery Festival** (☎ **902-963-7874**; Internet: www.lmmontgomery festival.com), held annually on the second weekend of August. Festivities include readings, a coloring competition at the local schoolhouse, and afternoon high tea served outdoors at the site of Montgomery's childhood home.

Anne of Green Gables Museum
Park Corner

Owned and operated by relatives of Montgomery, this museum is housed at Silver Bush, a name given to the home of the Campbell family who appear in two of her novels. The residence is decked out in period furnishings and a selection of the author's personal belongings is on display. The parlor, where Montgomery was married in 1911, is now a popular spot for Japanese couples to say their vows. You can relax in the small tea room, which serves hot drinks and homemade goodies, or enjoy a carriage ride (C$8/US$5.70 per family) along the nearby beach.

Route 20, 24km (15 miles) west of Cavendish ☎ *902-866-2884. Admission: C$2.75 (US$2) adults, C$1 (US70¢) children. May–Oct daily 11 a.m.–4 p.m., extended hours July–Aug daily 9 a.m.–6 p.m.*

Avonlea
Cavendish

Of the many amusement parks in Cavendish, only Avonlea, which reconstructs Montgomery's version of rural PEI, has any connection to *Anne of Green Gables*. The park comprises a general store, a church, farm animals, old-fashioned games, themed rides, and a chocolate factory (which wasn't in the book, but is a popular spot nevertheless). Throughout the day, costumed performers go about their business: milking cows, leading pony rides, giving dance lessons — and did I mention the chocolate factory?

Route 6, Cavendish ☎ 902-963-3050. Admission: C$17 (US$12.10) adults, C$15 (US$10.70) seniors, C$13 (US$9.30) children 6–12. Mid-June–mid-Oct daily 10 a.m.–5 p.m.

Green Gables Heritage Site
Cavendish

Within easy walking distance of Montgomery's childhood home is Green Gables, which belonged to her grandfather's cousins. This green and white farmhouse served as the setting for *Anne of Green Gables*. At the main entrance is an interpretive center; inside the picket fence, rooms in the main house have been restored and the barn recreates early farm life. Two of the most loved connections between the property and the book are Haunted Wood and Balsam Hollow, reached by short trails from the house.

Route 6 (just west of Route 13) ☎ 902-963-7874. Admission: C$5.75 (US$4.10) adults, C$5 (US$3.60) seniors, C$3 (US$2.10) children. May–Oct daily 9 a.m.–5 p.m., extended hours July–Aug daily 9 a.m.–8 p.m.

Lucy Maud Montgomery Birthplace
New London

This modest home is where the writer was born in 1874. The interior is decorated in corresponding style. Among personal effects on display is Montgomery's wedding dress, as well as scrapbooks she put together as a child.

New London, southwest of Cavendish on Route 6 ☎ 902-886-2099. Admission: C$2 (US$1.40) adults, C$1 (US70¢) children. Mid-May–mid-Oct daily 9 a.m.–5 p.m.

Site of Lucy Maud Montgomery's Cavendish Home
Cavendish

This is where the writer lived with her grandparents after the premature death of her mother. All that remains of the home are the foundations, but the well-tended gardens and mature groves of apple trees provide a peaceful retreat from the rest of Cavendish. A small museum and bookstore at the site are operated by members of Montgomery's family.

Route 6 (just east of Route 13) ☎ 902-963-2231. Admission: C$2 (US$1.40) adults, C$1 (US70¢) children. June–mid-Oct daily 9 a.m.–5 p.m., extended hours July–Aug daily 9 a.m.–7 p.m.

Cool things for kids to do in Cavendish

Amusement park–style attractions strung out along Route 6 between Cavendish and Stanley Bridge strongly contrast with the idyllic Avonlea so loved by Anne fans — but children will love them, and we all know that's the most important thing. Here's just a sampling:

- ✔ **Sandspit** (☎ **902-963-2626**) has old-time fairground rides including a roller coaster, carousel, and Ferris wheel, as well as bumper boats and go-carts.
- ✔ **Rainbow Valley** (☎ **902-963-2221**) features many rides for younger children and is extremely popular on hotter days for its waterslides.
- ✔ **Great Island Science & Adventure Park** (☎ **902-886-2252**) centers around a full-size replica of the space shuttle, with a science center, dinosaur display, and archeological dig sure to keep children occupied for the better part of an afternoon.
- ✔ **Mariner's Cove** (☎ **902-963-2242**) is the most challenging of Cavendish's many mini-golf courses.
- ✔ **Black Magic** (☎ **902-963-2889**) is mini-golf with a twist — indoors and in the dark.

Touring beyond Cavendish

Once you manage to pry the Anne fan in your family away from Cavendish, you'll discover that the surrounding area is well worth exploring. Take a walk from the village to enjoy the natural, rugged beauty of Cavendish's coast or drive east along the shoreline to Tracadie Bay and loop back on Route 6 to take in a mix of coastal and rural scenery.

Prince Edward Island National Park

This narrow park protects a sliver of coastline extending from London Bay in the west to Tracadie Bay in the east, as well as a separate chunk of coastline farther east near St. Peters. The park encompasses a varied landscape with wide beaches, attractive red sandstone cliffs, and rolling dunes. It can be accessed from seven different points along Route 6.

Swimming and sunbathing are the big summertime attractions for most visitors. The water is warm enough for swimming in July and August. Trained supervisors watch out for the well-being of those who take to the water at the busiest spots. The best — and busiest — beaches are those near Cavendish.

Starving art lovers, tuck in!

If not the most notable island gallery, then The Dunes, on Route 15 at Brackley Beach (☎ 902-672-1883), is certainly the most unique. Made up almost entirely of windows, this ultra-contemporary building is part gallery, part restaurant, and all tourist attraction. The island's preeminent painters, wood carvers, and sculptors have their work on display in a multilevel, spiral room, with a narrow stairway leading to a fourth-floor lookout. Hungry? The gallery restaurant outdoes itself with dishes such as Vietnamese rice noodle salad with grilled shrimp (C$12/US$8.60) at lunch and a roasted rack of lamb crusted with East Indian spices in the evening (C$21/US$15). The gallery is open May through October daily 10 a.m.–6 p.m. while the restaurant hours are 11:30 a.m.–10:00 p.m.

The Gulf Shore Highway, which begins as a northern extension of Route 13 through Cavendish, hugs the coastline, passing more park beaches, numerous lookouts (Orby Head is my fave), and a pretty picnic area at Cape Turner.

The section of park east of Rustico Bay is a lot quieter. Here you can enjoy a long beach walk, or take a morning stroll along the marshland behind the dunes in search of local birds, such as piping plovers and northern phalarope. **Brackley Beach,** at the north end of Route 15, has supervised swimming, change rooms, a concession, and an information center.

Rise early to experience Prince Edward Island National Park in its most picturesque and pristine state. Overnight, wind and water action creates textured herringbone patterns across the beaches and dunes and the rising sun casts an intriguing red glow across the entire park.

A National Park Day Pass costs C$5 (US$3.60) adults, C$4.25 (US$3) seniors, C$2.50 (US$1.80) children, to a maximum of C$12.50 (US$8.90) per vehicle. The **Park Information Centre**, just north of the junction of Routes 6 and 13 in Cavendish (☎ 902-963-2391), has park maps, posted weather forecasts, and natural history displays. It's open June to September daily 9 a.m. to 5 p.m. (July and August until 9 p.m.).

North Rustico Harbour

At the entrance to Rustico Bay, the tiny hamlet of North Rustico Harbour comprises a lighthouse and a smattering of trim homes lodged between the beaches of Prince Edward Island National Park and a small harbor packed with fishing boats. The picturesque setting attracts hordes of visitors, but somehow the village maintains a peaceful demeanor.

Down on the dock is **Rustico Marina & Interpretive Centre**, a small facility that catalogs local history. Native displays share space with exhibits on harvesting Irish moss, artifacts from local canneries, and a tank of live lobsters. The story of the Mi'kmaq, who left middens of shells on nearby Robinsons Island as evidence of 1,500 years of habitation, is most intriguing. Admission is a worthwhile C$3 (US$2.10) adults, C$2.50 (US$1.80) seniors and children.

Court Brothers (☎ **902-963-2322**) is one of many local operations that take visitors out to sea fishing for mackerel. Trips last around three hours and cost a reasonable C$25 (US$17.90) adults, C$15 (US$10.70) children, although the catch belongs to the boat. **Outside Expeditions** (☎ **800-207-3899** or 902-963-3366) launches sea kayak tours from a beach right beside the dock. If you've never kayaked before, the 90-minute trip is a great introduction to the sport. The cost is just C$40 (US$28.60) per person and includes instruction in basic paddling skills and the chance to view a wide range of seabirds while paddling the calm waters of the bay.

To get to North Rustico Harbour, take Route 6 east from Cavendish and turn left at the main intersection in North Rustico.

Chapter 20

Prince County

· ·

In This Chapter

▶ Soaking up Summerside

▶ Exploring Acadian culture

▶ Meandering around Malpeque Bay

▶ Heading to North Cape

· ·

Many visitors only tour the central portion (Queens County) of Prince Edward Island — they cross Confederation Bridge and head straight for Charlottetown, then venture north to Cavendish and maybe loop through Kings County before leaving via the ferry. But, to experience the island's less touristy side, you really should include Prince County, the western third of the island, in your itinerary.

The low-lying landscape of Prince County is mostly rural. It is surrounded by some of the Maritimes' best beaches, long sand dunes, and low, red cliffs. To appreciate the best of the west, stick to the coast wherever possible (Route 14 between West Point and Tignish is the highlight) and give the main thoroughfare — Route 2, which runs through the middle of Prince County — a miss.

What's Where: Prince County and Its Major Attractions

Summerside

Summerside, 71km (44 miles) west of Charlottetown, is the second largest city on Prince Edward Island and is the gateway to Prince County. While in Summerside, be sure to:

✔ Explore the **waterfront,** which features on a large marina and is home to summertime concerts

✔ Take in a performance at the **College of Piping**

Région Évangéline

Descendants of early French settlers are scattered throughout Prince County, including this string of villages west of Summerside. Learn more about their Acadian culture at:

- ✔ **Le Village de l'Acadie,** the recreation of an early 19th-century Acadian village
- ✔ **Musée Acadian,** the site of a historic meeting that kick-started a renaissance of this French-basded culture on Prince Edward Island

Malpeque Bay

The calm waters of Malpeque Bay are famous for oysters, but the area's natural appeal, its history, and its native culture can be appreciated by visiting:

- ✔ **Cabot Beach Provincial Park,** where two beaches are free of crowds that descend on nearby Cavendish
- ✔ **Green Park Shipbuilding Museum,** a quietly impressive attraction at the site of a once bustling shipyard
- ✔ **Lennox Island,** home to the Mi'kmaq, PEI's original inhabitants

Western Prince County

In western Prince County, potato farms dominate a rolling landscape that is lined to the west and south by sea cliffs. Local lures include:

- ✔ **Mill River Provincial Park,** home to a large resort and good-value golf course
- ✔ **North Cape,** at the end of the road and seemingly at the end of the world
- ✔ **Irish Moss Interpretive Centre,** where the real attraction is sampling a slice of seaweed pie
- ✔ **West Point Lighthouse,** Canada's only lighthouse to be set up as an inn

Summerside

Summerside (population 15,000) is spread around a south-facing harbor less than an hour's drive west of Charlottetown. The waterfront is the most appealing section of the city, although a recent rejuvenation extends to commercial buildings adorned with colorful murals.

Getting there

From the Confederation Bridge, take Route 10, then Route 1A, to reach Summerside in less than 30 minutes. The most direct route from Charlottetown is Route 2 through Kensington. Both these routes merge east of Summerside, with a well-signposted exit leading right downtown.

Staying in Summerside

A strip of motels on the eastern approach to downtown (within walking distance of the waterfront) offers well-priced overnight accommodations — just don't expect valet parking and room service.

Baker's Lighthouse Motel

$ **Summerside**

Rooms at Baker's Lighthouse Motel are no better than similarly priced choices on the east side of downtown, but children will enjoy the playground while you cook up a storm (or a lobster — pots supplied) at the outdoor barbecue area.

802 Water St. East ☎ *877-436-2996 or 902-436-2992. Rack rates: C$55–C$60 (US$39.30–US$42.90) double.*

Quality Inn Garden of the Gulf

$$–$$$$ **Summerside**

The rooms at this chain motel are nothing exceptional, but the downtown location is perfect for an evening stroll along the waterfront and kids will love the choice of outdoor and indoor swimming pools.

618 Water St. East ☎ *800-265-5551 or 902-436-2295. Fax: 902-432-2911. Internet:* www.qualityinnpei.com. *Rack rates: C$129–C$249 (US$92.10–US$177.90). AE, DC, MC, V.*

Silver Fox Inn
$$ Summerside

A distinctive 1892 Queen Anne Revival residence, this inn offers six comfortable guest rooms decorated in Victorian style. Tea and cookies are served each afternoon in the large living area. A tiered deck and well-stocked library provide alternative relaxation areas.

61 Granville St. ☎ *800-565-4033 or 902-436-1664. Internet:* www.silverfoxinn.net. *Rack rates: C$95–C$130 (US$67.90–US$92.90). AE, DC, MC, V.*

Dining in Summerside

Summerside has many restaurants, including a string of places along the waterfront, and none of them will break your bank account. If you plan on just one meal in town, sacrifice the water views and head for the nearby Brothers Two.

Brothers Two Restaurant
$$–$$$ Summerside CANADIAN

Locals love this casual place for a wide selection of dishes that go well beyond seafood (I tried the rotisserie barbecued chicken and loved it). Naturally, you can't go wrong with local seafood either. Try lobster pizza or a lobster club, or choose two favorites from a list (haddock, salmon, scallops, shrimp, and so on.), accompanied by potato, vegetables, and bread for C$19 (US$13.60). Choices are tables, booths, or seating out on a rooftop patio.

618 Water St. ☎ *902-436-9654. Main courses: C$11–C$24 (US$7.90–US$17.10). AE, DC, MC, V. Daily 11:00 a.m.–9:30 p.m.*

Exploring Summerside

Base yourself at the waterfront, where you'll find plenty of free parking and an **information center** (☎ 902-436-6692). The center is actually in a lighthouse, which you can climb for 360-degree views. Adjacent is the much larger Spinnakers' Landing complex, which has a small interpretive display that tells the story of the once-thriving shipbuilding business. Also here you'll find a pub with a waterfront deck, bike rentals, and evening entertainment on an adjacent outdoor stage.

College of Piping
Summerside

This college, the only one of its type in North America, is for people who want to learn Highland and step-dancing, or how to play the bagpipes. Students from around the world live in residences during the year, but for the casual observer, the college is also worth a visit. July through August, tours of the facility are offered Monday to Friday 11 a.m. to 5 p.m. This a great chance to learn about ancient Celtic culture and the skills involved in the various disciplines taught on campus. Mini-concerts, also free, are held daily at 11:30 a.m., 1:30 p.m., and 3:30 p.m. The nightly ceildh (pronounced "*kay*-lee") showcases the lively music of Ireland at 7 p.m. for C$12 (US$8.60) adults, C$11 (US$7.90) seniors, C$7 (US$5) children.

619 Water St. ☎ *902-436-5377. Internet:* www.collegeofpiping.com.

Région Évangéline

The Acadians were the first group of Europeans to settle on Prince Edward Island. When the British took control of the island in 1755, many of these French nationals escaped exile by hiding out in the remote western portion of the island. Over time, they resumed normal, mostly rural lives. Their descendants now make up over 15% of the island's population and are concentrated along the portion of the island covered in this next section — the southern coastline of Prince County, west of Summerside.

Getting there

Route 2 west from Summerside flies right through the middle of Région Évangéline. You can take Route 11 south at Miscouche to follow the coast to Cap Egmont for more scenic views, and then rejoin Route 2 at Mount Pleasant.

Staying in Région Évangéline

If you're looking for regular motel rooms or the services of a resort, plan on staying in Summerside or Charlottetown; for something unique, try my recommendation below.

Le Village de l'Acadie
$$ Mont-Carmel

An overnight stay at Le Village de l'Acadie, the recreated Acadian village described on the next page, is a wonderful way to immerse yourself in Acadian culture. Guest rooms are unspectacular — choose from those in the main building, a motel-style wing, or small cottages — although many enjoy water views. Aside from exploring the historic park, an Acadian restaurant (see below) supplies delicious meals; children will love swimming and shell-collecting on the adjacent beach.

Le Village de l'Acadie, Route 11, Mont-Carmel ☎ 800-567-3228 or 902-854-2227. Fax: 902-854-2304. Internet: www.levillagedelacadie.com. *Rack rates: C$95–C$119 (US$67.90–US$85) double. MC, V. June–mid-Sept.*

Dining in Région Évangéline

L'Etoile de Mer
$–$$ Mont-Carmel ACADIAN

A meal at L'Etoile de Mer is a definite high point of a visit to Le Village de l'Acadie. As you'd expect, it specializes in Acadian cuisine, based on recipes using locally available produce that date back many centuries. Be prepared for a hearty meal, including *poutine râpée* (pork wrapped in grated potato), *rappie pie* (meat pie topped with grated potatoes), *frites* (French fries), and chicken *fricot* (chicken stew), all exceptionally well-priced. During July and August the village hosts La Cuisine à Mémé, a nightly dinner featuring Acadian cooking as well as dancing and singing (C$35/US$25 per person). Some nights it is presented in English, others in French; call ahead to confirm.

Le Village de l'Acadie, Route 11, Mont-Carmel ☎ 902-854-2227. Main courses: C$8–C$16 (US$5.70–US$11.40). June–mid-Sept Sun–Thurs 8 a.m.–9 p.m., Fri–Sat 8 a.m.–10 p.m.

Exploring Région Évangéline

Trim homes, impressive churches — including **Our Lady of Mont-Carmel** in Mont Carmel — and flapping flags are signs that pride in Acadian culture is strong in Région Évangéline. Traditions are also showcased at two worthwhile attractions, Le Village de l'Acadie and the Musée Acadien — and I've included an eccentric non-Acadian sight as a bonus.

Cap Egmont Bottle Houses
Cap Egmont

Think you know the world's most obsessive collector? Think again. Originally put together by the late Edouard Arsenault, over 25,000 bottles have been cemented together to form three buildings, including a church complete with altar and pews, at this unique attraction. The surrounding gardens alone are worth the price of admission.

Route 11, Cap Egmont ☎ 902-854-2987. Admission: C$4 (US$2.90) adults, C$3 (US$2.10) seniors, C$1 (US70¢) children. June–Sept daily 9 a.m.–6 p.m.; July and Aug until 8 p.m.

Le Village de l'Acadie
Mont-Carmel

This recreated village is on the site of an Acadian settlement established in 1812. Buildings include a blacksmith's shop, a general store, and a schoolhouse, all built with logs. The village boasts an amphitheater decorated with murals that tell the story of Évangéline, an Acadian heroine who was separated from her husband on her wedding day and was not reunited with him until he lay on his deathbed.

Route 11, 1.6km (1 mile) west of Mont-Carmel ☎ 902-485-4371. Admission: C$5 (US$3.60) adults, C$2.50 (US$1.80) children. June–mid-Sept daily 9 a.m.–7 p.m.

Musée Acadien
Miscouche

Protected as a National Historic Site, this museum commemorates the trials and tribulations of the island's early French settlers. It boasts a permanent display of Acadian history, as well a remarkable audiovisual presentation that tells the story of their mass expulsion from Prince Edward Island in moving detail. Acadians gathered in Miscouche in 1884 to officially adopt the Acadian flag and an anthem, which gives the museum extra appeal.

Miscouche, Route 2 ☎ 902-436-2881. Admission: C$4 (US$2.90) adults, C$2 (US$1.40) children. July–Aug daily 9 a.m.–7 p.m.

Malpeque Bay

Malpeque Bay is a massive tidal waterway that almost splits Prince Edward Island in two. Famed for its oysters, it is ringed by pleasant beaches, the best of which are protected by provincial parks, and a number of historic sites.

Getting there

If you're coming from Cavendish, follow Route 6 through to Kensington, then take Route 20 north to Cabot Beach or Route 2 around the head of the bay. Tyne Valley, on the western side of the bay, is reached by taking Route 132 northeast from Route 2.

Staying around Malpeque Bay

Lodging around Malpeque Bay is limited, so reserve a room well ahead of time, especially for July and August.

Doctor's Inn Bed-and-Breakfast
$ **Tyne Valley**

On a rise above the village of Tyne Valley, this rambling 1860s home is more farm than bed-and-breakfast. It contains only two guest rooms and a single guest bathroom, but it is hospitable hosts Jean and Paul Offer and their wonderful down-home cooking that you'll remember long after you've gotten over having to share a bathroom. A full cooked breakfast, prepared in the old-fashioned kitchen complete with woodstove, is included in the rates. If you choose to pay the C$45 (US$32.10) per person extra for the four-course dinner, you'll enjoy appetizers and wine in the sitting room, followed by seafood complemented by wonderful salads in the dining room. Freshly baked desserts complete the cozy dining experience. Non-guests are also welcome for dinner with 24 hours' notice.

Route 167, Tyne Valley ☎ 902-831-3057. Rack rates: C$60 (US$42.90) double. MC, V.

Green Valley Cottages
$$–$$$ **Spring Valley**

If you're looking for an escape from touristy Cavendish, you can't do any better than these cottages in a rural setting. Green Valley is close to both Cavendish and the beaches of Malpeque Bay, while a ten-minute drive south is the Kensington Towers theme park. Each modern, woodsy cottage has a full kitchen, color television, and deck. Children will love the wagon rides and marshmallow cookouts around the bonfire.

The owners also operate **Malpeque Cove Cottages** (same contact information), which are perched right on the water beside Cabot Beach Provincial Park. Cottages are rented on a weekly basis only in summer, with nightly rentals in June and September.

Route 102 off Route 104, north of Kensington ☎ 888-283-1927 or 902-836-5667. Internet: www.malpeque.ca. Rack rates: C$110–C$175 (US$78.60–US$125) double. MC, V. April–Dec.

Exploring Malpeque Bay

Prince Edward Island itself is so small that the big foldout tourism map skews distances — you can drive from one end of Malpeque Bay to the other in just two hours.

Lennox Island
North Malpeque Bay

The Mi'kmaq, the original inhabitants of Prince Edward Island, had their 10,000-year nomadic lifestyle wiped out after Europeans arrived and cleared the land for farming. Around 1800, some had been persuaded to resettle on Lennox Island, which was later purchased for their people. Now linked to PEI by a short causeway, descendants of the Mi'kmaq still live on the island, living a mostly traditional lifestyle that includes fishing and harvesting peat moss. They share their culture with interested visitors at **Lennox Island Cultural Centre,** down by the main dock (☎ **902-831-2702**). It's generally open in summer daily 10 a.m. to 6 p.m., but call ahead to confirm these hours. Across the road is **Indian Art & Craft of North America** (☎ **902-831-2653**), where you can purchase Mi'kmaq baskets, pottery, and jewelry.

Take Route 163 east from Route 12.

Green Park Shipbuilding Museum
Port Hill

If you want to revisit the 1860s, when shipbuilding was Prince Edward Island's main industry, plan on a visit to this sprawling property on the western shore of Malpeque Bay. The mansion of James Yeo, who owned the yards, sits in the heart of sweeping grounds. It is fully furnished in Victorian style, including the top-floor cupola from which Yeo was able to watch over his workers. If you walk down to the site of the actual ship-yards, two wooden buildings and the slips are all that remain, although interpretive panels do a good job of describing the once bustling business.

To get to the museum, you pass through **Green Park Provincial Park,** protecting a low peninsula scattered with stunted birch and laced with trails leading along the waterfront.

*Route 12, Port Hill ☎ **902-831-7947**. Admission: C$5 (US$3.60) adults, C$2.50 (US$1.80) children. Mid-June–Aug daily 9 a.m.–5 p.m.*

Western Prince County

Western Prince County is an arrow-shaped chunk of land that comes to a point at North Cape. Potato farms dominate the landscape in the central portion of the region while small fishing villages and long stretches of uninhabited coastline beckon along the coastal areas.

Getting there

Route 2 splits western Prince County neatly in two, but you'll want to steer away from this highway and take the coastal route wherever possible.

Staying in western Prince County

You'll find dozens of cottage-style accommodations in the "Prince Edward Island Visitors Guide," but the following three spots stand out.

Rodd Mill River

$$ Mill River Provincial Park

Families will love this modern resort, the largest in Prince County, for amenities including a waterslide and pool, canoe rentals, and hiking trails. A bonus for golfers is one of Canada's top-rated golf courses. The rooms are adequate with the choice of park or golf course views. Both the main dining room and a casual bistro-cafe overlook the golf course.

Route 2, Mill River Provincial Park ☎ **800-565-7633** *or 902-859-2486. Fax: 902-859-2486. Internet:* www.rodd-hotels.ca. *Rates: C$125–C$150 (US$89.30–US$107.10) double. AE, DC, MC, V. May–Oct and Feb–March.*

Tignish Heritage Inn

$–$$ Tignish

Located in the village of Tignish, this lodging is a good choice if you're looking for inexpensive accommodation close to the cape. Built with locally fired red brick in 1868, its thorough renovation has removed any clinical feel from the former convent. Seventeen guest rooms are available, all with private bathrooms. Rates include a light breakfast and use of a kitchen.

Maple St., Tignish ☎ **877-882-2491** *or 902-882-2491. Fax: 902-882-2500. Internet:* www.tignish.com/inn. *Rack rates: C$70–C$110 (US$50–US$78.60) double. AE, MC, V. Mid-June–mid-Oct.*

West Point Lighthouse
$$ West Point

Have you ever stayed in a lighthouse? Here's your chance. Built in 1876 as a navigational aid to vessels entering Northumberland Strait, West Point is one of the oldest and tallest lighthouses on the island. It has since been converted to an inn with a coveted Tower Room, in the lighthouse itself, in addition to the Light Keeper's Quarters in the adjoining building. All nine guest rooms are furnished with handmade quilts and antiques; a restaurant supplies three meals daily. Book well in advance for the room of your choice.

Route 14, West Point ☎ *800-764-6854 or 902-859-3605. Fax: 902-859-1510. Internet:* www.westpointlighthouse.com. *Rack rates: C$90–C$130 (US$64.30–US$92.90) double. AE, MC, V. June–Sept.*

Touring through western Prince County

A tour through western Prince County is more about soaking up the scenery than visiting specific sites. The following are highlights of a driving tour that follows Route 2 as far as Mill River Provincial Park, then continues on Route 12 to North Cape, returning along the west coast on Route 14. This entire loop is around 400km (250 miles) and can easily be completed in one day.

- ✔ **Prince Edward Island Potato Museum,** in O'Leary, along Route 142 west of Route 2 (☎ **902-859-2039;** mid-May–mid-Oct Mon–Sat 9 a.m.–5 p.m., Sun 1–5 p.m.). Surrounded by potato farms, exhibits at this small museum catalog the local industry, which dates back to the 1830s when an Irish farmer planted the island's first spuds.

- ✔ **Mill River Provincial Park,** beside Route 2 at St. Anthony. This park is best known for its **golf course** (☎ **902-859-2486**), where the river comes into play on many holes.

- ✔ **North Cape,** 16km (10 miles) north of Tignish. Prince County narrows to a point of land at North Cape, with a lighthouse and long reef that becomes exposed at low tide. Nearby is the Atlantic Wind Test Site, where wind turbines generate electricity.

- ✔ **Elephant Rock,** 4km (2.5 miles) north of Norway on Route 182. Detached from high cliffs by erosion, this geological oddity lost its "trunk" in 1998 but the pinnacle of rock and the surrounding barren landscape is still well worth the effort to reach.

✔ **Irish Moss Interpretive Centre,** Route 14, Miminegash
(☎ 902-882-4313; June–Sept Mon–Sat 10 a.m.–7 p.m., Sun noon–
8 p.m.). A type of seaweed used in the production of ice cream,
Irish moss is collected by hand and on horseback from local
beaches. This small museum, operated by families involved in the
process, tells their story. Admission is C$2 (US$1.40). Attached to
the museum is the Seaweed Pie Café. Its namesake (C$3.50/
US$2.50 per slice) actually tastes better than you may think.

✔ **West Point Lighthouse,** off Route 14 (☎ 902-859-3605). Manned
from 1875 through to 1963, this historic structure has been converted to an inn (see page 287) and restaurant, but is well worth
just a casual stop. Part of the complex is a small museum describing the structure and its importance to shipping in
Northumberland Strait. The lighthouse is within Cedar Dunes
Provincial Park, where you can try your hand at digging clams.

Chapter 21

Kings County

● ●

In This Chapter

▶ Searching out seals in southern Kings County

▶ Striding the fairways of Brudenell River Golf Course

▶ Wandering through the shifting, singing sand of northern Kings County

● ●

*L*ike the rest of Prince Edward Island, Kings County is dominated by cleared farmland crisscrossed by rural roads. The biggest difference in the landscape is along the east coast, where the shoreline is more rugged than elsewhere on the island, as the red sea cliffs are replaced by a rocky, forested foreshore.

The region is encircled by a coastal highway that passes through all of the towns and parks detailed in this chapter. From Charlottetown, it follows the Trans-Canada Highway east to Wood Islands, the departure point for ferries to the mainland, then jogs north along the convoluted east coast before returning to the capital as Route 2. The entire loop is 374km (232 miles), easily tackled in one day.

What's Where: Kings County and Its Major Attractions

For the purposes of this section, I've broken Kings County in two, with southern Kings County and northern Kings County divided by the Cardigan River, roughly in the center of the county and draining into Cardigan Bay just north of Brudenell River Provincial Park.

Southern Kings County

If you've reached Prince Edward Island via the ferry from Caribou, plan on looping through southern Kings County before heading west to Charlottetown and Cavendish. Here a few highlights:

- ✔ **Rossignol Estate Winery,** which produces fruit and table wines at an oceanfront vineyard
- ✔ **Seals watching** on a boat tour from Murray Harbour
- ✔ **Montague,** a small village with a redeveloped waterfront area

Northern Kings County

Some of the island's most beautiful scenery is along the North Shore, where a coastal highway parallels uncrowded beaches and passes through untouched forests. Continue north from Brudenell River to reach the following attractions:

- ✔ **East Point Lighthouse,** standing guard at the easternmost point of Prince Edward Island
- ✔ Greenwich unit of **Prince Edward Island National Park,** where shifting sand dunes have enveloped the coastal forest

Southern Kings County

Mostly rural, the southern portion of Kings County is dotted with picturesque villages, fishing ports, lighthouses, and a number of provincial parks.

Getting there

From Charlottetown, take the Trans-Canada Highway (Route 1) east. After 20km (12 miles), Route 3 branches east to Brudenell River while the main highway heads south toward Wood Islands.

Between May and mid-December, ferries ply Northumberland Strait, linking Caribou (Nova Scotia) with Wood Islands just across the county line from Kings County. In summer, there are eight departures daily in each direction. Service in spring and fall is less frequent and no ferries operate in winter. No reservations are taken, so plan on catching a mid-week, early morning departure to avoid a long wait. The round-trip fare of C$49.50 (US$35.40) per vehicle, including passengers, is only collected upon leaving the island. (If you leave via the Confederation Bridge, a toll is collected there.) The service is operated by **Northumberland Ferries** (☎ **902-566-3838**; Internet: www.nfl-bay.com).

Staying in southern Kings County

The lodging scene in southern Kings County is dominated by small bed-and-breakfasts and family-style cottage accommodations. The following are my faves.

Forest and Stream Cottages

$ **Murray Harbour**

If you can go without room service and robes, and if you like the idea of cooking your own meals, then this is the spot for you. Set on a small lake, each of five cottages has an older but well-equipped kitchen, a separate bedroom, and a screened porch. Guests have use of rowboats (perfect for an early morning fishing expedition — trout for breakfast, anyone?) and children will love the shaded playground.

Route 18, between Murray Harbour and Murray River ☎ **800-227-9943** *or 902-962-3537. Fax: 902-962-3537. Rack rates: C$65–C$75 (US$46.40–US$53.60) double. MC, V. May–Oct.*

Rodd Brudenell River

$$–$$$$ **Roseneath**

This sprawling destination resort takes prime advantage of its bayside setting within the boundaries of Brudenell River Provincial Park. The unequaled choice of activities is what makes this resort a standout — two 18-hole golf courses, indoor and outdoor pools, tennis courts, bike rentals, canoeing and kayaking, horseback riding, and a full spa facility. Kids are catered to with their own activity program and a children's center. The main lodge holds 100 spacious guest rooms decorated in simple, contemporary style. Each has a balcony or patio with water or golf course vistas. Close to the main resort is a cluster of Country Cabins, which look rather boxy from the outside, but are well suited to budget travelers. Finally, each Echelon Gold Cottage has one or two bedrooms outfitted with king beds, a jetted tub, a full-sized kitchen, and a private deck with barbecue. Resort dining and drinking choices include three restaurants and a poolside bar.

Route 3, Roseneath ☎ **800-565-7633** *or 902-652-2332. Fax: 902-652-2886. Internet:* www.rodd-hotels.ca. *Rack rates: C$105–C$295 (US$75–US$210.70) double. AE, DC, MC, V. Mid-May–mid-Oct.*

Thought's End
$–$$ Panmure Island

The three motel-like rooms at Thought's End are unspectacular, but the setting is unbeatable — a 5.6-hectare (14-acre) property on remote Panmure Island, which is east of Montague on Route 17 and linked to the rest of PEI by a causeway. The island is ringed by beaches, and those fronting St. Mary's Bay are the most protected. Ask the friendly hosts about local boat tours.

Route 347, Panmure Island ☎ *866-838-4522 or 902-838-4522. Rack rates: C$89 (US$63.60) double. MC, V. May–Oct.*

Dining in southern Kings County

If you've just docked at Wood Islands, there is no better introduction to the region than enjoying a seafood feast — chowder, boiled lobster, or steamed mussels — from **Crabby's Seafood**, right beside the ferry dock (☎ 902-962-3228; open summer daily 11 a.m. to 7 p.m.) at one of surrounding picnic tables. Farther afield, plan on taking a full meal at Rodd Brudenell River (see page 291), or Windows on the Water in Montague.

Windows on the Water Cafe
$–$$ Montague CAFE/SEAFOOD

This old-fashioned eatery combines country charm with a prime waterfront location overlooking Montague Marina. You can dine inside where the ambience is warm and inviting, but if the sun is shining you'll want to be out on the large deck. I loved the chowder made with homemade fish stock and chockablock with haddock, clams, and scallops. It was lunchtime, so I skipped the mains (whatever seafood is in season, cooked simply) and dove straight into a generous serving of perfectly cooked apple crisp to finish.

106 Sackville St. ☎ *902-838-2080 Main courses: C$8–C$15.50 (US$5.70–US$11.10). AE, DC, MC, V. May–Sept daily 11:30 a.m.–8:00 p.m., July and Aug. until 10 p.m.*

Exploring southern Kings County

If you're approaching Kings County from the Trans-Canada Highway, take the coastal route from Charlottetown to Wood Islands, where the ferry from Nova Scotia docks.

East from Wood Islands

From Wood Islands, it's 9km (5.6 miles) to the first worthwhile stop, **Rossignol Estate Winery** on Route 4 (☎ **902-962-4193**), the island's only commercial vineyard. Its eye-pleasing location above Northumberland Strait plays second fiddle to the serious business of producing surprisingly good red and white table wines, as well as fruit-based wines and maple cider. You can try before you buy at the on-site wine shop, which is open June to October, Monday to Saturday 10 a.m. to 5 p.m., Sunday 1 to 5 p.m.

Fairways to heaven

Quietly, Prince Edward Island has become one of Canada's premier destinations for golfers. A solid collection of 25 courses makes the most of the rolling rural landscape and picture-perfect coastline, varying from rural nine-hole courses to world-class resort layouts. The best island golf courses are equal in quality and challenge to any others in Canada, yet greens fees (all under C$100/US$71.40) are a fraction of what you would pay elsewhere.

The Web site `www.golfpei.ca` details each island course while promoting accommodation packages that make island golfing an even better deal.

Here are my favorite courses:

- ✔ **Belvedere Golf Club** (Charlottetown ☎ 902-892-7838) is an old-fashioned layout that nurtured LPGA star Lorie Kane.

- ✔ **Brudenell River** (Brudenell River Provincial Park ☎ 800-235-8909 or 902-859-8873) mixes tree-lined fairways with open riverfront terrain. Thinking golfers are well rewarded at this renowned course.

- ✔ **Countryview** (Fairview ☎ 902-675-2800) is a sporty nine-hole layout with water views. It is surrounded by farmland, yet lies just ten minutes by road from Charlottetown.

- ✔ **Links of Crowbush Cove** (Lakeside ☎ 800-235-8909 or 902-961-7300) is routed around natural waterways behind North Shore dunes. Crowbush Cove is one of Canada's top courses.

- ✔ **Eagles Glenn** (Cavendish ☎ 866-963-3600 or 902-963-3600), although not overwhelming in length, is a challenging 27-hole, links-style creation through rolling highlands.

- ✔ **Glasgow Hills** (Hunter River ☎ 866-621-2200 or 902-621-2201) is in the middle of the island, but the ocean is in view from its hilly location. Be prepared for major elevation differences between tee and green.

Murray Harbour

This tiny fishing village 10km (6.2 miles) east of Murray River is a little off the beaten track, but is well worth the detour. The **Old General Store** (☎ 902-962-2459) and **Miss Elly's** (☎ 902-962-3555), both on Main Street, hold fine collections of antiques and gifts. Meanwhile, **Marine Adventures Seal Watching** (☎ 902-962-2494) departs the downtown dock three times daily for a short boat cruise to a large colony of seals. The tour costs C$16 (US$11.40) adults, C$14 (US$10) seniors, C$10 (US$7.10) children.

Pooles Corner

Pooles Corner, at the junction of Routes 3 and 4, is in the geographic center of Kings County (you'll often hear it used as a reference point for directions and distances). Friendly staff at the summer-only **Provincial Information Centre** (☎ 902-838-0670), right at the junction, will help you plan your onward travel.

Northern Kings County

If the weather is good, your time in the northern section of Kings County will be a highlight of your visit to Prince Edward Island. The beaches lining the Gulf of St. Lawrence are as nice as you'll find anywhere around the island, yet tourist crowds are minimal. The entire region is more lightly settled than elsewhere in the province; the largest town, Souris, holds a population of just 1,300.

Getting there

Route 4 is the most direct route between Pooles Corner and Souris, but you'll enjoy the scenic countryside on alternative Routes 311 and 310. From Cavendish, Route 2 enters Kings County near St. Andrews and veers inland to join Route 4 at Fortune Bridge. On any of these approaches, distances are not as long as they may seem from glancing at a provincial map. Souris is 82km (51 miles) from Charlottetown and 70km (43 miles) from Wood Islands.

Staying in northern Kings County

Accommodations in the northern half of Kings County are more spread out than elsewhere on the island, but the choices you do have run the gamut of prices — from one of PEI's best bargains to one of its most upscale (and expensive) inns.

A Place to Stay Inn
$ Souris

Once you get over the name, you'll discover that this inexpensive lodging has everything going for it — comfortable rooms, cooking facilities, television lounges, bike rentals, and a location within walking distance of the Souris waterfront. Beds are in downstairs dormitories or in upstairs bed-and-breakfast rooms that share bathrooms.

9 Longworth St., Souris ☎ *800-655-7829 or 902-687-4626. Rack rates: C$20 (US$14.30) dorm bed, C$65 (US$46.40) double. MC, V. March–Jan (after mid-Oct by reservation only).*

Inn at Bay Fortune
$$$–$$$$ Bay Fortune

Built as a summer retreat for Broadway playwright Elmer Harris, Inn at Bay Fortune is now an upscale, 18-room inn on the calm shores of Bay Fortune. You'll find the lodge and its well-manicured grounds rather aristocratic, and yet the ambience remains unpretentious. The elegant rooms are furnished with a pleasing mix of antiques and island-made furniture; some have wood-burning fireplaces.

The restaurant here has a reputation as one of the finest in the Maritimes. Enjoy views of the bay in a refined setting while dining on local seafood, carefully prepared using ingredients harvested from the inn's own garden. A full breakfast is included in the rates, or choose a package that includes dinner and a picnic lunch.

Route 310, Bay Fortune ☎ *902-687-3745. Fax: 902-687-3540. Internet:* www. innatbayfortune.com. *Rack rates: C$150–C$300 (US$178.60–US$364.30) double. MC, V. Mid-May–mid-Oct.*

Rodd Crowbush Golf & Beach Resort
$$$$ Lakeside

In the heart of one of Canada's top-ranked golf courses and adjacent to a magnificent stretch of sandy beach, Crowbush is one of PEI's premier resorts. Guest rooms are spacious and decorated in a casual, contemporary style. All have a private patio or deck and come with niceties such as bathrobes, television and DVD combos, and evening turndown service. Cottages scattered around the property are a luxurious splurge. Tennis courts, an indoor pool, and a restaurant specializing in modern Canadian cooking round out the resort. Although you pay top dollar to stay here, the atmosphere is refined-casual. The staff is service-oriented, friendly, and approachable. Always ask about packages that may include greens fees or meals in the price.

Route 350, Lakeside ☎ *800-235-8909* or *902-961-7300. Fax: 902-961-5601. Internet:* www.rodd-hotels.ca. *Rack rates: C$250–C$510 (US$178.60–US$364.30) double. AE, DC, MC, V. Mid-May–mid-Oct.*

Dining in northern Kings County

Inn at Bay Fortune and Rodd Crowbush Golf & Beach Resort (see above) both feature excellent restaurants that welcome non-guests. You can also dine at one of the following two choices.

Bluefin Restaurant
$–$$ Souris SEAFOOD

A great place to dig into a hearty seafood meal with the locals. The simple, wide-ranging menu has something to suit everyone — think Caesar salad, roast beef and mashed potatoes, and deep-fried halibut and chips. If you're not lobstered out, head to the downstairs section, where the lobster supper comes with all-you-can-eat seafood chowder and mussels.

10 Federal Ave., Souris ☎ *902-687-3271. Main courses: C$9–C$16 (US$6.40–US$11.40). Daily 7 a.m.–8 p.m. MC, V.*

St. Margarets Lobster Supper
$$ St. Margarets SEAFOOD

Unlike the lobster suppers in neighboring Queens County, the St. Margarets version is put on for residents as much as for visitors. It's served up in the local church throughout summer, although because they have no holding pond, the lobster may be frozen. The fixed-price meal includes a full lobster, freshly baked breads, delicious fish chowder and strawberry shortcake for dessert.

Route 16, St. Margarets ☎ *902-687-3105. Lobster supper: C$25 (US$17.90). Mid-June–mid-Sept daily 4–9 p.m.*

Exploring northern Kings County

You can easily hit the hot spots of northern Kings County — Souris, East Point, and the eastern end of Prince Edward Island National Park — in a single day, including stops. The road around the peninsula is never more than a few minutes' drive from the water, while rural routes cut across the entire peninsula, opening up various options for exploring the interior.

Souris and area

Souris (pronounced "Surrey"), 39km (24 miles) north of Pooles Corner, has a population of just 1,300, yet is the biggest town in all of Kings County. **St. Mary's Catholic Church,** on Chapel Avenue, soars higher than any other building in town. It was built in 1901 using red-colored island sandstone. At the west entrance to town is a beach and a concession renting kayaks and bikes.

Around 10km (6.2 miles) up the coast from Souris is **Basin Head Fisheries Museum** (☎ 902-357-7233), at the site of an abandoned fish cannery. The original wooden buildings, weathered by sun and salt, hold displays tracing the history of the industry as well as touch tanks and exhibits describing local sea life. The museum is open June to September daily 9 a.m. to 6 p.m. and admission is C$3.50 (US$2.50) adults, free for children. Below the museum is **Singing Sand Beach,** so named for the squeaking sound when you walk on the sand.

North Shore

The octagonal **East Point Lighthouse** (☎ 902-357-2106) stands on a low knoll at the easternmost point of land on Prince Edward Island. Built in 1867, the timber structure is open for inspection June to August daily 10 a.m. to 6 p.m. The attached lightkeeper's residence has been converted to a gift shop with a good selection of seafaring literature.

Take Route 313 west from St. Peters to reach the Greenwich unit of **Prince Edward Island National Park,** which is dominated by massive sand dunes. The unstable dunes are slowly moving inland, burying the coastal woods and leaving bleached tree trunks sticking up through the sand. The access road ends at an interpretive center (☎ 902-963-2391; June to October daily 9 a.m. to 5 p.m.) where the unique ecology of the protected peninsula is explained. To see for yourself, take the 4.5km (2.8-mile) **Greenwich Dunes Hiking Trail.** Allow 90 minutes to complete the loop. Admission to the park is C$5 (US$3.60) adults, C$4.25 (US$3) seniors, C$2.50 (US$1.80) children.

Part VI
The Part of Tens

The 5th Wave   By Rich Tennant

"WHAT DO YOU MEAN YOU FORGOT THE WHITE WINE?! YOU
KNOW DARN WELL I CAN'T SERVE FISH WITHOUT WHITE WINE!"

In this part...

Presented in a top ten format, the following three chapters aren't required reading, but I recommend you give them a look. Find inspiration in Chapter 22, which condenses the best Maritimes experiences. If you want a quick reference of the region's top restaurants (okay, not really — my favorite places to eat), check out Chapter 23. Finally, Chapter 24's rundown will make you the king of trivia, on ten Maritimers of note.

Chapter 22

Ten Maritimes Experiences

*I*n this chapter, I describe experiences that represent the best of the Maritimes — a combination of specific destinations and things to do throughout the three provinces.

A Day in Anne's Land

If you've read *Anne of Green Gables*, you'll want to spend at least a day exploring the area around Cavendish, on Prince Edward Island — the area Lucy Maud Montgomery waxed lyrical about in her famous novel. You can visit Montgomery's birthplace, stroll through the home in which she was married (or even tie the knot yourself), and walk — or skip for the full effect — along Lover's Lane through Balsam Hollow.

Drinking and Dancing

Maritimers love their beer (especially local brews such as Keith's) and they love traditional Celtic music. Combine the two in the surroundings of a local pub and you're in for an energetic night of fun. Nearly every town through the region has at least one pub, each with its regular clientele, but welcoming of visitors. A ceilidh (*kay*-lee) is an organized gathering that combines the two pleasures, often in a community hall or outdoor venue.

Fishing the Miramichi

Serious anglers from around the world are drawn to the wildly remote Miramichi River for spring and summer runs of Atlantic salmon weighing up to 13 kilograms (30 pounds). Fish populations have increased remarkably since a catch-and-release policy was implemented a decade ago. There are still lots up for grabs, but catching them is an art. Better your odds by hiring a local guide; many are associated with riverside fishing lodges.

If the fish aren't biting, head to the Atlantic Salmon Museum in Doaktown and read about other anglers' successes.

Going Golfing

Imagine striding the fairways of one of Canada's finest golf courses, staying the night just a chip and a putt from the 18th green, then teeing off again the next morning — all for less than you pay for a single round at a top city course elsewhere in North America. Golfing and golf packages are a relative bargain across the Maritimes, but Brudenell River on Prince Edward Island offers the bonus of activities for everyone in the family — think tennis, horseback riding, hiking, canoeing, and more.

Having a Whale of a Time

Hundreds of whales spend the warmer months feasting in the nutrient-rich waters of the Bay of Fundy. Species such as finback, minke, and humpback are commonly sighted, while the world's rarest whale — the North Atlantic right whale — is spotted by the lucky few. Tour boats depart from Digby Neck (Nova Scotia) and St. Andrews (New Brunswick) throughout the summer, lasting two to three hours. If the whales are playing hide and seek, strike up a conversation with your captain. Most are local fishermen making a little extra money in their downtime, and all are characters with a whale tale or two to tell.

Hiking the Highlands

Views along the Cabot Trail, which winds through Cape Breton Highlands National Park, are stupendous, but this "trail" is for vehicles (or cyclists who take their lives into their hands by traversing the narrow road by pedal power). You'll best appreciate the park's scenery if you move away from the road and hike along one of the walking trails. The Skyline Trail is a classic. Easily traversed in a half-day, it ends at a magnificent lookout high above the ocean. And if you're lucky, you may spy whales frolicking far below.

Making the French Connection

Acadian culture, which has its roots in the region's early French settlers, can be experienced throughout the Maritimes, but along the Acadian Coast of New Brunswick, you can live it in any number of ways. Visiting a museum — those in Moncton and Caraquet are best — provides a good introduction to the Acadians and their heroic history. But enjoying a concert at Village Historique Acadien or a home-cooked meal at La Fine Grobe Sur Mur, at Nigadoo, really brings the culture to life.

Sailing into the Sunset

No other boat is better known in Canada than the *Bluenose* (look on the back of the Canadian dime for a scaled-down version) and there is no more romantic way to spend an evening than under sail on the *Bluenose II,* an exact replica of the original. She has a packed summer schedule of public cruises throughout the Maritimes, with regular departures from her home port of Lunenburg as well as from nearby Halifax. You'll need to book well ahead of time to be assured of a spot on board — otherwise you'll be left waving from the dock.

Snapping the Perfect Picture

The combination of colorful subject matter and superlative scenery makes taking good photos in the Maritimes a snap. South of Halifax, picture-taking opportunities line up along the coast — the world's most photographed lighthouse at Peggy's Cove, the trio of bayside churches in Mahone Bay, and the colorful clapboard buildings of Lunenburg. On the rest of your travels, go beyond the obvious. In New Brunswick, have your family stand at a tilt in front of Moncton's Magnetic Hill and snoop around the narrow back streets of Saint John for a historic perspective. On Prince Edward Island, rise early to catch the first flush of light along the red dunes of Prince Edward Island National Park, and take to the back roads for rural panoramas.

Walking on the Ocean Floor

Okay, it's true in a literal sense. The action happens at Hopewell Rocks, on the New Brunswick side of the Bay of Fundy. As the massive Fundy tide recedes, it leaves the "ocean floor" bare around the entire bay. What makes this place even more notable is the dozen or so rock towers separated from the mainland by the forces of erosion.

Chapter 23

Ten Places to Eat Great Seafood

● ●

In This Chapter

▶ The cream of the crop of seafood restaurants

▶ Discovering what makes each place special

● ●

*F*ishophobes beware! Seafood dominates the Maritimes dining scene. Just about every restaurant offers seafood in some form or another, and many specialize in it. The food in major Maritimes cities is comparable in presentation and creativity to that in other North American cities, but it's offered at a fraction of the price. Aside from the regular restaurants, there are many small-town cafes that serve up seafood; you can count on the fish being battered, but lobster and mussels are usually boiled, and scallops sautéed. Finally, there are fish markets. Most coastal villages have one, usually down near the harbor, selling a range of fresh seafood — perfect for a home-cooked meal in your cabin.

And so, without further ado, here are the top ten places in the Maritimes to eat seafood.

Blue Mussel Café

Fresh ingredients, locally sourced whenever possible, are prepared at Prince Edward Island's renowned Blue Mussel Café with simple style. The highlight for many diners is what this restaurant *doesn't* have — a deep fryer. One local specialty is the soft-flavored Malpeque Bay oyster. Order them *au naturel* for the full effect. The restaurant setting is as memorable as the food — a small cluster of outdoor tables over the water is protected from the wind by a renovated wharf building that serves as the kitchen.

Butland's Seafood

If you're visiting Fundy National Park in New Brunswick, drive through to the adjacent village of Alma, where Butland's Seafood holds a prime position above the small harbor. Inside this lively market is a bathtub-sized container overflowing with cooked lobsters. They are pre-weighed, with prices (around C$10/US$7.10 per pound) marked on the claws. If someone has beaten you to the single picnic table out back, head back into the national park and enjoy lunch at any one of its numerous picnic spots.

Chowder House

How does a restaurant that hasn't seen a coat of paint for years and doesn't even offer table service make my top ten? Easy — by serving up huge portions of super-fresh mussels, crab, and lobster at ridiculously low prices. The location helps also, perched on a grassy bluff overlooking the Atlantic Ocean in the village of Neil's Harbour, on Cape Breton Island.

Five Fishermen

In Halifax, if you're looking to choose from a wide range of seafood in a stylish setting, make reservations at the Five Fishermen. Ensconced in an 1816 redbrick building that was originally a school — and, more infamously, a morgue for bodies of first-class passengers from the *Titanic* tragedy — tables are spread through numerous nautical-themed rooms. A massive wine rack holds pride of place in the center of the restaurant, and a century-old stained glass window is the feature in the main dining room.

Murphy's

Murphy's, in Truro, Nova Scotia, gets my nod for "The Best Maritimes Seafood Restaurant That's Nowhere Near the Ocean." Not only is water out of sight, the strip mall setting is unremarkable. Inside, the distinctly nautical setting includes model ships on the walls and fishnets hanging from the ceiling. Battered fish with a pile of perfectly cooked chips is the specialty, served up by no-nonsense waitstaff.

Muddy Rudder

The Muddy Rudder is nothing more than a ramshackle shed where orders are taken, a gas burner, and a bunch of plastic table settings on a grassed area beside the Cabot Trail. The seafood — crab, lobster, mussels, clams, and more — is dunked in a pot of boiling water to order. A truly unique Maritimes dining experience.

New Glasgow Lobster Supper

Lobster suppers have been held throughout Prince Edward Island for over 50 years. They originated as gatherings in community halls and church basements, often as fund-raisers for some local cause or another. The New Glasgow Lobster Supper is one of the best. It attracts quite a few locals, as well as visitors staying at nearby Cavendish. But there's plenty of room for everyone, with over 500 seats on two levels. Don't come here for the view (although some tables overlook the River Clyde) or the atmosphere (which is fun and informal). Choose this lobster supper for the food: a fixed-price meal of lobster, complete with all-you-can-eat mussels, seafood chowder, potato salad, and coleslaw. Just make sure to save room for the strawberry shortcake.

O'Neil's Fundy Fish Market

Digby, on the Nova Scotia side of the Bay of Fundy, is renowned for its fleet of scallop boats that harvest the sweetest, plumpest scallops you could ever imagine. At Digby's dockside fish market, they are sold raw to go, or rolled in flour and fried up on the spot. The market also sells Digby chicks, a chewy, jerky-style snack of smoked herring, as well as mussels, oysters, lobsters, and a variety of Fundy fishes such as halibut.

Seaweed Pie Café

At Miminegash, in Prince County, Prince Edward Island, a group of local women have formed a cooperative to harvest and process Irish moss, a type of seaweed that washes up on local beaches in big storms. Irish moss has traditionally been used as a thickening ingredient in ice cream and toothpaste, but the ladies of Miminegash market its nutrient-rich values for health-related products. Not all of it is shipped to outside markets. Some ends up in seaweed pie, a surprisingly delicious dish served up in a small cafe that is part of a larger interpretive center.

Shediac Bay Cruises

Add a little spice to your seafood feast by helping haul in the catch aboard Shediac Bay Cruises. With Captain Eric le Blanc at the helm, these trips leave daily from Shediac, north of Moncton, New Brunswick. The tour begins with an informative talk about the life cycle of the lobster and harvesting methods. The traps are then lifted onto the boat, the lobsters are extracted, and then they're boiled in preparation of an onboard seafood feast.

Chapter 24

Ten Famous People You Probably Didn't Realize Were Maritimers

In This Chapter

▶ Inventing the telephone

▶ Sailing around the world

▶ Belting out the tunes

● ●

*W*hile the stunning landscape is the Maritimes' most obvious asset, the people (universally known as "Maritimers") themselves are notable. Frank, friendly, and always with a story to tell, they contribute to making the region a great place to visit. The following Maritimers have gone on to greatness beyond their own borders.

Alexander Graham Bell

Prolific inventor Alexander Graham Bell spent his latter years at Baddeck, on Cape Breton Island, where his waterfront home is still owned by the Bell family. At the large museum in town, you can learn about his most famous invention, the telephone, as well as quirky facts, such as why he could never call his mom (she was deaf).

Stompin' Tom Connors

If you're not from Canada, you're probably not familiar with the patriotic tunes written and sung by this legendary musician, who was born in Saint John, New Brunswick, and raised on Prince Edward Island. Stompin' Tom has sold three million albums without ever having a song on the Canadian country charts and without ever releasing a song outside of Canada (who says "Bud the Spud" isn't radio-friendly?).

Samuel Cunard

Born the son of a Halifax carpenter, Samuel Cunard was the man behind Cunard Steamship Limited, the most recognizable name in ocean travel. In 1840, a Cunard ship made the first transatlantic passenger service, marking the start of the company's heyday. Today the company has just one boat in service, the *Queen Mary II,* the largest passenger ship ever built.

Lorie Kane

One of the most popular players on the LPGA Tour, multiple tournament winner Lorie Kane is one of the few big-time golfers who hasn't migrated south to Florida. She still calls Charlottetown home, striding the fairways of her home course, Belvedere Golf Club, when she's not lighting up fairways on tour.

Sam Langford

Generally regarded as one of the ten greatest heavyweight boxers of all time, Nova Scotia–born Langford stepped into the ring over 600 times through the first two decades of the 1900s. During his career, he fought in five weight divisions — lightweight through to heavyweight — but makes this list for his final fight, which he fought after having been declared legally blind. The result? He won. By a knockout.

Lucy Maud Montgomery

No other person in Canada has as well-preserved a childhood as this famous writer, who grew up at Cavendish on Prince Edward Island and used her early memories to create the character Anne of Green Gables, a lovable orphan girl. The paths Montgomery walked, the room in which she was married, and the unremarkable but much-visited farmhouse known as Green Gables make up Anne-fan favorites.

Anne Murray

With sales of 50 million albums and more awards than any other female singer, Anne Murray continues to entertain people worldwide with her sultry voice that blends pop and country. Murray was born in Springhill, Nova Scotia, and retains strong ties to the region through the town's Anne Murray Centre.

John Patch

Patch, a fisherman from Yarmouth, Nova Scotia, developed the screw propeller in 1832. It soon became the preferred method of propulsion in ships, more effective than either sails or paddlewheels. In 1845, a large steamship became the first to cross the Atlantic Ocean using his invention. In the later years of his life, Patch lost the rights to the propeller. He died penniless.

Harry Saltzman

Harry Saltzman had the movie mogul look: tubby, loud, and always brightly dressed. He also had the blockbusters to go with the look. Born in Saint John, New Brunswick, in 1915, Saltzman left home to join the circus at the age of 17, ending up in Paris during World War II. After producing *The Iron Petticoat,* which starred the unlikely duo of Bob Hope and Katharine Hepburn, he bought the screen rights to Ian Fleming's James Bond novels and then went on to produce the first nine Bond movies, the biggest espionage thrillers in movie history.

Joshua Slocum

Born and raised around Digby, Joshua Slocum left Nova Scotia for a life on the high seas at a young age. He is remembered today for one particular feat: being the first person to sail solo around the world.

Appendix

Quick Concierge

• •

*H*ere's a handy A to Z of practical information you may need on your travels through the Maritimes. You'll find contact information — including toll-free numbers and Web sites — for airlines, car-rental companies, and hotel chains, as well as other helpful tidbits. Best of all, this is one concierge you don't need to tip.

Fast Facts

AAA

The Canadian affiliate of AAA is the Canadian Automobile Association (www.caa.ca). Check the Web site for the location of regional offices or contact CAA Maritimes at ☎ 800-561-8807.

American Express

American Express has no full-service International Service Centers in the Maritimes. Instead dial ☎ 905-474-8700 for cardholder services. For lost or stolen traveler's checks, call ☎ 800-668-2639.

Area Codes

The telephone area code for Nova Scotia and Prince Edward Island is **902**. The area code for New Brunswick is **506**.

ATMs

The most common place to find bank machines is at the entrance to major banks. Check the back of your debit or credit card to see what network your bank belongs to, then contact Plus (☎ 800-843-7587; Internet: www.visa.com) or Cirrus (☎ 800-424-7787; Internet: www.mastercard) to find the location nearest to you.

Business Hours

Business hours vary throughout the Maritimes. The following is only a guideline. Banks: Monday through Thursday 9:00 a.m.–3:30 p.m., Friday 9 a.m.–5 p.m. Retail stores: Monday through Saturday 9:30 a.m.–5:00 p.m. Mall shops often stay open until 9 p.m. later in the week and open on Sunday from around noon until 5 or 6 p.m. In tourist areas, hours fluctuate greatly, and many shops close completely for the winter.

Credit Cards

For lost or stolen credit cards, contact the following: American Express (☎ 800-668-2639), Diners Club (☎ 800-363-3333), Discover Card (☎ 800-347-2683), MasterCard (☎ 800-307-7309), or Visa (☎ 800-847-2911).

Currency Exchanges

The best place to exchange money is a bank. Refer to the "Fast Facts" section at the end of each city chapter of this book for bank locations in major cities. Airports at Halifax, Moncton, Fredericton, and Charlottetown have currency exchange bureaus. Many Canadian businesses accept U.S. dollars — often gladly, but at a lower rate than a bank would offer you.

The Web site www.xe.com/ucc is a good tool for checking the latest rates.

Customs

Representatives of the **Canada Border Services Agency** (☎ 800-461-9999 or 204-983-3500; Internet: www.cbsa-asfc.gc.ca) are located at every major border crossing and at airports that receive international flights.

Drugstores

You'll find local drugstores listed in the "Fast Facts" sections at the end of each city chapter. Otherwise, ask at the front desk of any hotel or check the local phone book (look under "Pharmacies").

Electricity

Canada's electrical outlets put out 110 volts AC, the same as in the United States.

Emergencies

For ambulance, police, or fire department assistance, call ☎ **911**.

Hospitals

The location of local hospitals is listed in the "Fast Facts" sections of each city chapter.

Internet Access

Public libraries throughout the Maritimes allow visitors to use their computers for Internet access at no cost.

Most major hotels have in-room Internet access or provide access from a "business center." Bed-and-breakfast owners are often more than happy to let you send e-mail (especially if you say something nice about where you're staying).

Liquor Laws

You must be 19 years old to consume alcoholic beverages in the Maritimes.

A "licensed" restaurant or cafe is one that is licensed by the province to serve alcohol to those 19 years of age and older.

Mail

At the time of publication, stamps for mailing standard letters or postcards cost C49¢, C80¢, and C$1.40 other international destinations.

You can receive mail on the road by having it addressed to your name and "General Delivery," care of the post office in the town of your choice.

Maps

Each of three provincial tourism offices (see "Where to Get More Information" later in the Appendix) offers free information packages, which include a map that is sufficient for general touring.

Map Art (☎ **905-436-2525**; Internet: www.mapart.com) publishes a number of excellent regional and city street guides for the Maritimes. Rand McNally produces a softcover Atlantic Canada atlas. Bookstores such as Chapters (located in all major cities) carry these along with others.

Police

Dial ☎ **911** for emergencies.

Safety

The Maritimes is no more or less safe than anywhere else in Canada. You need to take the usual commonsense precautions for your own safety and personal belongings, just as you would when traveling anywhere else.

See Chapter 7 for details about driving in the Maritimes and Chapter 10 for tips on keeping healthy when you travel.

Smoking

Anti-smoking laws in all three provinces limit smoking in public places such as malls, museums, and sporting arenas. Many restaurants have barred smoking altogether, while others have set aside an enclosed area for smokers, or have put limits the hours patrons can light up. Hotels often have floors reserved for nonsmokers, while smoking at bed-and-breakfasts is nearly always limited to outdoor areas. Because ordinances vary from province to province and even town to town, you should check before lighting up anywhere.

Taxes

The federal Goods and Services Tax (GST) is 7%. Each Maritimes province tacks an additional tax on all purchases except food. The Provincial Sales Tax (PST) on Prince Edward Island is 10%, for a total of 17% in taxes. In Nova Scotia and New Brunswick, a provincial tax of 8% is blended with the GST to make a Harmonized Sales Tax (HST) of 15%.

The GST paid in Prince Edward Island and the HST paid in Nova Scotia and New Brunswick are refundable on accommodations and most consumer goods (except meals and gas) for non-Canadians. See Chapter 4 for details on getting a refund.

Time Zones

All three provinces are located in the Atlantic Standard Time zone (AST), one hour ahead of New York and four hours ahead of Los Angeles. From the first Sunday in April through to the last Saturday in October, Daylight Saving Time is observed throughout the region, along with the rest of Canada (except Saskatchewan).

Tipping

Tipping in the Maritimes is no different than it is anywhere else in Canada or in the United States. See Chapter 4 for details.

Weather Updates

The best online source of weather reports, complete with long-range forecasts, satellite pictures, and historical tidbits of meteorological data, is the Environment Canada Web site at www.weatheroffice.ec.gc.ca. If your hotel room has cable television, it will probably be tuned in to Canada's Weather Channel.

Toll-Free Numbers and Web Sites

Major airlines serving the Maritimes

Air Canada
☎ 888-247-2262
www.aircanada.ca

Air Canada Jazz
☎ 888-247-2262
www.flyjazz.com

CanJet
☎ 800-809-7777
www.canjet.com

Continental
☎ 800-784-4444
www.continental.com

Delta
☎ 800-221-1212
www.delta.com

Northwest
☎ 800-225-2525
www.nwa.com

Jetsgo
☎ 866-440-0441
www.jetsgo.com

WestJet
☎ 888-937-8538
www.westjet.com

Major car-rental agencies in the Maritimes

Avis
☎ 800-879-2847
www.avis.com

Hertz
☎ 800-263-0600
www.hertz.com

Budget
☎ 800-268-8900
www.budgetcanada.com

National
☎ 800-227-7368
www.nationalcar.com

Discount
☎ 800-263-2355
www.discountcar.com

Rent-A-Wreck
☎ 800-327-0116
www.rentawreck.ca

Dollar
☎ 800-800-4000
www.dollar.com

Thrifty
☎ 800-847-4389
www.thrifty.com

Enterprise
☎ 800-325-8007
www.enterprise.com

Major hotel and motel chains in the Maritimes

Best Western
☎ 800-528-1234
www.bestwestern.com

Coastal Inns
☎ 800-859-2486
www.coastalinns.com

Cape Breton Resorts
☎ 800-565-5660
www.capebretonresorts.com

Days Inn
☎ 800-329-7466
www.daysinn.com

Choice Hotels
☎ 800-424-6423
www.choicehotels.ca

Delta Hotels
☎ 800-263-8255
www.deltahotels.com

City Hotels
☎ 800-563-2489
www.cityhotels.ca

Fairmont Hotels and Resorts
☎ 800-257-7544
www.fairmont.com

Holiday Inn
☎ 800-465-4329
www.holiday-inn.com

Maritime Inns and Resorts
☎ 888-662-7484
www.maritimeinns.com

Ramada
☎ 800-272-6232
www.ramada.com

Rodd Hotels & Resorts
☎ 800-565-7633
www.rodd-hotels.ca

Signature Resorts
☎ 800-565-0444
www.signatureresorts.com

Super 8
☎ 800-800-8000
www.super8.com

Where to Get More Information

You'll find most of what you need to know for your Maritimes trip in this book, but if you're thirsting for more, try the following resources.

Tourist information

Each of the three provincial tourism offices operates visitor information centers at the major gateways to their respective provinces.

Provincial tourism bureaus offer free information packages and maps that'll boost your pre-trip planning. To get the goods, contact the following:

- ✔ **Tourism Nova Scotia** (☎ **800-565-0000** or 902-425-5781; Internet: www.explore.gov.ns.ca)
- ✔ **New Brunswick Department of Tourism and Parks** (☎ **800-561-0123**; Internet: www.tourismnewbrunswick.ca)
- ✔ **Tourism Prince Edward Island** (☎ **888-734-7529** or 902-368-4444; Internet: www.gov.pe.ca/visitorsguide)

These Web sites dish out information on specific cities, parks, and traveling in Canada beyond the Maritimes:

- ✔ **Canadian Tourism Commission:** www.travelcanada.ca
- ✔ **Fredericton Tourism:** www.fredericton.ca
- ✔ **Parks Canada:** www.pc.gc.ca
- ✔ **The Capital Commission:** www.visitcharlottetown.com
- ✔ **Tourism Halifax:** www.halifaxinfo.com
- ✔ **Tourism Moncton:** www.gomoncton.com
- ✔ **Tourism Saint John:** www.tourismsaintjohn.ca

Other guidebooks

Frommer's Nova Scotia, New Brunswick & Prince Edward Island complements this book perfectly. It covers destinations not included in these pages and offers a different perspective on those that are. *Frommer's Canada* is the preferred option for travelers planning on exploring the rest of the country. Another excellent resource is www.frommers.com, which offers travel tips, online booking options, and a daily e-mail newsletter filled with travel specials.

Making Dollars and Sense of It

Expense	Daily cost	x	Number of days	=	Total
Airfare					
Local transportation					
Car rental					
Lodging (with tax)					
Parking					
Breakfast					
Lunch					
Dinner					
Snacks					
Entertainment					
Babysitting					
Attractions					
Gifts & souvenirs					
Tips					
Other					
Grand Total					

Fare Game: Choosing an Airline

When looking for the best airfare, you should cover all your bases — 1) consult a trusted travel agent; 2) contact the airline directly, via the airline's toll-free number and/or Web site; 3) check out one of the travel-planning Web sites, such as www.frommers.com.

Travel Agency_____ Phone_____

Agent's Name_____ Quoted fare_____

Airline 1_____ Quoted fare_____

Toll-free number/Internet_____

Airline 2_____ Quoted fare_____

Toll-free number/Internet_____

Web site 1_____ Quoted fare_____

Web site 2_____ Quoted fare_____

Departure Schedule & Flight Information

Airline_____ Flight #_____ Confirmation #_____

Departs_____ Date_____ Time_____ a.m./p.m.

Arrives_____ Date_____ Time_____ a.m./p.m.

Connecting Flight (if any)

Amount of time between flights_____ hours/mins

Airline_____ Flight #_____ Confirmation #_____

Departs_____ Date_____ Time_____ a.m./p.m.

Arrives_____ Date_____ Time_____ a.m./p.m.

Return Trip Schedule & Flight Information

Airline_____ Flight #_____ Confirmation #_____

Departs_____ Date_____ Time_____ a.m./p.m.

Arrives_____ Date_____ Time_____ a.m./p.m.

Connecting Flight (if any)

Amount of time between flights_____ hours/mins

Airline_____ Flight #_____ Confirmation #_____

Departs_____ Date_____ Time_____ a.m./p.m.

Arrives_____ Date_____ Time_____ a.m./p.m.

All Aboard: Booking Your Train Travel

Travel Agency_____ Phone_____

Agent's Name_____

Web Site_____

Departure Schedule & Train Information

Train #_____ Confirmation #_____ Seat reservation #_____

Departs_____ Date_____ Time_____ a.m./p.m.

Arrives_____ Date_____ Time_____ a.m./p.m.

Quoted fare_____ First class _____ Second class

Departure Schedule & Train Information

Train #_____ Confirmation #_____ Seat reservation #_____

Departs_____ Date_____ Time_____ a.m./p.m.

Arrives_____ Date_____ Time_____ a.m./p.m.

Quoted fare_____ First class _____ Second class

Departure Schedule & Train Information

Train #_____ Confirmation #_____ Seat reservation #_____

Departs_____ Date_____ Time_____ a.m./p.m.

Arrives_____ Date_____ Time_____ a.m./p.m.

Quoted fare_____ First class _____ Second class

Departure Schedule & Train Information

Train #_____ Confirmation #_____ Seat reservation #_____

Departs_____ Date_____ Time_____ a.m./p.m.

Arrives_____ Date_____ Time_____ a.m./p.m.

Quoted fare_____ First class _____ Second class

Sweet Dreams: Choosing Your Hotel

Make a list of all the hotels where you'd like to stay and then check online and call the local and toll-free numbers to get the best price. You should also check with a travel agent, who may be able to get you a better rate.

Hotel & page	Location	Internet	Tel. (local)	Tel. (Toll-free)	Quoted rate

Hotel Checklist

Here's a checklist of things to inquire about when booking your room, depending on your needs and preferences.

- ☐ Smoking/smoke-free room
- ☐ Noise (if you prefer a quiet room, ask about proximity to elevator, bar/restaurant, pool, meeting facilities, renovations, and street)
- ☐ View
- ☐ Facilities for children (crib, roll-away cot, babysitting services)
- ☐ Facilities for travelers with disabilities
- ☐ Number and size of bed(s) (king, queen, double/full-size)
- ☐ Is breakfast included? (buffet, continental, or sit-down?)
- ☐ In-room amenities (hair dryer, iron/board, minibar, etc.)
- ☐ Other_____

Index

• *G* •

• *N* •

• T •

• U •

• V •

The Motel of the Stars

THE
Motel ᴼꜰ ᴛʜᴇ Stars

A NOVEL

Karen Salyer McElmurray

The Linda Bruckheimer
Series in Kentucky Literature

Sarabande 🕮 Books

LOUISVILLE, KENTUCKY

F

Copyright © 2008 by Karen McElmurray

Managing Editor
Sarabande Books, Inc.
2234 Dundee Road, Suite 200
Louisville, KY 40205

Library of Congress Cataloging-in-Publication Data

McElmurray, Karen Salyer, 1956–
    The motel of the stars : a novel / by Karen McElmurray. — 1st ed.
        p. cm. — (The Linda Bruckheimer series in Kentucky literature)
    ISBN 978-1-932511-66-6 (pbk. : acid-free paper)
    1. Grief—Fiction. 2. Loss (Psychology)—Fiction. 3. New Age movement—
Psychology—Fiction. 4. Kentucky—Fiction. 5. North Carolina—Fiction. I. Title.
    PS3563.C35966M68 2008
    813'.54—dc22   2008010564

Manufactured in Canada
This book is printed on acid-free paper.

Sarabande Books is a nonprofit literary organization.

This project is supported in part by an award from the National
Endowment for the Arts.

The Kentucky Arts Council, the state arts agency, supports
Sarabande Books with state tax dollars and federal funding
from the National Endowment for the Arts, which believes
that a great nation deserves great art.

For John, and for Jeff

Whenever you have two electrical fields together, there is another field that exists. No matter how many fields you have together, there is always present a group vibration of which everyone partakes.

—Jose Arguelles

Decoder, ancient Mayan calendar

Initiator of Harmonic Convergence

The Motel of the Stars

Chapter One

Beloved, let your eyes half close, and your heart beat
Over my heart, and your hair fall over my breast,
Drowning love's lonely hour in deep twilight of rest,
And hiding their tossing manes and their tumultuous feet.
　　　　　—from "Michael Robartes Bids His Beloved Be at Peace"

The Motel of the Stars

As Jason Sanderson drove the hours east for another foreclosure, he followed signs and directions for only so long. Then he pulled over to listen to cicadas and distant afternoon thunder. He stood in the summer grass, the Joe Pye weeds, tall and purple-blossomed, and remembered himself as a boy, fields where he'd slipped from church with the rest of them to smoke cigarettes and to sip stolen medicinal whiskey. He took in the scents of late August, too sweet wild roses and the pitch-tar smell of coal, and he inexplicably remembered other times. Thirty-some years ago. Saigon. The slick scent of gun oil. The garlic and hard candy taste of some girl's mouth. He stood in the quiet of strange roadsides and the past was more real to him than now.

He was good at what he did—a job in foreclosures in the eastern part of Kentucky. He began his phone calls to potential clients with questions about the weather and family, or with jokes that Rosa said were over the top. *What did the Dalai Lama say to the hot dog vendor? Make me one with everything.* And when it came down to it, to home visits and demands, he hesitated. He knocked respectfully, pretended he was on a social call and accepted cups of coffee meant as last-minute stalling measures before the signed and dated documents were produced.

Today's foreclosure was for a motel with a name that sounded like Rita Hayworth and Frank Sinatra. *The Motel of the Stars.* The folder the general manager laid on his desk some time back was crammed with more photocopies concerning that motel than he could have counted. Purchase orders and bills. Copies of overdue notices and notices of bank reclamation followed copies of threatening letters from lawyers, then notices from the credit bureau. Numerous calls to the owner of the motel, Frank Llewellyn, went unanswered. He had spoken once to a soft-voiced woman who had promised to send back payment, which had failed to materialize. *The Motel of the Stars*. Even with mirrored ceilings and magic-finger beds, the motel could not be saved.

He was supposed to know he was nearing Inez when he saw a store with a soda cooler out front here, a gas pump there. He was to see a sign for a coal refinery called Estep's and then a field cleared for a tent revival meeting. His general manager, who had the fervor of a televangelist and an obsession with stock market indexes, had especially pointed out the revival meeting. *They don't make them like that any more. A preacher who knows how to shake and rattle and roll. They can heal you, son.* He gripped the steering wheel as he pulled onto the road again, still studying the manager's hand-drawn directions.

At a crossroads about an hour back, there was to have been a yellow trailer and then a post office just before the right-hand turn onto a one-lane bridge. There had to be some overlooked landmark. *Where are you, sweetie*, Rosa would say at times like this, and he would realize he'd been standing at a window and hearing not a word she said about the new sofa slip cover. Where was he now? The signs, turn-offs, and deep green, late summer corn all looked pretty much the same. Who knew how long he'd driven or how far off the map he'd gone? Since breakfast, he had not been himself.

He remembered swallowing weak coffee and toast and how his jaw tightened as Rosa described tonight's gathering in honor of Sam. She'd been planning it for weeks. *You'll see*, she said. It would be a celebration of healing rather than of loss. There'd been an extra visit from the once-weekly cleaning lady. She'd bought sparkling juices for a toast. For appetizers, little cheese wedges wrapped in foil, olives neither of them much cared for, fresh bakery bread. *It was time*, she said, *to move on.*

Since before eight, he had moved east, past blue-green expanses of central Kentucky horse farms giving way to foothills. Barns advertising Mail Pouch Tobacco and family cemeteries lush with plastic roses abounded. Then there was parkway country and soon thereafter a town called Clay City and a diner for a bear claw and strong coffee. Only a few more miles from there and the parkway yielded to more stretches of road with passing lanes, more hills rising to small mountains, and then the mountain, that marked the entrance to Eastern Kentucky Proper. It rose, squat and deliberate, rock facings jutting and cedars reaching for a sky limited to his sight by other squat mountains soon to come. His heart tightened, beat faster, and his breath came quicker in the nearer proximity of country way too much like the hollows and mouths of hollows and heads of hollows that had long ago been his own home. And a couple of hours after that, a turnoff left him fumbling with his directions, looking for Inez.

You're scared, Rosa had told him at breakfast. He did have more than his share of fears. Depths of water. Steep mountains. Today he wasn't afraid of a thing. Today, something else gripped his heart, propelled him forward past mountain after mountain and sign after sign for little Eastern Kentucky towns. His heart beat and skipped and beat. After his stints in Vietnam, a whole slew of doctors had diagnosed everything from heart nodules to anxiety and counseled him to put his feet up, relax more. One of them even urged him to meditate. Today, he liked this feeling that carried him past town after town. He had exited the parkway a long while back and now houses dwindled in number, nothing but cornfields on one side of the road and fetid-smelling river on the other. *Happy. Feisty. Climax.* He sped up with the cheerfulness of these names through a hole-in-the-road town called Radiant.

Usually he listened to tapes of show tunes or to stations playing country oldies. *Trailers for sale or rent. Rooms to let fifty cents.* Now he flipped through AM and FM, but he kept coming back to hypnotic sounds that put him in mind of belly dancers. In honor of a festival called The Harmonic Convergence, there were flutes, a keening stringed instrument, and a radio announcer offering insights. *Follow the sounds of cosmic consciousness. Rhythms that vibrate to the sound of one universal mind.* Sanderson supposed the music was meant to be religious in some way, but religion wasn't right either, since that was hymnals and childhood prayers. Which was the one that always made him shiver? *If I should die before I wake, I pray the Lord my soul to take.* The memory of that prayer and the music both recalled his anger and he flipped off the air conditioner, leaned out the open car window, inhaled the pungent air.

This many years after his first wife's death, words she loved came back to him. *Pungent. Esoteric.* Columns called "Enrich Your Vocabulary" and "The Power of Words" were her favorites and she had loved any and every dictionary. Visual ones. Foreign language ones. She consulted bulky desktop versions and pocket editions at odd moments on family outings. She'd give Sam the gift of a sentence. *The pungent atmosphere left him feeling disconcerted.* Pungent. Sanderson savored the word now.

He loosened his tie, found a new radio station, part static and part country. Hank Williams. *Cause tonight I'm gonna see my cara mio.* Tonight he'd be home again, to fat new sofa pillows and exotic foods for a celebration. *Celebrate rather than mourn?* His son, dead ten years. One-handed, he slid his tie off, tossed it into the back seat, set off down the road again. That door had been shut a long time ago and he wanted it to stay shut, ten years' anniversary or not.

The first year Sam was reported missing at sea, Sanderson had felt numb. Numbness gave way to a grief that made him feel ashamed. Anger at no one in particular swirled in his heart. Rage gave way to uncertainty. He was perplexed when he studied his receding hairline in the bathroom mirror. He grew sideburns and a goatee and plucked gray hairs he'd never seen. He bought Grecian Formula, slimmer ties, and a cologne called *Incognito*. He took a night class or two, one in astronomy and another in poetry, and he wrote verse that his instructor said was sentimental. There were too many poems about butterflies, sunsets and love. He was never able to describe what he really meant—that image in his head of wings against a door, locked tight against something he didn't want to name.

He bought a place in Kentucky, in the center of the state. Took a new job. *Repossession case manager.* For the new house, he bought a gun case for the living room and stocked it with oiled rifles he never used. He took up golfing, a sport that had never much made sense to him, and he agreed to go on a number of blind dates arranged by his office coworkers. Shirley, a woman with nails bitten to the quick, phoned him three times after their Saturday afternoon coffee date, but he let the machine take the calls. There was Tiffany, who left salty-tasting blueberry pies on his desk at work, and Brenda, who talked him into attending a meeting the Fellowship of Christian Scientists. *Lisa. Judy. Lee Ann.*

Rosa, fifteen years his junior, worked at the real estate office. She had long red hair and she wore blouses buttoned to the neck, plastic glasses that hid her lovely green eyes. She was just separated when he asked her out for coffee, and he found himself telling her things he told no one—stories about Saigon, about hawkers' stalls and rainforests, about the times he'd drunk rice whiskey and wished so badly for home he could taste it. He did what he never did, told her the names of three buddies of his who never came back from the war. Two weeks later he met Rosa for lunch at the room she was renting in town. *Unbutton your shirt*, she said, and he'd never felt more at home in his own bare skin.

They married quickly, their wedding a small gathering in the home of Rosa's former high-school principal. There was a three-tiered cake and there were gifts of small appliances Rosa substituted for the less reliable ones he still owned from his marriage to Sarah. Rosa adored him, told him this often, told him how he had rescued her from her former country store owner husband, for one. And since the marriage? The last four years had vanished. *Evaporated into the atmosphere*, Sam would have said. Dinner parties with friends. Country music concerts, of which Rosa was fond. Trips to shopping malls for china and the latest patterns of stainless steel. Vacations up north. Recently, she was on a course of self-improvement, working on everything from her vowels—the way she stretched out *i* and *a* with a question embedded at the end of every sentence—to her entertainment skills, to her consciousness, with the help of pop psychology books and a regular Tuesday-night meeting for couples called *Energize the Inner You*.

Emotional Wellness Encounters, they were called, led by a counselor named Harry Simon, a man with frizzy gray hair and sparkling dentures who spoke of *inner peace* and *spousal communication skills* as if they were on sale at a discount store. Harry Simon, as group mediator, kept saying, *Let it go, let it go*, but Sanderson couldn't summon a particular time or place for *it*, though he was fairly certain what they wanted. Rosa wanted more than the war stories he'd told her. She wanted ones about explosions that could make the ground shake beneath your feet. Stories about gunfire and gaping wounds. Weren't you afraid, Jason? she'd ask him in the encounter groups and he'd feel himself grow sullen in his wish to tell no story at all. *Fear*. Were there words for it, those times he'd felt fear settle under this tongue?

Jason Sanderson, his father used to say, *make your bed*. Make your bed and lie in it. He had made his bed by now, and he knew that. Jason Sanderson, repo man. He lived where he lived, married who he had married, twice now. He had wanted children this time around, not one to replace Sam exactly, but some way for his name to be carried into the future. Rosa never exactly said no to this wish of his, but they had not discussed it either, not really. *We all have our dreams, our should've, could've, don't we, sweetie*, she said and sighed and left a kiss in lipstick on his cheek, then busied herself with a handkerchief. By letting go, he knew Rosa meant more. His past. Wife. Son. And more than them, really. How to let go of a son he could on some days scarcely recall?

A place he went, a removal that frightened her. That was what Rosa wanted gone the most. *Jason,* she'd say when she'd find him sitting alone, staring out a window or at a blank, white wall. He found himself shaking off lethargy and he turned, as if from a great distance, met her smile. Then he felt it most. *Vertigo.* An enormous height, a precipice. A dizzying fear and afterward an anger so intense it made him sick inside. If he sat still, some days, he thought he might just be able to step closer to it, the vast distance he'd traveled from his own heart.

Signs for a sorghum festival littered the Main Street of Links. That street was just a post office, a five-and-dime, and a fruit stand. A general store promised a Grand Opening and Hot Lunch. He hadn't eaten lunch yet and he could hear Rosa. *You live on snack mix and nervous energy, Jason.* Links was as good a place as any, so he drove the main street up and back looking for a place to get some coffee, and settled on a grocery store on the front steps of which sat a boy picking through a mess of weeds and greenish water in the bottom of a metal pan.

"That looks tasty, son," Sanderson said as he paused on the steps.

"Sang," the boy said.

"Pardon?"

"Sang, mister," the boy repeated, gesturing impatiently toward his lap and the pan. "Ginseng."

Sang. Ginseng. Sanderson turned those words over in his mouth.

"I don't think I'd know ginseng if it bit me," he said at last. He had a recollection of his grandmother and a trip to the woods to pick greens or to hunt up this and that herb. The boy plucked a gnarly root out the pan and cast it in the direction of his high-topped sneakers.

"Granny's got me going through everything, just about," the boy said. He plucked a tiny rock out of the pan, flicked it with thumb and forefinger. His hand had a tiny anchor tattooed on its back.

"She got anything to eat in there?" Sanderson asked as the boy set the pan aside and stretched his skinny, longish legs.

He followed Sanderson inside the store. Bolts of cloth and stray shoes and canning jar lids spilled from boxes here and there, and a woman crouched on her ankles near an open crate.

"Granny," the boy said. "Beans cooked yet?" He nodded in Sanderson's direction. "Customer's here."

The woman nodded as Sanderson made his way around the pile, and then she stood and gestured with one hand clutching a plastic baby doll.

"Pardon my housekeeping, mister," she said, her voice a wind-piped whisper that made him want to clear his own throat. As she peered up and down at him, he wondered why he'd carried in his briefcase.

"Got enough stuff in here to clothe the hungry and feed the poor too, mister." She tossed the doll into a box and nudged a heap of papers with one booted foot.

"That so?" Sanderson said as he eyed the store's shelves, stocked with the basics, soups and toiletries and animal feed. The store had a grainy scent of feed, a bitter odor that stung the nose.

"My daddy run this store up to the day he died and I don't reckon he ever throwed out nothing." She sighed and shook her head.

"You got a bite to eat around here?" Sanderson asked.

"Take my daddy, now, mister." She wiped her hands on an apron marked with grease spots. "You sit right there and tell me if a man needs to keep ary old soap scrap and snake skin he ever come by." She shook her head.

Across from the shelves were racks of items that must have been geared to tourists. Straw hats. Recycled Mason jars labeled Pickled People, which were small, decapitated heads with puckered faces, made of bits of cloth and cotton. Dried, weedy looking bundles were tacked to the tops of shelves or suspended from the store ceiling.

"Them's my herbs, mister," she said. She squinted and gazed up at the bundles. "Horsetail. Mullein." She gestured toward the lower shelves. "And I've got me a bunch of stuff laid up for this fall. Sang. Yaller root."

Sanderson glanced down at jars full of the gnarled roots the boy had been sorting through, and more. Bits of stalks and stems. Seedy looking pods. "Daddy's the one," she said, "taught me about healing. Ministering herbs. Laying on hands, when the spirit took him."

While she talked, Sanderson studied Granny's powdery-looking face and lilac-colored cotton dress. He noted her anklets, ones neatly turned down above her shoes. She could have been his own grandmother.

"Not that I took natural to learning what Daddy had to teach me," she said. "I was too fixed on running here and there and yonder. But he was a good man, my daddy. I'll give him that one." She sighed. "Raised six younguns," she said.

Close to the shelves was a cheese and meat cooler, a counter with a crock pot advertising beans and cornbread and, Sanderson was relieved to see, a hot dog warmer. He pried a charred-looking wiener off when it came around on one of the revolving prongs, piled on mustard and relish and onions from canning jars marked *necessaries*. The coffee was instant, and he dumped in three packets of sweetener.

"Mister, that your car?" the boy asked. He'd followed Sanderson back out onto the porch, where he stood eating and looking at the empty parking lot and the tail end of Main Street.

The boy was also eating a hot dog and the two of them regarded Sanderson's car, a black Pontiac with white wall tires and a license plate with the last name of a famous auto racer, one of Rosa's idols.

"You know the horsepower on that thing?"

Sanderson had to think a minute, and realized he no idea. He mumbled something about a V-8 engine, and munched his hot dog.

"How fast have you taken her?"

Sanderson, who used cruise control and had not driven without a seat belt nor played chicken with a road sign in about a million years said, "Oh, hundred, or thereabout."

"You ever ride anybody in that car?" the boy asked.

"My wife," Sanderson answered.

The boy licked mustard from his fingers. "She like cars?"

"Well enough."

"Enough ain't enough for a ride like that, mister."

"That right?"

"I can think of a bunch of folks could admire that car."

"I'll bet you could think of a person or two." Sanderson swallowed his hot dog.

It was well after noon by now, a heavy-looking midday. Sanderson checked his watch and stood, studying boy and car. Like Sam at that age, he was half boy and half on his way to being a man. Unlike Sam, he was dark-skinned, with blue-black hair. Fifties style, he wore his tee shirt sleeves rolled, with a pack of Marlboros stuck there. Too young to smoke, Sanderson mused.

The boy recited information about torques and engine types and drive trains, and the future glowed in his eyes—a shop all his own as an add-on to

the store. "If I'd had a car like that I could have gotten over there that quick."
He snapped his fingers.

Sanderson wadded up the hot dog wrapping paper and made a move
toward the porch steps.

"I could have gotten there quicker than the rest of them did."

"Over where?" Sanderson asked, pausing midstep.

Granny wedged open the store's screen door with one booted foot, gazed
up at the sky. "My daddy always said a sky like that one there's a sign."

"Sign of what?" Sanderson swallowed, once and twice. The hot dog taste
was still in his mouth, charred and gritty and he began to feel unaccountably
tense.

She leaned close, her scent sweet, like pouch tobacco. "Don't you know
nothing, mister?" She elbowed him.

The air now seemed to have a burning scent and he took out his
handkerchief, blew his nose. "I used to know a little," he said at last. "About
signs."

"Smoke's a sign of trouble or the Lord, one," Granny said as she pointed
up at wisps of grayish clouds traveling west, the way he'd come this morning.

With a sinking feeling, Sanderson peered up at the whitish sky.

"Most of it's settled from over that way, besides," she said and elbowed
him a final time.

"Over where?" he asked again as the three of them studied the haze. A
heavy feeling had begun to accumulate in his chest and he fumbled in his
pockets for tablets to settle his stomach.

"Over to the Motel," the boy said. "Over to Inez where they're at. Mama
and them."

"The Motel?" Sanderson asked and he paused at his car door. "Which
one would that be, son?"

"How many do you reckon there are in Inez, mister?" the boy said, looking indignant. He pulled the cigarette pack from his sleeve.

"What happened over there, son?" Sanderson asked, dreading the answer. The taste in his mouth had coincided now with the smoke-laced sky. The three of them regarded that sky and the woman pointed down the road in the direction he still needed to go.

As he pulled the car back onto the road, he could hear Rosa. *Don't you just find people like that a comfort?* The very thought made him sad. *Safety? Comfort?* His first wife, Sarah, filled their house with a variety of items in which she took comfort. Incense cones and burners. Prayer wheels. Candles to invoke safe spirits. At the same time she teased him about wanting the whole world to be safe, from his sock drawer to the details of the morning news. *Safety*, Sarah would say. *Don't you know that's a relative term?* And now Rosa, his second wife, had joined one self-help group after another, ones that promised safety for the inner child and renewed interrelational-communication skills. Their house was littered with things she called "old-timey." One whole den wall was devoted to a display of washboards and band saws and signs for *Martha White Flour* or *Bunny: The Best in Bread.* Don't you take comfort in your heritage, she asked him when he suggested that there were too many things, too much nostalgia.

His grandfather had been a First Baptist Church of the Redeemed Soul preacher, and Sanderson's earliest memories were of Saturday nights and come-to-Jesus sermons followed by dinners on the ground. The healing in his family wasn't the kind with herbs or divining rods, but, on occasion, his grandfather's rough-palmed hands touched souls. He remembered those hands. Gripping his chin, tilting his head to the sky. *Listen, boy. Listen to your maker.* And he had. During those Saturday night services he saw everything from anointing with oil to the way a man threw aside his crutches and danced underneath a sky full of lightning. His grandfather held out his hands, palms up, and declared it was thus that God could redeem. Later, when Sarah underwent every treatment they'd been able to find, radiation, the cleansing of cells, he had wished for those hands.

To heal himself after Sarah died, he moved with Sam from the mountains of western North Carolina to central Kentucky where he became regional officer for his repossession company. Regional Repo Man, Sam had called him, which left Sanderson with an image of himself in a super hero costume, defending his office against nonpayment and bad credit. Once Sam was gone and once he married Rosa and they bought a house in a gated community. To get home, he passed through a raised bar and a security guard who nodded to him each and every evening. *Mr. Sanderson.* How much more safe, Rosa wanted to know, could their lives be? *Gated.* Sanderson could almost hear Sam. *Facsimile. Pretend country living.* As much time as Sanderson had spent trying to batten down the hatches in his life, Sam had been the opposite. *Sam.* The exact opposite of that word. *Safe.*

Sam. Sarah. Rosa, her pronouncements about heritage, about healing and moving on. He wondered whether strong, dry hands, his grandfather's or anyone else's, might have, could have, pulled his son up from the waves of the ocean that took him. No one really had the power to heal, no less comfort anyone in this world. He drove on, approaching at last The Motel of the Stars under a sky that was, sure enough, thick with smoke.

He passed the Inez diner and then a hardware store and a trailer park. He drove reading the new directions the boy and his grandmother had given him, drove until he saw the Church of the Repentant, his new landmark. He missed the last sharp curve and had to slow down, back into a driveway, turn around. He passed the last five mailboxes, rechecked his directions, and took the last dirt road.

There'd been a fire the night before, all right. What was left of the motel looked careless and abandoned. He sighed and picked up his briefcase and stepped out of the car. Glass from broken windows crunched under his feet as he approached the side yard where there were the odds and ends of everything heaved out at the last second. A dresser with the drawers gone was upended near a metal foot locker; a plastic child's tractor trailer was melted and shapeless and lay next to what was left of a wooden-framed photograph of a dog. Now, only the last walls of the building itself were standing, and those were a charred substructure held together by pipes and thick, blackened wires. He could have found his way to Inez by smoke-scent alone.

He followed a path littered with before-the-fire cans and bottles that led behind the house. That's where the people were, less than a dozen of them, seated around the base of a huge willow tree, its trailing fronds singed. A worried-looking woman with foam curlers didn't meet his eyes. Near her was a younger woman in jeans and cowboy boots, and beside her an old man in a wrinkled wool suit jacket was crouching on his ankles, stirring ashes and dirt. He took his place at the edge of this group.

"Authorities been here yet?" he asked in the general direction of the old man, but no one spoke. He wiped his sooty hands against his trousers and stood, waiting. Already he could envision the investigation he'd have to conduct. Already he suspected arson and he thought of the forms he'd have to fill out, his own possible accountability. *Didn't you have an inkling? Not a clue about these people?* He could hear the bank manager now.

Then he heard the voices. Singing, from a rise near the smoldering foundations of the house. He stared in that direction, where there were two little girls. They wore cotton checked dresses, sneakers with the toes cut away, and their joined hands were lifted high as they danced in the burnt grass. Near them was a low wooden table and, beside it, a chair.

Pocket full of posies, the girls sang as they spun. *Ashes, ashes, we all fall down.*

From not too far away, someone called to the children. *Don't you all hear me? Get on home.* The girls laughed and whispered and hurried up a rise and their laughter died away in the distance. Sanderson set his briefcase down in the grass and approached the chair.

It was metal, its green paint scorched and peeling, and it held a woman, knees in her arms, head resting on her knees, a glimpse of her face the only thing visible from the folds of a blanket covering her. He felt as if he was spying upon a private intimacy, but he looked down into this face, which was shiny with sweat in the hot sun. She reminded him of photographs of Middle Eastern women covered by impenetrable veils, but more than that. The small pale and sooty face with its shut eyes, was both familiar and disconcerting. She seemed to be sleeping.

"His girl," someone said behind him.

"Pardon?" Sanderson asked. The old man with the wool jacket motioned to him. They walked several feet away from the chair, in the direction of the remains of the house.

"The daughter," the old man whispered. "Leastways his step-girl, her he had to deal with, once the mother took off. Back six years and more."

"What's her name?" Sanderson studied the huddled figure. Beneath the edges of the blanket, he could see bare feet and polished toenails.

"Lory," the old man answered. "She's about as odd-turned as he is, I'd say."

"Where's he at?" Sanderson gripped his briefcase, thinking of the coming encounter with Frank Llewellyn, the questions about how the fire had started, insurance premiums, responsible parties. Sanderson's head swam with the red tape it would take months to figure out.

"Reckon he's over at the shop," the old man said, gesturing in that direction. "Trying to calm down or sober up, one."

Sanderson straightened his tie, remembering the recent acquisition of the storage building and repair place. "I came on business, you know," he said. He studied the woman and the chair again as she shifted. The sight of her face, so incredibly still, tugged at him.

"Least he kept a clean room and she kept the books or something, upstairs where she stayed," the old man said. "Place did better than some of us expected."

"It's a shame it didn't do as well as the rest of us would have wanted," Sanderson said, and then was sorry for it. If he hadn't known better, he would have said the woman was peaceful, except for the deep lines etched beside her mouth.

"Sometimes you just have to leave a body be," the old man said, as if Sanderson hadn't spoken. He bent, fished a broken cup handle out of the grass. "Before it was a motel, son, that was a house. Not much of one, but it was there almost a hundred years."

They both stood looking in the direction of the woman. She was so still Sanderson could see the blanket rise and fall with her breath and he found himself breathing that way too, in time with the rise and fall of her chest. His own chest, to his amazement, felt calmer than it had all day. He stepped back from the chair, breathed deeply. On the table near the woman was an open dictionary, hardbacked and heavy, a random save from the fire. Its pages rustled in the wind and he wondered what page the wind would settle with, what word.

Between Towns

He called Rosa once, twice, on the way home, to let Rosa know he was on his way and to start without him. *Cell phones.* He fumbled for the thing again from his jacket pocket and thought of when Rosa gave it to him. *You can call me, this way. Any time or place.* She loved technology, state of the art appliances, had bought a television with digital programming for both the bedroom and the den, and he hated it. Devices. *Computers. Voice mail.*

"A sign. All of it," he said aloud as he punched his home line again. He did know signs when he saw them. Signs of a world close to a new century and a new century close to what, he wasn't sure.

"I wanted you to have time to shower and look presentable, honey," Rosa said when she finally picked up. There was laughter in the background, and music. She sighed. "Just get here quick as you can."

It had begun to rain lightly. He switched on the wipers and concentrated on their low movement, a point of focus amid the estimates and columns of numbers swirling in Sanderson's head.

While squad car lights circled over the site of the fire he made a call to the State Police, who arrived by the time he foresaw a list of things to be done. Follow-up meetings. Meticulous and often fruitless investigations. Insurance company contacts and an endless series of processing claims and disclaimers. There'd be a tallying of losses—amounts owed on the motel, liens on the repair shop. He'd started his questions already, at the scene. Has a medical authority been called? *They don't want nobody, no way. Nary one of them.* Where is the lien-holder at present? *I don't know nothing about no lien, but he's over to the shop, I reckon, medicating hisself.* Shop? There was no record of this shop, which the neighbors claimed was an auto repair place. In the shop, he saw a man slumped over a workbench.

"Mr. Llewellyn?" Sanderson said, his shoes scratching in the oily sand at the shop doorway.

Llewellyn barely raised his head in Sanderson's direction, settled his stare in the direction of those shoes. *Loafers,* Sanderson thought. They were polished, with shiny dimes in their tops.

"Mr. Llewellyn," he said again. "I reckon, sir, we've got a good deal to discuss."

Llewellyn stared again, this time at Sanderson's briefcase. Business cards were exchanged. Phone numbers and addresses were written down. And there was initial questioning. Casualties? *Everbody got out safe, thank the good Lord.* Who was in attendance at the start of the conflagration? *Attending which?* You know how this started, sir? *Can't never tell about a place this old. Coulda been a rat chewed through something.* There's suspicion of arson here, sir. We'll be filing a report.

"You'll have to ask her, mister," Llewellyn said. "She ought to do the filing her own self. She kept the records." He produced a bottle of whiskey and two motel glasses, at which Sanderson shook his head.

Her, he supposed, was the woman in the chair in the yard, but the long and short of it was, no one knew much.

The rain was now intense and he set the wipers going higher. He touched his cheek, checking on his shaving status, and caught the scent of his hands. *Ashes.* He sighed, thinking of the fire, of Llewellyn, and of the mysterious woman in the chair. And now this party ahead of him. He wanted to hide, think about none of it, but not thinking made him think of Sam.

What had Sam said about him? *You'd dig a hole to the other side of the world, Dad. If you could hide yourself in it.*

Sam, hiding from nothing, set out at seventeen to see the country via Greyhound, a journey he called quixotic. *I want to see America*, Sam said. *America by bus*. He sent photographs. Himself, posing with a pick and shovel with a trail crew for a national park in the desert, or in a country store where he weighed deer during hunting season. He hitchhiked to the coast of California to see the migration of whales from Vizcaino Bay and another time spent a year traveling with a backpack in the mountains of northern India, where he hoped to meet the Dalai Lama and question him about new theories of chaos and time.

Sam often reminded Sanderson of a music that mixed bells with harpsichord and a woman's chanting in a language he couldn't recognize. Sam had changed and changed again and changed back and was probably still changing, in an afterlife he once variously described as Nirvana, nebulous, or nothing at all. *Nebulous.* Now there was a word. Sometimes he imagined his son as a Hare Krishna in an airport or a shopping mall, with shaved head and begging bowl. But then the image grew more complicated. Sam with a begging bowl and a loincloth and Marine combat boots. Sam with combat boots and some other uniform that might indicate who he had become all over again. Sam who, incredible as it seemed, had twelve years ago ended up joining the United States Marines.

He heard Sam's voice again, this time right there, in between the swipes of the wiper blades and the pellets of rain. *You'd dig a hole to the other side of the world, if you could hide yourself in it.*

"What's wrong," he asked his son aloud, "with a little hiding?"

He tried to tune the radio to a news station. Maybe a motel fire was a big enough event to make at least the local reports. He could even end up on the news himself, with a mention in ensuing related commentary. But that, of course, could complicate the case.

He scanned past the weather, which warned that a stronger storm system was moving in up the coast from Florida, to South and then North Carolina. Ten years back, it had rained that night, too. He recalled the miraculous stories of that storm. A husband and wife had been trapped when hurricane-force winds and rain raised the level of a nearby river. Muddy river water filled the kitchen and they floated to safety on the back of a table.

He switched the station again and glanced at his watch, turned up the radio. *1997*, they were saying. *Navigate by the law of time. The correct time, the natural timing frequency.*

"This again?" He shifted forward, stretched his shoulders.

The Harmonic Convergence, they said, was divine intervention in the affairs of humanity. When the planets aligned, you could see through the center of the vortex that is history to the meaning of time itself.

The correct, natural timing? History? What did anyone know, what could anyone know, about timing? The motel was history. History and ashes. And that other night. He drove home from work, expecting to go to the airport, see his son, see Sam walk off the plane. He had been prepared that night for the initial shock of short hair, the uniform, how Sam would lift his hand to his forehead in a stiff salute when he saw his father. He expected that smile, the one that was as mischievous as a boy's, but crooked and somehow tragic. Bell's palsy as a boy. And tragic because it was full of history Sanderson didn't know, places he'd never seen, questions he didn't even know how to ask. Dark eyes and full lips, just like Sarah's.

He was near home and he was bone- tired. It was nearly seven-thirty now, and they'd have finished pre-dinner snacks and the fancy sparkling cider Rosa

32

had bought for the occasion. *Each one of us*, the radio said, *has an electrical body field that surrounds us, and a mind field that goes on to infinity.*

Had that been the problem? Electricity. Waves of it. His dreams, traveling in surges, in electric charges, multiplying, entering his own son's sleep?

For years, he'd had a recurring dream. He woke still seeing the dream's map lines that tied and untied, as if they were alive. The dream, he knew, was about Saigon. It was about himself, a kid again and sitting in the back of a Marine-issue truck. Just last night in the dream he sat beside another boy who lit a match and held it close to a photograph of some woman. *Guess who she is*, the boy said. *Just guess.* Sanderson's dream-mouth opened to answer, but only one word came out. Sam, he said. *Sam.* That was who the other boy was, his own son. Father to son, they looked at each other's familiar face, their skin shining with sweat and anticipation. *Wars*, a voice always said in this dream. *Wars and rumors of wars.* Brittle stars shone and the dream gave these stars names—*John Brown, Dust Light, Deacon Jones*. Firecrackers exploded and there were shouts, yellow and blue shadow, a chemical and smoke scent.

Sure, he had often told Sam stories. Stories of Okinawa. Saigon. Stories about training. About bends and squats and orders. About learning to hump seventy-five pounds on his back. There'd been history and specific places. *Binh Gia. Qui Nonh.* He had invoked the language all over again. *Gooks. Them. Not us.* He had talked just enough to make war seem easy, about strength and endurance, about heroism even, but on his worst days, Sanderson knew the truth. It was the dream that had enticed his son. The dream had a power of its own. It had traveled, alive and terrible. It had summoned his son to a war of his own, a war without a name at all, one in his own dreams, his own confusions. It had killed him.

The pavement ahead was shiny and wet, the rain now steady. He made a careful left off the interstate, passed the two signs before his exit. It was still light enough to see the banner Rosa had draped across the outer front door, crepe paper safely dry under eaves. *Welcome*, it said. She'd invited all their closest friends, neighbors, left and right, and a select group from his office, and hers.

The totalities of all our vibrations go together, the radio voice concluded. They make one pure vibration that is God. They create what is known as Harmonic Convergence.

Convergence. Past. Present. He imagined Sam, back again, alive and well and sharing a cup of coffee with him at the kitchen table, but when he added Rosa to the scenario, the vision disintegrated. *Dad*, Sam had written, *I know you need to rebuild your life from the ground up. But*. The letter had ended there, with *but*. It was impossible, anyway, when he tried, to imagine Sam at that kitchen table. Which Sam would it be? The Marine Sam? The thin young man, back from his travels to India? When he closed his eyes and tried to imagine his son, he could see no one face, no particular man in a certain body.

"Jason Sanderson," he could hear Rosa saying, "what are you doing driving with your eyes closed?"

His pass slid into the ticket counter at the front of their community and the usual gates swung open.

The Language of Letting Go

In the house in the North Carolina mountains where he once lived with Sarah, there'd been no dining room. They'd eaten at a long folding table covered with an Indian bedspread. His dining room now was crowded with people and food, buffet-style. A stack of dishes towered at one end of the table—Melmac stamped with country-quilt patterns Rosa used for informal dinner parties. He could smell dripping butter and spices that set his nose on edge. Rosa, a mint-colored dress clinging to her waist, met him at the door.

"Jason?" She took his hand, drew him toward the dining room. She was almost his height, and taller tonight, with heels. "We're just ready to start."

"You shouldn't have waited," he said, eyeing the room. It was a large space, with chairs now arranged along two walls, leading into a sunroom they'd added on last year. "You should have gone ahead."

"We couldn't, sweetie," Rosa said and squeezed his arm. "Not without you."

Emotional Wellness Encounter's Harry Simon, who was holding forth to a group of three women in the sunroom, looked up and waved in Sanderson's direction. "Looks like everyone's plenty comfortable," he said.

"We wanted you to say a little something," Rosa said.

"Now?" he said. "Couldn't it wait till after?"

"Sweetie, we've been waiting and waiting, and you missed the appetizers, so say hello to everyone, at least." She leaned close, brushed his lips with hers, and he tasted cinnamon.

He cleared his throat as Harry Simon rounded the dining table, heading in their direction. "Just hello, then," Sanderson said.

She hugged him, sniffed his shirt collar. "You smell like smoke."

"I'll tell you about it," he said, and then they walked side by side to the head of the table, where Rosa tapped a glass with a knife. "Everyone? If y'all could stop a minute I think there's someone here we've been wanting to talk to!"

She draped her arm about his waist, and he glanced around the room again, trying to think of what to say. His tiredness had deepened, and beneath that was a restlessness settling in his back, his legs. He'd never been good at speeches, dreaded those he had to make for reports from his division at the Savings and Loan office. He wanted to hide as the room fell quiet.

"I guess what I ought to do," he began, "is apologize for being late to my own to-do." He cleared his throat, glanced at Rosa, who did a mock bow in his general direction.

"But as lots of us in repo know," he continued, "it takes longer to take back something than to buy it in the first place."

Harry Simon lifted his fist and pumped it up and down. *Camaraderie.*

"And if I've listened the way I should to my wife," he said and paused, "this get together is about a lot more than that."

He scanned the bowls and plates and platters, the sweating pitcher of lemonade and another of iced tea. In the center of the table were two lit candles in the cut-glass holders he knew came from his own grandmother and between these candles was a framed photograph. His eyes and whatever else he'd tried to say paused there.

"More," he repeated.

The room was quiet, waiting for him to say what more meant, but he fumbled for words. He found himself peering instead at that photograph.

"More," Rosa repeated after him. "There's lots more that we all know we're here for. We all know what this day is."

Harry Simon was on the other side of the buffet table, and he raised his hands, clapped lightly and nodded.

"Today," Rosa went on, "is an anniversary," she began. "I don't want to say an occasion of loss." She paused and looked at Sanderson.

Sanderson was narrowing his eyes, staring harder at the photograph. His chest felt tight.

"Why's that there?" he asked. The frame held, he realized with a start, a picture of Sam.

Rosa looked embarrassed, but took his hand again, squeezed it. "It's okay, sweetie." The room grew quieter.

"A photo of Sam?" he asked again.

"It'll get clearer in a while," she said, and met his eyes. "Just wait a little." She picked up a plate, turned to everyone. "Before we talk more, we're here to eat some of this good food everybody's brought."

A line was forming for plates and utensils. She took his hand, and he moved along with her, lobbying for a place to get closer to the picture frame.

It was Sam. Right next to plate after plate of appetizers—little rounds of bread and poppy seed crackers spread with imitation crab, cream cheese, and a green he identified as shredded seaweed. The photo of Sam was one he remembered well. The particular toss of a head and the tousled child-curls. A missing-toothed mouth. The photo made him flinch as he picked up a plate and started walking, past deviled eggs arranged on a plate with lettuce and tiny tomato sandwiches, past broths and stews he didn't recognize, past a multitude of faces he hardly recognized.

He bent closer, examined a crock pot of soup and a card beside it.

The soup was identified as Asian Lentil and Rice, with a card, *The World*, next to it. And beside that, a photo of Sam, just as he remembered him after that time in India, his thin arms and his too-long hair, freshly dyed black. Another section of the table, devoted to Sam's military career, was arranged around a large bowl of vegetable salad. Here, there were two photos of him, one in dress blues, and another in Marine fatigues and helmet. And at the end of the buffet next to a bowl of deep-green molded Jell-O salad was yet another photograph, this one of Sam on a strip of North Carolina beach. What he was looking at, he thought, heart sinking, was a bizarre culinary history of his own son's life.

It was ridiculous, a travesty, an insult even. Photos. Cards with inscriptions. He could have sworn that a voice chimed in, right beside him. *Right out of a garden club magazine.* It was Sam. He heard the voice again, more bluntly. *And a New Age one, at that.*

Sanderson finally settled with his plate in the sunroom. His hands shook as he wielded fork and knife and settled back, remembering Sam. Five, maybe six years old. One night he refused to eat, until a trapped moth in a window was set free, and Sanderson refused to let the moth go until a hot dog was finished. Sam ate, and the moth, as Sanderson remembered it, never was let loose.

When Sam was nine, he went through a carbohydrate phase, eating only bread products in all their forms—sliced, toasted, fried, with not a trace of a spread, not a dab of butter. When he was twelve, he ate by color rather than content. For months, he ate red. Apples, strawberries, tomato sauces, and steak so rare Sanderson felt uneasy. At thirteen, it was potatoes in all their varieties. Mashed, salad, baked, even dishes of thin, raw slices he said tasted like apples. Why not eat apples, then, Sanderson had asked. *I don't like things to be confused,* Sam had said. By fourteen and finally fifteen, things were confused, the mutual appetites of son and father lost in Sarah's own inability to eat, some days, more than a cup of clear vegetable broth.

After that, when Sam hitchhiked cross-country, he left home with freeze-dried everything. Foil envelopes of peas and soups that promised a rich stew with the addition of a half cup of water. Sam wrote home about working in restaurants and eating off the plates of rich tourists. He traveled the world. When he came back from India, rail thin, his dark eyes huge and fierce, Sam was a vegetarian, a vegan, or something sinister-sounding to do with macrobiotics. He'd never know what Sam had done as a Marine, with food lines for Salisbury steak and white bread with gravy.

Farther into the dining room, Rosa was chatting with Harry Simon. She laughed, her from-the-gut chuckle, touched Harry's arm. If he weren't so befuddled, he'd have been jealous, although that, too, was ridiculous.

He remembered a friend of his father's. A funeral. The house had smelled of chrysanthemums and the casket had been set up right in the living room, next to a card table laden with casseroles and pies. He was ten. When he went in the kitchen for a glass of sweet tea, he had unexpectedly met the man's wife. *Johnny,* she had said, calling him by her husband's name. *Oh, that's not who you are.* Wakes and plates of food from neighbors and covered dishes at a funeral home. Plates of food in the name of the dead, to comfort the living. And this night?

He nibbled at the edge of a buttered biscuit, bit into a tomato sandwich, and then tasted a spoonful of lentil soup. There was an underlying sameness to each dish. Salty? Bitter?

"Get you something?" Rosa asked, pulling a chair up beside him.

He stirred his cheese grits. "I didn't know it would be like this," he said at last.

"This?"

"These people. The food." He gestured toward the other room and the laden table. "And the photographs, Rosa. On display. Like that. What were you thinking?"

"I have been thinking, Jason," she said and touched his shoulder. "For a long time."

"And this is what you end up with?"

She knelt beside his chair, looked into his eyes. "I really believe in it," she said.

"Rosa," he began, and then set down his plate.

She put her hand on his knee. "Ceremonies," she began.

"Ceremonies," he repeated. "Visualizations. Manifestations."

"A ceremony means something, Jason."

"That depends."

"Try to believe a little more," she said as she stroked his hair.

"Yes," he answered. "I guess that is the problem."

"Surrender," Simon told them, "can mean opening up. It can mean the pure light of joy and possibility. But we don't often understand that," he went on. "What it means to embrace happiness."

It was after dinner by then, and a much smaller group of them were sitting in Sanderson's living room. Simon stood near a table with three lit candles, one black, one red, and one white.

While Simon talked, Sanderson ate around the edges of a piece of pineapple upside-down cake, took a deep swallow from a cup of black coffee, unsweetened, a taste he usually hated. The bitterness braced him.

Black, Simon told them as he pinched out that candle flame. It was the color of loss, a time when nothing could be clearly understood, a time when grief overcame reason, and gradually overtook the heart. *Red*, he said, extinguishing that flame, was the color of fire. The color of coals deep beneath the ashes of memory, ready to ignite with pain, with loss that could not be transformed.

"Then white," Harry Simon said as he motioned to Sanderson. "White is the purest color of all. The color of letting go."

Sanderson sat still, staring at the front of Simon's tight-fitting Hawaiian shirt, its profusion of blue and yellow flowers above the white folds of

Simon's drawstring pants. White, the purest color of all. Like ashes. His fingertips had that scent, of a burning motel. Ashes. The taste from bite after bite of celebratory food.

There were seven of them in the living room—Harry Simon and his wife; Rosa; a couple from her office; and Wanda, Sanderson's assistant from the Savings and Loan office. She looked bewildered. Sanderson recalled the coffee breaks and her stories about her fundamentalist background—church services without even a piano to accompany worship. His own Sunday mornings had been at the Church of the New Resurrection, where he'd gone with his grandparents in Western North Carolina. "Amazing Grace" or "Softly and Tenderly" played in the background and the minister held out his hand, waiting for rededications.

Harry Simon waited as Sanderson and Rosa walked toward the bookshelf. His legs were weak, and though he'd eaten little, his stomach roiled.

"We believe," Simon began again, "in the power of Emotional Wellness."

He paused, held his hands over the last flame, reached for a ceramic bowl at the other end of the shelf. As they mounted the three steps to the upper living room, Sanderson could see two roses and two envelopes inside the bowl.

"Emotional Wellness," he continued as he set the bowl down in front of the white candle, "means living in the Present, living for the always necessary Now." He handed Sanderson a flower and an envelope, and the same to Rosa.

Rosa opened hers first, slitting the envelope along one end with one of her nails. Whatever the envelope contained, she moved slightly away from Sanderson, stood looking for a long time. She wept easily, and she began to do so now as she held another photograph first toward him, then out, so the others could see.

He recognized this picture immediately. It was a walk before sunset at the ocean, the violent loveliness of the sky, its reds colliding with purples and the hot light of the water. He remembered Rosa, wading farther and farther out, camera in hand. *Come on, baby,* she called to him. *The water is wonderful.* How afraid he was that day, his photographed mouth forming the word *No.*

"We invite you, Rosa Sanderson," Simon began again, "to release the past, its fears and misunderstandings."

Rosa stood close to the white candle, dipped the edge of her photograph into the flame. It burned surprisingly quick as she dropped it into the bowl Simon held out to her.

"And we invite you, Rosa, to soften this letting go with love."

She tore the petals from the rose's long stem, dropping them into the smoke.

We invite you, Jason Sanderson. As he opened his own envelope, he could taste it again. Ash. Ash on his hands, soot from the yard of a burned-down motel. Strange taste of ash on his tongue from a ridiculous meal. *Sam.* He pulled Sam, his son, from an envelope, stood looking at his boy's face, his cheeks flushed with wind and sun. How keenly he remembered that moment.

They'd been in the cluster of woods two fields back from their house then. There lay a small pond, green with algae in summertime, but clear with the early spring rains. He had tried to teach Sam to swim in that pond. He had been six then. The skin of his small arms was soft and pliant as he had picked his son up and waded with him, out where the water just began to be deep. Sam's back arched, his head tilted back over the water's surface. He let go and Sam's body balanced like a leaf for a minute, maybe less. Then his small legs kicked wildly, his arms flailing as he struggled, began to go down. Sanderson tried to pull Sam up and near his shoulder. But Sam pushed against him with surprising strength. His eyes, the lashes wet with pond water, stared back at him with defiance and only the slightest bit of fear. Sarah took the picture only minutes later, when the two of them stood holding hands at the edge of the water.

He knew the correct ceremony. How easy, really, to watch time flame up, bright and momentary into a bowl full of nothing but ashes. Just today he had brushed ashes from a metal chair, wiped his sooty hand against his trousers. Just today, he had held the word *bountiful* on his tongue and tasted it like joy.

Rosa reached out for him.

He turned her hand up to his face, stared at its emptiness. How intimately he knew her, the small, white scar that traversed her palm. He'd traced it with his tongue as they lay in bed together and promised each other comfort. Just today, he had promised himself to be happy, but as he looked at the photograph of his son, of Sam, it was too cruel, this travesty of healing.

"You don't know," Sanderson said into the blank space of Rosa's hand. He held that hand for a second against his cheek before he let it go. "You don't know the first thing."

He felt all of them reaching, their mutual hands full of ways to help him. *Help him?* He could very well help himself. None of them, he said as he crossed the room. None of them had the least idea what it meant. He headed upstairs, their voices following him up. *Not ready*, they said. *Too much for him. He'll be ready, in time.* He paused barely long enough to listen to it, the sound of the rain on a metal roof.

Rain, Ten Years Gone.

Ten years ago, the newspapers showed live oaks uprooted in coastal towns and families fleeing in one of the worst tropical storm systems in North Carolina history. Even in inland Kentucky, Sanderson fought heavy downpours to get to the airport, where the lobby that morning was jammed with passengers waiting for flights already an hour late. He had flown little in the past years, and airports and crowds made him uncomfortable. He sat by himself watching cleaning ladies push mops along the floors by the doors, where water seeped in with each exit and arrival.

Luggage carts rolled past as he looked again at the incoming flights. Sam's flight was listed, but rescheduled for arrival from Norfolk at nine. He checked and double-checked—nine-thirty, nine-forty-five. He paced, checking with the flight desk at five-minute intervals until they got busy with paperwork when they saw him coming.

"I'm sorry," the attendant said. "I just don't have a crystal ball. I can't look up there and ask for the weather patterns."

"You do have a telephone, don't you?" Sanderson asked.

"Air traffic control can't tell us any more than they already have, sir," the attendant said again. "They're waiting, just like us."

"Since when did you and air traffic control become parents? I'm trying to ask you," he said, "about my son."

His heart skipped a beat, and he took a deep breath, counting, as the doctor had told him. There were a dozen particle-board sections of the

44

ceiling, five colored squares in each of those. In these last years he had counted books in the Bible. Hours until lunchtime. Vacation days saved until the end of the year. Easiest to count? Communications with his son.

He could count the phone calls from Sam. The calls came sometimes once a month, sometimes once in six months. The letters were even more now-and-then, but he liked those more. He found himself spending time examining the way Sam underlined his name in his signatures. The way he signed his letters, sometimes, without the word love. He told himself that they loved one another, even if calls and letters merely gauged the changes between them. After Sam left home, they wrote letters that grew shorter, until those became postcards. *On the road. Kerouac would be envious.* He began to guess at which cities Sam lived in, which jobs he had or didn't have. Before this new military phase, he'd urged Sam's sporadic visits home. Sam was vague in his response to these invitations. *We'll see.* He still had that postcard, one with a picture of a canyon in some desert place in Arizona. Sanderson wanted this to be a hopeful sign in a relationship that was, whether he wanted to admit it or not, strained.

By ten-thirty he went to fetch coffee and, for distraction's sake, he wandered over to a late-night shoeshine vendor near the gate where Sam was to arrive. He settled onto a bench and stretched out his legs, studying a coating of mud from the airport's gravel parking lot on his shoes. One more sign of his grooming habits of late—stretched elastic or holes in the toes of socks. At least his shoes would shine when Sam arrived, if he could wait long enough. He fell to watching the various people seated and standing near him. A girl with leather high-tops and spiky hair. He imagined Sam leaning forward in his airplane seat, staring down into rain clouds, waiting for them to part. *You think a little rain can stop me from traveling?* He could hear Sam, as clearly as if he were there.

"I just can't understand it," a woman on the bench beside him said. Up close, her stiletto heels were scuffed and scratched.

Sanderson shut his eyes and concentrated on the rub and swipe of the

45

shoeshine. He was tired, and behind his shut lids he saw shapes, ones with small pinpoints of light—a sure sign of an oncoming migraine. He wished he were at home in his chair downstairs with a cool cloth across his forehead.

"I really can't," the woman persisted.

He glanced at her. She had light blonde hair and vivid makeup, red lipstick, blue shadow. Something about the makeup was off, like a poor camera focus. He could tell the woman wasn't speaking to him, or to anybody else on the almost empty bench.

"As if he'd care," she said.

Sanderson sighed, imagining a boyfriend, a husband, a lover's quarrel he was about to hear described. "Who," he asked reluctantly, "is *he?*"

"I've asked him and I've asked him," the woman said.

"What have you asked him?" Sanderson said softly, feeling like a guide through a place he'd never seen. A spot at the base of his skull began to throb.

"To listen, of course," she said. As the shoeshine worked their feet, she turned, studied him anxiously.

"Listening's a hard thing sometimes," Sanderson replied.

"Is it?" she said. "I mean, how hard is it to hear something when somebody has gone over it and over it? I've told him," she said. "I really have."

"He probably knows that," Sanderson assured her.

"You think so?" she asked.

"Sure he does."

She looked relieved, but Sanderson's left eye twitched. The headache was setting in, prompted by a disquiet that included whoever this woman was talking about and Sam, too. And to add to that, he had the odd feeling that there was someone he knew in the airport lobby.

The woman sighed. "Even if he heard me, I still doubt he gives a damn," she said.

He wondered if Sam himself gave a damn. It wasn't the first time Sanderson had waited like this. There was the time Sam, still a teenager, hitched a ride without asking and showed up three days later, after a rock concert in northern Michigan. Or there was the time Sam was visiting the new house in Kentucky and didn't come home until five in the morning. Sanderson was drinking coffee by the window when his son came in, reeking of cigarettes and liquor and he'd said, *For God's sake, I'm a man now, you know. I don't need any rules.* Sam had stalked off to sleep until mid-afternoon. Sanderson had wanted to tell him how it wasn't about rules, really, but about how lonely it had been to wait up for him, in a house that had of late grown larger in that loneliness.

"I mean, doesn't it matter when you tell someone you need something? Really need *them?*"

"Of course it does." The headache was making the woman's bits-and-pieces story at once maddening and soothing.

"I've been there, you know," she said. "I've *been there* the whole time."

"Where's there?" he asked, and he leaned back, listening to the rhythmic buffing of the shoeshine and the steady rain. Rain sounds blended with the woman's story, which was about, as he expected, jilting, disregard. Her apprehension mingled with his and he counted his heartbeats, the familiar skip and beat and miss. He wondered if Sam or this woman's lover, either one of them, knew how difficult it was to fill in the blanks in time.

Flight five-twenty, a voice said, *now arriving.* Before he knew it, the gate door was opening and he fumbled with his wallet for change.

He shifted impatiently, ready to hand the attendant his money.

"I haven't asked who you're waiting on," the woman said.

"My son," he said, just as he saw a man in Marine dress blues who took out a piece of paper, studied it as he looked across the lobby. Sam looked taller, broader, in the formal clothing and he felt as if he were ready to be introduced to a stranger. *That man,* Sanderson wondered. *That man is my son?* Hurrying now, Sanderson stepped down from the shoeshine platform.

He would remember with particularity a young boy with a huge black umbrella, how he opened it, shut it, opened it, the scattering of drops of rain as he walked past. He would remember how the tension in his neck and shoulders moved upward, settled, a headache blazing at the right side of his head, pain propelling him forward through the crowd. And he would recall with the greatest clarity of all how he saw the woman from the shoeshine stand in the arms of a man, her face exalted. *Exalted.* That was a word Sam had loved. It was a word that later, when Sanderson remembered that woman's joy, made him flinch.

"Sam," he called as he elbowed his way past people and suitcases. He was surprised at his own voice, which sounded timid and, unaccountably, embarrassed him.

The Marine held out an arm for a handshake, and as Sanderson reached he saw Sam's photograph. A blow-up of an identification card snapshot taped to a flimsy piece of cardboard with *Sam Sanderson* and a question mark written across the top. Sam, beneath a white hat with a brim and an insignia, looked stiff and uncomfortable. *Could someone tell me please,* he could almost hear Sam say. *Tell me what in the high heaven or hell is going on around here, anyway?*

"I'm Master Gunnery Sergeant Franklin O'Donnell," the Marine began. He paused and then continued, almost gently. "I'm here as a representative, sir. For the United States Marine Corps."

"Sir," the Marine said again. "There isn't much other way to report this, and I wish there was." He paused and removed his hat. "Your son is missing."

Missing, Sanderson thought. He blinked, pushing the headache back, focusing. *Missing?* Well, that was nothing new. Sam had taken the car once and not shown up for three days after a joy ride south for a bluegrass music festival in northern Alabama. He could have told them Sam would never stay put too long, even for the United States Marine Corps.

"He'll turn up," Sanderson said. He laughed. *I could have told you people,* he started to say. *I could have told you.*

"AWOL isn't a pretty word," he said aloud, "but I have to say I'm not surprised."

O'Donnell stood at a kind of awkward attention, hands and hat and photograph behind him. He was looking intently at nothing. "We've phoned, sir, throughout the afternoon. And since we couldn't get you, I'm here to act as support personnel."

"I never thought this was the thing he wanted to do," Sanderson said. "Not really."

"With the greatest regret," O'Donnell was saying, more formally now. "Lance Corporal Sam Sanderson has been reported missing as of eleven o'clock this morning."

At eleven o'clock this morning, Sanderson had been on the road, listening to country music on the way to repossess someone's washer and dryer. His son had been somewhere specific in the world then, too, and nothing, Sanderson was sure, could change that fact, not this quickly. "You never could tell," he said aloud, "where that boy would head off to, and I don't expect it's much different these days."

You need to listen, a voice inside his head said. "Helicopter maneuvers," someone was saying.

He felt himself backing away, step by step. Or was he? The Marine's face came closer to the edge of his vision, receded and Sanderson swayed on his feet.

I'm trying, he wanted to say.

"Offshore practice formations," the Marine was saying. "Engine malfunction."

Where's baggage claim, someone said. *Flight Forty-Four to Charlotte, now boarding.* He was trying to listen, but one voice crossed another, like map lines, like radio waves. *Missing, since approximately 0:1100. Missing from the manifest. One thing at a time*, a voice was saying, and it might have been his own, but it was hard to hear voices when it was so narrow, this place, this time. His heart was the narrowest of all. It left him no room to draw a deep breath, so he could think. What had that woman said? *How hard is it to hear something when somebody has gone over it and over it?* He tried to fix on that, on the going over and over. Water, they were talking about that. Ocean and temperatures and time. *Preliminary search procedures,* the Marine was saying. *Time will tell.* What could anyone at all know about time?

"Take me home," Sanderson said.

"Home," he said again. *I mean*, someone had just asked him, *doesn't it matter when you tell someone you need something?* But by then he felt the headache tighten its grip. He could no longer resist it. He felt like kneeling right there and then and emptying himself of questions. He felt like falling and he was ashamed of that. He was trying as hard as he could to catch hold of one voice, so he could stay standing, so he could understand. He was ashamed of not understanding. Ashamed of how his son's photograph was in another man's arms. He wanted to take it back, smooth its edges and press them, new, inside the pages of a book. *What book?* What did they mean when they said he was missing? He remembered a book, a dictionary, lying on beach sand on a towel. Pages riffled in the wind and he now wanted them to hold still so he could look up that word. *Missing?* He was right there, looking at them from a photograph. His son was in one place and time, safe and coming home, this very night.

He was ashamed for Sam to be held by a man who was not his father, to be discussed like something to be repossessed. He wanted to hold the photograph close to his chest but he knew a faulty heart had never been a safe enough place. *What did safe mean, anyway?* Who had said that before? Sarah? Sam? And who, now, was telling him everything could be fine, after all? *We don't know for sure yet. Nobody does.*

It was still raining as O'Donnell drove him home. They made a stop at an urgent care clinic where a shot of Demerol flowed like cold water into his blood, eased his headache, then made him antsy. It was all he could do to sit still in the passenger seat while O'Donnell maneuvered traffic. He was filled with dread of going home, of reading the report, completed just this afternoon and neatly folded inside a manila folder between them in the car's front seat. He dreaded the very chair he had been longing for earlier. He recounted the sixteen steps that led upstairs to bed, recounted his often fitful sleep, the dreams of Sarah's death. Dread and lethargy warred inside him and he felt like opening the moving door of the car, leaping out into some other life.

O'Donnell had been assigned to him for the duration, he said. *For whatever might be required.* And the following morning, there was the couple from next door, and one of them made coffee and toast and viscous, over-easy eggs. And by that afternoon, there was his sister, his sole surviving close relative, now that their parents were deceased. Janet visited seldom. She had never approved of Sarah, had never approved of what Sanderson had made of himself after meeting Sarah, of the fine opportunities, as she described them, for school and a bank presidency and who knows what, that he had sacrificed.

They sat for a long two hours, O'Donnell and Janet and Sanderson, at the table in the kitchen where they all looked at a recent snapshot of Sam taped to the refrigerator door and Janet looked at him more softly than he could remember since childhood. He studied her red hair and her dangling glass earrings. She was softer then he recalled, but a bit smug, too, he imagined, as if with this particular loss he'd come out the other side, moved beyond Sarah's death into something grander, more dramatic, a possible redemption from his, as she had once called it, pitifully ordinary life. Sam's disappearance was, after all, making both local headlines and the national news.

O'Donnell brought him very little, really. Nothing concrete but a few things of Sam's in a duffle bag. *We couldn't bring you your boy*, O'Donnell said, *so we wanted to bring you something.* Sanderson unzipped a corner of the bag, peered in. They had packed, not like he imagined military men might, with an emphasis on order, but with an intimacy a mother might have imparted. When he tried to open the bag further, reach inside, he touched paper, then hard edges, the graininess of leather. And deeper in the bag, cloth, glass, the smooth surface of a painted box. When he reached deeper into the bag, it seemed to him that each of these objects was warm in itself, then unbearably hot to his touch. He couldn't stand to go farther.

The only thing he wanted was to be alone, and that's where he was by late afternoon, covers and pillow over his head. Alone, so he could sort through what O'Donnell called *the relevant facts.* He closed his eyes and saw those facts, a list, as a column of arrears. *Fact.* At approximately 6:00 A.M. Crew Chief Abraham Scott ascertained that a severe storm off the North Carolina coast might compromise the helicopter-training mission. 6:30 A.M. Training mission delayed until further report. 9:00 A.M. The mission proceeded, regardless of reports of variable visibility and four-foot waves. The mission. Eight crewmembers, including Sam, under the supervision of said Chief Scott, plus adjunct pilots Spence and Adams. 10:00 A.M. His son, approximately three miles out to sea. 10:15 A.M. Smoke observed from primary mission helicopter by a second helicopter. Apparent engine distress. Distress? His son, missing now since 10:25 A.M. Seven crew members rescued, amid a trail of debris, and his son, missing. Missing now since 10:25 A.M. The prognosis, Sergeant O'Donnell had said, was good. *Your son*, he said, *is a strong swimmer.*

He left the bedroom door ajar, and their voices drifted up the stairs to him, low and conspiring. He drifted in and out with these voices. Their mantra.

Time, they said.

Controlled landing. Fire. Hypothermia. His only son.

Sam had once called so many things a mantra, anything that repeated itself, any clock ticking, any drumming of fingertips on a tablecloth. The mantra soothed him, lulled him, and he found himself between sleep and awareness. Not quite dreaming, but in times and places he knew.

His only son. Sarah had put molasses, or was it chamomile, in a warmed bottle, when nursing wouldn't soothe Sam, and Sanderson had walked with him for hours. How in awe he'd been of holding such a small body in his own, awkward arms. That small body changed in his memory, became older, resistant. A teenager's plans. *I will. I know. I want.* Became Sam, here and gone, gone to India, Nepal, gone to this city and that and nowhere. Became Sam, the Marine, upright, a newly muscled body, his eyes with a brittleness about them that made Sanderson uncomfortable. Sanderson slept for a while, dreaming. Sam, a Marine. Himself, a Marine. Boys. Men, standing by a well. And a girl with thin arms holding a basket of coconut halves. *You buy? You buy?*

When the phone rang, its ring jarred, didn't match the pattern, the rhythms of sleep he'd begun to ride. He answered the same time as Janet so that it was almost impossible to distinguish one voice from another. On the other end, a woman's voice. A girl's. Beneath the smoke screen of drugs and his own fear, he remembered little of that conversation, later.

The voice was musical, sad, and it scraped against his heart. *I'm sorry, sir. I'm sorry.* And another voice, more distinctly. Janet's. *Who is that on the phone? Jason?* He'd thought, for a minute, that he knew the voice. That girl. The one Sam had come back from India with. What was her name? How little he'd known about the girls Sam had courted, the ones he'd said he loved. *Who is this?* And somewhere else, O'Donnell, taking charge. *We should handle all extraneous enquiries. Security reasons.* And the click of the receiver. Had he dreamed it, that voice? *I loved him, too.* Like a child, insisting. A woman, bereaved.

Sanderson lay curled on his side beneath the blanket Janet tucked around him. She smoothed back his hair, kissed his cheek. *Just never you mind, now,* she said. *Just never mind.* He could have told her it wasn't him who was a child again. That was Sam, nine years old and standing on the outskirts of a field. Sanderson coached T-Ball then, and Sam, too young to play, was a batboy. Sanderson remembered Sam's thin legs, the shoes he wore, ones with reflector stars on the heels. Sam, saying, *See, I can run faster than any of them.* His child's face, nine years old and chasing balls that arced high. Janet kissed his forehead softly, much as she had done long ago, when he was just a boy.

Try as he might he could not remember his son now. Sam was a man, but did he have a mustache these days? A tiny earring in one ear? No. Military training did not allow such aberrations. Sanderson thought there was a scar over Sam's right eye, but he wasn't sure. Sam, who had *that* look, as Sarah used to call it—something between sardonic and charming. How would anyone's face look beneath waters so cold, fifty-six degrees cold, ocean-cold, at night?

Heavy with the sleeping tablet Janet had given him, Sanderson focused on the voices—Janet and the Marine Sergeant, talking in the hall. *They aren't going to find him. That's the truth, isn't it?* Janet said that, or O'Donnell did. *Who knows what can happen in this universe we have inherited.* Sam had said that, when he'd just come back from that ashram he'd visited in India. Voices came from the radio she'd turned on to soothe him. *The Harmonic Convergence,* that voice said. *The following of an inner voice, the only way to break the cycle of fear and destruction, the crisis of the modern world.* The modern world. His son, adrift there.

He could taste them, bitter sleeping tablets and water from a bathroom cup. Nearly asleep, but not quite, and so he counted again. Footsteps in the hall. The words to prayers. *Now I lay me down to sleep.*

After the Celebration

After the sound of departing guests and the clatter of dishes into the kitchen sink, Rosa slid into bed beside him. She fit her knees into his, her arms around him. *Won't you speak to me, Jason? Won't you talk to me?* She kissed the back of his neck, but he moved away from her. Her body tensed with hurt.

"I meant to do good," she said.

He lay still, listening to her voice.

"Are you asleep, sweetie?" She moved closer to him.

"No," he said at last. "I'm not asleep."

"It wasn't what I thought it would be, I guess." She paused. "But I love you. You know?"

"Yes," he said. "Yes. I know that."

She curled her arm around him, whispered to his back. "And you know, Jason. I can't do it all. I can't fix the past and love you now, too."

He shifted, rearranged the covers. "Tomorrow," he said. "We'll talk tomorrow."

She was quiet for a little. "You're glad, aren't you?"

"Glad?"

"Glad I'm trying."

"How are you trying?" he began, his voice loud to his own ears in the still room. "I know you're trying, Rosa." He touched her hip and she took his hand.

They fell silent and he listened as her breathing evened, deepened with sleep. He turned, studied the bedside clock, turned again, replayed the last minutes of the evening, how he'd walked, run from the room. *No,* he'd said, feeling much younger than the Sam he remembered from that photograph, the one of his son in his arms.

He slipped from bed. Down the hall from their bedroom was a room that wasn't Sam's, not really, but he thought of it that way most of the time. It was just a room in a house Sam had never lived in, a room where Sanderson went to read a book or write a letter and stand in a place that held mementos. Swimming trophies of Sam's from high school, and a framed certificate for an essay that he'd written in elementary about water conservation. Photographs too. There weren't many of Sarah, since this made Rosa uncomfortable, but he framed just one, of the very afternoon she delivered Sam, a home birth he feared. Mother and son, sitting on a glider on a porch. He stood for a while without the light on, his eyes getting adjusted to the way the room looked through moonlight from the window. Then he switched on a desk lamp, and he stood staring, his breath caught and held.

Everything was gone. Trophies. Certificates. The Mexican flag Sam once used as a blanket for a twin bed, had been replaced with a pale blue coverlet, the pillows stuffed into ruffled shams. The dresser photographs of Sam, the boyhood one with a dog, the one of him in jeans and a tee shirt and a backpack, the one of him in Marine dress blues, they were all nowhere to be seen. Everything that had been Sam in this room was gone, old things replaced with new. *Emotional Wellness. Letting Go.* He turned those phrases over and over on his tongue as he stared at two pale blue china figurines atop the dresser.

Not the duffle bag. He knew where that was, and not even Rosa could have found it. In the top of the closet, at the back of the highest shelf, was a board that slid back into a crawl space in the ceiling, and he'd put the bag there, contraband, hidden from Rosa or himself, he wasn't sure which. He moved a chair, flipped on the closet light, and climbed. Since the night Sam was reported missing, he hadn't looked at these things, had only now and then unzipped the bag, slipped in a card, a note, a memento he wanted to keep. He carried the bag to the bed.

His heart was pumping, set in motion by the cups of coffee after dinner and he took deep breaths, held them in, but that only caused the beating to take a new form, anger that entered his arms, legs, the palms of his hands. How could Rosa have done it? This room. A shrine, she called it before. *Veneration. Devotion.* Sarah had shrines in her bedroom, those first months he'd known her. Small altars made of shells and stones and bright pieces of colored glass, to venerate the angels of desire, she said. They had made love once on a rug in front of an altar made of old shelves draped with angel hair and holiday lights and she had kissed his bare chest with a solemnity she called *love's devotion.*

He knew the items in this bag as well as he knew the palms of his own hands. A pair of olive green flight gloves. An olive green cotton tee shirt. White, boxer-style briefs, olive green socks. Dog tags. A written inventory of his own son's body.

The body. A well-developed Caucasian male with facial features nearly obliterated by marine animal feeding and an advanced state of decomposition. An unembalmed body. Cold, with rigor absent, and lividity not fixed. Scalp hair, short and dark. Eyes. Nose. Entire upper gingival and portions of lips, missing, as a consequence of marine animal feeding. Upper central incisors and right lateral incisor. Separated from their roots and in the back of the oral cavity. Upper chest and neck. Marbling, consistent with decomposition. Head. Diffuse hemorrhage. Centered over vertex of parietal lobes. Hands, to the level of the wrists. Ankles. Extensive skin slippages, algae overgrowth. Washerwoman's skin. Genitalia. Normal, circumcised. Back. Abdomen. Remaining portion of the extremities. Unremarkable, except for a tattoo on the right arm, in the shape of a rat carrying a double-barreled shotgun. The cause of death of Lieutenant Corporal Sam Sanderson. Blunt force injury complicated by drowning.

His hands shook as he took out the next items. Two envelopes with Sarah's scrawling handwriting on their fronts. *Sam.* His boyhood things, his later, teenaged interests. Notes and clippings and news articles and poems Sam had loved. He'd not looked at many of the photographs, as if looking at them would make those particular times stand still, vanish. One photo was of Sam standing alone on a rock overlooking a lake, and was another of him and a woman, both of them costumed, masks and capes for a Halloween ball. On the backs of the photos were phrases, not in Sam's handwriting. *A perfect point in time.... The exact color of anything at all.... The beginning of love's apocalypse.* There was half a bottle of men's cologne, gone brown with age, an herbal variety that reminded Sanderson of embracing his son, their awkward, last-minute greetings or farewells, as elusive as a scent. Near the bottom of the duffle bag was a corduroy shirt with a tear in one sleeve. He sniffed the torn shirt, imagining it smelled of ocean salt.

The next item was a red, embroidered bag made of velvet so worn the fabric was shiny. Sarah's. He untied the bag's strings and emptied its contents. There was a lacquered box, hand-painted with roses and deep green fronds of an exotic grass. A gift for Sarah. *It's from India,* Sanderson had told her, when was it, a month after they met. The box fell open as it hit the bed. *Bones.* He picked them up, one by one, feeling his stomach surge, his head grow light. The bones were fragments—the fluted remains of a pelvic bone, a tooth, a section of what was probably a finger joint—and he bit down on the inside of his lip. Sam's body had been recovered after ten days in the ocean, and he'd done what his own son's will had asked, cremation described in language as cryptic as his own life had become. *Ashes to ashes, dust to dust.*

Sanderson remembered a diner, another box. Bones lying on a Formica table. His son, back from India with stories to tell about a river and cremation of the dead. What had Sam said? *I picked up a bone, held it to the moonlight. It was a perfect human bone.* Sanderson picked up one of these fragments, held it to his cheek. It felt dry and brittle and the texture, strangely, made Sam new to him. Sam, when he was first born, had slept between them for weeks. *Hadn't he?* Hadn't he loved his son, loved his son with all his heart and the good Lord, too? Who had said that? Someone so far away in his own past he couldn't remember a time or a place.

The last item he took from the bag was a wooden-framed photograph. A young woman in a white blouse and white skirt. A girl really, her hair long and pale blonde. She was standing on a beach somewhere, her arms raised above her head, her body lithe. He flipped the frame, unfastened clasps. The photo and a yellowed piece of paper fell out. Sam's handwriting, and lines of a poem Sanderson didn't recognize. *I hear the Shadowy Horses, their long manes a-shake, their hooves heavy with tumult. . . O vanity of Sleep, Hope, Dream, endless Desire. . . .* Sanderson held the photo to the bedside light. *Lory*, the name in large, flowing letters. And below that, an inscription. *A remembrance of her childhood, from Lory Llewellyn, the girl touched by lightning.*

Chapter Two

Lightning:

1. An abrupt discontinuous natural electric discharge in the atmosphere. 2. A sudden, usually improbable stroke of fortune.

The Origin of Fire

She still has his black wristwatch, the one with a word engraved on its back. *Lightning.*

Sam. The last time she saw him, he came to Inez with plans for a trip to Grandfather Mountain. They'd buy wine if it stormed, he said. Their cups would catch lightning so they could drink straight from the mouth of God. *God was nothing but a vortex, and they'd stare right into his eye.*

A few days later, Sam Sanderson was dead.

And now, ten years later, she lies still in her room in The Motel of the Stars and listens to the radio, a special about the anniversary of the Harmonic Convergence. *This time won't come around for another 26,000 years.* Three A.M. She swings her legs out of the covers, lands her feet against cool linoleum. *The Harmonic Convergence is coming back again.*

She remembers the first Convergence well. August 16, 1987. The earth, she was promised then, was ready to enter a cleansing period. Global Awakening. Unity through divine transformation and love. Renewal of the human race from the cellular level on up. There were spiritual gatherings everywhere, from Seattle to Radiant, Kentucky. And now, on August 17, 1997, it was back again. *The Harmonic Convergence,* the radio says. *Ten years closer to the 26,000 year cycle of evolution.*

She tunes the station in, listens. *The biosphere is a finite, limited thing; it can only take so much stress.* This is true. In the motel's lower floor, a corner of a back room is sinking. At the base of a wall, she has felt damp, smelled mold. Five years ago, she called a building inspector and he gouged at the wall, inside and out. He took earth samples and measured and prodded. *Termites at the very least,* he said. And at the very worst? A gloomy picture. The foundations would need to be dug out, the motel jacked up a good foot and supports put in and substructures bolstered. She'd not needed him to tell her the worst. Decrepitude was here already. Her stepfather, holed up with scotch straight up from the bottle out in the garage. Inez, its one road in and the same road out and the same sorry customers. Traveling salesmen and short-haul truckers who knew the back roads. Her world? Diesel fumes and inertia.

She lights a candle on the shelf near the computer, sits, pushes the monitor button. She can have the world with only a touch. Wars in other countries she's never seen, rumors of wars in places as unlikely as caves beneath the earth. And light? With a computer's power, she can travel to Asiatic islands for sunsets. She can look up the latest in electroscopic research concerning anything from heart disease to black holes in space. She can grow lighter, advertisements tell her, by ten pounds in a matter of days! And the screen itself was a marvel of light. *Contrast. Intensity. Gamma Rays. Brightness.* Sometimes when she holds her hand like this, fingers extended and the blue screen light shining through, she feels the same amazement she'd felt long ago on a mountaintop.

Google. Ask.com. She can find anything, even news items about the day of the coastal storm that killed Sam. The forecast for that day, and the two days following. Clearing, then cooler. And the crash itself. Boats and airborne vehicles, an archived AP release read, continued to patrol the area, about three miles offshore and fifty miles north of the city. Preliminary search procedures confirmed that a routine patrol mission, involving three CH 46 helicopters, had resulted in engine malfunctions of an as yet unknown origin. But the computer can't summon him, can't bring back Sam

Sanderson, that interval in her life, her happenstance lover from a bus across America.

She lights a second candle, a third, a fourth. The room glitters as she sits again and checks e-mail messages in both her accounts. New messages? Old messages. Endless possibilities. She knows almost no one from either of the address lists she keeps, or only impersonally so. On one account, there are addresses for paper goods orders for the Motel of the Stars, and for the companies from which she orders plastic cups and tiny bars of motel soap. And on the other account are a growing list of people she has met through briefly visited chat rooms. Sufferers of Obsessive Fears, the name of one such group, and there she met a man named Tom. *I am getting better,* Tom's message of this morning says. *I am. But I still struggle sometimes,* he says. *Today, for example. I woke convinced that God was dead.* Another group is for animal lovers, and she has countless files with attachments. Photos of dogs and cats and Asian pigs. *I'll be all alone,* a woman named Kim has written, *when my dog dies. Tell me what to do.*

The chat room she visits most is for the SI's. Self-injurers. Self-mutilators. She thinks of Indian women and their hennaed hands. Of London, street corner punks with fifteen earrings and holes in their tongues and arms tooled by tattoos. *People who self-injure,* the Internet says, *have not developed three important self-capacities: the ability to tolerate strong affect, the ability to maintain a sense of self-worth, and the ability to maintain a sense of connection to others.* She is no self-injurer. She merely revisits the site of old wounds. Refashions the trajectory of long-healed scars. She knows that.

And yet she understands these people. *The Manic-Depressives. The SI's. The OCD's.* The merely lonely. On her computer's files there is a list of her own various and sundry worries. *Weather,* the list begins. Hurricanes and eddies of water and funnels rising from the sea and winds full of ocean water, ones that reach the apartment above a motel where she has lived for almost twelve years. Weather could spill her out like a pebble in a fish tank. She fears the ocean and its inexplicable horizon and the ebb and flow of its tides. Currents, she has read, are deflected as a result of the Earth's rotation. One current on the surface generates another beneath the surface and another and another until ocean waters whirl. *Vortices*. They are such whirlpools. *Whirling motions. Masses in flux. Occupations viewed as simultaneous, concurring.* She fears things lost or broken, things once possessed and now misplaced. She once looked for hours for a missing earring, retraced her day's steps, motel to post box to the store and an uphill path through the woods to the motel and back, again and again, on the lookout for the earring's deep red stone.

Love. She can add that to her lists of fears. Love is supposed to be as easy as the Website where you can order desire—a vial of vitamins, unknown herbs. The screen promises safe sex. Provides warnings about unsafe sex that can produce death or worse. But with the computer screen she has played the edge. Five-minute erotic films for free. Hard-core porn, personal ads to which she can respond or not, the latest pictures of lingerie. Once she'd been exploring the Internet and she found a Website for made-to-order, anatomically correct men. *Stress-free, disease-free companionship*, the ad promised. *Cheaper*, they said, *than most alternatives*.

One afternoon a blonde man with cigar checked in to the motel. She was holding a stack of computer manuals, a bag of groceries, and had a winter coat draped over her arm. Smoke rings settled around her shoulders and the next she knew she was on her hands and knees, retrieving potatoes and bottles of spring water. The blonde held her shopping bag while she glanced surreptitiously at his gold hair, his white eyelashes. She later rehearsed the scene in her mind, the dry tongue at the base of her neck, the unzipping and unbuttoning, the belt buckle that jangled to the floor. For months, she was caught in a never-ending cycle of worry. *What about that new bruise on her thigh? Her lymph glands seemed swollen. She had her third headache in a week.* She made three appointments at her regular physician, three more at the downtown clinic, and another two at the free clinic. As unlikely as lightning striking a person—a one in 3,000,000 chance—but was she safe? *He had a tattoo on his middle finger. Weren't tattoos a means of infection?*

Behind her, candles flicker and the Harmonic Convergence preview goes on. *We must speed up our personal processes of spiritual awakening and prevent self-destruction of the planet.* How to speed up her own spiritual awakening, to understand that word, destruction? There was no way, Sam once said, to avoid the future, no way to escape the cycle of death and life and death. *Death.* She has surfed the Net about death and found sites like the Death Clock or a site selling special Legos that assemble as history's greatest torture devices. There's Death to Spam. There's the Death Test, which promises to tell you how long you'll live. *Near-death, pro-death, heat-death, sudden death, Black Death, Happy Death, Blue Screen Death.*

Suicide. There you get hits for everything from a girl punk band to messages from international centers for health and wellness. *Before you consider suicide,* they say, *consider us.* Warnings of the afterlife. *The consequences of one's decision in this life must be confronted in the next.* Methods? *Drowning. Poison. Air in veins. Painting of entire body.* There are chat rooms about plans and near misses and repeated attempts. Nowhere, she tells herself, has she seen a story about anyone who killed themselves by never leaving the upstairs room of a wayside motel.

Fear. She's been dying of that for years. She's been dying of that since Sam, almost ten years ago. *You cannot predict the day of your own demise.* Who told her that? Some Indian mystic in a stall in a marketplace in Delhi, or some reader of Tarot on a Paris back street. It doesn't matter. She does know the day of her own death, has known for it for years.

On the anniversary of The Harmonic Convergence she will climb to the top of Grandfather Mountain. The sun will rise and shadows will converge on the face of the deep and a thousand souls will meet at the foot of the mountain to celebrate and she will dive. She will plummet from this world and enter whatever one is next. She has waited ten years for this.

She lights one last candle, sets it atop a shoebox underneath the window. She opens a desk drawer, takes out the papier-mâché box, the one from India that Sam Sanderson once filled with bones and ash from the foot of a temple to Kali. She drapes a blanket over her shoulders and slips downstairs. Outside, the grass is moist with dew in the spot she chooses beneath the willow tree.

Cars pass on the road beyond the Motel. Cicadas. A voice from a house somewhere. *Harry, let me sleep now, you hear?* Then silence as she sits in the metal chair and thinks of women kneeling by some river. *The Ganges.* Clothes slapping against rocks. Brackish water drifting by and the women watching, their faces hidden by veils. Her own face is hidden now in the shadows of a wayside motel, and she can do anything. Open the box full of ashes and bone. Inside, that box smells of chalk and she dips her fingers inside. Hesitates. A mockery of those women maybe, but she does it anyway. Marks her cheeks and beneath her eyes, kohl made of bone dust. She could be those women by rivers-faraway, hidden by purdah, full of their own secret desires.

Candlelight shines down from The Motel of the Stars. Downstairs her stepfather is drinking himself to sleep, while she should be thinking of clean rooms and keys. Upstairs, the radio is still playing, promising the alignment of planets, galactic clusters, the convergence of subatomic particles in her very own soul. In this world of the stars she has everything she needs, though sometimes on nights like this she needs a little more.

She got it from her stepfather, the tiny knife she keeps in the box of bones. Some stock-sale find forgotten on his work bench, lost in the midst of auto parts and thick, old oil. She has cleaned and polished the one whetted blade, a blade so thin it could make a sound like music keening if she tapped it. Like Tibetan bowls whose edges you skim, over and over, until there's that wave of sound in harmony with the universe. Touch this knife just right and it too can make that sound. It makes that sound now as she touches the blade to the underside of her arm. She graces her body with three fine lines she draws on her own flesh. The blood that wells up is beautiful enough to make her catch her breath.

Lory Llewellyn folds her knees into her arms and stares at the sky and heat lightning. She thinks of that. Of lightning. Of childhood, its rhymes and spells. *I wish I may I wish I might.* Of seasons turning into years, night becoming day and day becoming night, and on and on into a future she no longer wants. Nothing, not a computer screen, not wishing, not memory or desire or faith can bring back Sam Sanderson. *Sam,* she whispers, *tell me who you are.*

Divinity

Lory Llewellyn can clearly remember her love of dictionaries and thesauruses, the encyclopedias and almanacs, the year she was eight. Too young, her mother said, for fancy-schamanzy words, but she loved them anyway, the contrasting definitions. Awe. *Terror and wonder*. Attenuate. *To weaken. To make slender, fine*. That year she also read everything she could find about storms and light. Light, she read, was as necessary to the body as water or air.

They lived then, her mother and her real father and herself, in the mountains of Western North Carolina. Mountains surrounded her, ones she'd never seen. *Pisgah. Snowy Bald. Clingman's Dome*. That year she was eight they took a family vacation to see Grandfather Mountain, a place so majestic, her father read to them from the guidebook, the Cherokees called it *Tanawha*.

"We will sup," he said, "upon nectar amid clouds inhabited by Gods."

"Come again?" her mother replied as she stuffed clothes for Lory and father and her own best dancing shoes into a red suitcase.

"Tanawha," he said, "means resting place of God." He tamped down the cherry tobacco in his pipe.

"I'll settle for a resting place for these," her mother said as she snapped the suitcase shut. She sat on the bed, wiggled her bare, plump feet in the air.

"Get the heel part on that one," she said as her father took one foot, and then the other in his hands and rubbed.

"Tanawha," he repeated, gazing out the trailer window. The word sounded

70

like wine, forbidden and bittersweet when she'd stolen a sip from her mother's glass.

Their Pontiac was a blue her father called *lapis lazuli*. It had rusted out spaces in the back floor through which she could see the highway as they headed toward the mountains. As she traced their route on the map in a guidebook her father bought, she studied herself in the visor mirror, her ordinary nose and the mouth they called a cupid's bow. She pointed out scenic attractions and historic markers her mother would love, but they drove straight through since her father was set on reaching Grandfather Mountain by nightfall.

Can't we just surprise ourselves, go the way the crow flies or something? Her mother insisted, so finally they stopped at a refurbished log cabin with a display of flintlocks and butter churns. *Historical truisms.* Her father told them this and pointed with disdain to everything made from apples: carved wooden bowls, fried pies, and dried apple dolls. They bought jars of apple butter and a box of divinity candy.

After that it was time to put their feet up. A motel and dinner. They stayed that night in a motel with a restaurant offering soup beans and cornbread for supper and, in the bathroom, milled soaps with birds of various colors on printed tissues. *The Red Bird.* For economy's sake, her mother said, they would share a room, one so close to the sign that Lory counted flashes of red light spilling across her bed through the blinds while she listened to her parents talking. They thought she was asleep, but what she heard were words, ones she translated into a more palatable language. Voices rose and fell with cool air from the open motel windows. *Romanticizing. Misnomers. Pipe dreams and promises.* From the highway outside, car lights intersected fingers of red light crossing and re-crossing her bed as she fell toward sleep. *For two nickels and a ticket to nowhere I'd trade in every one of the last five years.* In the distance, she imagined a mountain,

71

thick green branches and fireflies. *What pleasantries*, her father said. *To sing me sweet good night.*

Midmorning, she woke to weak sunlight from a cloudy sky. Her father opened the blinds and then sat on her bed with the guidebook and a red felt-tip marker.

"Grandfather Trail," he read aloud. "Let's try that one."

The book described an upper mountain ridge trail running in and out of wind-dwarfed spruce and fir, across rock walls and pinnacles, into open spaces with views of mountains in every direction. Across from them, Lory's mother groaned and burrowed in the covers, a pillow over her head. Her mother had talked, yesterday, of outlet malls and of a wax museum on a stretch of highway that included a place where you could dress in historic costumes for family photos. Now, her bare legs and her bobby-soxed feet swung over the bed's edge.

"We'd better pack a lunch, is all I can say."

The trail began at the Hiker's Parking Area, near a Visitor's Station where her father bought a book detailing history of flora and fauna of the Blue Ridge Mountains. He questioned a ranger about topographic maps of Grandfather Mountain while her mother stocked up on brochures and leafed through tourist's coupons for restaurants and a Mountain Ghost Tour.

"Where you folks headed?" the ranger asked. He looked dubiously at her mother's shoes, which were rubber, wedge-soled sandals with large, plastic daisies across the toes.

"Grandfather," her father said. He was wearing a white dress shirt and a red tie with a pattern of ferns. The white shirt was wrinkled, particularly at the shoulders, beneath the straps of an Army day pack he'd brought to carry their lunches.

"The Trail, you mean?" By then, it was a quarter after two and he frowned as he studied his watch.

Guidebook still in hand, her father thumbed through the pages, read aloud from the trail's description. "It was along this trail that two centuries ago French explorer and botanist Andre Michaux broke into song, thinking he'd reached the highest peak in North America."

"Two and a quarter miles of it, sir." The ranger looked again at her mother, who was near a display of indigenous wildflowers, and again at her father.

"And here," her father continued, pointing to another page. "John Muir, Naturalist, from the Grandfather Trail. The face of all heaven, come to earth."

"You'll think it's heaven, come about five o'clock, on one of them extra steep parts," the ranger said. "Look here," he said.

He stood, pointed to the trail map behind his desk. He pointed out an easy hike called the Woods Trail, with sixty-seven varieties of flowers and plants. He pointed out the Black Rock Nature Trail, with views of a swinging bridge, and Grandfather Mountain to the Southwest. But her father had a stubborn set to his mouth.

The ranger jotted down their names, their vehicle number, and the time. When Lory looked back, he was watching as they crossed the Visitor's Station porch, then made their way across the parking lot.

They lingered at wildflowers pictured in the guidebook—fire pinks and rhododendron. Lory made a crown of violets and stuck a blossom in her father's shirt collar and even her mother seemed happy. She sang rounds of the "Twelve Days of Christmas," and they laughed that this was off-season as their small and off-key voices disappeared into the thick green foliage on each side of the trail as they climbed. Through openings in the trees they glimpsed mountains and deep blue, late afternoon sky. Two and a quarter miles were nothing, her mother declared. She'd skipped that far. She'd danced that far, even, in the early days, when she was courting her young men.

By nearly five o'clock, according to her father's calculations, they were nearly to the crest—the point that promised, as the guidebook said, *such spectacular views that the Indians had wept, as if at the sight of God.* But he had been saying they were close to the crest for an hour and more as they climbed parts of the trail that grew steeper for long stretches, then sharply so. They balanced themselves against tree roots, took frequent rest stops at flat stones. At points the trail was made of nothing but dry, crumbling rocks, and after that they nearly leapt from one large stone to the next. A rock facing leveled out for some distance and her mother chose a smooth stone and sat. She mopped at her forehead with some toilet paper from the Army pack, took a swig of water.

"And just why," she asked, "am I doing this?"

"This?" Lory's father asked. His face was red from the climb and sweat circled the underarms of his white shirt. "It's good to hydrate when you're exerting yourself."

"Not that, fool," she said. Her hair, short and dark, set with tight curls from a recent permanent wave, was wet with sweat. The curls seemed sinewy, a mass of angry black coils Lory tried not to think of as snakes. "I mean climbing up a shit-load of rocks in the middle of the damned summer, just so you can get *the view.*"

"It's not just *a view,*" he said. He planted his hands on his hips. *View* came out a like something unsavory he needed to spit out. "It's the resting place of God."

"God," she answered, her voice, usually throaty from cigarettes, higher pitched. "God?"

Before they could say more, Lory heard voices, ones with crisp foreign accents, from the rocks above their heads, and soon a man and a boy appeared. The boy was short and stocky, with plum-colored pants that ended at his knees. The man carried an enormous aluminum frame pack with a

74

sleeping bag tied to it, with cups and canteens suspended here and there. He planted his hiking boots firmly.

"Other visitors," he said, holding out his hand in the general direction of the three of them. "To Tanawha."

Lory's mother laughed shortly, but her father brightened. "Tanawha! A fellow devotee." He held out his own hand and the two shook politely. "How much farther, sir?"

The man waved dismissively. "A short walk." He took out a pocket watch from his vest, snapped it open. He looked surprised, then peered up at the sun, which had lowered in the last hour. "Not far," he repeated. He studied Lory's mother's wedged shoes, and her father's red tie, which had come unknotted and hung limply from his collar.

"We'll be down by sunset," the boy said. "We want to set up camp." He was carrying a pack nearly as large as the man's.

"And you?" The man unzipped a small bag at his waist, took out a zip-locked bag of nuts. "Surely you will accompany us, at such a late hour?"

Lory's mother looked eager. "Surely," she repeated as, ahead of them, the trail seemed steeper yet, the rocks gray and unfathomably solid above them. A long-winged bird circled. Thin shadows had begun to cast across the rocks and the sky was a deeper, dusty blue set with gathering clouds.

The final climb was to a crest looking out over mountain upon mountain, a chain of smoky peaks edged with red and black as the sun fell. It was almost dusk. They were too exhausted, the three of them, to comment upon the way mist now gathered in the valleys below, filling pocket upon pocket of space until clouds, full and darkening gray, rose and reached across the horizon. *Tanawha*, her father said, determinedly, as if this word could keep back clouds and what was, more and more evidently, evening. Later, Lory remembered her parents and their voices, rising and falling. *Now what, mister tour guide? Your fault. Listen to me. Listen to me.* The voices carried on the heightening wind down the trail they'd struggled up, carried the long way back to everything they had known before, motels and trailers and late-night arguments about, her father said, the cost of wine and cigarettes and the price, her mother said, of romanticizing the world.

They found an overhang of rocks where they huddled together as the summer's heat turned cool, their bare legs against stones. Rain fell softly, a shower that gathered, became quiet lightning in the distance, then the rumble of thunder circling back. Her parents sat, one on each side of her. *You didn't used to be this way. Remember how much you loved the way roses smelled, wild ones, in that field behind the house?* They hardly noticed when Lory shifted, wedged her hands, hard, against her ears. *Well I'm that way now. That way?* They hardly noticed when she slipped from between them, felt her way out to the edge of Tanawha. One of them called out to her to be careful, to count her steps, there and back again. As she went one step farther to what felt like the edge of everything, she heard her mother's voice. *What way is it to want more out of life than a two-bit trailer and a promise?* The night ahead, long and cold and rainy, was forgotten. She was forgotten. They were lost, like they always were, in the sounds of their own voices.

Tanawha. God, not resting at all, stood so close to her, she could have tasted him like sweet water in a metal cup. She shut her eyes and imagined a white robe in the wind and how God caught the edge of this robe and held it above her head, a tent where she could rest. The thunder was louder now, and with it, hard little pellets of rain. She stood still, frightened and amazed, as the lightning gathered power, settled around her in a tight circle of white-yellow light that took her in. Years later she'd read about it—how lightning could become an entity of its own, could become a sphere, a ball of energy so powerful it could envelop those it touched. Her own long hair stood out around her head, a charged cloud, and her fingers wound through the long, waving strands. Her hair, her mother used to say, was like corn silk. Now it was lightning-lit, coarse and full of electric-blue air.

Lit air sparked along her bare skin, at the back of her neck and down her arms, stroked, played, cut into her with a touch so fine she shivered. Once in an apartment where they'd lived, she found a space at the back of a closet and made a soft, rose-colored nest from which she'd awakened hours later to her mother's voice. *Where'd you get to this time?* Fiber-glass, her father said and her mother scrubbed her, hard, in a metal tub full of tepid water. Lightning entered her that way, now. A cobweb of light that lay on the surface of her skin cut its way in, delicate and brilliant.

Lightning gave way again to thunder, thunder sounded, and the rocks and the sky shook as she stared up, expecting the world to come crashing down. Prayers. She knew plenty of those, ones about food and light bills and when they'd move next. She knew the beginnings of others. *Now I lay me down to sleep. Hallowed be thy name. Alleluia. Amen.* She made up prayers of her own as the rain fell and as the charge of lightning crackled in her spine, in her palms, on the tip of her tongue. *Let them love each other. Let them love me. Love.* Over and over, the one word in which she most wanted to believe. The word that could mean everything, if only it were true. Years later, she'd cut her own flesh, keen-edged probes, questions asked of her very own skin. *Are you still there?* She'd search for it for years, the radiance that touched her that night she awoke to lightning.

Chapter Three

Shadow:

1. A dark figure or image cast on some surface by a body intercepting light. 2. Darkness, especially that coming after sunset.

The Black Dog

Sometimes Sanderson woke Rosa in the middle of the night and told her about the dream. *Again, sweetie,* she'd say and hold him until he felt her ease back into sleep. It was five o'clock now and he lay still remembering that dream again. A war. A truck. Himself and a boy who could have been Sam. This time, a woman had appeared, leaned in to the truck bed. *Hush now,* she said. *Don't be afraid.* Then the dream-world exploded and a blaze of light woke him.

He moved nearer Rosa, parted strands of her hair across the pillow, asked her questions. *Petals? Photographs? Did you think it would be as easy as that?* He studied her face—her mouth parted in sleep, the lilac veins beneath her eyes—remembered how he used to wake her in the mornings. The bare skin of her back, a birthmark there in the shape of an exploded star, touch of his tongue to her neck. Now he held back. The past was the past was the past. She believed that. And yet he heard it, a voice in his head he couldn't deny. *How close we are when we touch,* he thought, *to bone and blood and a beating heart, our own and another's.* Who had said that to him once? He reached out, his hands close to Rosa's skin. *Laying on hands.*

Instead he thought again of his dream. *Hush now. Don't be afraid.* It could have been her voice. Lory Lllewellyn. The woman from the motel fire. The long-ago girl who had loved his son. The photograph from the duffle bag. One and the same. Faces coalesced in his memory into one face, that girl who had been with Sam at the airport that day when he'd come back from India.

81

How had he not recognized her, even if it had been almost twelve years? She'd never breathed a word, never called nor sent a card. *How are you? I'm fine. I used to love your son.* Had slept with him in his very own house, if Sanderson recalled clearly.

He had scarcely recognized Sam, at first, that day at the airport. He'd seen a shaven-headed figure raise one skinny arm and wave in his direction. Just back from India, Sam wore loose fitting cotton trousers belted in at the waist with what looked like rope and, as Sanderson drew closer, he realized with a shock that this thin person was his own son. And the girl. Lory. He had met a few of Sam's girlfriends, beginning in high school after Sarah's death. They seemed ethereal, most of them—slight women with pale eyes who looked adoringly at his son.

Lory Llewellyn then had a shoulder-length mass of hair, a tiny red jewel beside her nose, and she wore half a dozen or more brightly colored bracelets and slippers made of untanned leather with absurdly pointed toes. Hers had been an absent face, cool and detached and yet oddly speculative. She reminded Sanderson of those paintings of women Sarah had loved, Modigliani women, as she looked up at Sam and said, *Is this the place?* Sam smiled at her, as if they had some secret Sanderson would never know. Sanderson shook her hand and later, his palm had the scent of some scented oil. *Meet Lory,* Sam said. *The luminous heart of the world.*

Or had Sam said that at all? When Sanderson tried, later, after the initial meeting at the airport, and after a disastrous lunch with Sam and Lory and himself, he couldn't accurately recall who had said what. Perhaps it was Lory who had said something about light or luminosity and the world. *Back from the luminous heart of the world?* Or something else. *Back from the world, the heart is luminous?* He envied her, this woman who had looked long and deeply into the face of a son Sanderson had never fully understood. Had loved, but lost long before his death. *Held back from the world, the heart cannot be luminous.* Trying to remember made him feel as uncertain as he'd felt that day when he'd seen the two of them step into the airport waiting area, then again when they'd shut the door to the basement room they shared together that night. The next day they were gone. *Directions unknown,* Sam had said, while the girl had mumbled something about a quest. Quest? *The miracle of vortices.* Vortices? *Portals,* Sam had answered for her. Doorways to what, Sanderson wanted to know. He didn't remember Sam's answer, but there'd been portals, all right. Doorway upon doorway.

Downstairs, the kitchen counters were covered with remnants of last night's party. The guests had emptied bowls and stretched plastic wrap over plates of partly eaten desserts. Before grinding fresh coffee for the morning, he began to stack plates, emptied half-full cups. *Meticulous.* Both his wives called him that. He emptied grounds into the coffee press, boiled water. Today, Doris could do the cleanup. Doris, who came weekly to clean, always left an empty soup can full to overflowing with cigarette butts on the steps to the back deck. He imagined her finding the place cards from dinner. Sodden with dressing, one from the edge of the counter read, *Gently Sleeping at the Bottom of the Sea.* The words left him tight inside.

He filled a thermal cup with coffee and slid his feet into some deck shoes, set out for the pagoda near the lake. Halfway down the block, there was Mr. Benton, already out unwinding his water hose, ready to water his tomato plants against the August heat and he waved as Sanderson walked toward the lake. The streets were all like this one—blocks of neat ranchers, cultivated yards. *This close to the ocean,* Sam said when he saw the new house Sanderson had chosen with Rosa after their marriage. *And you go for a place with a piped-in lake.* Sanderson had made his rituals here—the small lake, the paved path for his early morning stroll.

The lake was an expanse of water surrounded by an asphalt path, and it made him feel safe to sit beside it, on a bench near the swans and geese. This morning the water was murky and he stared at it, trying to see past algae and a yellowish layer of summer pollen. He imagined wading out, the safe edges of silt and cattails giving way to some center point of deep green and impenetrable depth where he could let go of them. The dream images. The woman's voice. The truck's open tailgate.

Rosa had grown up believing in the significance of dreams and the importance of omens, but what about this Rosa, the new one devoted to Harry Simon and his Emotional Awareness Encounters? When they were first married, she'd come to his house to cook him her specialty, meatloaf and twice-baked potatoes. After dinner, they danced to old songs like "Hello, Mary Lou," then lit candles and lay in bed, holding each other. He told her about Sam and Sarah and himself, and Rosa had made him feel safe, made him feel young, like anything and everything was possible, yet he knew what she'd say about his dreams, these days. *Dreams*, Harry Simon would say. You had to encounter yourself in the pages of your dream journal every morning. *The gateway to our souls*, Rosa said one evening when she came back from a session called *Working Dreams: Make Nighttimes Pay Off!!* He could see Harry Simon's plump face now, his hands stuffing the envelopes with pictures of Sam.

He sipped his coffee and he concentrated on the bench on the opposite side of the lake. Yesterday's anger was stirring in him and he peered at the lake shoreline where a stray dog, a small, thin one, waded in and lapped. She was a black silhouette against the water.

Sam begged for a dog when he was eight, until Sarah drove downtown and they picked out a puppy from the local animal shelter. The puppy had been beneath their feet at the dinner table, at the foot of Sam's bed, at the door when anyone came home, and had failed to be bothered when Sanderson shouted no as it gnawed its way through everything from the morning paper to his own new tennis shoes. The dog had feared nothing, until that fall when they took their annual family vacation to the shore. Sanderson remembered the two of them, boy and dog, as they stood at the edge of the waves—how wild-eyed and resistant she was as Sam walked with her into the waves. The dog had outlived Sarah, and had stayed behind when Sam left. The dog was still with him when he moved to this house with Rosa who, with her love of white carpets and refinished floors, had insisted that the dog sleep in its own house, not theirs. She'd been none too receptive to his wish, at times, for another dog to fill the void left when a kidney ailment forced him to put her to sleep.

He drained the cup and stuck it in his sweatshirt pocket, whistled until the stray came running from the shrubs a hundred yards off. She shook herself and sat, waiting. He found a scrap of paper and the stub of a pencil in his sweatshirt pocket, to write down the name and phone number of the dog's owner, but she was collarless. Sanderson and the dog looked across the lake and he wondered what lay at the bottom of such murky water.

He came back in the house through the kitchen, the black dog trotting behind him. It crouched, wagged itself near the counter, where he was surprised to see that Rosa had loaded the dishwasher and wiped down the counters. She was tuning in morning news on the set beside the microwave.

"Jason," she said, just as the dog stretched itself.

"It was down by the lake."

"Obviously," she answered, studying the muddy paw prints across the kitchen floor. She covered one stockinged foot with the other.

"Stray," he mumbled. The dog cowered now, gazed up at Rosa with its dark eyes.

"Garage," she answered, and bent, grasped the ruff of the dog's neck. It yelped as she tugged in the direction of the door. While she escorted the dog out, Sanderson stood watching an interview about something called the planetary moral emergency.

The crisis of this age, a bearded man with round glasses was saying on the television, *is that we market the past. Only by understanding the past can we come to a full awareness of the value of our times and our own lives as they unfold.*

"You going to call the Humane Society?" Rosa asked as she came back in, picked up her coffee cup.

"Isn't Doris coming today?" he asked, changing the subject and gesturing toward the cleaned counters. "Doesn't she take care of the dishes?"

"She'll be here about ten," Rosa said. She set the dishwasher going.

"Why so late?" he asked. Rosa often did part of the work before the woman arrived. She'd vacuum the den or carry out old newspapers and start a load of laundry, and then he'd come in from work and find Doris still there, doing a leisurely dusting of the living room while a soap opera played.

"I thought maybe we'd leave a little later," Rosa said. "Have coffee and talk." She handed him a necklace, raised her hair and turned, waiting for him to fasten her.

"Talk?" He fumbled with the delicate chain and when he was finished Rosa reached up and stroked his cheek. He had not yet shaved.

"Toast," she said.

"I haven't made it yet," he said, glancing hurriedly at the clock. Ten till eight. They never left for work until nine, but he was usually ready with breakfast, his meal of the day, by this time.

"No, silly," she said. "Toast. Your face. I used to touch my daddy's face in the mornings before he shaved and it always felt just like that. Like toast."

The tenderness he often felt when she referred to some taste or scent or touch from her childhood fused now with the thought of last night. Photographs and candle flames.

"Jason," she said, still touching his face. "We need to talk." On her face, guilt was a girl's, and he was even more aware of how young she really was.

"About?"

"About last night."

"Yes," he said. "I wanted to talk about that, too."

"It was too much, too soon, I guess."

"Or just too much." he said, choosing which words he would use to describe how he felt last night, how he felt this morning, the tightness in his chest gathering, taking hold.

She reached for the coffeepot, filled her cup again. At the window on the other side of the counter she stared out at the drive, and at a bird feeder Sanderson put there last spring. "I guess that's just it, Jason," she said. Her voice was soft and she kept her back to him. "Things being too much."

"Things?" he asked.

"Things," she repeated. "Us."

He moved behind her at the window, started to touch her. "Yes," he repeated. "Us."

"Last night," she said, keeping her back to him. "I meant what I said, Jason. About moving on. It wasn't just words."

Words. Some of the words from the place settings from last night came back to him. *Gently Sleeping at the Bottom of the Sea.*

"What was it then," he asked. "If it wasn't words?" His own voice sounded distant, and the tightness deepened, widened.

"I feel like I'm floating, Jason," she said. "Floating along with you, between the past and the future, and I can't put my feet down in the present long enough to know where I am or where you are. And I want to know. I have to know."

A strange metallic taste was in his mouth. He swallowed, spoke, said what he least intended. "Is there someone else?" he asked, though he was certain this was farthest from the truth.

"Jason," she said, turning from the window, looking sad. "You know that's not it."

She'd said she felt like she was floating, and he felt like that now. The taste of metal converged with the tightness inside him and he swallowed hard.

"Jason?" She sat opposite him, reached for his hands. "Don't you understand what I'm trying to say?"

He sank into a chair, touched the grapes and oranges, hand-painted wooden fruits in a bowl at the center of the kitchen table.

"I want things to be better. Like they used to be, and more than they used to be." She was staring right at him, her eyes wide and serious. "New," she said. "I want them to be new."

She held his hands tighter, but he couldn't speak. The metallic taste was stronger, had moved to his throat where it burned as it slid down into the center of his chest.

"Last night," she said. "I *know* it was a new-fangled way to say something my own mama used to say, after my daddy died."

"And what was that?" he asked, not meeting her eyes.

"Can't live with one foot in grave and one in the land of the living, too," Rosa said, and she took one of his hands, laid it against her cheek.

"Is that what I'm doing," he asked.

"I didn't mean you, Jason," she said. "I meant me." She laid his hand down on the table. "I'm so sorry, Jason," she said, studying her fingers. Her nails were newly painted and like her toes, were a deep, muted red. She looked at him, and then away. "God, I'm so sorry," she said again.

Floating, she'd said. He was floating now. Anger. Panic. Confusion. He pushed to the top of these feelings, said what came to him in a voice that was stifled, airless. "You should be."

She started. "What did you say?"

It was hard to listen to her, no less speak, but the words guided him, took their own shape. "I'm sorry," he said. The words sounded bitter.

"For?" She was sitting at the edge of her chair now.

"That I had to participate," he said at last, "in such a travesty."

"What do you mean?" Her polished toes were white as they dug into the kitchen linoleum as she leaned toward him.

"How could you," he asked. The words came out singly, one by one by one, neat categories of them. "Put all of it on display like that? Me? Sam? You, for God's sake?"

She was defensive now. She stood, paced between counter and table. "Last night," she began. "Last night, I said what Harry meant me to say."

"I'm sure you did," Sanderson said. Sarcasm was at the edges of this, but he plunged on. "You mean what Harry Simon says. Or what all of them mean. Those emotional basket cases. Those vultures."

"Jason."

"It's true," he repeated. "They're vultures. They prey on others for their own emotional depth."

"And you," she asked. She stopped pacing, faced him. "You touch me these days, and you're a ghost."

"A ghost?" he asked. "Ghosts, angels, vision quests. More claptrap."

"I do believe in ghosts," she said. She reached for his hand, her voice lower, gentle. "I'm living with one."

"You knew when you married me I'd lost my son."

"Yes," she said. "I knew. I just didn't know you'd be a ghost, too."

"For better or for worse."

"Oh, Jason." She stood, her hands at her sides. "You're someplace else, living some life I was never part of, and I don't know what to do."

"Do what you want."

"I meant what I said." She stood near his chair, cupped his chin her hand. "Something has to change."

"That's what I want," he said. "To leave it behind. All of it."

"That isn't the point," she said. "Just leaving things and forgetting about them."

He leaned against the table, forehead against his palm.

She paused between table and counter as she looked at her watch. "Jason," she said again, but then shook her head as from the garage came the sound of persistent scratching. The dog, begging its way back in.

He stood at the kitchen door as she backed the sedan down the drive. She stopped, lowered the window, leaned out and waved in the general direction of the house. What were the last things she'd said before she'd left the house? *I need some time, Jason. You need some time.* She spoke of separate vacations, a beach house she could rent from her realty company. A few weeks, she said. She needed time. Of that much, she was sure.

She lifted her suit jacket from the back of the chair. "We'll talk some more later," she said. "Tonight," she said as she hesitated and then kissed him on the cheek.

There was a shelf to one side of the window where Rosa kept glass ornaments—redbirds and cats and hoop-skirted women—and a few items of his. He picked up a plate and held it to the sunlight to illuminate the pale orange flowers. He had bought that plate in Okinawa, in the war. He could remember streets behind a ramshackle guest house, the litter of vegetable peels, cart after cart of brilliantly colored fruit, the taut muscles of pigs strung from their back legs. The woman at the hawker's stall had teeth that were a deep beetle-nut red. *Fat American soldier*, she'd called him with a laugh that made him want to hide from the sun's sticky heat and the crowded market.

Outside, he lifted the garage door, set the dog free, and then made his way to the back yard, where he sat at the picnic table. The yard was large, with boxwood hedges on all three sides and a portable swimming pool with its cover still on at the far end. He'd been meaning to clean that pool for the entire summer. He'd been meaning, also, to trim the boxwoods, but could never remember the best part of the season for that, and he studied them, their ungainly year's growth. He started as a cold, wet nose pushed against his leg under the table. *Go on, get on home.* The dog crouched in front of him, her ears cocked, one of them chewed and raggedy. Instead of chasing her away, he held out his half-empty coffee cup for her to lick.

It was true. He was a ghost, and Rosa was losing herself right along with him. In the first months of their relationship, when he told her about himself, she had held him when he couldn't cry. Even now, these last weeks, she reached for him across the cool bed sheets, as if she wanted to draw him back from some far. And he, too, had tried. Sam. *Incalculably sweet as rain.* Sarah called him that. Sam, lost in the ocean. Still floating there ten years after his death, and he, Sanderson, was drowning in the wake. He wanted to try to tell Rosa such things, but the taste in his mouth drowned out the words.

He pictured Rosa alone in this house, her polish-toed feet, bare and luxuriating in the white carpet down the hall. He pictured the evenings she'd have, the way she might fall asleep, as she sometimes did, with a video ended and the blue television screen humming. And later, pink night light from the corner of their bedroom would fall across her as she slept, dreaming of her own quiet heart.

The dog lapped at the last of the syrupy bottom of his coffee cup. He could almost hear them talking to him. Women's voices. Lory Llewellyn, finger raised to her lips in his dream. *Hush now,* she said. *It's time,* Rosa said, *to let your soul be still.* And Sarah? *Do you really believe the heart can be changed, just by something as small as dying?*

Chapter Four

Fire:

1. A state, process, or instance of combustion in which fuel or other material is ignited and combined with oxygen, gives off light, heat, or flame. 2. Greek fire: any of a group of inflammable mixtures; wildfire.

The Road Out

Harmonic Convergence. What had the radio said? *August 17, 1997.* Attunement of the planets. Union of life forms. The morning after the fire, Harmonic Convergence sounds like something ludicrous, like tiny men with tiny guns. *The Day the Earth Stood Still.* They think she is asleep, but she is sitting in a metal chair and planning how the Harmonic Convergence, this time, will be the road out.

Neighbors and her stepfather and all the rest of them saved what they could from the Motel of the Stars, pulled this and that from clothes hangers, threw chairs and end tables into the yard. Someone, somehow had picked up a dictionary and left it open to a page. *Devastation.* A word underlined in red, and they thought it agreed with her. That she was devastated. In shock. That she had, what was a better word? *Flipped out. Lost it.* She isn't even unhappy, really. She wasn't unhappy even when the window of her room grew brighter and brighter and the whole place went up like kindling, nor when old man Sykes and the other one were standing by her chair and discussing her like she was whatever was leftover from the fire.

Turning. That's what she thinks about as she sits in a metal chair and listens. Neighbors. A man whose voice she recognizes. Planets turning in a void not black, but ebony. Blue-black. Sable. The sun, nothing but air with a visible edge. Earth. Venus. Mars. Planets gliding past. 93,000,000 miles from the sun. 67,000,000. 140,000,000. Celestial bodies moving one note to the next via the sound of the universe. What word for this sound? Neither vowel nor consonant suited that imperceptible spin of stars and planets, suns and moons moving through time, through gaseous substances, through a prevailing emotional tone. 950 degrees hot. 364 degrees cold.

She herself has moved with the heat of desire, with the cold of avoidance. With the speed of light. From a green metal chair in the sun, she is a repository of memories of light. Light, traveling in wave upon wave through space and time, no straight line, in spheres, a whole family of curves and surfaces touching other curves and surfaces. Sunlight through a trailer window in the aftermath of rain. Fire and light in a temple at the top of the world. Sunlight and shadows on Sam Sanderson's face. The world struck open with lightning.

Lightning strike could cause damage to synapses, or weakened tissues in some place that really matters—the brain, for example, or the heart. Memory loss. *Disasters,* the article called incidents involving lightning. *Airplane passengers see ball-shaped lightning the size of a basketball enter their craft and chase an attendant up and down the aisle. Boy sees lightning strike seventy-five yards from garage, watches it rise to one foot above ground and follow a path to his feet and up his body.* She could acutely recall her own experience with lightning, the way light had entered her, leaving her skin feeling luminous. *Luminous.* She once looked it up again and again. *Gleaming. Shining. Incandescent.* She wants luminous back again.

Harmonic Convergence. August 16, 1987, the first time. Interviews in Seattle. In Eureka Springs, Arkansas. In Asheville, North Carolina. In a sequence of cities cross country, ones they called vortices. People gathered in these cities by the thousands and brochures promised peace and love and everything in between. *We are all parts of God from time upon time,* they said. She remembers love beads and prayer wheels and tee shirts with rainbows. She remembers Sam Sanderson, how he once filled her heart like firelight. That night ten years ago they planned to go to the top of Grandfather

Mountain: *Harmonic Convergence*. When it came back, the original face of God, would it come back like a flash of light?

Chapter Five

Due to living in the wrong time, humanity is creating a planetary moral emergency. We cannot really expect to have a new millennium without a new time.

—Jose Arguelles

Horizon

Sanderson called in, told them he had to have a week. *A week? With this motel business? I've seen your desk.* He packed the essentials—socks, one pair of slacks, two flannel shirts. A journal. He'd just set the lacquered box in the seat behind him when the dog leapt in the open car door, made her body heavy when he tried to push her out into the drive. He told himself he'd drop her off somewhere, at the pound or a vet's office, but now as he headed toward Inez, she poked her snout out the window and her long ears blew back in the wind from the open windows. At least neither he nor the dog would be there when Rosa came home this evening.

It was now midday according to the dashboard clock. Doris had already arrived by the time he left and he dodged her questions. *You don't look so good, if I have to say so. Take it easy today, Mr. Sanderson?* He drove in silence, with just the wind from the rolled down windows and the sounds of passing cars. His only plan: drive to Inez, find Lory Llewellyn, talk about Sam, get her to tell him something about this son of his who'd professed to love her. He'd drive some more after that, until it was dark enough for a motel and go on from there tomorrow. Drive to the coast maybe, spend some time walking sand and surf and thinking about what the girl had to say. Would that be Emotional Wellness?

As he retraced yesterday's route, he tuned to a local station and smiled as he heard the headlines. *Temperatures in the mid nineties by end of week. Chili cook-off this Sunday at United Methodist, Cairns Road.* There was an announcement of a birthday for a 103-year-old woman, then the promise of a barbeque supper at a local church. He turned the volume higher, remembering a church cakewalk he'd gone to with his grandmother, the taste of coconut cake. Local news gave way to national. Summits in the Middle East. Continuing research on a cure for AIDS. Stock indexes. And a feature on the forthcoming ten-year anniversary of The Harmonic Convergence. *None of us,* they were saying, *are inherently linear. We are all gifted with the ability to know time, true time. Natural timing is ours, if only we know how to look.*

He flipped the window controls up against the hotter afternoon air, set the air going, wondered about timing, about natural times for this, for that. *Why?* He wanted to ask Rosa that, this morning at the kitchen table. *Why have we come to this?* But he hadn't asked her that, nor had he called, from a gas station, fifty miles back. He left the cell phone behind and he hadn't even left a note, though he tried. Twice he began and finally came up with almost nothing. *You're right,* he wrote. *I do need to find myself again.* Then he reread what he had written and heard his own father's voice in his head. *Find himself? You're right there, where you've always been, son.* Instead of finishing the note he sat rehearsing what she had said to him yesterday. *You touch me these days, and you're a ghost.* What did she expect from him? There was no natural time for love or loss, not to mention death.

He was only fifteen miles from Inez, if he remembered this stretch of road correctly, when he noted that the red temperature light was flashing. He studied the temperature gauge as it crept up, wavered. He regretted that he was so ignorant of the workings of an automobile. Hadn't the owner of the burned-down building called The Motel of the Stars been a mechanic, or what passed as one in a hole-in-the-road town? The gauge would last that long.

The radio switched from local news to bluegrass, banjoes and fiddles, and he fooled with the buttons in search of something calmer, more suited to the late-afternoon light. He hummed along for a few bars of a Frank Sinatra song, scanned past some shopping-mall jazz, and was just fine-tuning a public radio station when a red and black bicycle streaked in front of his car. He slammed on the brakes and the tires spun and slid as he missed the bike by mere inches.

The last thing he saw before the car halted, one wheel deep in a rut to the side of the road, was the face of the boy. One hand still gripped a Popsicle as he straddled the fallen bike. His grape-stained mouth was open with surprise and Sanderson, sitting still and with his own hands clutching the steering wheel, met his eyes. He gunned the car in reverse, forward, and then sat, staring, until he was aware of his fingers, clammy and stiff on the wheel. He pushed open the car door and swung his legs out. The car was tilted, in a deep hole filled with sharp-looking cans and bottles.

"Didn't y'see me, mister?" the boy shouted, though he was no more than a few yards beyond the car.

Sanderson had no memory at all of the bicycle, and he realized he was shaking, in his legs and in his hands, which still felt the grip of the steering wheel.

"Son," he said, starting toward the boy, who, he was relieved to see, was righting his bike. "You all right, son?"

The boy glared at him, tossed his Popsicle stick in the general direction of the car. The two of them looked ahead down the road, lined with trees and a few buildings—a diner on one side, and on the other, railroad cars that had been converted to a hardware store. In between were houses where, now, heads poked out of doorways. A woman in a plaid housedress and an apron came flying.

"Mick," she said, her arms, which Sanderson noted were covered in a fine white dust that looked like flour, encircling the boy's plump shoulders. She glared at Sanderson, and at his car.

The car, its front wheel settled in the rut, looked exaggeratedly new as the woman and the boy studied the car, the glossy deep blue exterior, the vanity license plate Rosa had ordered with his initials and hers and a background of state flora and fauna. All the same, the car's engine was sighing and hissing, with a trail of steam coming out from under the hood.

"Look's like you've got you a problem, mister," the woman said as she drew the boy toward her, put her arms around him protectively. "You all right, Micky?" she asked, grasping the boy's chin, raising his face so she could see him.

Two men, one in a soda jerk outfit, the other in coveralls, approached from down the road as Sanderson fumbled with his wallet. He had the sudden image of the Triple-A card, left behind on the dresser, where Rosa had last laid it after locking the keys in the car.

Sanderson looked down the street, past the few buildings, and saw more road.

"Look's like you're aiming to stay a while," one of the men said.

The five of them, boy and mother and men and Sanderson, stood looking at radiator steam rising toward the town's horizon.

At the least, a new tire rim, and at most a thermostat and radiator repairs, all for the repo man. The shop they took him to was Frank Llewellyn's and Sanderson stood there, looking on as Llewellyn unhooked the car from the tow truck. Llewellyn, who wore a bright red nametag monogrammed with *Red* and a tiny devil holding a mug of beer, gave no immediate indication he recognized Sanderson.

The building was part auto repair shop and part something else, storage for dry goods, judging from the boxes marked *Desk Supplies* and boxes of motel-style facial soaps. One corner was set up with a folding cot strewn with thin blankets and a mound of clothing, and a rabbit-eared television set on a metal tray, so the place was also what now looked like home. While Llewellyn poked and prodded under the hood of his car, Sanderson walked the length of the workbench, which was laden with manuals and oil filter wrenches and an assortment of bottles, most of them whiskey or gin, and a few brightly colored jars, one with an oily label stamped with roses. *Eau du Toilette.*

While Llewellyn's hands and face were streaked with set-in residues of oil and grime, he also was, as Rosa would have said, a looker. His once-blonde, now thinning hair was cut into layers and beneath the top of his coveralls Sanderson glimpsed the collar of a green dress shirt. A looker who had seen better times. His eyes, a watery, light blue, opened wide when he spoke, and his mouth seemed weak, exposed.

"You're right lucky, I'd say," Frank Llewellyn told him. "Lucky thing you come up on that ditch when you did, from how hot you've been running." The dog, who had followed Sanderson into the shop, sniffed at Llewellyn's leg, and he scratched her ears, let her lick his hands. "Nothing much the matter from you and that ditch but a bent rim, and we'll have to hunt one of them up at the junkyard, but you could've done worse. And the thermostat."

Sanderson typically either left his car to be serviced or had Rosa drop the car off at the dealer on her way to the office. He knew little about cars, but he now discussed broken axles and tie rods. The thermostat was shot, that was a fact, and it wouldn't have done him a bit of good to run his engine hot, not in August. Not to mention that he'd come in a hair of running Micky down and that, Llewellyn told him with a wink, would have deprived all of them of a twelve-year-old with a lot of promise and gumption enough to run errands for just about anybody, even if he was in your face every minute of the day, asking for a quarter for everything from an ice cream to a pack of Marlboros.

While Llewellyn talked from under the hood, Sanderson let the dog out through a door in the back. The lot there was scattered with debris—tires and oil pans in which unidentified objects soaked and stray auto body parts, doors and bumpers and a seat from a school bus. The dog sniffed and wandered to a thicket of bushes. Back inside, Sanderson studied the walls. A wall to one side of the workbench was typical enough—a poster for Bosch plugs, a calendar with a girl in a string bikini atop a Harley. Another wall was more startling.

Photocopies, untouched by grease and oil stains, were taped and tacked everywhere. *Lightning, the Brilliant Miracle.* One page gave a scientific definition. *The visible electric discharge that happens between rain clouds or a rain cloud and the earth.* And thunderstorms. *Violent rainstorms, producing thunder, lightning, and frequently hail, form when violent updrafts push hot, humid air high into the cold, upper atmosphere.* And thunder. *The discharge of lightning is seen in the form of a brilliant arc, sometimes several kilometers long, stretching between the discharge points. The discharge also sets up a sound wave that is heard as thunder.*

Some of the pages were ink-stained, covered with handwriting. *A possible new type of lightning, called a red sprite, is a dim, reddish-colored burst that lasts only a few thousandths of a second and can be many kilometers wide. A second type, a blue jet, is a blue, cone-shaped burst, brighter than a red sprite. Blue jets erupt from the center of a thunderstorm at speeds of up to 6,000 kilometers an hour.* Sanderson looked closely at a large color blow-up of streaks of lightning, with a title in blue and yellow, at its bottom. *Lightning in the desert sky outside Tucson, Arizona.* The photographed lightning was a resplendent bridge from earth to sky.

Boots crunched in spilled oil and the sand scattered to soak it up. Frank Llewellyn held the just-pulled thermostat.

"Now this one, mister," Llewellyn began. "This'll take longer than that tire rim, for sure. Have to send clear up to Radiant. Or Lexington, could be."

Sanderson sighed as the two of them stood and looked at the wall and its various taped-up pages. "And how long do you think that might take?"

"Tomorrow," Llewellyn said. "Next day, worst case."

At least, Sanderson thought, he'd have more opportunity to talk with the girl. He reached up, traced the photograph of the Tucson lightning, the zigzags and fine threads of light.

"You'd have thought she'd collect something that would make a little more sense. Cat's-eye marbles," Lllewellyn said, wiping his hands on his pants legs and peering at the wall. "I used to collect those. But I reckon lightning is as good as anything."

Frank Llewellyn pointed out clippings Sanderson might have missed. A story of a fisherman from farther down the coast who was convinced he'd seen God and heard the voice of heaven when lightning struck his boat. A report from a local elderly woman who was said to have been cured of blindness by a lightning strike.

"My son knew someone who liked lightning. A girl."

Llewellyn reached for a clipboard on the workbench, flipped through its pages. "Yeah. Girls and stars and such. And drive-in movies, for that matter. My ex used to like to go to drive-in movies when it stormed."

"Your ex?"

"Met her at a diner, and lost her at a motel." He chewed on the eraser end of a pencil, scribbled on a folded-back page.

"You have kids?" Sanderson asked, studying the pictures of lightning again. What had the photo's inscription said? *From Lory Llewellyn, the girl who loved lightning.* He remembered the motel and a green metal chair, the woman and her soot-covered face.

"Can't say I do. Wife liked traveling salesmen a little too much. Or traveling with them, I mean, and I guess I never was much good at family." He scratched the dog's rear, right in front of her tail. "Not for lack of trying."

"That must have been rough," Sanderson said. "Losing your wife like that."

"Lots of things are rough, mister. That thermostat, for one," Llewellyn told him, retrieving the thing from his coveralls' pocket. He examined it briefly and handed it over.

Sanderson turned the device over and back, sniffed it. It smelled like hot wax. "My son," Sanderson began. "He knew this girl named Lory."

Sanderson watched Llewellyn's eyes open wide, that same startled and tired look. "You know Lory?" His brows arched and he listened as the dog scratched at the door. He peered at Sanderson over the clipboard.

"It's strange," Sanderson went on. "My son, Sam. He wrote about her. In these papers of his, I mean."

"Why don't you ask your boy about her?" Llewellyn let the dog in, then considered the clipboard again. He took a pencil from his shirt pocket, scribbled.

"I would," Sanderson said. His heartbeat quickened and he breathed. "But he was killed. Helicopter crash on Marine maneuvers."

Llewellyn took Sanderson in, and then shifted to the estimate he was calculating. "Losing a son, now," he said. "That's hard, mister. Any way you look at it. Maybe that's another reason I'm no family man. Can't lose what you never had."

Sanderson reached down, patted the dog when she trotted over to him.

"Marines, now," Llewellyn said. "I always wished I could do something like join the Marines or go overseas. Volunteer to help somebody. I always did have the utmost respect for a body could serve."

"I never knew why Sam joined," Sanderson said. "It was the last thing I ever imagined him doing, really."

"They end up like that," Lllewellyn said. "Family. Doing what you least expect. Take her now."

Sanderson wasn't sure who he meant, the wife or the daughter, but he fished in his back pocket for his credit cards and his wallet. "That's why I came here, you could say," Sanderson said. "About her." He held out the photograph, the one of Lory Llewellyn as a little girl, her bare feet dangling.

Llewellyn studied the picture for a little, glanced at the wall of photocopies.

"It's her, isn't it?" Sanderson asked.

"She was a sight as a child." Anger crossed the man's face and was gone so quickly Sanderson could have imagined it.

"I was hoping to talk to her. See if she could help me."

He handed the estimate to Sanderson. "Reckon a good rim and a radiator flush is about all the help I can give a body, most days," his voice softer, almost gentle. "Can't speak for her."

"I was hoping," Sanderson began.

"Yes, sir," Llewellyn said. He held the photo toward a light bulb dangling on a wire from the ceiling. "Can't tell where a body will end up. Me, I used to imagine I'd end up somewhere really fine. New York City, Europe, maybe."

"Is she here somewhere? Somewhere in town?"

Llewellyn dusted the photo against his sleeve, handed it back to Sanderson. "If you're looking for Lory, mister," Llewellyn said as he glanced at the clock again. "You've come about a day and a fire too late."

"What do you mean?" Sanderson said, flinching at the word *fire*. Surely Llewellyn would recognize him now as the man who'd come calling to repossess his motel.

"Night before last I lost everything I had to a fire, except for this place. She took off the next morning."

"What's that?" Sanderson asked. *Took off*. He thought of jets. Of helicopters.

"Wasn't much of an auto," Llewellyn went on. Auto, he'd said. *Ought. Oh.* "Old piece of shit Pontiac. Belonged to her mother."

"Where'd she go?" Sanderson asked.

"Her?" Llewellyn answered, and then laughed. "No telling, I'd say. First she goes around the world and back, then she sits here in Inez for over ten years, like it was the last place on earth and her too scared to come out of her room to see it."

"And then she just took off?" Sanderson asked.

"Could be about anywhere and nowhere, on some mountain, finding God."

"Say, mister, you're that fellow was out here yesterday, ain't you?" Llewellyn said suddenly. "That insurance feller," he repeated.

"I guess so, " Sanderson said as he stared at the estimate, its row of figures, and at a headline on the wall. *Lightning.*

"My luck," Llewellyn said, studying Sanderson.

At three, he left his car at Llewellyn's shop and, dog in tow, made his way down the one main street. It was close to six-thirty, and he tied the dog to a sign outside a diner where he headed in for coffee and a vegetable plate and, as he glanced out the diner window, wondered where he'd spend the night. Could there be more than one motel in a town this size? He sipped coffee and talked to the counter waitress, who refilled his cup and answered his questions.

"Yeah, I know Frank Llewellyn, and that wife of his both."

The wife. A mother-turned-competition for the girl, so Sanderson heard. Wore baby-doll pajamas in the middle of the day and you could hear her shouting, could have been at Frank Llewellyn or the girl either, once she came back around to live. Things like *Good for nothing but one thing, and you and me both know what that is.* Though it was the mother who took off north with some salesman in house wares. There'd been stories, of course. About Llewellyn and the girl. A man, alone with an odd-turned young woman, even if she was his own stepdaughter. Her, pretty as you please. And the way the fire must have started, up at the motel.

"Him chain-smoking in bed, waiting for his wife to change her mind, and that girl locked up in her room doing who knows what," she went on. "I'm surprised the place hadn't already gone up like a cracker box."

"What's Lory Llewellyn like?" Sanderson asked.

"Lory? She was odd," the waitress said. "That's for sure."

"Odd?" Sanderson asked.

"I don't know," she said as she totaled his bill. "Been to all those foreign places, and there she was, keeping motel records. Worked the computer ninety-eight hours a day." She lowered her voice confidentially. "You could see her," she said, "sitting up there in that room, staring out the window like she was waiting for her eighteenth birthday to come back around."

"And where is she now?" Sanderson asked.

"I think she headed for the hills," the waitress said. "Some craziness. Something in harmony with something, though I couldn't tell you what it was."

"Harmonic Convergence," Sanderson said under his breath as he paid up and recollected the radio advertisements. The true timing of the cosmos.

"Do what?"

"I said, is there another place." Sanderson cleared his throat. "Another motel?"

"Place for the night, huh?" She tapped a pen on the counter as he handed her a few ones for a tip.

"Yes," he answered. "Just the one night."

"Not much around here," she said as she stuck the bills in her uniform pocket. "Unless you count Goldie's place. She lets a room sometimes." She scribbled a name and a rough map on a scrap of paper and handed it to him.

Goldie Tiner. The woman. The boy on the bike.

"Don't get me wrong," she called after him as he headed out. "Frank Llewellyn ain't a bad kind, nor the girl neither. Nobody's bad, I reckon."

Her voice followed him onto the street. "Just some people're more scared than others."

As he sat on an itchy wool sofa across from Goldie Tiner, he thought of lawsuits and possible accusations. *Hit-and-run, near about. Reckless driving for such a fancy car*. She signed his name into a thick ledger, gave him a rope for the dog for the back yard. Then she sat across from him, rocking furiously in a vinyl-bottomed rocker as she told him everything and more than he wanted to know about Mick, the boy, who as it turned out, hadn't been home since earlier that afternoon. He'd ridden off, she said, on that red and black bicycle, and had neither phoned nor left a word with a soul in any house up and down the road.

"And I swan," she said as she rocked and thumbed through the pages of a large, black-bound Bible. "Boys his age. Running here and yon, up to not a lick of good."

Sanderson mumbled something about boys being boys.

"Might have done him some good," Goldie replied, "if you'd really'd hit him with that car of yours."

"I wouldn't go so far as that," he began, but she interrupted him.

"No, I wouldn't wish him harm," she said, "not for all the gold in China."

She was what Rosa would have called beside herself, then beside him as she took a seat on the sofa. "It's ain't like he's my very own, you know."

"He's not? I thought he was your boy."

"Like it," she said, "but not." She'd taken him in when a cousin had taken to drink. "Let me show you," she said, "what becomes of raising a boy."

She reached for a glossy-covered book from the coffee table. There were photos of herself—a girl then, pin-curled hair and a sailor shirt, sitting on a porch swing beside a boy her own age. Then there were county-fair beauty photos of the cousin, a wispy, dark-haired girl with bright lipstick. Later photos, the cousin, married, to Goldie's own boy-beau. And the child? There were photos of that, too. A baby being washed in a sink, hands dispensing water over him from a pan. And then photos of the baby, grown to the boy himself. The same one from the road, this time smiling and sitting in this very room, his eyes wide, off-kilter and staring at something unseen in an opposite corner.

"Guess he's most of what I've got, these days," Goldie Tiner said.

"That so?"

"I never did marry," she said.

"No?"

"No kids of my own, and none to come at this point."

"You never know."

She looked at him with her sad eyes, shook her head. "Don't time fly, mister," she said. "What is it the good Lord says? Time goes, and healing too, all waiting for the Lord."

The room to let was at the end of a long hallway with a separate bathroom, a rusty sink and a light that came on when he yanked a chain. The hall was lined with low cabinets covered with thick plastic and, beneath that, dolls in various stages of disassembly. Those, he mused as he turned over again on the bowed mattress, frightened him more than a lawsuit. Doll half-bodies. Dolls, armless or legless. Two large doll heads, weighing down either end of the plastic on one shelf, cascaded their doll hair toward oiled board floors.

"Don't mind my doll-pretties," Goldie Tiner had told him. "I'm fixing them up, one at a time, some of these days."

"Fixing them?" he had asked as she steered him toward the last door at the end of the hall.

"Can't tell," she said. "Collect them long enough and you might just find you a whole one in there somewheres."

Later he dreamed of a doll with gnarled arms and one too-short leg and he dreamed voices, high-pitched ones from throats made of plastic and wood. Outside in the hall, the floorboards creaked and he sat upright, listening, his heart beating fast. At last, he slid his feet into his unlaced shoes, felt his way out into the hall. The bathroom door was ajar and enough light shone along the walls that he could feel his way along fine. His hands caught at the edges of plastic, came to rest a time or two atop the sharp, hard features of the doll faces. Pointed noses. Bristly hair.

Just as he'd about reached it, the bathroom door swung open and he could see the boy, the red and black-bicycled one named Mick, standing before the bathroom mirror. He posed, a cigarette in his mouth, his cap first shoved forward, over his eyes, and then turned backward, bill-side low over the back of his neck. He turned, this side and that, and Sanderson could see the jagged line of a cut down one cheek. Sanderson could almost hear him thinking. *Two, three more years. I'll be right out of here, then. Yes, sir*. Then he stepped out into the hall and, before he saw anyone else was there, he stood still for a while, looked right and left at the stretch of plastic-covered dolls. What was it he said? *You all waiting on me? You better be, I reckon. I could steal me an arm or two, I sure could*. He stepped further into the light from the open bathroom door and saw Sanderson. Without hesitation, he smiled, raised his hand to his lips, made a whispering motion. Then he walked toward Sanderson, stood close to him. He peered up into his face.

"Well, she got her one," the boy said as if he were describing a fish.

"One?"

"Roomer," he said. "She don't get many, with the motel and all."

"I guess I'm one, all right," Sanderson said.

"Mister?" the boy stepped closer, peered up from just below Sanderson's mid-chest. "You're that one that cain't drive too good, aren't you?"

"You could say that."

"So she's got more'n just me and these dolls here tonight." He moved closer to Sanderson.

"I met your aunt," Sanderson said, stepping away. This was a boy, he reminded himself. It could have been Sam, late-nights, sneaking in, in his sock feet. "Your aunt's worried about you."

"She ain't my aunt."

"Your mother, then?"

"She ain't that either," the boy said.

"She was worried, all the same."

"She always has to have something to worry about, besides them dolls."

"You mean a lot to her, so she says."

"She always has to carry on about something or other."

"Carry on?" Sanderson asked. "She seemed genuinely concerned."

In the low hall light, the boy's disheveled hair and bleary-looking eyes gave him look of an old man. He made a short sound like a laugh. "Some things you have to get used to, don't you?"

Somewhere far below them, another door creaked open. Muffled footsteps started down another hall and soon they could hear a television.

The boy raised his head, alert as an animal. "We've woke her up now for sure."

Sanderson and the boy stood and listened to the television and to music. What was that old-movie song? "Summer and smoke." The boy pushed past Sanderson, quietly shut a door.

There was no way he'd sleep now, so he went to fetch a jacket. He'd untie the dog, walk a little. Out and down the dark street, dog's leash in hand, he walked past the few houses and the now closed diner where he studied the window's display. Photographs. The diner's original owners. A helmet-haired woman in a cook's apron and a younger, prettier woman with red-lacquered nails and a cigarillo. Light from the one main streetlight cast over these photographs and over plastic roses in vases, over small, ceramic statues of dogs and Jesus, over a laminated copy of Today's Menu: Mashed Potatoes, Meatloaf, Brown Gravy. The Tuesday lunch special. And in the middle of it all, an open Bible on a stand and just enough light to see that, too. He made out a verse. *Then shall the lame leap as an hart, and the tongue of the dumb sing: for in the wilderness shall waters break out, and streams in the desert.* Behind him, the streetlight buzzed and zapped and shut off at intervals, but there was light all the same, a glow from the damp late night air itself. He walked and this light reminded him of looking into windows of his grandmother's house long ago. Beveled windows, the old kind that made the air full of lines and waves and a kind of translucent smoke.

The dog nosed the ground eagerly outside the garage where he'd left his car and Sanderson stopped there again. The one window into the shop was dust laden, but there was light here too and he looked in to see the same workbench heaped with everything Frank Llewellyn owned. The light came from one side and it was television, the rabbit-eared set he'd seen earlier, with Llewellyn himself sitting on the cot nearby. Sanderson started to rap at the window, but the television held him. Black and white, this light. And a song, the same one from the hall in Goldie Tiner's place. *Summer. Smoke.* He could barely hear through the window, but there were distinct words this time. *I'll love you every evening, love you as the summer dies.* A dusky, late-night cabaret voice, a woman's. As he watched, Llewellyn got up, knelt by the television. Sanderson was too far away to see the woman's face, but he knew her anyway. White-blonde hair, just so, a toss of curls and a single wave over an eye. The eyes? A close-up there, eyes so dark they revealed nothing, no small inroads to the heart, nothing but a wink, a flirtatious lowering of those thick lashes. The face? Just a pale moon, glossed lips, microphone close to the mouth. Nothing else visible in black and white, the features indistinct with static. But Llewellyn knelt there, traced the outline of her. *I'll love you like there's no tomorrow and never, no parting by day, no parting by night.*

Behind Sanderson, the streetlight zapped and wavered, sent down fingers of light. If the light had been hands, Sanderson mused, they might have stroked the back of his neck and made him shiver. A love song. *Love.* He thought of Rosa, wondering where he was. He thought of Sarah, and of Sam. Had he told his son he loved him, that last visit before he died? He thought not, and he wondered if he had, if it would have made a difference. He watched the way Llewellyn held his hands against the screen, like he was waiting for some television miracle.

The dog was in his back seat again the next morning, twenty miles outside of Inez. He'd started to offer the dog to Frank Llewellyn, but at the last minute she'd leapt into the car, planted herself behind him on the driver's side. Down the road fifty miles, he pulled over, searched under the seat for something to pour water into from the bottles he'd filled at Goldie Tiner's. And that, in the end, was where he found a folder full of clippings. He imagined Llewellyn putting the folder there, a kind of map to guide him along.

Lightning, one cutout of a headline said, *doesn't usually strike people.* Lightning hit mountaintop trees. A series of photographs cut from magazines showed snaking branches afire, blazing white. In a journal called *The Mountain Horizon*, an article described the enormous odds of lightning-strikes for buildings or airplanes or churches, for golfers or workers in open fields, for children on swing sets in playgrounds or for fisherman. Anything, the article warned, could be a conduit.

August 17, 1997, the headline of another article read, *Anniversary of the Harmonic Convergence.* Lighting will strike in its full Glory, this article read. Grandfather Mountain would be a vortex of power. The sky would open. Truths would be revealed. Light and power would collide. On top of that mountain, on August 17, 1997, the past could be laid to rest and the future, full of light and the energy of the forthcoming Millennium, could be revealed. *Grandfather Mountain.* Sanderson remembered it well. He climbed up there with Sarah when he first knew her. They packed food and wine, and her mouth tasted sweet as they stood on broad, flat rocks overlooking the valley, as they held hands and promised to love each other. Warm rain fell and he tasted that, too, on the palms of his own hands.

Sanderson turned the car back west. *Grandfather Mountain*. Sanderson thought of that one mountain, the slant of it, tall and black and rising from clouds. Lory Llewellyn might be there.

Chapter Six

Black Hole:

A theoretical massive object, formed at the beginning of the universe or by the gravitational collapse of a star exploding as a supernova, whose gravitational field is so intense that no electro-magnetic radiation can escape.

Heart Chakra

Lory Llewellyn drives mostly on Interstate, but also through a network—two-lane roads, small city congestion, roundabouts of small towns. The route unfolds in an old movie, the pages of an historic map with a bold line that guides west and north. *Grandfather Mountain*. She is certain she remembers the exit from her childhood. It's nearly seven o'clock, too late to stop for log cabin tours, but in time, she hopes, for a room.

She hunts for The Red Bird along the usual strip of shopping malls. She is tired and she peers at sign after sign. This must be the area she remembers, but The Red Bird is nowhere in sight, so she settles for a place called Betty's, near an all-night diner and a homemade-fudge shop. Betty's sign advertises that it is family-run and, more interestingly, that it is Devoted, with a capital D. Lory imagines slippers and a robe in the room. She imagines a bedside table and Jehovah's Witness literature.

In the registration area, she rings a bell once, twice. The large, dark room smells of curry, but also lemony and clean. Behind the desk, she sees the family part of this place—a large photograph of a gray-haired woman in a vivid blue sari, beside a man Lory recognizes as Rajasthani, with his elaborate red turban and his curled, waxed mustache. At the base of the photo are lit incense cones and votive candles beside a huge vase of silk flowers and tiny figures of Ganesh and Hanuman.

"Yes? Yes?" A woman emerges from behind a doorway hung with material from a sarong. She is dressed in Western clothing—tight black jeans, cowboy boots. The only indication that she, too, is Indian, a red bindi sparkling with silver glitter.

"A room," Lory says as she takes out her wallet. The registration will require a vehicle number, an address, and she thinks about each of these. The Pontiac is from a distant past involving her mother, who drove it last to and from a nightclub called La Petite Femme. After that, it was towed to Inez, where it sat behind the garage with, as her stepfather said, enough gas and oil in it to give it a get-go and a heartbeat. The car's approximation of running is a miracle and it has no current tags. And her address? *Ashes. Foundation stones.*

"Lapis or emerald?" the woman asks.

"Pardon?" Lory says. She stops rummaging in her bag. The woman is leafing through a spiral-bound notebook, one with colored bits of paper sticking out from its edge.

"We code the rooms," the woman says in that way Lory remembers as Indian—a rise and fall of the sentence, a slight back and forth nod. "These are your choices." She stops at a section of the notebook that has a rose-colored tag, thumbs back to another with a tag that is deep green. "The lapis is yours," she says, "for thirty-seven dollars, and the price of breakfast is additional. The emerald is slightly more. Fifty-three. But with complimentary tea and biscuits." She turns the notebook in Lory's direction.

The notebook not only has tags and sections, but photographs of each room. Lory pauses, stares at one room. In rolling script: *Lapis.* The bedspread is vibrant blue and a dark blue rug is on a tiled floor crisscrossed with lighter shades. The room descriptions lists hues. *Lavender. Turquoise. Ice.* Even the walls are cloudy blue, even more so with the pixilated computer print-out. Blue swims in front of her, one vibrant color that reminds her of lake water.

A small stone set in one side of the woman's nose sparkles. "What is your pleasure," she asks, as if she expects a firm answer. She is not impatient, but she taps a page depicting the emerald room. "Slightly more," she says. "But worth it, for the heart."

"The heart?" Lory asks.

"Green," the woman says. "The color of emotion."

Lory feels like laughing. She recalls a chat room she entered once, one called *Chakras and Choctaws: The Native Way to the Spirit*. Discussions recommended rituals, sweat lodges, sage burning, drumming. The goal? To reach an understanding of various spiritual centers in the body, each of which was assigned a certain color. *I saw the spirit of my dead aunt once*, a man wrote her. *It was the color of spilled oil.*

"Green," the woman says again. "For the cave that is the chest and the chest that holds the heart." She places her hand over her own chest, meets Lory's glance with her dark eyes. "Your heart," the woman says. "So tired."

Lory counts the money in her wallet. She wonders about other motels on the strip, imagines the road outside, the hum of late-night traffic. She thinks of The Red Bird and sighs. Emerald it is.

Her stomach is rumbling so she stops at a vending machine for snacks. Along with nuts and crackers, there are other choices in brightly colored packs with Hindi names: bags of curried and roasted chickpeas, dried papaya, and something called black pepper pappad. She chooses these, which are spicy and slightly stale wafers, but she is hungry, and she munches on them as she finds her way down a path behind the main building, to a longish building where she sees one or two windows lit. The blinds are gold and deep orange with lamplight and she can just see her own room's sign, a metal plate on the door. *Emerald. Number Two.* The room key is actually a key in the true sense, an antique one on a ring, and she has to try the lock twice as she shivers in the mountain night.

The room is at least five or six hues of green. She sets down her pack, lies back on the bed, her shoes still on. Her shoes. High-tops, are themselves what used to be Kelly green. Other names for green? *Olive. Khaki. Pea.* She stretches out across the bed's checked spread, turns down the mint sheets, feels for the television remote in the bedside table. For ten years she has lived in a motel room, has had solitude and had time for thinking. She fights an urge to go back to the registration desk, ask them if she can check her e-mail, even for a fee.

She wants nothing from this evening but rest. Or old reruns. *My Favorite Martian* or a fifties sci-fi film about sea creatures various and green. What she finds, when she settles back against the pillows with the last of her black pepper pappad, is a blank screen that shimmers with a color that is, unquestionably, emerald. *Emerald Cities. Deep green pants suit with bell bottoms her mother used to wear.* She presses buttons on the control, but the screen stays blank and green, then condenses to a flat, emerald box which expands again to a face—the older woman in the photograph behind the registration desk. She is now wearing a fashionable green sari and she smiles and folds her hands. *Namaste,* she says. *Be at peace.* There are no other channels. *Imagine,* the woman says, *an image of the sun behind your eyes.* Imagine the sun, a wheel of light that turns and pauses, pauses and turns. This is the wheel of time, the cycle of order and balance in the mind of God. Balance and God, Lory thinks, have become an oxymoron.

She'd seen God often enough, with Sam. In New York, an ordinary man in a business suit had teeth filed to small, sharp points, and he held a sign that read, *God Is Not Only Dead, He Isn't Even a Memory.* In Paris, she'd stood with him at the Basilica of Sacre Coeur, listening to a litany. It was noon and they looked up to the top of the basilica. Light, blue and deep red from the stained windows on each side of the nave, filtered onto her face and on Sam's. *Deliver us from darkness, Blessed Mother,* the nuns sang, and she stared up at the Mother, her dead son in her arms. In New Delhi, they'd gone in a booth that sold colorful puppets that danced and played brass horns and they'd never seen anything so delightful. But a sadhu had peered through the curtain that led to the street. He demanded baksheesh, his hand with a knife through its wrist, the wound clean and bloodless. *Such*, he said, *is the price of enlightenment.* Since then, she's questioned the price of God many times. She's surfed the Web with her questions about the divine, found everything from whygodwhy.org to a site that reads, *Hi! I'm God. How Are You? Get Out of My Way!*

The televised woman says there are seven vital centers, divinely planned doorways through which the soul has descended into the body and through which it may ascend by a process of meditation. The woman's black eyes study her, her plain face adorned only by her red bindi. When all the chakras are whirling, the woman says, when they are open, bright and clean, then our system is attuned to God. Lory places her hands on the base of her spine. What the television screen and this woman could never know is that this journey is planned already, has been planned for years. Lory Llewellyn can close her eyes and follow the chakras by a map already written on her skin. A map of scars.

At her spine's beginning, she feels a delicate zigzag. An ordinary scar from childhood, a fall on a sidewalk or a slide down a tree. It's a scar she doesn't remember with particular intimacy. But this chakra, the televised voice says, governs our physical existence, our bodies and our health.

The second chakra, near the womb, is one she knows much better. On a snowy afternoon after she'd lost her virginity, a college professor told her light was nothing remarkable, really, when it could be perceived by the mere human eye. She drew the longest cut on her body yet, a shallow line across her abdomen, and she felt such tremulous power with the flow of her own blood. *A painting on a cave wall.*

Her hands travel through other chakras, along the ridges and planes of other scars. The third chakra, the solar plexus. Fourth chakra, her heart. *The chest*, the woman says, *is the seat of love, tenderness, compassion and honesty and its designated color is green.* Lory holds her hand closer against her heart, and thinks of a lush, green place she'd visited with Sam. India? Thailand? A rainforest. A trail leading to a waterfall where they bathed in water so cold she ached.

The scar at her throat is tiny. A rosebud. A miniscule leaf. This chakra represents human will, the television says. At the site of her sixth chakra, her third eye, there is no scar at all, though she has imagined one, a rakish tilting scar, a third eyebrow, a pale gray thread leading upward, vanishing into her hairline where there is the last chakra, the seventh. This, the television says, is the connection to our higher selves. Wisdom. Integration of our eternal selves with our current physical selves. *Our umbilical cord to "God."* She touches this last chakra, this last unhealed wound now. She thinks of the way Sam Sanderson looked when he was sleeping. The taste of his mouth, first thing, when he woke. If he touched her now, he could follow the maps of scars here, there, could come to rest. *Here. Just here.* Now the woman is talking of the condition of the modern heart. *The shutting off of one or another center of the self*, the woman is saying, *is a spiritual condition which must be addressed.*

Lory Llewellyn lies touching herself and she knows this is a cliché, a woman alone thinking of lying in her lover's arms. She is a woman in love with a long dead man, one who might be swimming right now in water as blue as this light. *We have forgotten*, the woman says, *the map to our own hearts.*

Certain Facts about Light

No-good lying dog. That was what her mother called her father the year of the disastrous climb at Grandfather Mountain. He took off soon after that, leaving only a note that said nothing about where he was going or when he'd return. They kept his picture in a frame on the kitchen shelf, but it soon receded into a foreground of bottles of cologne and soda pop and cheap, sweet wine. Her mother started coming home later and later, her lunch-counter uniform smelling like oils and salt. One afternoon her mother came home and found Lory in the way-back of the yard, lying beneath a tree in a fresh pile of leaves. She was waiting for rain, she could have said, but her mother bent over, shaking her free of the good-smelling fall leaves. *Just like your daddy*, her mother said, yanking her up. *Leave you to your own self, and no telling where you'll end up.* Her mother's eyes were wild and shiny, those of a stranger who wandered in by mistake and who would soon leave again.

One night, she woke with the phone ringing and her mother saying, *Honey, you be good now, until I get home.* Her mother liked cokes with cherry syrup and no ice, but ice now clinked into some glass and she was laughing, *You're big enough to stay by yourself, anyway, aren't you?* Lory felt her way down the trailer hall with all the lights still off, felt her way outside into the yard where stinging drops of rain fell. *My good girl*, her mother had said, humming some juke box song. When it rained the trailer park smelled like rust. Water, dank with winter, trickled through the bare branches of trees. *Awe?* She was merely cold.

That autumn her mother married a traveling man who sold everything from cosmetics to antifreeze. He liked to diversify, he told them, and brought her mother samples of facial cleanser some weeks and miracle laundry soap the next. He was from Inez, a little town in the mountains of Kentucky, though lately he lived in a city where you could really shake your behind. He was ready to follow the sunset. For the wedding party, they decorated the trailer with balloons and outlined the word *love* in the back yard with small paper bags filled with sand and lit candles. While the rest of them danced to country-western until the wee hours, she sat in the yard near one of the sand candles, her hand held above the flame. *Luminous*. She turned her hand back and over, trying to see through to the bones.

Following the wedding, she filled her room with so many candles in so many leftover wine bottles that her mother laughed, at first, and said she'd help them cut back on the fuel oil bills. She experimented with light, with wires and radio batteries or magnifying glasses and sunlight, and her new father gave her names like *girl genius*. She liked the way he said this, and the way he wore cowboy boots that clicked on the porch steps. He listened to big band records and danced with her and her mother. He called both of them fine little ladies and swung them around and around until Lory saw stars.

Later, experiments annoyed them. Her mother, who had taken to planting the back yard with neat groups of marigolds and pruning the water sprouts from the trees, complained when she left circles of ash and charred wood from late-night fires. *You're about to burn up the whole damn planet,* they said. And her stepfather complained that too much reading, the books about electricity and weather, wasn't good for you. He took the books from her and shut them with a snap, turned his records up high. His hand reached beneath the covers one night when she had fallen asleep reading. She could hear him breathing in the dark. *Are you awake?* he asked. *Are you awake?*

They moved to a city near the ocean to be closer to her stepfather's sales office. They lived in a hotel that rented by the week, but she loved the beach in the afternoons after school. At dusk, she ran for miles along the shoreline, but even with the crash of waves and the gathering of storms on the horizon, she often felt as if she were standing as still as an animal caught in headlights.

One particular night, her mother was working and her stepfather offered to buy the two of them dinner near the beach. *We don't get enough time,* he said, *just you and me.* He drove them in his company car, a black sedan with a hula-girl air freshener fastened to the rearview mirror, and they ate at an open-air seafood hut where they served crabs, the first time she had them. Her stepfather wanted scotch and soda, but draft beer was what they served, in a frosty mug he laid against her bare arm. He fed her sips on the sly while the two of them tossed bread scraps and crab shells from the deck to the gulls. By the time they finished three beers, she found herself liking the tic in his left eye, something that always unnerved her before.

After dinner they walked to the beach for snow cones. The huge sun was on its way down to the ocean, the day balanced between light and night-time. Couples walked dogs and children. Evening bathers from nearby cottages and joggers all passed them and soon they were alone on a strip of shore down from a large dune. Her stepfather sat on a piece of driftwood, stripped off his loafers and socks, and she stopped too, took her sandals off and scrunched her toes in the cooling sand. The clear sky was softening from brilliant blue to rose. A fierce red spread from the horizon to the shore as the sun set, leaving the sky lit by the city in the distance and the electric light above the dunes.

They watched fishing boats cruise the horizon with their searchlights. Her stepfather lit a cigarette, tossed his match toward the surf. He offered her a taste, an acrid smoke that set her coughing. He grabbed her hand then and they walked to the edge of the water, crouched on their ankles. *Look,* he said.

He raked his hand back and forth across the sand as the waves receded. At the edge of water, moist sand shone with pinpoints of light. *Phosphorescence. And you and me, we're freeing them up, right now.* He, who she had previously known only for his briefcases and his sample bags of Evening in Paris and White Shoulders, now ran with her along a strip of glittering sand beside the ocean.

The tide freed trails of light along the sand where their bare feet skimmed the surface of shining water. She forgot she ever lived with him and her mother in a hotel room with thin walls, forgot everything but how enormous the sky seemed when she threw her head back and looked at the stars, reciting to herself the only two constellations she knew. *Orion. The Seven Sisters.* He drew her to him, his cold tongue pushing hard against her teeth. *Hey, what the hell's the matter with you?* He called after her as she ran in the direction of home.

She prayed some nights, after her stepfather's kiss, but she never saw the power of lightning again. Instead, her mother grew more and more suspicious of the shortness of her skirts and the curliness of her hair, of the way her breasts grew. *Perky*, she said. *Good for nothing but one thing, and you and me both know what that is.* Lightning, the sky, the ocean, all of them could be held out in the palm of God's hand, but what did she have in the end? When she walked along the beach after that afternoon, she thought of the taste of her stepfather's mouth, looked at the ocean and wondered what it was she couldn't see beneath the waves and the flat horizon. Lightning was nothing but the scent of rust.

She was sixteen when her mother took to looking at her critically. *You wouldn't have caught me dead in that get-up when I was your age,* she said when Lory wore a halter top or shorts her junior year of high school. By then, her mother worked most nights serving drinks at La Petite Femme where she had invented a new name for herself, *Monique*. Her mother's hair was bleach-blonde and the bright blue contacts she bought gave her the same frightened stare as one of the plastic dolls they gave away at a beach carnival.

Lory finished high school, working all the while at discount stores and diners. *Do everything you can for a person and then they drop you like a hot rock*, her stepfather said when she came in late from a night shift. Her mother often spent whole nights now at *La Petite Femme* and her stepfather, whose business had slipped considerably, sipped Scotch and waited in their moldy basement apartment. *Think you're too good to associate with the rest of us*, he said to no one in particular. She saved her money, some of it in a Mason jar she buried underneath the porch and some of it in a hundred dollars worth of stocks she picked at the bank, a protection against the future she told herself. And it paid off. By the fall of her eighteenth year she was on her way to a state-supported college where she planned to study the growing field of computer technology and to never go home again.

On the first day of a class called Physical Science the professor entered carrying his tabletop podium, one shoe unlaced. While he stood at the window and stared down at the campus lawn, she took notes about constellations and found herself sketching his profile—a white-haired man with near-sighted eyes she would later hear him say were cerulean. He talked with them about luminous displays. *Auroras,* he said, *are rapidly shifting patches and dancing columns of light, seen most often in polar regions when charged particles from the sun interact with gases in the earth's atmosphere.* He showed them slides, one day of an aurora outside of Fairbanks, Alaska. Other days they were of more ordinary things catching light—a stone in a riverbed, a lightning bug at night. *A firefly,* he told them, *produces a chemical called luciferin that reacts with oxygen to create light.* And lightning? *It originates 15,000 to 25,000 feet above sea level when raindrops are carried upward and sometimes converted to ice.* Her notebook soon filled with facts and figures and the margins were ornate with his initials, drawn in script and laced with lightning bolts.

As fall turned to winter, the number of students in the class dwindled and many who stayed slept while the professor charted graphs on the board for the light curve of a variable star. The classroom grew close with the hissing radiator heat, but it was then that she began to find him fascinating. *Ms. Llewellyn,* he would ask. *Can you define for us a wavelength?* Or, *Ms. Llewellyn. Can you review for us the final thoughts in last week's discussion of frequencies?*

Eight weeks of a twelve-week semester were spent exploring what he called *The Story of Light.* Incandescence and luminescence. Refraction and reflection. *The speed of light,* he told them, *was calculated in 1983 as 299,792,458 meters per second.* They heard about ultraviolet photography and photochemistry, about photosynthesis and the photoelectric effect. *Bodies,* he said, *which do not themselves emit light are seen by the light they transmit or reflect.* She ordered his book, *Attenuated Shadows: Illuminating Phenomena,* traced the glossy pages of the book and its numerous diagrams with her fingers and felt oddly hopeful.

One afternoon, even though it was snowing and classes were canceled, she waited outside his office with a rough draft of her term paper, an essay she called "Mysterious Presence: An Ordinary Girl Encounters the God of Light." Half an hour past the scheduled conference time, she sat nervously across from him at his desk while he read what she'd written. His office smelled pleasantly of cherry tobacco and sweat.

Before he marked her essay, he heated water for tea. She savored the sweet, black taste as she sat in a chair beside his and watched his hands. His hands were soft-looking, with a map of blue and green veins across their tops. He marked her sentences, the misuse of commas, the inaccurate use of phrases. *Reverential awe. Don't just tell me this or this, Ms. Llewellyn,* he said, bracketing paragraphs for her elaboration. His face, she was surprised to see as she watched his expressions of interest or confusion, was pink and as smooth as a child's, and she stopped herself just as she was ready to reach out, pull away a tiny square of tissue marked with blood at the corner of his mouth. *Show me,* he said, motioning her closer as he underlined her inclusion of words like *God* or *sacred space.* There was a part of the brain, he said, that registered moments when sunlight seemed holy, and another part for translating such moments into pure feeling. But it was her job, he said, to find the correct terminology. To correctly translate experience into fact.

Dry snow gathered at the windowpanes when he tapped the final page with his red pen. As he heated more water for tea, she searched for words to describe the sacred. *It's the way light strikes your fingers as you write. It's the way you hold a pen.* She told him about that day on top of a mountain and the sphere of lightning that touched her. He told her about the less scientific but profound ways he too had come to know light. *When I was a child,* he said, *my mother hung prisms in my window.* He watched wavelengths traverse the length of the bedroom wall, and he measured them with his bare hands. *White light from the sun,* he said, *is made up of all the visible wavelengths of radiation.*

In her memory it was she who touched him, she who held him, afterward, her neck stiff against the arm of his tweed couch. Years later, she remembered him as ridiculous, his pants down around his socked feet. His eyes, without their thick glasses, were watery and much less blue. *Sweet light of Jesus and Mary!* He'd said that as there was the quick intake of breath in her ear. Nevertheless, near Christmas break, by the time they had met in his office a dozen times, she believed not so much that she was in love, but that she had at last found another person touched by light.

For weeks nine and ten and eleven of that semester, he was her lover. After all, he knew every definition, every machination of light. *Illumination. Radiance.* They made love in the afternoon once, with every light on and sunlight through the windows. She saw for the first time how old he was, the spider veins next to his nose, the yellowed incisor that poked out when he smiled. His skin was papery, thinner and thinner in her imaginings of him when she left his office. *Sweet light of Jesus, of Mary,* he said again and again in her ear. The afternoons turned darker as winter peaked and she wondered what it was that her own body felt. *Nothing. Nothing.* He was married, a rambling has-been. None of that mattered, but still her pleasure receded, a scent turned to old socks and stale smoke.

She went home for Christmas to Inez, the little Kentucky town they now called home. Her stepfather's job was gone due to a poor sales season and her mother was at work in one more diner. *You don't come from nothing but a hole in the road,* her mother said and paced while her stepfather drank at the kitchen table. *And now you've gone and drug me in there with you.* She went over for the thousandth time all the places she could have seen, the things she could have done if she hadn't had to hide herself away in a trailer park, raising a daughter all by her lonesome.

At night, during those weeks of Christmas break, Lory stayed up late and read and reread her notes on the definition of light. *An electromagnetic radiation in the wavelength range including infrared, visible, ultraviolet, and X rays and traveling in a vacuum with a speed of about 186, 281 miles per second.* Was that the truth? In her memory, light came in shivering fragments. What did they tell her in Introduction to Philosophy? *To be meaningful, statements about the world must be reducible to the simple facts. Metaphysical, theological, and ethical sentences are factually meaningless.* Fact. *Light is followed by dark.* Fact. *The absence of light is dark.* Fact?

And color? There were only three basic colors in the spectrum—red, green, blue—but any color was possible, given the right addition or subtraction. All the primary colors at once meant black, whereas the addition of mere light from these same colors meant white. How white it felt, the pure electricity on her skin, that night of the mountain and lightning. What she will know is this: there was one brilliant moment in her past and now, try as she might, the time in between had vanished.

Janus

By the time Lory graduated, her mother had saved enough money from tips and whatever back in Inez to open a motel. A family-run place, she said, hinting that with Lory's college education she would be perfect for keeping records and paying and putting off the bills. *And him,* her mother said. Her stepfather had grown thinner and wore sleeveless undershirts around the house so they could see his skin, yellowish and hanging loosely from his bones. *Well,* her mother said, *he hadn't been much to write home about, but she thought he could change a sheet or two.*

Her mother's waitress uniforms and her stepfather's scotch were becoming selective memory. Even her memory of lightning was less clear now, and she sometimes doubted she had ever experienced true brilliance. A syllogism. *Part One.* Light is often brilliant. *Part Two.* Brilliance is sometimes disappointing. *Part Three.* If brilliance was disappointing, therefore *what?*

She worked that last year in college, everything from a night checker at a grocery mart to a morning newspaper route and she'd pawned things she didn't need, a wristwatch her stepfather gave her for graduation, a necklace made of fake pearls her mother had given her for her sixteenth birthday. At the last minute, she sold the telescope too, the one she herself had bought with Top Value stamps. *See the stars*, the catalogue had said. *Each and every one of them.* Now she'd have to depend on the naked eye for all those long imagined meteor showers in the desert by night. She'd have to find out for herself that stars and planets looked the same, a thousand miles away from where you started. She bought a ninety-nine dollar Greyhound ticket to the west coast, one way.

Those first 500 miles from North Carolina to Conway, Arkansas, the highway unfolded like a black armband undone. She wanted to feel something for the family she left behind, her mother and the stepfather and the memory of her real father, but it rained and as it rained she drank vending machine coffee at every concession stand for five stops running. With each rest stop, a part of her stayed behind and the part of her here, now, counted road signs and miles to the next town. *Winslow, Arizona. Winslow and Meteor Crater and Flagstaff.* She stayed awake for the next 500 miles, a song replaying in her memory. *Standing on a corner in Winslow, Arizona, such a fine sight to see.* The bus hummed with voices.

Midafternoon. Oklahoma. At a bus stop near Oral Robert's praying hands, a working-class family of six got on. There was a mother and a father, a grandmother and children and bags and baskets and a crying baby and, at dusk, they offered her peeled beet-colored boiled eggs and a red-hot sauce in a dish to dip them in. The father, in a language half music and half English, told her a story about Vietnam, about all of them walking, an evacuation of some sort, and a child, their second, being born in a ditch full of water beside a road. He'd studied to be a medical doctor. The kind of doctor who could fix hearts.

"Then the world blew up," he said. He held out his thin hands and arms to show her the size of the disaster that had befallen his family, smiled with his flat, black teeth. His hands were as beautiful, her mother used to say, as someone who could play piano in the dark.

Morning and New Mexico and the desert surrounded all of them, the two soldiers beside her, in front of her an elderly couple with cameras and shorts and cheap, flowery shirts. She'd imagined the desert, the one in cowboy movies with parched dirt and thirst, but this wasn't like anything except the ocean at sunrise. Red desert earth and clouds, fat and perfect, their shadows following the bus. Tumbleweed alive and drifting across asphalt hot to the touch. Her boots stuck to it when she stood outside for a smoke.

At dark, her head against an armrest, legs and arms folded, she stretched out in two seats all her own. When she woke there was heat lightning in the distance, and she could see all of it, sky to earth, the storm still maybe a hundred miles away. Was that moment a sign? *He came with lightning, as brilliant as night and the desert.* She wrote this as a poem in her notebook after he got on at that next stop. He was not necessarily attractive and she liked that. Nothing about him was ordered from a catalogue for travelers—no Gore-Tex boots or travel guide in an all-weather vest pocket, just a beat-up canvas backpack. When he bent to tie his laces, his hair, a nothing color between gold and silver, shone in the bus lights.

She folded her jacket, leaned against the window while he settled into the empty seat beside her, his pack under the seat, a book jammed full of papers wedged between them. He took out a fistful of papers and an ink pen.

"Bus seats," he mumbled and she studied him out of half-closed eyes. "Only two sitting positions known to a human being."

He moved his knees to the left, right, leaned into the aisle armrest so that his hip lodged against her side. The book's spine dug into her thigh and she picked it up. *This is Your Brain on God* was the title, just visible in the light from the aisle. She thumbed through drawings of monks seated around a sand painting.

"Just how," she asked, "do we recognize a brain on God?"

He was asleep, that quickly, and she glanced at him again, the back and forward movement of his eyes. She studied diagrams of the brains of animals she didn't recognize, glanced at a sketch of a pyramid with an eye and meticulous arrows pointing up until she, too, drifted into sleep.

The next rest stop, a parking lot and a tourist center, was for Death Valley. The center was locked tight, so she headed off into the cottonwood trees and picnic tables. Headlights shone on the highway and lightning was closer now, illuminating large rain-filled clouds.

"Resonance."

The voice startled her and she stepped back, peered into the trees.

"I love how lightning resonates." Her seatmate from the bus moved out of the shadows.

"It does." She stood some distance from the table. "From the thunder."

"I love how it resonates inside you." He stretched his legs and leaned back, looking up at the sky.

She sat on the opposite side of the table.

"The lightning," he said. A web of light spread across the sky, then vanished. "It reminds me of words." He took out a cigarette, lit it, dipped the match in sand.

She'd not noticed it before, the pocket of his denim shirt, embroidered with pale yellow and white eyes of God. "Isn't lightning no words at all?"

He was thin and small looking against each flash. "It's nothing at all. Like words, or most of them."

"What's your favorite word?" She leaned on her arms on the damp table.

"Lately?"

He offered her a cigarette, held out a lit match. "Brittle," he said at last. It means both *delicate* and *easily broken*."

"I love how words do that." She savored the word. "Mean two things, and almost one thing, all at once."

There was thunder this time, and this time a snap and a streak of fire as a not too distant tree was struck. A few drops of warm rain now fell.

She studied him, the small drops of rain in his hair.

She rubbed her hands up and down her arms. She was cold in the wind that had risen with the rain. "Here," he said. "Take this." He stood, took off his jacket, handed it to her.

In the distance, buses honked and they ran back to the line full of passengers, damp and wired on caffeine and middle-of-the-night conversation. She thought of a phrase from a movie, a book whose name she couldn't recall. *Time in between.* He took Kleenexes from his pack and blotted rain from her hair, and she was surprised by how easily she let him do this.

As the bus rolled west, he told her about how he wanted to travel the world, go to India and farther than that, to a temple devoted to Kali where he'd ask a blessing for his own mother's soul. He told her about how he had tried but failed to believe in God.

"Aren't these eyes God?" She traced the design on his jacket.

"Decoration," he said. "New Age finery."

"I don't believe you."

"You know me well enough? To believe or not?"

She slipped the jacket off, laid it over her lap. "Not exactly."

"What does that mean?"

"I do feel," she paused. "That I recognize you somehow."

He too, traced the embroidered pattern on the jacket. "That's a cliché, isn't it?"

She told him about her history of light, about Grandfather Mountain and lightning. They sat next to each other, their heads touching, their eyes closed, yet she realized that after this one long night she still hadn't asked his name. *Sam*, he told her, and she liked the way those three letters felt in her mouth, the way she fell so easily into his company, easily enough to ride all the way to the coast together.

As he slept, she studied his face in the bus-light. The one side of it, even in his sleep, smiled almost sardonically while the other half was slack-muscled and gentle. Later, he'd tell her about the chemistry of Bell's Palsy, how it was simple really, a viral infection that damages or destroys the facial nerve. He'd tell her that there was a treatment. A mere beam of light could make him just like anyone else. He'd draw for her the many-branched nerve, its course from brain to face, and tell her how he preferred himself this way. A reminder, he'd say, of the duality of this world. On the bus that night, she thought of Janus. The God of two faces looking in opposite directions. God of doors and gateways, of beginnings.

The next day they stepped off into a crowded LA terminal and she went with him, the first city bus to take them to the ocean. They pooled their sleeping bags and Swedish cook stove, snack mix and a cheap bottle of wine, and camped on the shore. The near full moon gave them enough light to climb down a path leading from a precipice, past fallen trees and boulders, to reach a stretch of smooth sand far enough back from the water. The surf was wilder here than she had seen before and they listened to it roll forward and recede. The ocean was like a mural he'd seen once, one glowing haze of color.

He described other sacred places, ones he had seen or wanted to see. Sunrise from the back of a van on the way to see the town where Einstein was born. Mountains. Holy rivers. The ruins of temples and the dust of pilgrim's bones. Sacre Coeur and the voices of holy sisters raised in supplication. *Varanasi*. Light settling on the water at the bathing ghats. Bones at a temple in the heights of the Himalayas. God existed, he was sure, but only in the borderlands.

These were the places he wanted. *Vortices*. Wind on a deserted street, how it could gather up the least thing. The pages of a book in your lap. A crumpled piece of paper from a notebook. The world gathering to a center. As they lay on their unzipped sleeping bags, she held her breath, alert to each shift of his arms.

141

Listen, he said. The ocean was quieter now, with the changing of the tides. That stillness, he said, could be the center, the calm in the centrifugal motion of a vortex. I want to ride that down, he said. *The edge of the still point.* Gulls called out in the night and mosquitoes circled and the ocean grew darker. *Sam Sanderson,* she said as they fell asleep. *Tell me who you are.*

Chapter Seven

Sunlight is what makes life possible by fueling photosynthesis, and sunlight can penetrate only the first few hundred yards of the ocean's great depths. Lower, a few creatures might still eke out a living by scrounging the organic detritus that drifts down from the surface of the sea. But thousands of feet down, in the utter blackness at the ocean's bottom, there could be practically nothing.

—The Light at the Bottom of the Sea

A Film Interlude

Sanderson stopped for a day, then two, in Hendersonville at his sister's house and that was where he stood now, in her front hallway, listening. From the back yard the dog barked and moaned. The house was too orderly for his own visit, no less for a dog to rampage through. Even the collections of photographs with mats to match the wallpaper were arranged chronologically.

There was one section of very old photos, some of them daguerreotypes. His great-grandparents on his mother's and father's sides. His grandmother, standing in a dirt yard, holding a guinea hen under one arm. A building, almost a lean-to, that he recognized as the one-room schoolhouse his grandfather attended. And his grandfather himself, stern-looking in a wool suit and suspenders, on the steps of some clapboard church. Someone scrawled a phrase at the bottom of this photo. *Bringing the Lord to West Virginia and Kentucky.* His grandfather's strong hands held a Bible skyward.

There was also Sanderson's own, more recent history. Just back from the service, in a uniform that made him look stout. With Sarah, right after their marriage. And Sam in a blow-up swimming pool with Sarah wading after him, her arms bare and strong in a bandana halter-top. Sam in a variety of posed photographs, everything from junior high-school graduation to the high-school swimming team. The most recent photo was taken at the reception after Sarah's funeral. Sam was jammed into a suit and tie, blonde-headed from the months they spent at the ocean, before Sarah died. He was fourteen, but with his crooked face and his grief, he looked older, angry with whoever was taking his picture. Sanderson was uncomfortably certain it had been himself. *Do you think she'd have wanted it like this?* Sam meant the church full of lilies and a service right out of a hymnal. No, Sanderson thought now, Sarah wouldn't have wanted it like that at all.

"He was a fine boy, Jason," Janet said. He hadn't noticed she was in the hallway until she patted him on the shoulder. His sister, Sanderson thought, had always been, in moments of emotion, a patter.

"Sometimes I think he still is," Sanderson paused. "Fine, I mean. That he's just hidden somewhere, and that he'll show up one Saturday afternoon and offer to show us slides of the world."

His sister leaned in, kissed him on the cheek, and Sanderson caught a scent he thought he recognized. Vanilla? Or something his mother used to wear. *Midnight Allure.*

"How long can you stay, sweetie? We haven't even talked about your plans."

"I'm thinking about driving up near Boone," he said. "Tomorrow morning. A little road trip to where we used to go, when we were kids."

"August," Janet said. She looped her arm through his. "A good time to head for the hills." They stood together, studying the photographs, and Janet reached out, flicked a speck of dust from the photograph of Sam.

"You've done real good, Jason," she said. "And you'd be doing even better if you'd give that Rosa a call."

Sanderson hadn't phoned Rosa since he left home. He'd thought about it every few minutes, but what had she said? *I feel like I'm floating. Between the past and the future.* Both of them needed, he thought, to come to earth. "I'll call her," he promised. "This evening. No later."

"And in the meantime," Janet said, leading him toward the breakfast nook, "we've still got plenty to catch up on, you and I."

Breakfast nook. Household office. Family room. Every room in the house came with a noun and adjective. And there were small notes affixed to this and that. *Watch inner lining on shower curtain, with two dots and a loop for a smile. Pillow shams on top, small pillows underneath.* Directions for what should be done if one found one's self alone in a given room for too long. *Books on shelf. Tape in deck.*

He arrived at nearly five the first day, much to Janet's surprise. Tom will be so disappointed, she said, after she quizzed him about Rosa and he said something evasive about a trip Rosa had planned with just the girls, and about a little trip back home, just for himself. But what good luck after all, that Tom, Sanderson's brother-in-law, was out of town at a conference. There would be more time for the two of them. Time? Sanderson walked the dog at eight. She had tai chi at nine. There'd been a trip to a wine shop and a specialty food store, ten to eleven. Lunch at the club at twelve. Golf at two. More dog walking, then drinks before dinner. After dinner, at a Chinese restaurant, with four of Janet's real estate office cohorts, he escaped to his room, exhausted, where he skimmed some pages for today's film discussion group. *How to Read a Film,* the book was called. *Be aware,* the book told him, *of the truth of even the most ordinary details.* Or was that his fortune cookie?

In the breakfast nook, he sipped coffee while Janet buttered croissants at the counter with one hand and answered phone calls with the other. *Janet.* He could hardly believe she was his sister, nor that he had seen her only, what was it, three times in the last ten years. Each visit seemed memorable to him because of the enormity of the circumstances, and because of Janet's hair color. When she'd come to be with him, after Sam was reported missing, her hair was a red he remembered as fiery. And when she and Tom had come to the back yard party that Rosa had put together a couple of months after their wedding, Janet's hair was a startling blonde. Janet seemed to take an immediate and distinct dislike to Rosa, as if she could read between the lines and uncover all she needed to know about background, country store and county roads included, when Rosa played Hank Williams and "Hey Good Lookin'" and danced Sanderson around the yard beneath the bug lights. *Your hair's as pretty as honey on toast,* Rosa had called out to Janet. These days, Janet's hair was a polished silver, with bruised-looking undertones of lavender.

"You never did watch your waistline, did you, Jay?" Janet said as she watched him stir three spoons of sugar and a generous dollop of cream into his second cup of coffee.

Jay. He hadn't been called that in years, or by anyone, ever, really, except his mother and Janet. "I'd almost forgotten you used to call me that," he said.

Janet smiled and sat across from him with the plate of croissants. "You're looking more like Daddy, every day."

"Frederick Rosemont Sanderson," Sanderson said as he pushed back the lapels of an imaginary jacket and looped his fingers through imaginary suspenders. Their father, soft belly and all, had been a dresser, right up until the final days of his seventy-second year, when he died in his office at the Hendersonville Bank and Trust.

"You're more like him than you know." Janet stirred a spoonful of cream into her own coffee and studied him. "In more ways than one."

"What do you mean?" Sanderson asked. He scooped jam onto his croissant and then winced as he took his first bite. Unsweetened. The healthier variety.

"Oh, your profile, for one." Janet held out her hands in two triangles, like an artist, and studied his face. "Same Roman nose."

"I guess that's something to be proud of?"

"Same pig-headedness," she said, looking, this time, down the tunnel of her two hands, like a telescope.

"I beg your pardon?"

"I called Rosa, you know," Janet said suddenly. "Last night, late."

He'd seen Janet having a hushed phone conversation with someone he later suspected was Rosa, but still he was annoyed. "You did what?"

"Just a brief call. To check in."

"Thanks for checking in with me first," he said. He pushed his plate back, drained his cup.

"Honey, you hold onto things, just like Daddy did," Janet said. She reached across the table, laid her hand on his. "I'd bet you my last five cents that you've got Sarah's picture in your wallet, right alongside Rosa's."

Sanderson went for a third cup of coffee, even though, already, he felt his heart flutter. He'd lie down later, he told himself. Rest for a spell. *Center himself*. Isn't that what they called it in the tai chi class? He did have Sarah's picture in his wallet—she had daisies tucked behind each ear, and she was so young, she was like someone he'd never met.

"I loved Sarah," he said.

"And I loved Daddy," Janet said. "And Mother, too. And I'll love Tom, right up to the time one of us is nothing but earth and dust. But we have to lay the dead to rest sometime, sweetie." She laid her hands flat on the table, leaned toward him when he sat down again with the coffee cup. "And that means Sam, too, you know."

Sanderson spooned sugar into more. This cup was so sweet and hot it burned in his throat, but he took a long swallow. "What do you know," he said before he meant to, "about having to forget your only son?"

Janet bowed her head and sat staring at her hands.

Sanderson sat staring at his almost empty cup and the configuration of sugar and coffee grounds in the bottom. *Fortunes*.

"Do you remember," he asked her suddenly. "The way we used to look for fortunes?"

"Fortunes?"

"You know. Dropping the Bible to whatever page or verse. Seeing what it'd tell us to do."

"I do," she said. "I remember that."

"There was a time you were in love, or thought you were. That Dillard boy in tenth grade. You must've dropped that Bible ten hundred times."

"I'd forgotten him."

"And then there was the time we snuck off up to that woman who read photographs. Up near Burnsville."

"That fat lady? The one in the trailer?"

"Her," Sanderson said. "She said you were bound for higher places."

"Higher places." Janet laughed. "All this time later, and here I am, still in the mountains."

"Maybe that's what we should do now. Find us a fortune teller or two."

"Why's that?"

"I guess everyone but me," he said, "knows the best way toward my future."

"The best way?" Janet asked. She didn't look at him.

Outside, the dog howled again and he imagined her, the long black muzzle raised to the sky with her urgency.

The afternoon film group did not meet, as he had expected, in some conference room at the local public library. Instead, they drove the distance over to Asheville and he found himself walking up streets he recognized and in a bookstore he knew so well he looked for Sarah behind the counter in the cafe. Even Sarah, he believed, would have been startled by the tattoos of tropical birds and the lush green hair of the waitress who served him. Since morning, his heart had raced and settled, but he ordered cappuccino, since Janet was having that. *Go with the day.* He ordered a low-fat muffin.

"This place doesn't seem like your deal," he said to Janet as they made their way downstairs, to the room where the film would be shown.

Her white hair was back in a French braid, and she wore a black linen jacket. She looked immaculate and as much like a visitor in the store as he did. "The selection is excellent," she said. Under her arm, he glimpsed her day's purchase. *Selected Poems of W.B. Yeats.* He left her looking at *Cooking with the Herbs of Southern France* while he looked at a display where a sign with neat calligraphy read, *Harmonic Convergence: Order is Emerging Out of Chaos.*

The display was laden with guides to the solar system, planetary maps and *Songs,* a CD case read, *for Astral Observations.* There were biographies of Copernicus, studies of the predictions of Nostradamus. Near those was a book called *Love, Joy, Bliss,* which was full elaborate Maori paintings of spirals in ordinary natural objects like shells and unfurling leaves. He flipped forward more to a chapter called "Soul, Mind, Body" and read a few lines here and there. *The process of identifying with all three of these phenomena, along with other spiritual practices, ultimately leads to an identification with the soul as the Essential Self.* His head spun and he put the book down. A local newsletter described a gathering of possibly a thousand people for the upcoming ten-year anniversary of, the headline read, *Convergence: Let's Align What's Out of Phase.* The gathering would be the largest in this part of the state since the first celebration. *August 16th.* He glanced at his wristwatch. It was already the eve of the Harmonic Convergence.

"You ready, Jay?" Janet peered over his shoulder. "This is certainly the place if you want New Age," she said. "It's about all I can do to keep up with old age."

Downstairs, they passed through a plastic-beaded curtain into a room with metal folding chairs and a screen that reminded him of a schoolroom. A woman in a brightly colored batik pants suit hurried up to them, kissed Janet on alternate cheeks.

"Janet and Jason," she said, as if she'd known him all his life.

Janet waved her hand from one of them to other. "Jason, this is Sue Ann, one of my dearest friends, and the most selfless human being on the face of the earth, I might add. She organized these films for us."

"Labor of love," Sue Ann said. She hooked one arm through Sanderson's and another through Janet's and led them over to a table against one. "Everyone!" Sue Ann clapped her hands above her head. "We have an honored guest," she said.

As the group filled little plates with cheese and crackers and cauliflower, he wondered if, later on, he'd be asked to comment on the movie. What was this one again? *Night of the Hunter.* He'd never heard of it. At least no one here had asked him a question about Sam.

It was before nine when he removed the pillow shams and turned down his bed, unlaced his shoes, folded his clothes neatly onto the back of a chair, started to pull on his pajamas. *His nightly ritual, come hell or high water.* Rosa laughed when she said that, but with a certain way of smiling afterward.

"On second thought," he said aloud.

He eased into bed in just his boxers, something he hadn't done in years. Rosa teased him about his methodically brushed teeth, his neat sets of striped and checked pajamas. Now he slid his bare legs from side to side on the cool sheets. "Yes," he said, again aloud.

From the yard he heard the dog howl once and again, then fall quiet, and he imagined her heavy body settling into some soft spot of leaves and grass. *What in heaven's name do you need a dog for, Jason?* Janet asked. She suggested the SPCA or even a sign at the bookstore about a dog, free to a good home. But the dog had been presumptuous in her dog-love. She'd hitched a ride with him, and she held on this far in a journey that he was now uncertain about. He'd keep the dog, at least until he was home again. He'd made that much of a decision about his life, he thought as he rearranged the covers, refolded the top of the blanket against his chest. The room smelled strongly of potpourri and as his eyes began to itch and burn, he burrowed under the pillows. *It's sweet, Dad. How you could just climb in bed and pull the covers up and stay there, forever.* What Sam had said was true. He usually had no love of surprises.

He began to recite names in his head, a game he played with Janet when they were children, and one that Rosa teased him about. *It's an adventure, honey,* she'd say about the beds and breakfasts or seaside hotels he found uncomfortably reminiscent of other people's excretions. Part lover and part mother, Rosa held him for as long as it took for him to fall asleep. *Okay,* she'd say, *what'll it be tonight?* He silently listed the names of everything from the books of the Bible to vegetables. *Genesis. Exodus. Leviticus. Radishes. Rutabaga. Rhubarb.* Long after Rosa's breathing grew steady, he would himself fall asleep, dreaming of ghosts he could not exorcise by day.

In no particular order, he remembered scenes from the afternoon's movie. He remembered tattoos of love and hate and a switchblade knife. He remembered children's voices. *Hing, hang, hung.* He remembered the dark shape of the preacher riding against a huge full moon. The ethereal face of Lillian Gish in a sky full of stars and children's faces. Children's faces. Sanderson remembered his own face and Janet's. How old had they been? Ten or eleven, but not old enough, they were told, to see the body of their grandfather, where he lay in a casket in the front room. They snuck in anyway, and they touched the cold flesh of their grandfather's face. *Blessed are the pure in heart,* Lillian Gish prayed, *for they shall see God.* He'd been baptized when he was twelve, in a muddy creek behind the church and afterward, wrinkled his nose. *If that's what God smells like, I don't want any.* How cruel children were. In the movie, the legs of a murdered woman lay inside a basement entrance, and children gathered around. *Wherefore by their fruits, ye shall know them.* His own innocence, Sanderson thought, had been lost in increments. In a floating world of grieved and grieving. And in the film, a boat's flight down a river, past an owl and a turtle and a rising moon. *It's a hard world for little things.*

153

As he fell asleep at last, he remembered light and water and a woman's hair. *Her hair waving soft and lazy like meadow grass under flood water.* And on the shore, a girl in a red sarong. A girl smiling, her teeth reddish-black and in her arms, a basket of coconuts and their fleshy whiteness. Her mouth became another mouth. Sarah's? Rosa's? That dreamed mouth became a painting. Women, their mouths ripe and laughing, standing by the long chain to a bucket from a well. Their mouths spewing the rapid song of dream language.

The mouth of God, a voice said. Sanderson was in a helicopter with Sam on the bottom of the ocean. He was trying to breathe and move a large crate that had Sam trapped and he could see kelp waving and fish swimming and hear what sounded like music. *Leaning, leaning, safe and secure from all alarm.* It was all so real. He could feel his lungs aching, full of cold water, as he struggled with the crate. It was too heavy and his clothes were heavy with sea water that held him, pulled him down, with Sam calling for help he didn't know how to give. Then Sarah was there, handing him a rope and saying, *Let him rest.* Or it was Rosa, holding out a lifeline. *Can't live with one foot in grave and one in the land of the living, too.* Janet repeated what she'd said that morning. *Jay, be good to yourself.* Some voice, Rosa's or Janet's or Lillian Gish's, rummaged inside him and he woke again to the quick beat and beat of his no longer sleeping heart. It said, *Listen.* It said, *Remember.*

Chapter Eight

Sight:

1. The power or faculty of seeing; perception of objects by use of the eyes; vision. 2. One's range of vision on some specific occasion. 3. Mental perception or regard; judgment.

A Little Harmonic Preview

Across an expanse of field crowded with tents and bonfires and dancers and vendors and even a magic show on this eve of the Harmonic Convergence, she can just glimpse a Ferris wheel as it meets the skyline above the distant carnival grounds. She's only been here since the afternoon, but she's heard murmurings about the carnival. *Commercialism at its most banal. A sacrilege.* She will never forget one carnival and a Paris Ferris wheel. Along Place de la Concorde she and Sam Sanderson once drank red wine and rode the rocking airborne cars until two A.M. Her plan now? At dawn, on the day of planets and convergence, she wants to climb Grandfather Mountain and remember him again, remember him once and for all.

The crowd is large, 500 or more, and above it drifts the scent of wood smoke and Thai stick, curries and Moroccan stews. There are Indian mystics and shamans and spiritual adepts. There are leaflets which advertise medicine wheel ceremonies, Kiva sacred rites, vision quests for transformation and healing, and connection rituals to Mother Earth. There's a patina of tofu and essential oils and truth, but there's also bartering, New Age and otherwise. Tables are laden with Cherokee prayer rugs and silver and turquoise rings. Tee shirts are plentiful. There's the $14.95 version that reads *Harmonic Convergence: Another Universal Gathering, 1987 and 1997.* Twenty bucks buys one with a puckish-looking boy sitting on the edge of a crescent moon strumming a mandolin.

There are also sales in reading the future and the past, in rebirthing and

157

interplanetary lives. She's wandered the field again and again, and been offered palm readings to determine patterns for her next cycle of seven years. Tarot decks abound. *Egyptian. Chinese. Motherpeace.* Or hypnosis, to encounter her previous incarnations. Rebirthing means a yak wool blanket on the ground and a woman who encourages couples to hold one another and let go and let God. And UFO stories. *I was taken,* she overhears a woman with fiery hair who is selling her memoirs say, *right out of my bed to a council of elders from an unspecified galaxy and that was when I felt my son quicken in my womb.* Diogenes, Lory thinks, searched the streets of Athens for one honest man. This gathering doesn't feel dishonest, but there is a sense of expectation so heightened that it would be a major disappointment, she thinks, if the night passes without some valid sign, some manifestation. The crowd is large and its excitement has been building, shifting.

Since afternoon there has been dancing. Furious drumming and stamping of bare feet and African dancing in the center of the field on the tamped-down grass and a chanting, straight up at the hot, clear sky. *Come down. Shine down on us. Sun. Moon. Stars.* Sweat-drenched women have removed their shirts and danced, bare-breasted, necklaces of shells and coins swinging from their hips. And after that, a contingent from the Southwest led a processional portending the Day of the Dead. They were wailing as they carried a bier laden with sugar skulls and roses and a model of planet Earth. The center of the field became a bonfire, one small enough at first for children to leap across, daring the flames to touch them. The bonfire reached heavenward, its flames higher than anyone. Dogs rounded it and slunk back, frightened of the intensity of this kind of heat on an August afternoon. Sufi dancers, their eyes reflecting firelight, circled in their long white skirts. There were Fancy Dancers twirling their shawls and stepping, one and two. *Dance,* someone shouted. *Dance the unity of the galaxies. Dance the unity of the world!*

At dusk she joined in, took her shoes off and held the hem of her white skirt up, danced with the stab of dry grass on her bare soles. They danced contra and flamenco. They danced rock 'n' roll and then a slow, bluesy waltz. They danced singly and in pairs. In threes and fours and more. She took the hands of a man with a black fedora that had seen better days and let herself be twirled as he swung her until the field careened, a dizziness she wanted. She wanted to dance until that tight knot in her gut, the one she'd felt for years, loosened, then disappeared. To dance until her blouse was transparent with sweat. To dance until she could throw her head back and laugh like that woman, there, or that man, the one who took her hands and sashayed with her, right and left. Instead, she thought of the way her palms felt, marked by the touch of strangers.

Now it is nearly dark. Someone is playing a flute and she hears the fretful voices of children. *When are we going home? When will the planets meet?* Near the bonfire, a circle has gathered for a storyteller, so she wraps a blanket she's brought from the car around her shoulders and settles on her ankles and thinks about time. *Time.* She remembers Sam Sanderson and how they once had to wait for a bus from Varanassi. It was so hot she sat by the roadside, drinking barely cold, sweet drinks as hour passed into hour. When? Sam demanded of the ticket-seller. When exactly will the bus be here? She asked a man with an empty rickshaw what time it was. Time? he said. Ask the blind woman. A woman with rheumy white eyes smiled at her and pointed up at the white-hot sun. In Varanassi, hour dissolved into hour and there was no time at all.

The time now is true dusk. From the other side of the fire, she can see the face of the storyteller, a tall man in a beaded robe. That face is black and white, a stark paint that unsettles her, and his eyes, shiny black in the firelight, seem to be staring at her and no one else. He raises his arms, the robe spread wide. *This will be a night of souls revealed,* he says. *A night like the dance of ghosts.* She sees, after all, that he is looking this deeply not at her, but into her, and into others huddled near her. *A night of songs and disguises,* he says. *Of winds and mountains.* The wind is cool and it has a scent of earth that makes her want to cry, but she can't. She pulls the blanket tighter around her and wonders whether, if she tries hard enough, she could disappear.

He talks about the earth. Mica that sparkles in the sun. Coal. Granite. Sandstone. Rough, smooth, slick and shifting, the shapes of the earth. About a summer sky, its naked blue at midday. About water. How it has no shape until you hold it in your mouth. He talks about seeing all these things with more than the eye, with the third eye, with the eye at the center of the self. He talks and his sound of his voice has the color of charcoal. It catches in her throat, makes her want to speak. He chants. Sings the story of light. Of the time light was stolen from the earth by an old man. Only Raven, the trickster, was brave enough to steal this light back and set it free as he flew up and out through a smoke hole into the sky.

She knows Sam Sanderson fell through a hole in the world and couldn't climb back out. *A black hole.* She has seen it many times since he died. A dark, foreign eye. The square when the computer screen shuts down. A hole has been torn in the ozone and carcinogens now fall through like dust in sunlight. In the rend between continents and cultures, a virus, insidious and quick, could find its way into anyone's veins. Or a plane could appear out of nowhere, slam into a tall building where people are doing meaningful things—loving one another, selling stocks and bonds—and nothing is left, afterward, but a hole that collapses in on itself, story after story. Light, the storyteller says. The world's salvation.

She wants to remember a time when light saved her. Fireflies in a blue Mason jar. Candles in sand bags on the edge of a lawn. Phosphorescence by the edge of the sea. Wants to remember lightning and its charge in her hair. But she feels small and insignificant next to the tallness of this storyteller and his arms reaching up through the shadows of flames.. How vast the sky is, and the black shape of the mountain, and the reddish moon. She can almost hear planets sliding through their courses in space. If she tries, she can almost hear him. *Sam.*

Reliquary

It was late 1985 when Lory Llewellyn woke in a cheap and good guest house in Katmandu and studied Sam Sanderson's crooked face in the early light of morning. Sam at this hour was a boy, his lips full and soft with sleep. His eyes fluttered and he yawned.

"Are you awake?" he asked. He stared out of the blankets at her.

"Almost." She draped her arm across his waist.

"I had the dream again."

Summer heat already rose from the streets of Katmandu, but for now, in the cooler respite before noon, she moved close, fit her body against his, knees into knees. "Tell me."

It was always about his boyhood. His mother, Sarah, was packing a suitcase with squares of bright cloth and smooth stones and the bleached white bones of sea birds. *I'm leaving now and this time I'm never coming back*, Sarah told him.

"The dream," Sam said. "It's her and not her. Her voice. So real."

"She is real," Lory said. "Here." She touched his chest, his heart.

"I want more than that," he said. He lay still, looking out at the balcony, the light of morning. "It's why we're here."

Here. *Katmandu*. Wood smoke curled the roofs of houses where fires cooked curries and mutton. Hawker's stalls peddled patchouli and musk. She'd held her breath against the scents of urine from a viaduct, against warm blood from a butcher's stall. Now, she left Sam sleeping again and made her way across the stone floor, squatted over the toilet, dipped cold water to clean herself.

Outside on the balcony she leaned over, watched Katmandu wake up. On the balcony below their room she heard strangers waking also—throats being cleared, coughs, spitting of betel nut into the street. Taxis revved and wild dogs barked. At the tourist's restaurant down the street, a man in plastic sandals and a dhuri emptied a pan of dishwater into the street. They'd eaten at that place yesterday.

She'd eaten two heaping plates of gado-gado, dipping her fingers again and again into vegetables and a muddy peanut sauce. Near their table, as they ate, she read news from a bulletin board for travelers. *In jail six months for smoking dope and no sign of a hearing. Send food.* In the back of the restaurant, a grandmother smoked a hookah, and the scent of hashish and tobacco deepened the gnawing she'd felt since their plane landed three days ago. She licked her hands for the last traces of sauce, swallowed cup after cup of milky, sweet tea. Later, as her stomach rebelled, they sat for hours on the steps of the Bodhnath Stupa, the temple of the white dome.

"This is the place," Sam said.

"The place?" she asked, thinking of all the temples and gardens, shrines and sanctuaries highlighted in *Nepal on a Shoestring,* their guidebook.

"Imagine this world," Sam said, "as transparent as skin."

She watched a man urinate near a post carved with Hindu Gods. There was the marketplace in one direction, the snowcapped mountains in the other. She looked at Sam's hands, gesturing in the empty air. She swallowed again, a sour-sweet bile. "Transparent?"

"We can see through," Sam said.

"To?" she said, though she knew what he meant. The air smelled of the living body. And of the body's demise. Earlier they'd seen a woman with full red lips and waves of blue black hair walking up the alleyway. She was wailing a name. *Ahmed. Ahmed.* A death chant, Sam said, but Lory knew it was a name. She could almost see it, the soul of some departed lover trailing after the woman, holding on to her red veil.

The distance between this world and the next, between a living that made her flinch and a dying no one concealed, was indeed nothing but beautiful silk. Just yesterday, they'd walked down by a stream in the public park and she'd seen a dead dog lying there, its blonde fur matted with mud. It was nothing, Sam said, but a dog. And it was nothing but a dog, and that was the thing. She'd seen men vomiting against the walls of holy temples. She'd seen the golden face of Buddha, in the same park, thick with human feces. The body and its refuse, bodies themselves, even sacred ones, held in seeming disregard.

Katmandu. A whole world within a world, no ironic safety of Bangkok high rise shopping malls, blast of imported American rock'n'roll, air-conditioned hawker's stalls. Here she is the foreigner. They take photographs of her and her light hair, so she dyes it in the bathroom sink, dyes it chalky black. Katmandu, pretty, and not. She passed an open doorway where three men crouched on their ankles around the body of a butchered goat. She smelled warm blood and their knives rose and fell, quick, quick against decay in the heat.

Two days and already she had discovered that this was a world that moved, was never silent, with no external aloneness. Quick voices were everywhere. *Change money. Hotel good and cheap. Come see. Just looking.* Everywhere the touch of hands, shoulders, press of hips in a packed bus, a man with the blackened stumps of fingers asking for baksheesh. Quick steps around red betel-nut splashes in the street. Ringing, ringing of a bell in a public square without a name, a sadhu, laughing, naked, his scrotum swollen large as grapefruits. Everywhere, moving, the push of crowded marketplaces hung with mutton and hot peppers, moving, the itch and pull of her bowels, parasites that would hatch in a month or in six.

And now, on this early morning on this particular guest house balcony, the whole world was shifting. The streets of Kathmandu were already her past, her future unfurling, stretching itself like a cobra from a woven basket, and she could do nothing but follow. A membrane, fine as silk, Sam said, between one world and the next, between beauty and terror, between love and nothing. Taxi motors revved, a child was crying in the street, and today they'd start north on a trek toward Muktinath, just across the border from Tibet.

She leaned over the wooden railing, then called behind her into the room to Sam. *Are you awake?*

By seven o'clock they were in the marketplace to buy bus tickets to Pokhara, where they would begin their two-person trek. On the restaurant bulletin board, they read accounts good and bad of trekking that way, without guides to take them north toward Muktinath, across the border from Tibet. *Beware of robbers*, one note said. And another. *Find Tatopani and bask in the hot springs, if they aren't washing clothes.*

They ended up on the roof of the bus, lodged between two long metal pipes and a group of farmers balancing a large, metal tank. The bus itself, low-riding and spewing smoke, was a slick-tired and rusty version of those she remembered from elementary school.

One of the farmers gestured, held out a packet of cigarette tobacco and some papers. His fez was red and a bright yellow and blue and it had slipped low over eyes that appraised her, the bare skin of her calves at the edge of her long black skirt, her bare shoulders from the sleeveless shirt she'd worn. Everywhere, yesterday, she'd seen women who were covered—those in burqas from head to hands to feet, their black eyes the only thing visible; Western women, some in loose-fitting pants and long-sleeved blouses, bought cheap from the market, others in hiking boots and jeans; Tibetan women with their brilliant turquoise and coral necklaces and nose rings, their arms

165

layered with shirts and jackets. She'd known she should cover herself, had felt rather than seen the stares, yesterday, when she'd worn her cotton pants that came midcalf. But how hot it was, in this pre-monsoon time. They'd known that too, from the guidebooks. *How hot can it be?* Sam had asked that, and now she watched him wipe beads of sweat from his forehead, take off his sweatshirt and tie it around his head like a turban.

She reached for the cigarettes and papers and the man nodded, smiled at her as she laid these things in her lap and bent over them, guarding the loose tobacco against the air. She rolled two thin cigarettes and lit one of them as they navigated the narrow streets out of Katmandu. The bus was slow-moving on the outskirts of town, and picked up only slightly more speed as the main road gave way to part pavement and part dust and gravel. She inhaled the tobacco, held it in. Yesterday, as they wandered through alleyways and past the door of holy places closed to Westerners, they'd been offered hashish, for a price, by a boy no more than eight, and they'd smoked and laughed in the courtyard of the guesthouse underneath a tree heavy with cloying blossoms. Now tobacco's harsh smoke made her sway inside as the bus climbed the mountain road. The bright sun bore down, more by the mile, and the cup of tea from the stall near the bus stop—a syrupy, pinkish liquid—churned inside her.

In their guesthouse lobby she'd met a woman from England who'd been to Nepal once, then to India, and then back again to Katmandu. In India, she said, she had taken up walking barefoot and a parasite had entered her body though the soles of her feet. Unnamed, such parasites, though the guidebooks told of their effects—giardia, dysentery, malaria. Without names, as well, most of the trees on the often barren hillsides the bus was passing, as well as the villages beside the road, perched precariously on the steep sides of the mountains, as it wound around curve after curve. She held on tight to the rope leading from the metal pipes to the water heater and tried not to look over the side of the bus as it swerved.

Sam was talking to one of the men at the far end of the rooftop and she could see his long hands. He was making a large, round shape in the air, and gesturing down the road, then up at the tallest of the mountains on the horizon, as if to indicate where they'd be going soon. The farmer with the red fez shook his head.

"There is no need," he said.

Sam looked at him and nodded, waiting.

"There is no need to pursue death to the ends of everything," the farmer said. He held out a clenched fist. "It is here," he said, then he held his hand, palm up the sky, and then behind them.

With the sweatshirt wrapped around his head, the lopsidedness of his face was more pronounced. The faces of the other men were also deeply lined from the sun, but Sam, in his white shirt and faded jeans, was like a cutout of a man from another place pasted into the midst of these Nepalese, most of them with bare, calloused feet, all of them dressed in bright reds and blacks, jackets, vests.

Just at the edge of the next village, a larger one, the bus neared a low-hanging electrical wire and she heard Sam yell out to her at the last second. She ducked, as did the men. *Allah*, they chanted, as they passed underneath the wire, which was frayed enough for her to see bare metal.

The Nepalese light was relentless, leaving the top of her head and the tops of her bare shoulders tender. She drew her legs into her arms beneath her long skirt, thankful for the covering. The tea churning in her stomach had translated to nausea so that she closed her eyes, counting, one and two and three, until the next wave hit. Behind her sunglasses and her closed lids, she still saw the shapes of the passing mountains and like the bus as it dodged potholes and swung into curves, these shapes swerved, rose and fell until she leaned far over her side of the bus, heaving. Below her, a window slammed shut.

The bus slid to a stop in front of another guesthouse.

"Eat now," the farmer said. He held out a faded red cloth, a handkerchief from his flask of water. "Eat and feel better soon," he said again as she rose, dizzy in the hot sun.

Past, present and future were diaphanous, with only a transparent division in between as day passed into day and they trekked the Nepalese dirt road. It was no more than a footpath leading north, but they would cross plains changing to gorges and rivers spanned by spindly swinging bridges. Monkeys watched them from wild trees. They broached the Middle Himalayas and came within range of a town called Mustang, and then a village called Muktinath where yaks were herded through the streets and a celebrated temple had been raised for the Dalai Lama. After one more village, they climbed, not the magnificence of the Great Himalayas, but a lesser mountain whose name she would later not recall. There, they found the village of Marpha and another temple they'd heard about, from a fellow traveler in a London hostel. He claimed to have walked there from the farthest southern point of India, to see the face of God. *Beyond the end of everything,* he called this temple at the top of the mountain beyond Marpha. *The place where pilgrims go to worship, and to die.*

Past, present, future. In her pocket she was carrying a Tarot deck she'd bought in Paris in a shop called *Le Monde,* where an old man with one eye covered by a scarlet velvet patch did readings. Her future was The World, a card with the earth at one edge, the ocean at the other, and an ecstatic dancer in between. The old man closed his one eye. *What is here is there,* he said. *What is not here is nowhere.* Another card showed Persephone at the threshold of the underworld. *Descent.* Again the old man laid his hand on the card, but this time fixed his murky gold eye on Sam.

The trail turned steep and rutted, and then became flat, reaching across stretches of gravel and loose, dry soil. She wrapped a wet bandana around her head against the heat as they passed spouts extending from the mountains at turnouts beside the trail. Before they reached the village of Tatopani, they followed a procession—two Sherpas and a woman with her face covered by an embroidered shawl. The two men were carrying a body on a platform made of woven straw and leather, with crude wooden handles. The body was a woman's, her bony feet and silver bracelet-ornamented ankles sticking out from a blanket.

Lory and Sam climbed behind the procession for miles as they left gifts for their dead. Lory marked time by counting small piles of grain mounded on top of smooth stones, where painted red arrows pointed the way up. After two days, the procession disappeared and she counted, instead, the villages they reached, the cold Nepalese sodas sold at the villages wealthy enough to boast of guesthouses for Western tourists. Some days there were no such villages, and they ate watery soups colored yellow with a handful of barley at wayside huts. Once they'd stopped at a hut perched on the edge of a cliff where a woman was combing with her fingers through a child's hair. *Chapati,* she said. *Quick, quick.* The woman lit a fire and made them these breads of flour and water, and the dusty taste soothed the sickness that had begun to follow her, a ghost of the pink tea in Katmandu.

Sam took on more of the weight of her pack as she grew nauseous and as fatigue traveled into her arms and legs. Gritty wind blew down the steep mountainsides, and she counted now how many times the wind left her feeling so light she could have been born up on air and brilliant sunlight, over the next ridge, to the next town of mud-brick huts and wood smoke fires. The guesthouses had holes in the centers of their roofs for smoke from their cooking fires. One night pinpoints of pain woke her, small bed-bug nips on her legs and back, and she lay looking up through the fire-hole into the hot sky. *Touch me, Sam,* she said. *Hold me.* His breathing was slow and steady.

The next day they rounded a bend in the trail and found a pack mule abandoned at the edge of a ravine and she approached it, held out her hand. *Here now. Come here,* she said, and it tumbled over its own weight, head over legs, its hooves sparking against stones on the way down the steep cliff side. *Kali.* That was the Goddess of destruction, their guidebook said. The Divine Mother of Love who danced in ecstasy as the world turned to ash. *When death comes,* the Parisian Tarot reader had said, *one must greet it without fear and with a minimum of grief.* When it died, the pack mule's eyes darkened and she shivered.

Such death was insignificant in this world that grew more foreign to her by the day. In a village called Tatopani, she sat beside a hot spring, stuck her feet into moving water lukewarm and cloudy from soap bars and clothes beaten against the rocks. And at night, in a guest house, she cleaned her bowl of dhal and rice, and then headed to a latrine where she steadied herself as she looked down into a pit teeming with larvae.

Sam stayed awake later and later, and kept her awake with his questions. *Where was that woman buried, or was she buried, and how? What did the red arrows mean? The grains of corn?* Sam scoured the pages of their guidebook for any bit of information. She also wanted to know things. How soon would the rains come? How far to the next village? But Sam's questions, the intensity with which he asked them, left her wondering who she was lying next to in the dark. He turned the few Nepalese words he knew and looked in their *Nepalese for Beginners,* but the only word for death he could find was *Gorakshe:* a mountain known as Graveyard of the Crows.

In five more days they reached Marpha, the last village of all, the village at end of the world. Houses were the color of the faded earth, dust-rose under the scorching sun. They climbed higher, beyond the end, up a trail toward a temple in the clouds, up to air so thin her lungs ached. They passed a sadhu in a black, ragged robe and they passed a family, a mother and two girls dressed in fine red saris. They passed mounds of stones piled to knee-height, tributes left by pilgrims from as far away as Madras. They passed a hut on an edge of a cliff with a child crying alone in a steep yard and more children and a mother who walked out and stared. One of these children, a boy, walked behind them for a while, his hand held out. When she stopped, he opened his hand, palm out, and in it was a small dead bird.

The temple of bleached white stone sat at the top of the mountain, with more mountains, magnificent and unreachable, beyond that. The temple, its disrepair a thousand years old, was surrounded by fallen columns, by gifts of garlands, gifts of the bones of animals. In front of her, a family worshipped. A mother in a crimson sari knelt before a stone basin of stagnant water. A sadhu knelt, made an offering of yak butter to the Gods. Prayer flags strung from the trees whipped in the thin, hot wind. And everywhere, on the walls, roof, shut doors of the white temple, there were carvings of love and destruction. Lovers. Mouths open to receive both God and other mouths, tongues full of desire. Women bent, their bare buttocks offered to hands and hips, to the thrust of a penis carved in stone. Kali, her stone likeness above a doorway, neck bedecked with human skulls; Shiva at her feet. Kali. *Beyond fear. Mother of limitless peace.* One of her arms held a sword, another a severed human head. Another of her four arms was to remove fear. Lory looked up into Kali's open mouth. Kali. *Manifestation of time. Absolute night.*

Sam knelt and took the lacquered box that had been his mother's from his pack, opened it. He scattered dried rose petals at the feet of the Goddess and said his mother's name. Lory crouched on her ankles, as she saw the other pilgrims do, and held out an offering, a palm full of dust.

Each night, in a map of guest houses stretching the miles they trekked back south, Sam Sanderson made notes on scraps of paper. The notes were random lines, glimpses of small things he'd seen. *Nothing but the wing of a bird floating on top of water from which we fill our bottles to drink.* Or there were lines from poems, only some of which she recognized. *O vanity of sleep, hope, dream, endless desire, the horses of disaster plunge in the heavy clay.* They had grown more and more silent.

They slept, night after night, but not together. Night after night, he touched her and she touched him as his breath rose with passion, her body reaching the edge of climax. It was easy enough to turn away from him, touch her own body with her own hands. What did she desire? For him to reach out to her, to touch some far, small space inside her. And what did he desire? She believed, more and more, that the lover he wanted was one she was afraid to name. *Kali. Keres. Cerridwen. Hel.* Women of darkness and death.

In a Kalopani guesthouse their sleeping bags were on the floor near a window overlooking a courtyard. They could see the startling rise of the moon over mountains so vast she could hardly believe they had walked up one such mountain, 11,000 feet into the clouds. She remembered a summit beyond Marpha, how sunlight exploded from behind clouds and the distant, snowcapped peaks and now, in this guesthouse, she wanted to touch her lover, to translate this remembrance into the ordinary desire of her own body. She touched his face. His two-sided face. *Who are you, Sam Sanderson?* Before she knew it, he was inside her. He moved and she moved and they cried out, him, her, and he said some word, a name maybe, but it was not her own.

Once in a science class she'd had when she was a girl, they'd experimented with their hearts. How many times, the teacher asked them, did their heart beat in a minute? How many times did their hearts beat in an hour? In a day? In a year? Some nights when Sam touched her, she felt him counting, beat by beat, the rhythm of her heart beneath his fingers.

Later, on the balcony, she sat by herself watching bats race toward the heavy summer moon. They had already laid plans for traveling farther south, back to India where, in the pre-monsoon heat, other lovers, too hot and restless to touch, would sleep far away from one another on cots in the street. There were miles south yet to trek and tonight she was cold, inside and out.

A week later, they were crossing a huge plain with the Himalayas in the distance, white capped against a blazing blue sky. She counted off names of God as she walked. *Soul. Infinite Mind. Spiritus Mundi.*

In two weeks or three, they will be recuperating in an Indian town called Pushkar where there is a lake. At night Sam, too hot to sleep, will walk beside the shore and gather human bones to fill up his mother's lacquered box and he will say, *anything*, his voice fierce, *can be transformed.* But he does not say how, or by what.

Today, as they crossed a plain in sight of the Himalayas, his hair, nearly white in the brightness of noon, shone as he disappeared into vortices of sunlight and dust. Could any God keep anyone safe in such a fierce and mysterious world?

Chapter Nine

Still:

1. Motionless; stationary. 2. Subdued or low in sound; hushed.
3. Free from turbulence or commotion; peaceful; tranquil; calm.
4. Steadily; constantly; always.

Carnie

Words woke Sanderson. *I want to thank you all for your support during the recovery of my son's body that he might be brought home.* Words from a speech he'd made when Sam died, from a thank-you card, or some letter of condolence. He opened the bedroom door, slipped out into the hall, down the steps, stopped in the kitchen to fill a empty bottle with ice water for the dog. He left Janet a note. *Leaving now rather than waiting. I can't sleep.* He wanted to drive out the rest of the night, he told himself. He wanted to drive until there were no words to follow him.

The dog leapt up from the nest she'd made in the corner of the yard and bounded toward him, full of patient dog-love, making no sounds, no howls at the moon, which was nearly full. She followed him, quiet and leashless, already knowing her spot in the back seat, passenger's side. He rolled the window down and her head peered out and her ears flew back as he drove.

Grandfather Mountain. Less than two hours north, in time to find a motel for the rest of the night. Road signs and park signs and mile markers later, what he found was a wrong turn and an unmarked gravel road that went on and on and, in the distance, the lights of an all-night carnival. He stopped the car in the tall weeds and he watched through the trees the multicolored wedding ring of light that meant the Ferris wheel, listened to faraway laughter and music, a gentle rock 'n' roll, song words he could just make out. *Reminisce about those times, try and take them out, but they play to you again and again.* He sat listening with the car windows rolled down, and then after a while stepped out into the dark, poked around for something to use as a leash for the dog.

There was no path to the carnival, but there were the Ferris Wheel lights, so he pointed himself in that direction. He was wearing shorts and deck shoes, no socks, and soon he heard the whine of mosquitoes. The dog was barking at something, a flash of red eyes in the weeds, but it was too late to find a pathway now. He shone his flashlight and the dog whimpered low in her throat as he pushed forward through brambles and a spiky mesh of thorns. He held tight to the dog's rope as, behind him, a couple of cars spun gravel, their mufflers loud and their radios turned to full blast. The cars headed on, and soon there were carnival sounds, closer now. *Get your cotton candy. Hot buttered popcorn.* He couldn't recall when he'd last walked at night, stars above him and a mystery ahead of him, without Rosa or anyone else he knew, and he navigated ahead to the sounds of voices. Soon there was a clearing and a chain stretched across with a sign. *All-night Carnival! Lester's World of Light!*

It was a tourist's heaven. At a concession stand, he ordered a burger for himself and one for the dog and wandered through a crowd that was amazingly substantial for almost midnight. He elbowed past high-school kids with their late-night dates and truckers back from their hauls, even a mother or two with children hankering for the merry-go-round of garishly painted elephants and camels. Sanderson and the dog wandered past a ring-toss booth, a shooting gallery, and a trailer that promised to house *A Mountain Gallery of Horrors.* He stared long and hard at a poster for hairless black bears and two-headed rainbow trout. He found souvenirs galore. Refrigerator magnets. *Been there, done that. Harmonic Convergence, 1997.* Snow globes with glitter falling around Planet Earth. He bought an Harmonic Convergence sundae made of freeze-dried ice cream.

CARNIE

At last there was the Ferris wheel. *A wedding band of light*, Sarah called it once at a state fair. She'd thrown her head back and laughed when they reached the top, held her arms out and shouted up into the air. *We can have everything. Everything.* He couldn't recall riding one with Rosa, though he remembered well what she called him at moments when exuberance overtook him. *Silly, sweet thing.* Sweet, the taste of ice and fruity syrups from a snow cone stand. The dog lapped at the paper funnel. Sweet, this night's adventure as he tied the dog's rope to a table leg near the ticket stand and paid for two consecutive rides. He stepped into the car, fastened himself in, leaned his head back, breathed. Far below him, the dog barked, sharp and wary of this moving circle of light.

Chapter Ten

Illumination:
1. Sometimes an entertainment, display, or celebration using lights as a major feature or decoration. 2. The luminous flux incident per unit area, express in lumens per unit of area. 3. Intellectual or spiritual enlightenment.

The Book of the Dead

Lory Llewelyn can remember their hole-in-the-toe shoes when they arrived from India those ten years and more ago, but as hard as she tries, she can never remember their faces. Sam must have looked tense that entire long day and into the next. A flight from Bangkok to Seattle. Another flight from there to the local airport near where his father, Jason Sanderson, lived. *The old must fall away, the new emerge.* The Parisian Tarot reader had said this.

The memories of India remained, its temples and cows draped with jasmine, mutton carcasses hung above open sewers, press of bodies and incessant voices in the Delhi streets. And before that the weeks in Nepal, and behind that other worlds within worlds, traveler's worlds. Past wasn't present and present wasn't past and her future became the roar of a landing jet and then the startling quiet of a small town airport where Sam's father rushed forward to greet them.

Father and son reached for one another's hands, then awkwardly embraced as a feeling she could not yet identify was exchanged.

Jason Sanderson was a plump man who wore suit pants and a jacket, a striped sports shirt with a wide blue tie from a decade earlier. "Sam," Sanderson said. His voice was tense, uncertain. "You're really home."

"Yes," Sam answered. "Almost."

"Are you tired?" Sanderson took one of the packs from Sam, shouldered it. "You must be." He paused and glanced in Lory's direction, cleared his throat.

"Don't know if I'm tired," Sam said. "Or just afloat. Both of us, I'd say." He reached for Lory's hand. "Meet Lory. Lory Llewellyn."

Sanderson's hand was cool and sweating, but his grip was strong. "Lory," he said, and then repeated the name. "You're home too."

Sam, who had said his father preferred to be known as Sanderson, had called his father inapproachable. She would have immediately chosen a different word. *Hesitant.* As if he were on the verge of choosing a word, one he'd thought about carefully but felt embarrassed to say. *Embarrassed.* Yes, he seemed embarrassed, almost shy in front of his son.

"Home," Sam said slowly, as if he tasted the word. "Back from the luminous world."

They took back roads. Sanderson called this direction *the old way*, and he drove slowly, a too careful negotiation of the curves and meanderings of the road. They went past fields and tobacco barns, past horse farms and miles of hand-built stone walls erected by slaves in the Civil War, near a country church advertising a gospel sing on the coming weekend. As Sanderson maneuvered the large car over a very narrow bridge, he narrated the place, its history, but in an odd way that Lory enjoyed. He told them when this board or that had gone missing in the bridge. He told them about the various levels to which the creek had risen after the winter thaw, the types of debris he'd notice on the creek's banks. She stared at the bridge and thought of another one, rope-suspended, over a gorge in Nepal. A gray monkey had screamed from a tree near the river two hundred feet below her. Now they passed fields of goldenrod and asters, a North Carolina late summer.

"I don't know where to begin asking you about it," Sanderson said.

"It?" Sam asked.

"India." He flipped the air on a higher setting and buttoned his jacket. "I can't even imagine India, except for some picture out of *National Geographic.*"

184

Sam lit one of the short yellow Indian cigarettes he'd taken to smoking, and a bitter odor invaded the new leather smell of the car.

"That's right," Sam said finally. His voice was tired, but Lory recognized an edge of sarcasm. "Yes. That's exactly how it was."

"I saw a documentary the other day," Jason Sanderson began. "*India, Between Epic and Media.*" He pushed the power lock on Lory's door and she jumped. "The old ways and the new. I imagine that."

"Yes," he said again. "Something like that."

Lory laid her hand against Sam's back. The road had narrowed and was densely overhung with boughs of already crimson leaves. "It's so quiet here," she said.

Sanderson pushed another power button and Sam's window descended a bit. "Do you mind the windows down?" he asked. "I like plenty of air."

She drummed her fingers lightly against Sam's shoulder. "Do you know this road, Sam?"

"He ought to know it," Sanderson said. "He used to hitchhike out this way nearly every weekend, the last year of high school. Visiting some buddy of his."

"This road always reminds me of Sarah," Sam said at last. He had one arm draped across the large backpack beside him.

"Your mother?" Sanderson asked as he steered loosely with one hand and began to pick at invisible pieces of lint on his slacks. "I'd forgotten that you called her Sarah."

"She loved drives in the country," Sam continued. "She always wanted to stop and pick flowers to dry."

"She always wanted to drive somewhere," Sanderson said.

"And she always wanted to live near the ocean," Sam answered. "But we never quite did that." He lit a second cigarette.

"She loved the mountains, too," Sanderson said quickly. "Grandfather Mountain. Sam, do you remember the time we went there?"

"You always ask that," Sam said. "I don't think I was even born yet."

Sanderson paused, as if this were an impossibility, then shook his head. "No, I guess not. I guess I'm just remembering your mother."

Sam didn't say anything. "I remember she always wanted to go to India," he said at last. "She wanted to scoop sand from beside the Ganges and find talismans to bring back with her. Do you remember that?"

"Talismans," Sanderson echoed. He leaned forward, stretched his shoulders. "She believed in them. Believed in signs and wonders. She always called them that. *Signs and wonders.*"

"She believed bones were magic," Sam said. He flicked cigarette ash from the car's window. "Shamans believe you can dry bones and bleach them and ask them about the future."

"I've never wanted to know about that," Sanderson said. "The future. It's all I can do." He paused and didn't go on.

Sanderson glanced from the road to Lory, then back again. "Has Sam told you about his mother?" he asked. He sounded quieter, uncomfortable.

"Yes," she said. "He's told me a little."

"He never wanted to be at home after his mother passed." Sanderson's mouth looked tight and his eyes looked sad.

They drove some miles in silence, and Lory pulled a sweater out of the day pack at her feet and huddled into it. The car was cold even with the field they passed glaring white in the heat. She was glad when Sanderson pointed out a sign flashing in the distance.

"Let's get a little bite," Sanderson said. "Plane food doesn't stick with you."

The roadside diner was called Fred's and was a red and white, squat building. "Son," Sanderson said as he paused at the top of the diner steps.

They took a booth where Lory sipped ice water and where Sam lit a new cigarette before the last one was half-burned. They were quiet, and

Sanderson pored over the menu even after the waitress took their orders. It was as if, she thought, they'd all forgotten how to speak. There was a language for the places they'd been, and there was a language for this moment. She tried to think of words to describe this day, and the ones that came before it. *Fecund. Waiting.*

"Tell me about what it was like," Sanderson asked, as he had in the car.

"I can try," Sam said.

"Just tell us," Sanderson said. "Pretend you're telling a story."

Sam smiled, shook his head. "Once upon a time in the desert," he began.

"Sam," she said. She tapped him on the leg. "Be real."

"Real?" he asked. "I thought I was."

"You know what I mean."

Sanderson sipped his iced tea, studied the two of them.

"Just give him the layout." She traced the general shape of India on the table, like a map. "The Travel Guide to India version."

Sam ground out his cigarette. "All right," he said. He laid his hands against the booth's table, sighed.

He could be entertaining and he was at his best now. He described the bus that brought them from Katmandu to Benares, and he diverged from that part of the journey to give them a brief history of when and how the name of the city had changed, Benares to Varanassi. He described a second bus they'd taken, or a third or a fourth, one that took them north, out of the greatest part of India's summer heat, to the lake country of Srinigar, and then back south again to sun that shone even hotter, in the deserts of Rajasthan. And after that, the cool white and the enormity of the Taj Mahal. And, at last, the plane ride, brief and hectic, that took them to the beaches of Phuket, southern Thailand, where they nursed their travel wounds.

Lory sipped weak coffee, listened and added details in her own memory, ones she didn't share with Sam's father. *It was hot.* She tried to reconcile the lazy coolness of the diner, a circular fan humming on its counter, with the heat she remembered. *So hot I'd lie in my room at night, with a wet towel over me and the fan on and then off again as the power came and went.* She remembered sounds from alleyways. Prayers to the east. Drums and bells from the temples around the lake. Stray dogs and how they'd follow her, their eyes red, when she slipped out to the streets for the cool, those nights. Nothing really asleep in a heat of which she had never felt the like. She thought of words for all that he was describing. *Potent. Expectant.*

Sanderson poured dressing on a salad, shook his head. "That's something," he said. "More than I could do." He paused. "Did you get what you wanted," he asked. "In all those places?"

"Get?" Sam asked. He lit another cigarette. "I haven't added it up quite like that yet."

Sanderson persisted. "I'd have to have had a reason for going."

And what is your purpose here? She remembered the times they'd been asked that on buses and trains and on visits to holy shrines.

"Maybe I wanted a definition rather than a reason," Sam said.

"A definition?" Sam's father peered at them.

"To experience a place most of us never reach." Sam leaned back into his corner of the booth, stared at his hands.

"All those places." Sanderson shook his head again. "I'd have been scared out of my wits."

"Maybe it's good to be scared sometimes."

"Is it?"

"Like that one night. You remember it, Lory."

She took his hand and held it beside her on the booth's seat. "Which place?"

"We were in Pushkar."

"Pushkar?" Sanderson asked. "Go-carts maybe?" He laughed, then looked sorry he'd done so. "Tell me."

"It's a holy city," Lory said.

Sanderson squeezed lemon into his water, added a packet of sugar, sipped. "Maybe I have heard of that."

"There's a lake. They bathe there," Sam said. "Remember that, Lory? All those women washing themselves beneath their saris."

"Yes, Sam," she said. "I remember."

"You remember," he said.

"Yes."

"You were asleep that night and I got up and went for a walk," Sam said at last.

She'd heard the story and she lowered her head, waited.

"I took off my shoes and went wading."

"Sam," she began. She willed him not to say too much.

"I felt something under my feet."

"Like what," Sanderson asked. He looked uncomfortable now. Lory could almost hear him. *Do I want to know this?*

"A bone. A human pelvic bone."

"Bones?" Sanderson took a long drink of his soda. He stared at his half-eaten sandwich.

"If you're going to tell him, Sam, just give him some context." She sighed. It was too late now.

"Context?"

"Why the lake is what it is."

"Context it is." He met his father's eyes. "They cremate the dead."

"In a lake?"

"Sometimes," Sam said, and then paused. "They don't cremate them."

"Sam," Lory said. She squeezed his hand firmly once and again. "Maybe this isn't the time for all of this. Not all of it," she repeated.

"The ones who can't afford it," Sam went on. "They put bodies in the water."

Sanderson laid his napkin across his plate, pushed it back.

"And they float away."

"Is that what you wanted to see?" Sanderson's voice, Lory thought, was not unkind. "God knows it can't have been."

"And what does anyone," Sam asked as he pushed his own plate to the center of the table, "really know about God?"

Sanderson flushed. He looked both embarrassed and angry, and also at a loss for words. "I know God holds the cards," he said at last.

"Which ones?" Sam asked.

Sanderson didn't say anything at all for a minute. "I don't know which cards, Sam." He paused. "Maybe we aren't supposed to know everything about life and death and in between."

Sam looked at his father, shook his head. "I still want it," he said.

Sanderson sighed. "What?" he asked. "What is it you want?"

"Everything," Sam said, and then he repeated that word. "Everything."

Chapter Eleven

Vortex:

1. A whirling mass of water, air, or fire, esp. one in which a force of suction operates, as a whirlpool. 2. A rapid rotatory movement of cosmic matter about a center, regarded as accounting for the origin or phenomena of bodies or systems of bodies in space.

Dancing by Moonlight

Sanderson rose with the Ferris wheel car beyond the crowd and looked up at Grandfather Mountain and at pinpoints of lights from chalets perched on other, more distant mountainsides. There was an expanse of open field with huge words strung in lights. *Harmonic Convergence.* And stars, most of all. The car lifted him up to a sky where stars and heat lightning flashed. *Lightning, the Brilliant Miracle.* He remembered that from a newspaper clipping and he thought of Lory Llewellyn. She was there somewhere, below him or beside him in the far reaches of the mountains, or close by in a town within easy reach. *The girl who loved lightning.* He thought of Lory and Sarah and Rosa and Janet. The women he knew most. *Knew. Had known. Might know.* He wondered if all of them, somewhere, somehow, were with him now in the swaying of a carnival ride, looking up at the sky and its heat lightning, its presentiment of a summer storm.

He met Sarah that year he came home from Vietnam. *1971. 1972.* Ambiguous years. Tender ones, too. His heart ached when he stepped off the plane in L.A., not because he heard triumphant applause nor because of some proverbial waves of grain, but because the runway, for him at least, seemed a long, empty stretch. His father was there, his mother and his sister, but something else was not. Part of him was left behind in a country he did not want to remember, in faces he refused to name, in their deaths. He stood there at the airport feeling the embraces of his parents and of Janet and feeling, conversely, nothing at all.

193

Good to have you home, son, his father said. His father's hands were desk-job soft but they gripped Sanderson's own hands with determination. Sanderson longed for touch, that was it. His grandfather practiced riverside immersions for baptisms, healings, and the laying on of hands. Sanderson longed for that then, for some strong hands to lay themselves there, at that exact point, and ease the way his heart beat, fast and heavy.

In his first year home, Sanderson worked at an odd job or two, a hardware store, a department store office, until he found himself living in a one-room apartment above a bookstore in Asheville and attending a business college where he'd been accepted for an accounting program. He had plans. *Plans. Outlines of the future.* And much confusion. Some days, he planned to hone his skills at math with vocational school training. Numbers he'd always been fairly good at—the clean addition and subtraction, the tidiness of columns of statistics. Then he'd inherit his parent's restored historic home in Hendersonville, a house his high-school sweetheart was already redecorating. *That screened porch,* she said. *Can't you just imagine us sitting on a veranda with a fountain and cocktails, instead?* Other days, the boy Sanderson wanted no future, no plan at all.

The high-school sweetheart was as perfect as a row of figures, except for an impatience he noticed most when they went places, like the drive-in movie when he was home for long weekends. *Not now,* she'd say, smoothing her skirt and scooting away from him on the front seat of the car. *How many years did you say school will take,* she'd ask, crossing her arms, her charm bracelet jingling. She broke up with him before he got his degree, having taken up with a hometown gastroenterologist who was already set with an office and a steady stream of intestinal disorders. That was when he met Sarah.

Part of the bookstore was a small café where on some Saturday nights a guitarist played. Upstairs, Sanderson sat staring out the window as bluesy notes and laughter drifted up to him in his apartment. He preferred his own quick cups of instant coffee and fried toast for his morning breakfasts before class. When his high-school sweetheart sent him a postcard from the Smokies from her honeymoon, he found himself restless, pacing the floors. Downstairs, he ordered a large black coffee and a cream puff and settled in at a table with his advanced statistics homework.

That was the first time he saw Sarah. It was the sixties and Sarah looked it, with her peasant blouse, a gauzy skirt sewn with tiny bells, and sparkly, pointy-toed red shoes. Her most startling characteristic, he thought later in his room, were her remarkable eyes. *Royal blue*, she said, years afterward.

Why she should have chosen him, he never really knew, though he suspected it was something between pity for what looked like a lonely life in the apartment upstairs and fascination with a man and a life so different from the one she led. He was, she said, a war hero in penny loafers and she was no bra and skinny-dipping. Come summer, he found himself taking only one class, and then dropping that. He took a job with a landscaping crew, some friends of Sarah's, and enjoyed it thoroughly, the feel of his own muscles, the way his palms grew tough with work so that when he touched her the first time he marveled at the contrast, the roughness of his hands and the amazing softness of her breasts. She was his first lover though he was not hers, and he tried not to dwell upon that fact.

She loved obscure novels by women writers and she painted fabulous canvases lit with remarkable blues and yellows and reds. *The colors of the earth*. Once at night they made love on the floor of the fiction aisle in the bookstore adjoining the café, then later, as they lay naked near the window, she read aloud to him from a mystery novel by a British woman writer from the last century, a story of ghosts and inheritances and heiresses in love. *Aghast, he lingered, watching the ethereal form of the woman ascend the steps, closer and closer, until he felt her ghostly fingers at his collar, her ghostly breath mingling with his own.*

195

One night at the end of that summer, they drove out into the county outside of Hendersonville until the two lane road turned to gravel and fine, white dust. They ended up parked near an abandoned house. *Come on,* she said. *There's not a soul anywhere.* Inside, the front room was empty except for a rusted trunk filled with photographs so old they were brittle. There were photographs of women sitting on a glider in a yard, of dogs and a deep snow, of a swinging bridge hanging from its snapped cables. Sarah took out a yellowed lace dress, pulled it on over her clothes, posed in front of a mirror. They pushed aside a pile of old books from the trunk, sat side by side on the floor.

Sanderson raised his flashlight to the ceiling, made an arc of light that trailed across their hands, their cigarettes, the whiskey bottle they passed back and forth. He held the light steady at Sarah's face, moved slowly down her bare arms, around her mouth.

"Come on," she said. "Dance with me."

Sarah put one of his hands on her shoulder, the other at her waist, and they moved, triangles and lines across the paper-strewn floor. Sanderson hummed a half-remembered waltz. Blue, something about blue and a river, a song that made him think of huge empty rooms, floors so shiny they could almost be water at night. Sarah made up words to his song and sang them. *Stars, they shine and change, like you, lover, like you.*

Sanderson didn't understand her. Not until later, that same night, after they headed outside, weaving a little. He kicked over a forgotten canning jar on the porch, heard it fall on the soft ground. Felt out each step down into the back yard overgrown with blackberry vines and coral berry and wild roses. Shadows of abandoned ladders stretched from the bare boughs of apple trees.

At the back of the field behind the house was a pond where, still in their clothes, they waded in at the edge of murky water smelling of mud and cattle. Sanderson pushed off from the bottom and swam out, his mind cloudy with whiskey. He floated as a heron plunged down from a far tree, wings held back as it skimmed the water. Weightless, Sanderson moved through water, above water, above the county roads they'd driven that night. And above other roads, ones he'd already seen, and ones he had yet to imagine. He saw himself back at home behind a desk, neat piles of newly minted dollar bills in vaults behind him. He saw himself alone at night in a rented apartment, his notebooks and his lists of things to do arranged on the kitchen table. Get signature for add-on class. Find out procedure for early graduation. Apprenticeship applications. His life was an unknown and yet carefully planned journey, a whole country of possibilities, ones he supposed he could well predict. And ahead of him was Sarah, an unknown country unto herself.

Feel, she said. She took his hand and laid it there, against her belly, already soft with pregnancy. She treaded water behind him, hands on the buttons of his shirt. It eased off, sank like a skin they no longer wanted.

Sanderson later looked back on his former plans with a mixture of bewilderment and, mostly, love. His father, wary of his son's life goals, as he called them, did not make him successor to bank president. There was a succession of office jobs that did and sometimes did not call on his skills in accounting. The job that he ended up taking and keeping and capitalizing on as his professional expertise was in repossessions at the local loan and finance company. *How can you repossess something*, Sarah had wanted to know. *Don't you have to possess it first?* Privately, to lighten the situation at hand, he coined phrases for that job—raking in the kitty, reclaiming the wages of excess—but Sarah did not find them humorous. When he got to the house or apartment where he'd come calling with a bill of goods, it was as easy as when you went for a coat and hat with the claim check.

When he came calling with foreclosure notices, when he turned into a driveway or knocked on a locked screen door, he had the uncomfortable feeling it was his own life that had been repossessed by circumstances he no longer understood at all. Repossessed. Or subtly shifted. As the first years of their marriage progressed, the ecstasy of a night swim turned to bemused responses to his stories of days behind desks, customers, mortgages, loan applications. Sarah, the artist, became wife and mother. Year followed year. His wife became a somber woman whose eyes he did not always know how to read. His son, baby turned child turned wide-eyed adolescent boy with an off-center face from the Bell's palsy he had the year he was ten, studied him morning and night. *Who are you?* Sam would ask as he leaned, elbows on the sink while Sanderson shaved, mornings. *Who are you?* Sanderson could not, for the life of him, have answered such a question.

When they rented a family cottage after Sarah was diagnosed, they loved the salt air and distance. Sarah sat out on the beach below the cottage and read novels while he and Sam fished at the edge of the ocean. Sam was fourteen then, and he'd run back and forth from cottage to chair to ocean, fetching all of them cool glasses of sweet tea or little necessities, as Sarah called her medicines, timed at different prescribed intervals throughout the day. Late evenings, they'd play card games, or rent bad science fiction videos from the local market. Then, come nine or ten, Sam would withdraw to his own room, leaving them time for themselves.

Those nights, he'd close the windows against the ocean breeze to keep Sarah warm. She leaned against him saying, *You know I'll still take care of you.* Of me, he had asked. Of me? And she had answered him. *Do you really believe anything can be changed, just by something as small as dying?* He held her close while storms brewed over the ocean.

This is the real thing, she said, holding his hand, her eyes full of a kind of awe. They stood on the deck overlooking the ocean and talked of nothing, of shrimp boats trawling in the distance, of lights along a fishing pier at the end of the island, and she laid her head against his shoulder, told him all the possibilities. The prognosis, the months she would have, the treatments, the odds for survival, or not. She went to bed early and called to him later, asking for a glass of ice water, and before he could help it he felt annoyed, by all of it. He looked at her face, her suntanned cheeks, the gold hair just beginning to turn gray, and was unable to imagine that she would ever change at all, descend into anything called sickness, ascend into anything beyond his reach, beyond the reach of the life he had come to count on. *We're going to have to go the whole gamut,* she said, *of living, and of dying. Isn't that what love is for?*

Later that very night, a storm shook the house with the force of thunder and light. He woke to the bed empty beside him and, barefoot, he padded to kitchen, the back deck, looking for her. It was on nights like this one she loved to swim, far swims out into the ocean. *I want to disappear, the ocean is so dark.* He went down and stood at the edge of the sand and water, frightened and calling out for her, and suddenly there she was. She held her arms out, wanting him to lie down with her near the tide, but later all he could recall was walking alone far along the beach until just before sunrise.

Sanderson rode out his second ticket on the Ferris wheel, then went a third round, a fourth, until the ticket hawker stared at him and looked in annoyance at the dog, who yipped and tugged at her rope each time the wheel descended and stopped for a new circuit. For whom had he grieved more? Sarah? Or himself, his own skin and the bones inside, skull and ribs and hips, and how once she was gone they seemed to hold nothing but empty air. Anyone who could have walked inside his body after Sarah died would have known that nothing came together like you thought it would. He'd been like the smoke and ashes of a once living soul. Sarah's. Sam, too, was now a ghost, long assimilated into some universe, into some afterlife Sanderson feared his imagination was too limited to understand.

Chapter Twelve

Vision:

1. The act or power of anticipating that which will or could or may come to be: prophetic vision. 2. Computer vision: A robot analogue of human vision in which information is received by one or more video cameras and processed by computer. 3. An experience in which a personage, thing, or event appears vividly or credibly to the mind, although not actually present, often under the influence of a divine or other agency.

Vortex

Once they left Jason Sanderson's house, Lory and Sam spent two weeks in an ashram in Vermont and learned to chant, to lift their palms to receive passing souls. South again, they worked for a few weeks as gardeners at a cemetery for Confederate soldiers in Lynchburg, Virginia. Evenings, they did rubbings on tombstones of soldiers and slaves. *Ashes to ashes, dust to dust,* one inscription read. *The work of all our hands.*

They caught a ride with a man who claimed he'd been a guitarist for a heavy-metal band, but he'd given that up when he'd sold his guitar for a pie. A pie? Sam asked. Yeah, the guy said. A pie and a pack of playing cards and a shack beside the ocean. The ocean, the guitarist said, was unsafe these days. It was the habitat of sharks and killer whales and poisonous jellyfish that wrapped around your legs. He left Lory and Sam beside a highway out of the Everglades with a backpack full of books. *Keep these,* he said. *You'll need them.*

Sam called these books a serendipitous find. *The Tibetan Book of the Dead. Man's Search for Meaning. The Existential Quest.* There was an anatomy text and he used it to memorize systems, circulatory, skeletal, neurological, as if they were maps through the body to the soul. There was a copy of a book of drawings by Blake, *The Soul Exploring the Recesses of the Grave.* And there was a book about plagues, old and new. A journal entry described the 1937 Black Death. *Such fear and fanciful notions took possession of the living that almost all of them adopted the same cruel policy, which was entirely to avoid the sick and everything belonging to them. By so doing, each one thought he would secure his own safety.* 20,000,000 died from this plague, caused by flea infestations of the black rat. 1918, the Great Influenza. In Kansas, an Army cook named Albert Mitchell reported to an infirmary with a low-grade fever and a mild sore throat. By noon, 107 soldiers were sick. Within two days, 522 people were sick. Within seven days, every state in the Union had been infected. By April, French troops and civilians were infected. By mid-April, the disease had spread to China and Japan. By May, it spread throughout Africa and South America. 25,000,000 people died. Sam Sanderson knew these facts like he knew the backs of his own hands.

They drank whiskey that warmed their blood. Red wine. Cognac. They stayed no one place long. They worked for two weeks as caretakers in a New Orleans cemetery where they camped out when Sam burned prayers for the dead. Homeless, they slept on Miami street corners and on park benches near the ocean, stole cameras from gift shops and took photographs on beach after beach. *Why can I hear it here, of all places,* Sam asked. *A death angel's wings?* After that it was summer. At last moving West, they met an artist who mixed her paints with the ashes of cremated desert animals. They settled for a few weeks in her studio, and then moved on to on a reservation in Arizona, where they visited a medicine man who drew a diagram in sand. *Here,* the medicine man said as he pointed at the middle of this diagram, is *the center of the world.*

Sam's center of the world was like the end point of a shell or like the center of the spirals she'd seen in drawings of the walls of Celtic tombs. Sam's pursuit of a world center was his own personal Holy Grail. She felt lucky, most days, to be allowed on the journey, but it frightened her when she saw the books he pulled out of the backpack these days: *Secret Underground Bases and You: Effects of Extraordinary Circumstances on Ordinary Lives.*

The book was a detailed accounting by a former nuclear scientist about what she claimed were secret underground military bases in a variety of North American locations. She had researched for years and had recorded personal accounts, her own and those of area citizenry, in particular in Dulce, New Mexico; Grand Mesa, Colorado; and Groom Lake, Nevada. The bases were built with the assistance of a secret budget amounting to over twenty-five percent of the gross national product. *Dulce*, the author said, *goes down over 2.5 miles deep.* Sam read further from the account of that base. *I found myself,* the author said, *in a large cavern full of outer-space aliens, otherwise known as large Greys. Eventually, we encountered a whole underground base of them and found out they'd been living on our planet for as much as one million years.*

That book was how they ended up in the Arizona desert. She had grown up imagining deserts as a wasteland, a barren expanse, but they hitchhiked to within a few miles of the city of Sedona.

Right away she saw a world in a palm full of sand. *Caliche*, the guidebooks called this earth, the red and brown and white of it that sparkled as she scooped it into her hands. Soon she felt it on her scalp, tasted it on her lips as her tongue shaped new words. *Arroyos. Dunes. Canyons.* Sand, the book also said, covered only about twenty percent of the Earth's deserts. Here the sand was alive. Sand sheets. Sand seas. Dunes. Red rocks made of sand, home to the Gods. Fans of sand blew against her sleeping bag in the night and in that sand, small, thick leaves crushed to salty water between her fingers. In the distance, horizon, howls of wolves. Wind and little eddies of dust.

They camped their first Sedona nights at Cathedral Rock and by flashlight in their tent they read its legend: *The native legend related to Cathedral Rock tells us that the first man and woman argued all day and all night. When they finally appealed to the Gods for a solution they were placed back to back, but together, so they would each retain their own vision and direction.* She felt her tired legs and arms and heart expand, contract. They had traveled thousands of miles to reach this spot, her back to Sam Sanderson's, his back to hers. *Man. Woman.* She inhaled the pure desert air and made a wish. *The center might be here.*

Chapter Thirteen

One way to define a desert is as a geographic region with an arid climate with a deficiency of precipitation received on an annual basis relative to water loss by potential evaporation from plants. Another approach is to classifying deserts is to divide them into five distinct types: tropical, coastal, inter-coastal, cold-winter, and polar.

—*Desert Analysis: The Quest for Training Areas*
U.S. Military Academy

The Palm of a Hand

Sanderson walked toward a huge bonfire at the center of the Harmonic Convergence gathering. A woman with an eye patch and a turban handed him a flyer that he peered at in the light from numerous smaller campfires. Brothers and Sisters, the flyer said. *Celebrate the advent of a new age! Convene with us at dawn! World Meditation for Universal Peace!* Sanderson shoved the flyer in his back pocket.

He passed a table laden with blankets from Mexico that made him think of Rosa. Since their marriage, she'd bought so much pottery and so many baskets and hand-woven throws at craft fairs, he told himself he was no longer lonely. *Doesn't the house make you feel safe?* she asked. Baskets and afghans, maybe, but the last gathering she'd taken him to was a psychic's fair, where she'd urged him to use the services of a medium to contact Sam's spirit. *Let him know you're at peace.* That's why he was here now, to make peace. Universal peace? His best hope was a little patch of earth where he could stop awhile and think, once he'd found the girl, once he'd, *what?*

He sat near the firelight, but the dog didn't make it easy. She pulled on her leash near the sparks and smoke, and the hair on her back bristled at the sight of a man with a beaded robe and face painted black and white. She growled low in her throat and Sanderson drew the leash tighter, but patted her too.

To his right was a family of father and mother and two red-haired girls, all of them bedecked with love beads and hand-made garlands of flowers. As the mother danced, tiny bells jangled at her wrists and ankles. In the opposite direction, a man with blue-black skin was inhaling from a glass pipe. Sanderson had gotten stoned a time or two with Sarah and a few times in the service. *It gives the soul wings*, Sarah had said of the sweetish smoke, but he'd never liked the way it made his head lighter than his body and his heart flutter. He took the pipe, held the smoke in.

Closest to the fire were women with bare breasts, their nipples glittery and silver. A humpbacked old man with a poster on a stick he was waving as he circled the bonfire once, twice, again. *The end of time is nigh.* And the oddest sight of all. A boy, naked except for two pieces of cardboard taped together around his middle. The cardboard was painted white, with stripes, and Sanderson shook his head when he realized the boy was in costume as a bar code. Sanderson, in his deck shoes and polo shirt and a Nepalese woven jacket taken from Janet's closet, wondered what to do with his hands. *Harmonic Convergence*. This was it?

"One thing I hate," a voice at his elbow was saying, "is when somebody sets out to rewrite the Bible."

"Pardon?" The woman standing near him was short and plump, so short she came no higher than just above his waist, and her hair was set in plump, sausage-like curls. She raised a toothless face to him and frowned.

"The way I heard tell of it was that woman partook of the apple of knowledge of good and evil," she said. "If they was any stealing of light and so forth, that was what done it."

The woman slapped one small hand into another as the storyteller went on to describe a character called Raven, the trickster, who stole Earth's light back and then escaped through a hole in what Sanderson supposed was a hut.

"And another thing," the woman said, frowning again.

"What's that?" Sanderson asked.

"How they go about changing the names of people and the like," she said. "In my good book, the Devil's the Devil and a serpent is a serpent by any other name. I don't see where they get this trickster business."

Tricksters. Serpents. Light. Sanderson had the feeling that essentials were being turned around, but he wasn't sure, at the moment, what these were. His head was beginning to feel lighter and lighter. Smoke, he thought. From the fire. From the glass pipe, which he'd tried once, after all, as it made the rounds of the bonfire again.

Light, the storyteller was saying. *The only salvation of the world.*

"Jesus," the woman said, a statement that invited no further commentary. "The good Lord is indeed the light and truth."

"On good days," Sanderson answered and the woman frowned up at him again.

"Don't matter," she said. "Good days. Bad days. It ain't your choice, mister."

Just as she poked him in the leg again with a determined and sharp elbow, the dog growled again and pulled forward, faster than Sanderson could rein her in with the leash. The woman stepped back and held her plump hands out as fists, glowering at both Sanderson and the dog.

"Well I never," she said. "You just better watch yourself, mister. No telling when the light'll call you home."

Chapter Fourteen

On Earth, the nearest things we have to black holes are vortices. Tornadoes, for example, can suck up trees, roofs and trucks. If the vortex rotates much faster than the light can move, any ray that strays too close to its center will get caught and dragged inexorably inwards. So just like a real black hole, the vortex has an event horizon beyond which escape is impossible.

—New Scientist

Cathedral Rock

Summer, 1986. Home was an adobe house on the outskirts of Sedona, Arizona. On a patio outside the front door, she planted herbs, rosemary and lavender. There were three rooms with thrift store chairs and a couch with broken springs and mirrors on every wall. Fat strings of garlic from the farmer's market, beeswax candles jammed into empty wine bottles, dishes, clean and stacked. It was a real home, if she looked at it the right way and it allayed her fears about the future. She even had a job, the noon shift at Johnny Guitar's, a café with Mexican blue-plate specials and under-the-table deals for peyote, eagle feathers, and salves made of sweet grass.

In the kitchen, she stirred a crock pot full of beans and cumin and garlic she'd set going at dawn, when Sam left for his job with a Sedona company that sold healing desert tours. *Enjoy yoga and hiking amid sacred red rocks. Open your heart to the peace within in Sedona's vortex energy.* The day was already so hot steam gathered on the cracked kitchen windows.

Sometimes she counted off the days that brought them here. *India. Nepal. The Graveyards of North America.* And now, this resting place. She could almost hear Sam. *Don't you know,* he'd say if he were there. *Nothing rests, not really. The world simply spins and spins and only if we're lucky do we reach any center at all.* And yet they'd taken root in Sedona. *Indian paintbrush,* he called her, smiling. Some days he helped her weave threads of beads in her long hair and he touched her, for the first time in months. But there were other times.

Like that time at The Sundowner, a Sedona blues bar; they were dancing face-to-face, his smile vanished, just like that. Sam's hands on her hips. His lips against her neck. She followed him outside where he stood looking up at the amazing panorama of desert stars. *I'm tired*, he said. She put her arms around him, held him, but he pushed her away, hard. *You just don't get it, do you? I'm sick of all of this.* How sad those nights, when Sam became a stranger.

As she walked toward town, she studied the horizon—crisp sky, red-rock mountains, sand and highway against which she opened her arms. *I embrace you.* Sedona newsstands were full of books that urged such affirmations, which she had begun to practice with some trepidation. Sam mocked these easy sentiments and today she also felt their flatness. Today, the air, which always smelled of sage, had an undertone of chemicals. The raw, edgy scent they said was waste from the power plant made her walk faster, her ankle bracelets jingling.

The road she walked was a popular side street, Flaming Arrow Way. A couple of vehicles passed her, and she smelled exhaust from the old Renault before it pulled over in front of her. Two Hawks leaned out, rolled down his truck window to the sounds of guitar and bass.

"Too hot to move," he said. Two Hawks, a.k.a. Arty Winters, had a tattoo of Ganesh on his fleshy upper back.

"Sure too hot to walk." She pushed aside a large sack to make room on the front seat.

Two Hawks grinned, turned up the radio. "Been playing Hendrix all morning. Laced with a little metaphysics," he added.

"I hear this is the day for it," she said as she studied the bag between them. "For metaphysics."

"You got that right," he answered. "You like my spirit catchers?"

Coke bottles. Blue wine bottles. The bag had every color and shape inside. Two Hawks saved bottles for spirit trees; she'd seen them a time or two. *Tie all the ones you save onto the branches of a tree and the wind calls your name down the bottle necks,* he said.

"Does it do that?"

"What's that, darlin'?" He was smoking, cigarettes that smelled like cloves.

"The wind. Call your name." The window on her side of the truck was stuck halfway down and hot air fanned onto her.

"It listens," he said.

She breathed the hot air in, conscious again of that acrid, sweet scent.

Two Hawks reached down, cranked up the radio. They were playing Hendrix in the background. *Purple Haze.* In the foreground was a sultry voice she'd come to recognize. Sedona Stella, television and radio disc jockey all in one. The New Age version of Tokyo Rose. Her mission? Seduce Sedona into believing in a consciousness greater than its own. *The universe at its most basic level,* Sedona Stella crooned, *is nothing more than an immense pattern-generating function.* It was only a two-mile ride to Johnny Guitar's, but there was time for Two Hawks to fill her in on Sedona's up-and-comings.

He told her about food festivals and music festivals and psychic fairs. A celebration at Cathedral Rock, that very night. Steaks on the grill and every kind of health food. Macrobiotic. Gluten-free. And blues, besides. "The Red Rockers," he said, describing the Louisiana-based band that had been imported for the occasion. "It's one of a series. A preview celebration of the Harmonic Convergence," he said. That's what Stella Sedona was describing. The Harmonic Convergence. A little more than a year from now.

Lory knew about the Harmonic Convergence, how it was expected that by August 1987, thousands of believers in peace and spiritual cleansing would descend on Sedona to witness the alignment of the planets. She watched the shops of Sedona appear one by one and she wondered what all the verbiage meant. *We are just one small part of the universal pattern,* Sedona Stella was saying. *Convergence.*

They were at the café now and she paused before she stepped out onto the sidewalk.

"He's a good guy, that Sam," Two Hawks said. He'd scooped up a red bottle from the floorboard and he held it out to her. "But you never can tell what the wind might bring."

The café's slogan was on a sign above the bar. *Chili rellenos hot enough to make you cry.* Vienna and Emma, two sixties pals, had also given the place an ambience from *Johnny Guitar,* a campy Western filmed in Sedona, circa 1953. Vienna was the owner and hostess who wore tight black jeans and riding boots that clicked across the tiled café floors. Emma, the cook, was as small boned and fierce as Mercedes McCambridge. And Faustin, the Havasu bartender, could have been Sterling Hayden in another life. Today, they were all sipping Coronas behind the grill and sneaking tokes in the walk-in. The Harmonic Convergence Preview was in the air.

On a television over the cash register were the usual lunchtime local updates. Sports. A Sedona Little League Team in a park. A news spot of booths and tents near Cathedral Rock. And Sedona Stella. *When we study the cosmos and the universe and the galaxies that surround us,* she said, *we also study the worlds within. Loss. Love. Harmony.*

Lory laid down a platter of nachos and a Long Island Iced Tea for a woman in a caftan who was doing palm readings.

"I don't see the desert in your future, sweetie," the woman warned as she took Lory's hands in her own. She peered at both palms. "I see oceans. A mountain."

"A black dog," she said. "A black dog to find you in space and in time."

Space. After the two sips of Bloody Mary and one toke when she took the trash out back, Lory thought Sedona Stella looked like a swami. An eye in the palm of her hand. Tattoos of constellations across her stomach. *Cathedral*

Rock, Stella said. *Tonight. An initiation into the alignment of the stars, the planets, us.*

By three o'clock the crowd died down. They made more Bloody Marys and the air was thick with herbal cigarettes. Out back at the dumpster, she'd smoked part of a joint with Faustin, and she'd inhaled that chemical-whatever-it-was in the Sedona air, and she'd come back floating. The café now had a surreal gloss, a heightened reality.

Like they did every afternoon at four o'clock, they ran a reel to reel copy of *Johnny Guitar*. An old projector sat atop the pickup station and as the film sputtered to a start Vienna did a two-step with the broom across the floor. They all knew the plot. Shots of prairie flowers and Johnny Logan astride a horse. There was a stagecoach robbery and a murder. There was Emma Small and the Dancin' Kid. Everyone heading for the hills. A posse. A lynching.

She was spinning, a little sick, and the movie had begun to repeat itself in her chest, its mixture of McCarthyism and Feminism all rolled into one. Her mouth tasted like metal as she swallowed the rest of a Bloody Mary in one long gulp.

"You all right there, girl?" Vienna asked.

Lory filled the peppers and salts. Wiped the kerosene lanterns. She held her breath against her head-spins.

"How's that Sam?" Emma asked.

"Doing good." Lory balanced two plates on each arm.

She had gone with Sam to Vienna's and Emma's house more than once now. *Watch out for that man,* Emma said to her the next day before her shift. *He's a looker, you know.* Lory said she knew Sam was attractive, but Emma said that wasn't it, not by a long shot. *He's looking, sweetheart. Looking here and there and everywhere but at you.* He'd never be unfaithful to me, Lory said. *That wasn't what I meant, sweetie,* Emma said and shook her head. *Not at all.*

The television was on again. Weather at noon. A storm was brewing from the east, the meteorologist reported.

"Maybe it'll be a doozy," Faustin said.

Rain. Only now and then in the desert, but when it came, it rained in sheets and walls. Water so hard it could sweep you away.

"Maybe not such a bad thing at a summer festival in the desert." Faustin said.

Maybe, she thought, the Sedona air had that taste because of rain. The lack of it. Its possibility. She imagined a crash of thunder, the deluge to follow. *More people die by drowning in the desert*, their Arizona guidebook said, *than of thirst*. She wanted it to rain and rain. She wanted to stand at the base of Cathedral Rock with Sam and bury her face in his arms. At the end of a day in the desert sun, he smelled like wind and salt.

She slipped outside, took a seat on the curb by the street. She was half drunk, vodka stinging in her throat, and there was still that chemical taste in the air, like sipping cologne. *Harmonic Convergence.* She stared up at the sky. Still clear, no gathering clouds.

At nearly midnight, when they headed to Cathedral Rock, it was raining a little, a fine, warm mist, so they huddled against each other in the back of a panel truck full of Sedona revelers, half of them in disguise. A woman in a burqa. A warrior with a dime store feather headdress. Two Hawks had his long hair tucked up in a battered sombrero, and he handed her a bottle. She sipped and threw her head back and saw them. Cliffs ascending, descending, dizzying distances, up and up. The truck bounced and dove along a rutted road called Verde Valley that led to the red rocks of Sedona.

The woman in the burqa was an Italian-Bulgarian named Uranita. Her name, she said, came from the planet Uranus, from which she received translatable poems. She'd moved to Sedona for its community, one dedicated to the study of the history of the universe, particularly vortices. *Masculine/electric energy. Feminine/magnetic.* Feminine vortices were soothing, healing energy, part of the Earth. Masculine energy was outward-energizing.

She handed the bottle to Uranita, who sipped and passed it on and then grabbed Lory's wrists. "Try this," she said as she rubbed Lory's hands together, palm to palm. Heat. A tingling that moved from palms to arms to chest.

"Cathedral Rock," Uranita told her, "enhances."

Enhances what, Lory asked, but Uranita was addressing the whole truckload now. They were all trying it, their palms, the touching of foreheads, third eyes, heart chakras. *Can't you feel it,* Sam asked. *How alive everything is?* Roman candles and sparklers and spinners in blue and gold and red exploded. The tingling from her palms settled in her mouth, moved into Sam's and back.

A storm was gathering, threads of light rising from beyond the rock cliffs, connecting this cliff to that one. So far, the sky was quiet, but thunder rumbled way across the valley and she shifted closer to Sam. He was holding a rain poncho over his head and she burrowed inside, their own still tent where he too was sipping a bottle. He spilled the potent liquid into her mouth from his as the truck jolted to a stop and they piled out into a huge open field at the base of Cathedral Rock. There were lights strung up across poles, tents with campers huddled near camp stoves and under umbrellas. Two Rastafarian-haired men huddled, adding kindling to a blaze.

The heart of the world, Uranita said as she walked away. Her own heart was racing, blood tumbling, one chamber to the next. Her head spun, settled, as she focused on a broad streak of lightning across the top of Cathedral Rock.

There was power here. A presence she'd felt before in cathedrals in Paris. In the morning light on the Taj Mahal. *Sam,* she called again. *Sam?* He was nowhere. Clouds moved across the towering rock cliffs, leaving shadows like giant wings in their wake. *Desert birds.* Did they fly at night? The chemical scent of the air had intensified and she swallowed it, felt the scent slide down inside her, take hold.

She headed across the field. Sand turned to small stones and then rocks and boulders large enough to sit on. The gypsy scarf she was wearing was sodden with rain and she wiped her wet face, sucked thirstily at the edges of the cloth. This rain was a fine mist, but the lightning had an urgency and the thunder afterward answered sooner. The storm was going to peak soon, break overhead; she wanted to find Sam.

There were others nearby, costumed and not. A witch in a pointy hat. Two Hawks, the Mexican bandito.

Wound tight, he tapped his booted foot against the boulder. "Storm's gonna converge us right into next year. Make us see things."

"What things?"

Her tongue felt heavy and his plumpness beside her felt heavier than that.

"Whoosh. The Lone Ranger and Tonto dancing in the sky."

Words echoed in her head and she swallowed them in.

"Sam," she said at last. "You seen Sam?"

Music from the tents and parked cars carried down the cliffs. Song words. *Crazy. Crazy for feelin' so lonely.*

"What was in that drink, anyway?" she asked.

"Drink?" He studied her. "Hmm."

"Mescaline?"

"Darlin'," he answered. "Not a thing in that bottle but a little sweet wine and some desert water."

Not a thing. "That couldn't be."

He looked at her again. "Watch yourself now. Rains coming. Comes fast in a place like this." He jumped down from the boulder.

"Had to be something," she said again.

He was calling over his shoulder as he walked into the shadows. Did she hear him right? *Nothing in that drink but a little vision or two. A little Harmonic preview. A little Convergence of the twain.*

She began to climb, the same song following her. *Crazy for feeling so blue.* Far below, an open field was full of faces looking up at the sky and waiting as the cliffside began to turn white and gray with the first hard-falling drops of rain. "Sam," she called as loud as she could but her voice disappeared in another crash of thunder.

She skipped the trail and scrambled up a dry wash, climbing steadily and quickly. Soon she was on the west side of a saddle, and then she veered left, another short but steep climb that carried her to a ledge between two rock towers. The rocks were growing slippery and her sandals slid, found footholds, and she was cold now and breathing hard with climbing. Birds, black shadows, dashed in between the rock facing. Night birds, calls keening in the distance between rolls of thunder. The lightning had become full and rich. It divided the sky, pulled it open, an instant in which anything at all could be witnessed. *The face of God.* The sweet-wine drink and its visions made her see him beforehand, Sam, up there, standing on a ledge without her, coming to decisions about the world. *Alien visitations. Underground cities. Light and stars and eyes of God.* What of the world did he see, without her?

She hurried now. She was as close to the peak as she could get when she reached his silhouette at the edge of the cliff. *Sam?* She shouted this against a wind stinging with sand and rain, strong enough to make her crouch low, brace herself.

"Sam," she shouted again and pushed herself up, a half-crouch, nearly a crawl on her hands and knees. He was there after all, sitting on a part of the ledge so narrow she gasped. When she reached him, she grabbed hold of his hands. Touched the bare legs below his cut-off jeans. His skin was as cold as hers.

223

"I've been looking," she called to him as she pulled herself up beside him. *Looking for you.* She started to say that, but her mouth was dry, her tongue incapable of words.

"Sam?" Rain pelted against them in the rising wind and her words whispered. "What is it?"

He wasn't looking at her. He was looking up at the sky and out and down at the valley, the enormity of Sedona and the desert and beyond. His eyes. How could she see them in the dark? The light in his eyes and their black, expanded pupils. And now that she was up here, at the final height of her climb, she too was expanded. Waves exploded behind her own eyes. And the taste of the drink. It collided with the air's acrid taste and as waves of nausea sent her reeling, she reached for him, leaned into his shoulder. *Look.* Had he said that? She felt the word leave her own mouth, and then saw it on his lips, felt its shape as she laid her hand against his face and the coolness of his lips.

"Look."

Above them, stars. Obscure ones. Antares, shy but brilliant orange. And the celebrities. The Milky Way, diva of the evening sky, a star-studded highway stretching north to south. A billion stars, at least. Mars. And Venus, surpassed only by the sun, the moon and the lightning's thin touchdown.

Below them were the distant lights of the town she traced with her fingers, a pattern in which she located this street, that one. The café. The road she'd walked home. Adobe houses with lights above kitchen tables and ordinary lives. Other roads in their neat alignments, the lights of trucks and cars hauling north or south, west and back east. And beyond that square buildings and landing fields. A radio tower's flashing, red and off against the sky. A voice, musical and severe, chiming from that tower. *Crazy for feeling so lonely.*

"What are they saying, Sam?"

A voice from a megaphone. *What're those crazy hippies doing over there to*

Cathedral Rock? Harmonic Converging, my sweet ass. And beyond. A military base with planes touching down or taking off, well-lit metal birds, a concordance of power that made her dizzy. *Look*, he said again, and she wondered which particular point of light he was showing her, which path and where, the phantasmagoria of lights below her and the acrid taste of rain above. The world was churning. *Crazy.* The scent. It was gasoline now, and creosote, and a vileness she couldn't name. It was in her mouth and she tasted the dregs.

"Don't you see?" Sam said. "Don't you see now?"

What she thought she saw was beating helicopter wings above their heads. Blades wet with rain whirling into their faces. A funnel of wind. A gas mask, some clandestine military spirit gazing down on their world. The helicopter, hovering above them. But she would never remember anything she saw that night, not clearly. It could be anything, this memory of brilliance. *Lightning. Electronic magnetic charges.* A craft from some other universe altogether. Clouds of blue smoke and a scattering of something like confetti. In place of clarity, she'll remember incidental images. Blazing fountains and sparklers and Roman candles. A funnel rising into light. A spiritual elevator taking them up into a vortex. *Takeoff.* Just like that, the helicopter was gone, leaving in its wake a hollow taste in her mouth.

And Sam. Still sitting beside her.

"It's real," he said, his voice more excited than she'd ever heard it.

Real. He'd told her the rumors. Quoted passages from the authorities. Underground facilities in Sedona. An underground city in case of nuclear attack. Government direct satellite communication. Secure communication links with the outside world in case of disaster. Secret reconnaissance missions to check on the daily undertakings of ordinary lives. Mysterious helicopter flights had indeed been documented. Even she knew that. And that, he said, was what they'd just seen. A glimpse of the dark heart of the world.

Firelight

War and its conflicts, the storyteller is saying as drums beat and the Harmonic Convergers dance in the firelight. Beside Lory Llewellyn is a florid man with jet black hair and a red sarong. *What's your name, sweet one?* he says. She is not sweet. She is as bitter as the past that follows her, a black dog.

"Sam," she said, that night when he stood in the door of the Motel of the Stars in his khaki slacks and polished boots. He took off his cap and set on her own head. She turned it inside out and back, staring at a band dark with wear. "Sam," she said again as she traced the cap's insignia with her finger. *Semper Fi.*

She remembers his stories. Twenty-five mile hikes across swamps. Twenty-four miles with full combat gear. Half marathons with one hundred pounds on their backs. The barracks floor and walls decorated with the Grim Reaper, with drawings of skeletons, black spades, and cobras. A motto right by the door. *Give you pain, give you hurt, we believe in killing first, can't no other compete with us. Death Dealers turn bones to dust.* He'd been, Sam said, only experimenting before in the lore of dying. Mere intellectualization. This was the real thing.

One day, he said, they herded them into a concrete-block hut with the windows painted black and made them take off their gas masks, made them breathe vaporized pellets of tear gas thrown by the handful out of a jar. *Breathe,* the drill sergeant said. *You can't leave until you breathe!* They were in the total dark and their hands shook as they pulled away their masks, as fumes stung their skin. Some of them cried and spit and some of them ran back out. Those, the ones who couldn't take it, were tackled or chased and they lay there on the ground. They rolled over, played dead. They were dead for as long they were told.

The week Sam disappeared, it rained for days, part of a storm pattern up and down the coast. Seventy-six miles of coastline were closed. There were news reports about a helicopter downed in the ocean. A Marine, lost at sea off North Carolina's coast. She knew right then it was him.

The red-saronged man has a silver ring in his ear. His laugh is strong and full. He is close to her, too close, so that she can see his eyes in the firelight. He touches her hand and she pulls away. How long since she has let herself be touched?

There are hours yet before dawn.

She looks across the firelight again and who she sees, this time, is not a storyteller at all. She sees Sam Sanderson. His hair is thinning back from his forehead and he wears aviator glasses and slacks and a striped jacket. He has, she sees as he steps into the full light of the fire, a pouch of a belly that makes her heart ache. She feels her breath coming quicker and she stands, ready to raise her hand or make some sign, but he has not seen her.

Chapter Fifteen

The Harmonic Convergence was an announcement of the forthcoming end of time as we know it and a preparation to move from the third-dimensional reality of space into the fourth-dimensional reality of time. Some call this Heaven on Earth.

—Announcement of the Forthcoming End of Time

Palmistry

The night was enormous beyond anything Sanderson had seen. Sanderson's hand tightened on the dog's leash and his heart skipped, beat, skipped. It was her. He was almost sure of it. Lory Llewellyn. In his mind, he still saw the woman in the metal chair at the motel fire, or one with long black hair, pale skin, and a nose ring. Back from India with Sam. This woman standing on the other side of the bonfire, was running her fingers through her short, dark hair. She looked straight at Sanderson, and he looped the leash around his hand, through the crowd to the other side of the fire.

Fractured light and chaos. The storyteller was still talking as Sanderson pushed his way through, glimpsing the back of a head. Dark hair. She was dancing now, a movement of elbows and arms, the striped-cloth man taking her hands, moving with her in a circle of dance close to the fire. The storyteller's voice rose as the music of drums and bells rose, an hypnotic chant. So many dancing bodies that he couldn't see her.

A tall, thin boy with a sallow face close to him on his right, a little girl in cut off shorts and a burly-bodied man in front of him, blocking his way, and the dog, tense now, straining ahead of him.

The earlier sweet pipe smoke had quickened in his head and he could barely see his way forward. *War and its solutions,* the storyteller was saying. The Harmonic Convergence, he said, was a chance to realign not only the planets, but history itself. Sanderson pushed forward again, the dog straining against him, pulling him back and around. To one side, a large man in a leather jacket and on the other, the dancers, a line of them now, weaving, snakelike, undulating away from and then toward the firelight. Where was she?

"Troubled?" a voice asked.

He looked down at a small woman, her skirt and long, black scarf dragging the ground. She peered at him.

"I just need to," Sanderson began. He stood still, his head spinning, not sure what he meant to say next.

He couldn't focus now on anyone in the crowd as embers exploded from the center of the fire. He clutched the dog's leash.

"I'm looking for someone," he said.

"I see that."

She was holding his free hand now and he moved to take it back from her, but she held on, turned the hand palm up, near her face.

"I see you are familiar with discord," she said. She traced, this time with her nail, the outline of the Marine Corps insignia on his arm.

Sanderson remembered the psychics' fair he visited with Rosa. Readers of tea leaves and crystal balls. She opted for a palm reader and had stared at her hand, the whole drive back home that day. My lifeline, she said to Sanderson. *My lifeline is the strongest one she'd ever seen. Isn't that something?*

"A palm reader," he said. "Could you tell me something?"

"Perhaps," she said.

"I'm looking for someone." He scanned the crowd again for the girl.

"That's not it," the woman went on. "What you're looking for."

"How do you know who I'm looking for?"

"You're looking for something," she paused, laughed. "With wings."

"Excuse me?"

She pointed at his hand again. "Something soft, beating against a locked door."

"I don't understand," he began.

The woman shook her head. "It's you," she said. "You must open the door."

At some great distance, the storyteller was still talking. His voice out of the shadows. *Soon we will reach it. The Zero Point, where everything we think or desire will instantly manifest. Love and fear. Our intentions will be of utmost importance.*

The woman took hold of the edges of her long skirts, started toward the fire. "The woman," she said with a last turn of her head. "She's here. The woman you seek."

"What? You know her?"

The long black scarf tossed over the woman's shoulder and she disappeared with a wave of her hand. "It's never too late," she called back to him. "To open the door to yourself."

How tired he was. Sanderson stared out over the crowd of now slow-moving dancers. The storyteller's voice and the sound of drums and bells gathered in his chest, thick and heavy. *Lory Llewellyn?* She was nowhere to be seen.

Chapter Sixteen

Combustion:

1. The act or process of burning. 2. Violent excitement; tumult.

Uncanny Likenesses

It couldn't have been Sam. She is sure of it now that she is far enough away to catch her breath and see the man for who he must have been. Sam Sanderson's father. Enough like Sam in some ways that even here, at this safe distance, the likeness of their faces makes her chest ache. She could have spoken to him, couldn't she? How afraid she'd felt at the mere sight of Jason Sanderson, a man who is part ghost.

He was a ghost, Sam Sanderson, the one she thought she knew back there in the desert. During their last days in Sedona, Sam Sanderson was more in love than ever, but not with her. He sat up nights, poring over books about nuclear attacks and high-risk security measures by the American military, any book he could find that revealed secrets hidden beneath the Sedona deserts. When she looked at his two-sided face, she told herself there was still an opening for herself, but in truth a new vocabulary came from his mouth, a hard set of words and sentences and plans that left him unrecognizable. *Military complex. Window of vulnerability. The power of God in a technological age.* And love? She'd ask. He often fell asleep in the same chair where he'd been reading, or slumped at the kitchen table. Where, she'd ask. *Where are you now?* He was deeply in love, but not with her, not with any certain person, any certain place.

She takes off her pack, sets it at her feet, and crouches there on her ankles. This is where she'll spend the night, so she unzips the pack, pulls out a rain poncho, feels in the bottom of the pack for the things she'll need, come morning. She spreads the poncho on a bed of leaves, curls herself beneath her jacket, stares at the full moon. Sam Sanderson would have loved such a moment.

But he is not here. Sam fell through a hole in the world, a black hole he loved more than her. He fell in love with knowing the unknowable. With war, even. She still remembers what he told her, about boot camp. How he learned what mattered in war. Not rounds fired nor the mere cacophony of artillery. It was the hit that counted most. The impact of a bullet hitting flesh. The anonymous face. The expression you learned not to see as the body fell. The detachment from that face and its particular smile, its particular look of terror or regret, its history that wasn't your own. The face of the enemy was not a face. It was dead already.

He is dead. Dead and gone. But still she remembers that last night she saw him. That night before he fell into the sea. She remembers street light trailing across the bare skin of his arms. How warm he felt. *Convergence.* That word lingers inside her and even now she almost believes it, that the world could be made harmonious.

Chapter Seventeen

Shadowland:

A land or region of shadows, phantoms, unrealities, or uncertainties:
the shadowland of the imagination.

Still Night

After Sanderson circled the parameters of the bonfire twice, he went farther toward the line of trees, searching for the girl until he was lost. He stumbled on a campsite where two dread-locked young men offered him sips of whiskey, a sleeping bag, and finally directions back to the now-darkened carnival grounds and his car. He was tired enough to have slept anywhere, but the car seemed safest and he was thankful when he reached it. *A substantial car*, Rosa had said when they picked out this particular model. It was true. Settling in the back seat, the dog licked, a sound like water lapping a canoe, and in the front he found that there was not quite room to stretch his legs out.

He closed his eyes and wanted no words, but they came to him. *Butterfly wings against dead-bolted doors.* He was still a boy when he'd written that most sentimental of poems. He'd given it to Sarah, a gift. Sanderson turned, face against the car's seat, turned back. He huddled under his jacket, feeling cold, and then settled, staring up through the dashboard at the night sky.

He saw the girl's face across the light of the bonfire. He saw the fortuneteller, the toss of her scarf over her shoulder as she walked away. *I see you are familiar with discord.* What words had he once scrawled in a notebook? *Heat of a jungle, rockets and mortars, death riding inbound.* Discord. Saigon. His pretty poem was about that, too. He drifted, part dream and part restlessness, and saw himself, like he always did. Himself, as a boy. And once again, beside his dreamed self was another boy who lit a match and held it close to a photograph of a woman. *Guess who she is*, the boy said. *Just guess.* Sam, and the woman, this time, was Lory Llewellyn. She pointed down from the truck at a street where women in red sarongs walked through explosions and waves of white and yellow and blue smoke. She took his hand and stared down at the complex of lines and creases on his palm.

Then she wasn't Lory Llewellyn, but a particular, red-saronged girl, someone's daughter from a village in a jungle, a girl lying on the ground. *Coconuts.* Halves of them from her basket lay beside her, their white milk mixed with blood. Tall grasses shadowed her, but he could see her mouth. Open. Her eyes darted up and back. She was pushing down hard with her hands against her pregnant belly and he was fingering a hand grenade.

He woke hard, his shirt clinging to his back with sweat.

He was nineteen years old then, and not yet finished with boyishness. But was that the real truth of it? He remembered now a sound so loud his ears went numb and with that, little pieces of something hot floating down, striking the ground like pellets hitting water. He was a boy and he lay there wishing for home, wishing for his hometown, wishing hymn words and his grandfather's hands. *When sunlight through darkness and shadow is breaking, Jesus will come in the fullness of glory.* He remembered how the girl was crying and how he wanted to help her. Wanted her to be quiet. Wanted not to die. He wanted to lie in the deep grass, hide himself until all of it was over.

It isn't too late to remember, a voice said as he shifted in the car's seat. The dog was on the floorboard now and she raised her head, licked his face gently. The voice? It was the fortuneteller, calling to him over her shoulder. *It's never too late,* she'd said. *Never too late to open the door to yourself.* His heart and fluttered and stilled.

He pushed open the car door, stepped out into the late-night, early-morning wet grass. The air—and he was unsure somehow if it was early morning or still night—was damp enough that he could rub his eyes awake in it. The full moon was up there, white and whole. And on the other side of the sky, the sun was not yet ready to rise. He stretched up into the light, swept his arms down to his socked feet. He'd forgotten to slip his shoes back on.

Letting in the Light

Grandfather Trail By Moonlight. It's been years, but she knows the trail, its switchbacks and overhangs and precarious ledges, like she knows the palms of her own hands. It's unimportant how close she comes to this or that drop off into space, this or that rock face into which she might career headfirst. She works her way by scent. *Here.* A square inch of earth her mother touched a million years ago still has a fragrance, a cologne-memory. *There.* Smoke. Her father's pipe burning, his mouth sending smoke rings up. Her own child's scent of chocolate and oranges.

And everywhere, Sam. He is a ghost that leads and she follows, past chasms in the dark. *This way*, he says. *You're almost there.*

A Glimpse of White

Sanderson climbed and held fast to the straining dog's leash. Leash laws. He'd read that somewhere about Grandfather Mountain trails. There'd be laws at home, too, for dogs running unsupervised in yards and around the lake. A temporary fence. He'd put one of those up when he got back, if he kept the dog around for a few weeks or month until he found it a home. He could just see it. The white-carpeted front hall and Rosa standing there with her arms crossed as the dog did her muddy-pawed dance. Maybe she'd consider the dog an Emotional Wellness Encounter. *Dogs provide emotional stability for the lonely and can be a tremendous stress-reliever.* He'd read that somewhere. He imagined telling Rosa about the dog in the back seat of his car as drove away, as he drove here, to Grandfather Mountain.

Dead-bolted doors. As he climbed a particularly steep rise, he remembered that phrase from somewhere. From Rosa. Who, he asked himself, was locked away from whom? How to determine the intricacies of one heart shutting off from another? Rosa, absorbed in her New Age adages about intimacy. *Let go and let God. Surrendering the past.* Or Sam. Always looking over the next hill, down the next road, as if a place or a job or a food with an exotic name had anything at all to do with really, really living. But who was he, Jason Sanderson, to say anything about being really alive? At the beach and afraid of the ocean. In the ocean and afraid of the depths. In the depths and afraid of what? *Love. Memory.* And the girl. Which piece of the puzzle was Lory Llewellyn, in this unlocking of the past?

It was a miracle that Sanderson had glimpsed her at all as she slipped out of the brush, started toward the back of the field and this trail. He had followed her for an hour, then two. He wanted to watch her at a distance, this woman his son had loved. Loved? Did he know that for sure? Traveled with, then. India. The desert. He stopped getting any news of them after the desert. As if what Sam had sent could be called news. In one small box with a wax seal, a small brass monkey with a curled tail that unlocked with a key. A brief letter on onionskin paper from a place called Jaipur. *The Taj Mahal resounds with power.* After that, there'd been the brief visit home, and then months and months of silence, except for a couple of postcards with notes about moving east or moving west to desert places with spiritual truths. He'd seen Sam just once more after that post-India visit home, and then Sam had been in full military regalia.

The girl? He'd seen her only once ever, really. Why then, did he seem to recognize her now? The tilt of her head as she looked up at the sky. The way she shifted her pack higher on her shoulders. Then the merest trace of her. A slip of cloth from her skirt around a bend in the near-dark. She was like that postcard he'd gotten from Sam, just the once, from the Southwestern deserts, red cliffs and an empty skyline and one line on the back. *We hope that we've found it, at last.* What had Sam found with her, this woman now just a glimpse of white in the distance?

Chapter Eighteen

Lightness:

1. The state or quality of being illuminated. 2. Thin or pale in coloration. 3. The relative degree to which an object reflects light, especially light of complementary or nearly complementary colors.

Zero Point

He'd lost track of Lory Llewellyn now, and he let the dog off the leash, hoping she'd locate a scent. She ran and nipped at the air with pure joy and soon she was sniffing at everything in sight. She ran ahead, disappeared into the shadows, finally made her way back to within a few feet of him, as if urging him on. And he needed urging. He had never thought it could be this difficult, the climbing, the breathing.

He'd done all of that and more, he told himself, in the war, which testified to his former ability to survive anything. *Wet socks, skin rash, wide open sores, gun oil and pungy pits.* He laughed at himself now, an aging repo man with stiff joints chasing a dog and a mystery woman up a mountain ridge. Someone, he thought, needed to repossess him. Thank God he'd not succumbed yet to night blindness.

The trail was astonishing. Rock walls and pinnacles, open spaces with shadowy views of mountains unfurling in every direction. He stopped, peered with his flashlight and skimmed a page from the trail guide he'd taken from Janet's house. *Route follows crest of Grandfather Mountain.* A little over two miles, but he felt like he'd been walking for the entire century. He stopped on a level stretch, perched on the edge of a rock and unlaced his shoe. A blister. Two maybe.

By the time he'd fumbled in the depths of his knapsack for Band-Aids and a sip of water from his canteen, the dog was nowhere in sight. He climbed atop the rock where he'd been sitting, peered into the trees, and whistled through his forefingers, a sound that circled back to him. Nothing. Feeling ridiculous, he whistled and shouted. *Dog. Dog?* How to call a dog with no name? Nothing but night sounds. The crackling of dry leaves. A creature in the underbrush. Random bird song. The truth of it? Running through sniper-filled trees, how had he been so brave, that other self, that boy, Jason Sanderson? He shouldered the knapsack.

To his right or maybe to his left in the far distance he heard the dog, a high-pitched and excited barking, and he stepped down from the rock, started toward the sound in one direction, and then the other. He felt confused and momentarily panicked as he started out on what had at first seemed like the trail, and he backtracked, once, twice, certain he'd gone the wrong way. He was off the trail altogether, that much was certain, with the ground beneath him mostly stones and bigger rocks after that.

He thought of helicopters with spotlights, search parties, news headlines about an eccentric businessman lost in the woods. *Braille.* Was this how it felt to read by signs and symbols? His feet sought entryways between the larger rocks and his hands reached, made certain that the way before him was clear. He breathed a sigh of relief when the dog barked again, closer at hand this time. *Dog?* He called again toward the shadows and set out in what seemed like a correct, more upward direction where the trail might lie again. How had they moved when he was in the jungle in the war? Compasses? A breadcrumb trail along the ground? The barking grew more frantic, quicker and more demanding, and then stopped altogether.

She's surefooted along the inclines and descents as she finds the right place to veer off the trail, the right opening in the rocks to a crevice she shimmies down. Pebbles scatter ahead of her and she slips once, braces herself against the rocks, finding handholds in crevices and in the sturdy roots of trees. Ten feet down or a little more, and she feels her way to a rock outcropping with an overhang. *Here.* Maybe it's the place. Tanawha, she called it that day when she was a child. She remembers her parents, their voices in the distance. *You didn't used to be this way. Remember how much you loved the way roses smelled, wild ones, in that field behind the house?* She was invisible then and she's invisible now in the last part-dark before the sun rises.

She finds a hollow space, sits and traces cracks and indentations on the boulders behind her. Opens her backpack and sips water from a bottle, tepid and rust-tasting. She's patient as she waits for daybreak and as she studies the sky, a day that hasn't made up its mind. There's a cover of clouds, thin and gray-threaded across a patch of the last evening stars. And there's a flash or two of what could be real lightning, a harbinger, or nothing more than heat-residue, a promise of the August day to come. There's still enough dark for the candle she's brought, and she strikes a match to that, melts wax on a smooth slice of shale, fixes her candle beside her. The light casts fine.

She takes things out of her pack. A blanket. The papier-mâché box. She holds this for a while, feels the ebb and flow of painted lines along the box's rim. A knife whose handle she kisses, and then laughs at the sentimental excess. Too much to have brought photographs or letters. Clippings from the news. *Navy divers recovered the body of a Marine who had been missing since he went down off the North Carolina coast.* She's pared her life down to this. A knife from an Inez discount store and a box of bones.

Sunrise. It spreads across the mountains, touches the rock overhang above her head. Thin and crimson.

At the summit, he paused, remembering the promise he'd made himself, years and years ago and then again, that night after Rosa's celebration of letting go. He remembered the feel of the lacquered box he'd taken out of his son's duffle bag, and he took that box out of the deep pockets of his khaki shorts now. As he held the box close enough to see in the dim light, the color

251

of the box struck him immediately, a blow to his chest that took his breath and set his heart beating. The box was a deep, azure blue and he remembered Sarah when he first knew her, in a scarf, a gauze shirt, the blue threads of her Indian print skirt. When she grew ill, her floating dresses were too large for her, ones that hid her puffy body. Rosa wore blues sometimes, but those were blues as crisp as stationary, as clean as new sheets. He held the box close to him, next to his heart for a minute before he pried open the lid, held the contents next to his nose and sniffed.

Skeleton-in-a-box. This residue that smelled of chalk and ash. Bones. *The dense, rigid, porous calcified connective tissue forming the major portion of the skeleton of most vertebrates*. Sam would rattled off such a definition at this very moment, then stood back, finger on the side of his crooked face, head tilted, and asked some metaphysical question. *Did the soul reside in the body for some time after death?* Sanderson touched a bone fragment, stirred a finger through the debris at the bottom of the box, held that finger to his tongue, tasted and then shook his head, ashamed of this small violation.

For a decade a military-issue bag had held the flotsam and jetsam of his son's life, all the mementos he possessed, and here he stood, ready to fulfill an obligation, tasting his son's remains. If only he could cry. But he could not weep, and he would celebrate as he had planned. He would let go. Instead, he held the box close to him just a little longer.

She takes the lacquered box from her pack and sits with it a while in her hands and memorizes the box's shine, its intricate pattern of Indian blossoms. With the box balanced in one palm, she opens the hinged lid. *Rose dust. Talc. Powder of bones*. She thinks of that temple in the far north of India, how Sam knelt to worship strange Gods.

A trace of bone powder lifts into the wind before she casts the rest of it out over the precipices. Dust from the bones of strangers floats above the valley and toward the mountain peaks. She remembers when she and Sam followed the funeral bier of a woman up a trail in the mountains of Nepal. They followed the woman's family, watching how they laid offerings of grain and stones at turns of the trail. In her memory something followed them for days afterward around this bend and that. Now, smoke drifts up from the valley. This August morning is almost chilly and she rubs her arms to stay warm. How long has it been since she's believed in anything as mercurial as a ghost?

He'd reached the summit without even knowing it. True light was setting in and with it he could see a chasm just in front of him, a steep and rocky slide down into what looked like yawning pit. He sat for a while, still holding on to the lacquered box. When he opened it again, he stared at the ashes and bone fragments inside and told himself again that this, so pitifully little to be a human body, had been his son.

The service for his son had been a military one with restrictions, since Sam had been neither hero nor a survivor of active duty. What honors, he wondered at the time, were bestowed on someone who had only been lost at sea? He remembered little of that service. The ceremonial folding of an American flag. A woman wailing. A hymn. *Just as I am, without one plea.* The sound of a boy's shoes, kicking against the back of a pew.

Around him now, birds chattered in the lightening trees and a distant plane hummed against the sky. And beneath that another sound. A voice. He shook himself, startled. He cupped a hand next to his ear. The sound was low-pitched, muffled by some distance. The dog? Or another, more human noise. He strained forward into the gray light, listening intently.

He got up, called. *Dog?* He inched forward toward the incline of rocks, settled onto his hands and knees, straining to see over the ledge, down the incline where he glimpsed the black dog leaping out into space, disappearing down a stony incline to nowhere.

Day rising over one more mountain. As she burrows in, an animal making itself small inside the crevice's nest of rocks and debris, she can almost taste the brightness. She has taken off her shoes, peeled down to an undershirt, rolled up her pants legs. New sunlight makes it way up her bare legs, warms her stomach's bare skin. *Light.*

Her life has been made of light. *That force in nature rendered luminous by the operation of the organs of sight.* Light though windows of an office during a late afternoon. Light in deserts and the panoramic views of foreign cities and through the deep blue of a cathedral's stained glass. Light rendering the hair of her lover so beautiful she was afraid to wake him with the slightest touch. And on this very mountaintop? Lightning touched her, entered her forever.

She remembers her mother on that long-ago day, how she stood looking at the mountains, already wanting distance to drink her in. Her eyes had grown more fierce and tired by then. *Do you have to be so odd-turned,* her mother often asked. *Isn't it enough that I have to feed you and him both?* When her mother left for good, she took everything she owned but a beat-up blue Pontiac and left a note that read, *see you for the next round.* She remembers hours alone in a back yard, a hedge and an apple tree where she found a rusty stretch of chicken wire and scratched her hands tugging at it. Later, she held her arms out to wash them clean in the afternoon's rain and she savored it, the liquor-sharp stinging. No one, not even Sam, could heal her.

And now? She cuts clean and quick and she touches her forehead, her cheeks, her blood-smelling hands.

What he heard below wasn't animal, but a voice after all. Or something in between animal and crying. *Are you okay?* He looked down at a ledge with a clear space of gravel and weeds. *Sam? Is it you?* His own voice coming back to him? It was her. Lory Llewellyn.

Sanderson leaned as far over as he could, called down again. What came back was the dog's subdued whine. He stood, assessed where he was. An outcropping of huge rocks stretching fifty feet toward a ledge, and the wide valley and mountain upon mountain. Dizzy with the height and the distance, he inhaled, held his breath. The dog. She must have leapt into thin air, chasing birds or shadows or who knew what.

He studied the edge of the boulders, found it at last, a crevice just wide enough for a body to ease itself down. There was the merest suggestion of a path, one made of slate and loose stones, and he inhaled again, vertigo seizing him, his legs and his gut weak, he thought, as a baby's first steps. He couldn't. Couldn't move forward or back with a thousand feet down or more, nor could he leave her there. His legs, foolish and afraid, seized hold, held fast to that spot of relative safety, the edge of the abyss, and he wished for it. Rescue, ropes, picks, axes and a trail crew. *That foot. There. That hand. To the right.*

He shook his head to clear it, forced himself to move toward the path, if he could call it that. It was nothing more than a niche, really, and scarcely wide enough for a child's body to ease through no less his own. He sucked in his gut before he began to step down, his feet sideways now, inch by precarious inch. The rock crumbled as he braced himself with his hands against the smooth sides of the boulders, The rocks, at least, were steady, and he calmed himself by counting backward to the number of years they must have been there. *One thousand years. Two thousand years. Stop.* And the names of stones. He recited those, one by one, as many as he knew until he was calm. *Granite. Limestone. Slate.* He'd lowered himself to a real foothold now, a place wide enough where he could plant both boots solid on what passed as earth. And then he was through, standing in a narrow crevice of sorts, a narrow spot no bigger than shoulder-width.

Sliding sounds down the rock, and behind her closed eyes, a black shape crosses the sun. The angel of death? A scrambling of claws and an animal's panic.

Near her, there's a scrambling to hold on, a scattering of stones, something sliding past her and balancing precariously at the very edge of the outcropping. A creature scoots for traction, and she half-sits, reaches, and it jumps toward her at the last instant with the scent of fur and leaves.

A dog, its hair short and wiry. She catches hold.

It's okay, Sanderson said as he reached the ledge. There was just enough room for him to stand, and to kneel beside her. Lory Llewellyn. He still couldn't decide what to call her. Girl. Woman. He flinched when he first saw them, streaks of red on her white skirt, cuts along her bare legs, her arms, on even her face.

He slipped off his knapsack, spilled its contents next to the girl. He fumbled with the canteen's top, splashed water onto a handkerchief.

"Here," he said, holding out the cloth to the girl. She didn't move, but she was alive, that much.

Awkwardly, he knelt beside her, still holding out the cloth.

"Here," he said again, then realized his voice was booming, loud enough to echo. *Here. Here. Here.*

And the box. He'd spilled the papier-mâché box and he leaned far over the side of the rock ledge, helpless as the box careened down, vanished for good. He buried his face in his hands. How ashamed he was. He could have sprinkled the ashes years ago, someplace Sam might have loved. Beside the ocean, he thought, and then rescinded the thought as soon as it came to him. The ocean. It had taken Sam for good, and now this, a gray funnel of ash in an eddy of wind.

His hands shook as he turned again to the girl. He was begging her now. "Tell me what to do," he said. "I don't know what to do."

The smallness of her where she was sitting, the black dog in her arms.

She is small. An atom, a molecule, a fractal of light. She is as small as the hard kernel of grief she has carried in her own heart. Some dream of a speck in the eye of an unfamiliar God. She buries her face in the dog's soft fur.

Now not a trace of wind from the valley, no sounds in the distance from the celebrants of the Harmonic Convergence. He pictured them, awake now. All of them kneeling as if in prayer, waiting for an esoteric answer. Maybe Rosa was there. And Janet, doubtless she was somewhere, her eyes scanning the crowds, looking for her brother. He could nearly see her, beckoning to him. *Go home, Jay. Go home.*

Home? There'd been none, not for a long while. His dreams told him that, their maps circling and stopping before he saw himself, a boy in a Vietnamese village a million miles from home. A boy hiding in a thicket of ropy vines beside a girl who hardly looked fifteen, a girl in a red sarong lying on her back on the ground, her dark eyes veined with gold and green. A frightened girl giving birth. Her legs sprawled apart as she bit down on a stick, a strap of canvas, a knife. A baby's dark head crowned, but what he thought of was the way the gunfire sounded, that close. Hush, he told her. *Hush.* He was a boy in a uniform afraid of dying, as frightened as she. Hush, he said again and he pressed down hard against her open mouth, pressed until he couldn't feel her breathing anymore.

And now, below him, a valley of revelers. *Harmonic Convergence.* Universal peace. He could tell them, he thought bitterly. There was no such animal. No peace. No accord with anything, not even of a man with himself. He had only to look at this girl to prove it. *Lory Llewellyn*. She lay there holding the black dog and shivering and he could think of nothing to do for her, nothing at all.

She holds on. Holds on tight and makes a wish, like some forgotten birthday with a candle.

He was trembling even more than she was and when his hands touched his own cheeks, he found tears he didn't want. No wonder, then, that he seemed to hear words. *A voice*. Was it Sarah's? *Be gentle. Be kind.*

Had he been gentle? Certainly not with himself. With Sarah, with Rosa? And Sam. He could have washed his son's body, blessed him for the afterlife with his own living hands, but now he could only hope his son died quickly, there in the waves at the bottom of the ocean.

He touched the girl's forehead, stroked her hair. Her skin was clammy, cold. And yet he could feel it, the pulse of life. He put his hand on her shoulder, shook her. *Gently*. He was capable of that.

O vanity of Sleep, Hope, Dream, endless Desire. The poem Sam loved. Surely, she thinks. Surely there's more at the bottom of the world than that.

He thought he had forgotten how. The gentle way he unfastened her hands, her fingers, one by one. The dog, freed, inched away from her, but gently too. Inched to his side, where Sanderson reached down, touched the warm fur and said, *There. Steady now.* The dog shook herself, a quick and decisive ruffling of fur.

This girl, he thought. Her life. It was in the shadows underneath her eyes. The sad turning-down of her lips. He watched her eyes moving behind her closed lids and that small a thing, that movement, made his heart ache.

258

"Listen," Sanderson said to her at last.

"Tell me," she said. "Tell me how."

The sun has risen fully now.

Chapter Nineteen

The South is pouring down roses of crimson fire...
—from "Michael Robartes Bids His Beloved Be at Peace"

Convergence

Native Americans called the mountain Tanawha. Home of the Creator. Home of the Gods. *Grandfather Mountain*. This day, it is home to the Harmonic Convergence. North has unfolded night above them and in the valley below there are revelers. Faces are rinsed with cool water and feet find their shoes. A braided-haired man at a campfire turns slices of bread, pleased with their rich, buttery scent while, nearby, two little girls, awake and excited, dance with their hands joined. They circle and toss their heads back and sing. *Ashes, ashes. We all fall down.*

In the parking lot near the field, two women have been driving all night. They stretch, rub sleep from their eyes. They wonder how long it will take to find him. He is brother to one, a husband to the other, and they love him, a mutual love that has occupied them in their conversation throughout a long night of driving winding mountain roads. The one woman has learned something like humility during this night drive. Her sister-in-law, so she has believed until now, has risen on the coattails of her brother's life, gone from country-store wife to lakeside, gated community. She's softened toward this woman, her brother's young wife. They've stopped at diners for coffee and they've listened to country music until the wee hours. *Crazy. I'm crazy for loving you.* A thousand faces in this field and one of them, they know, is Jason Sanderson.

"We'll find him," Janet says. "And we'll take him home."

Rosa loops her arm around her sister-in-law's waist.

Light illuminates the field. Vendors are already proffering their wares. T-shirts proclaim *The Implicate Order. The Submanifest State of Being. The Quantum Field.* More campfires, bright and hissing, flare up and there is the scent of herbal teas. Of incense and sage. There is laughter and the counting of rosary beads. And there are prayers to Brahma, Allah, Tao, Great Spirit. Coffee cups fill and unfill.

Far above the field, on a summit at the head of a trail, a black dog has just scrambled to the top of a steep rise over the valley. The dog scratches and sniffs and peers over the edge of the rocks, where a man stands on a rock ledge, remembering his dreams. *Wars*, a voice in these dreams always says. *Wars and rumors of wars.* As always in that dream, he is young again and he is sitting in the back of a Marine-issue truck. Outside that truck, brittle stars always shine and the dream gives these stars names—*John Brown, Dust Light, Deacon Jones.*

The man is kneeling beside a young woman, and he sees how gray threads her fine blonde hair. Unaccountably, he wants to touch her face, to lay his palms against her eyes. He remembers his grandfather doing just that, laying on hands, sending up hymns of praise. He himself used to believe in such wisdom as touch and its holiness. He wants to believe now that when he takes his hands away, she will be different. She will smile, cease to bear the sadness of his son's loss.

By 2012 we will have entered the Fifth Dimension. Believers in the field below this man are certain of the fact, but the man has only the faintest notion of what dimensions really mean. Believers are certain that there are such things as dimensions. Layers of time. They are folding their hands in morning benediction, thankful for bread, for butter, for jam. And above them, in that dimension, are the ghosts of times past, faces of lost loved ones. *See,* the braided-haired man says as he watches the shadow of a hawk diving up from the tree line, disappearing into the clouds.

Far above them, on a rock ledge, a young woman listens to the high-pitched, barking of the dog she held in her arms moments ago. Congregations have gathered. Planets have aligned. She wanted to die today, but she has instead been outwitted by a sound. A humming. An harmonic tone. She can almost see them, people thousands of feet below her who have come here for sunrise on this Harmonic Convergence anniversary day. They are kneeling now, these hundreds of souls. They are looking up at the summit of Grandfather Mountain and they are watching the way light moves across the rock face of the mountains.

He shifts on his crouching ankles, follows the line of her vision. What does she see?

Dust. An eddy of dust from a box hidden for years at the back of a closet. A man hidden for ten years inside his own grief. Dust spins and dances its way farther and farther out into the distance.

"Do you see him, too?" she asks after a while.

He watches a funnel of dust disperse into sunlight and surprises himself with the name he doesn't utter.

"You're the girl touched by lightning," he says at last.

She looks at him, startled.

"Can you make me a promise?" he asks.

"Here and now?"

"A small one." He sprinkles his handkerchief with water, bathes her cheeks and her sad face and he thinks, one more time, Sam is whispering in his ear. *Transfigured.* Lory Llewellyn could be that.

She leans against his shoulder as he helps her up. "A promise for someone I don't know?"

"Just for now." She is so light against him, he is startled. "Be safe," he says.

Today he will guide her down the trail, back through the field of celebrants. He will drive south and east and he will take her home. That much he knows. *Home.* A bountiful possibility, Sam would have called it. He imagines how they might spend their evenings, doing something as simple as making dinner, some ritual of an evening's ordinary events. All of them. Rosa and himself, the dog and this stranger. This woman who loved his son.

For now, he cannot say whether love is, after all, a blessing he might hold in his hands.

Acknowledgments

Many thanks to all the friends and loved ones who have listened to, commented on, or read parts of this work, especially Lorraine Lopez, Carlyle Poteat, and Cindra Halm. Thanks also to my colleagues, past and present. Berry College gave me invaluable time during my time there as Writer-in-Residence. Georgia College and State University and its MFA Program has provided the challenges and rewards of workshops, readings, and conversations with my students by the lake. To all the folks at Sarabande, particularly Kristina McGrath, I offer heartfelt thanks for the best revision advice ever. And, of course, my love and thanks to Johnny.

Jackson Tucker

The Author

Karen Salyer McElmurray, who has been a landscaper, a casino employee and a sporting-towel factory worker, is in her current life a writer and a teacher of writing. She is the author of *Surrendered Child: A Birth Mother's Journey*, described by *The Atlanta Journal-Constitution* as "a moving meditation on loss and memory and the rendering of truth and story." The book was the recipient of the 2003 AWP Award for Creative Nonfiction and a National Book Critics Circle Notable Book. McElmurray's debut novel, *Strange Birds in the Tree of Heaven*, was winner of the 2001 Thomas and Lillie D. Chaffin Award for Appalachian Writing. Her work in both fiction and nonfiction has also received support from the National Endowment for the Arts, the Kentucky Foundation for Women, and the North Carolina Arts Council. McElmurray teaches in the Creative Writing Program at Georgia College and State University, and is Creative Nonfiction Editor for Arts and Letters.